MGM's Grand Hotel: *surely the most glamorous, possibly the most entertaining, and arguably the definitive Hollywood movie.*

Ethan Mordden

THE HOLLYWOOD STUDIOS

*House Style in the
Golden Age of the Movies*

ALFRED A. KNOPF NEW YORK 1988

THIS IS A BORZOI BOOK
PUBLISHED BY ALFRED A. KNOPF, INC.

Library of Congress Cataloging-in-Publication Data
Mordden, Ethan, [date]
The Hollywood studios.
1. Motion picture studios—California—Los Angeles—History.
2. Motion pictures—California—Los Angeles—History.
3. Motion picture industry—United States—History.
4. Hollywood (Los Angeles, Calif.)—History. I. Title.
PN1993.5.U65M64   1987   384'.8'0979494   87-40488
ISBN 0–394–55404–3

Manufactured in the United States of America
First Edition

To the memory of my friend Bill Tynes
1956–1987

The author wishes to acknowledge the support and guidance of his collaborators. Bob Gottlieb, first of all, not only came up with the idea for the book but pursued the project during what may have been his Most Interesting Time, in the last days before he became the Ultimate New Yorker. My secret agent Joan Brandt fields sterling advice and a bracing English accent, though her collection of Coronation Mugs isn't a patch on mine. Copyeditor Mildred Maynard did a brilliant job of tidying up the manuscript, with a memory for repetitions of ten-dollar words that is truly phenomenal. Last and foremost, editor Victoria Wilson took over the book with smarts and charm, for both of which I herewith present my sincere appreciation.

CONTENTS

THE HOLLYWOOD STUDIOS

INTRODUCTION

What Is a Studio?

In the summer of 1908, the unsuccessful actor and playwright D. W. Griffith paid a call on the American Mutoscope & Biograph Company: Biograph made movies, and Griffith was looking for work. The company kept its studio in New York, at 11 East Fourteenth Street, near Union Square, and what Griffith found at that address was a typical Northeast urban stone-and-stoop affair of five floors, narrow at the face and deep at the sides, the basement peeping half a story over the street.

This was a movie studio in the early days of the industry. Erected to house a tony family, the building had been sold and hired out commercially when Society pushed north along the swank avenues,

Fifth and Madison. Stores now squatted in the lower street front. Biograph's officers, film cutters, PR people, and shippers occupied the upper stories. Wardrobe, prop storage, and the dressing rooms shared quarters at the back of the cellar. The former ballroom, at the rear of the *piano nobile,* was cluttered with rolls of canvas and pots of paint, lumber and tools, the overhead mercury lamps and the movable arc lights, and the ungainly Biograph camera itself. Here was where movies were made.

This was not the entire Biograph caboodle. Developing and printing were handled extramurally by a private concern, and outdoor scenes, weather permitting, were shot in exotic, madcap Fort Lee, New Jersey, just down Fourteenth Street and across the Hudson by ferry. Studio shooting and location work were very different experiences, for the cramped and dingy insides of American Biograph, now dark as a cavern, now burning with light, meant hard labor. The field trips to New Jersey were something of a romp.

Of the history itself, of participation in an undertaking that was to expand into America's mythology of self-esteem, courage, loyalty, and compassion, few of Griffith's Biographers—or anyone else in film except Griffith—had the slightest inkling. It was not that they lacked the imagination to foresee *The Wizard of Oz, The Grapes of Wrath, Casablanca,* or *Bringing Up Baby.* There was simply no reason to assume that what they were doing was permanent, like farming or plumbing. Or if it turned out to be permanent, no reason to assume that anything other than Biograph would ever happen.

Movies, at about the time Griffith came to Biograph, were a questionable entertainment for the working class, inferior by intention and execution to even the shoddiest touring edition of the most uncouth play. Movies were ground out, like bent-fork diner hash, of leftover bits of things: old melodrama plots, dustbin clothing, poses from the classics. The director was neither dramatist nor poet but simply a foreman in the manufacturing of film: choosing the subjects, assembling the cast, and calling out the moves—an auteur in the most practical sense but the least artistic one. The cameraman was little more than a janitor of light. He had not art to make but a job to do: catching the action. The performers were mainly unemployed thespians tiding themselves over. Given the broad proportions of the theatre scene of that era, and the movies' lurid reputation, it seems likely that only the most untalented (or unlucky) theatre people would have ventured into cinema. At that, virtually none of them was identified by name or permitted to project the sort of original and recurring image that was later to establish, say, Clark Gable or Bette Davis or W. C. Fields. Nor was there anything like a producer in the best sense of the word, as a good witch who initiates and encourages an idealistic project. There was no need for producers of any kind, or for visionary directors, observant cameramen, or alluring stars, any more than there was need for such artisans in a paper-box plant or a flour mill. When Griffith came to Biograph, movies were a product, moviemaking a business like any other. Thus a movie studio, first of all, was no more than a place of business: the factory.

You're waiting for me to get on with it, to raise my curtain on the sexiness of Paramount, the crabby hustle of Warner Brothers, the paradoxical MGM glamour that can check both Joan Crawford and Greta Garbo into its grand hotel. You're waiting; yes, okay. But I think we have to comprehend a little history to discern the possibilities in the studio system, to learn why studios that grew up in the same place and age developed so differently, each from each. Curtain going up, I promise you, very presently.

Movie factories such as Biograph not only ran on assembly-line procedures but looked on any attempt to vary the results as absurd. Why propose some ideal of more fully delineated stories, more lyrical camera work, more naturalistic presentation? Once you find an efficient method of manufacturing paper boxes or milling flour, you don't think of ways to make the operation more complicated or expensive. You pursue your method, rigidly and indefinitely. A studio, then, is not only a place of business, but a theory of business economics, a belief in so much capital down yielding so much in receipt. A studio is a fixed budget.

The possibility of maintaining a budget, however, was sabotaged by the movie public's enthusiasm for certain of the unnamed performers. This one with the toothy smile, that one with the brazen confidence, a gamine, a lad, a dire contessa, a pleasingly fumbling hero. Something broke through the restrictions of the one- and two-reel stories, the veil of anonymity, the business as usual. Something *wasn't* usual; or, rather, was uniquely usual, the same only better, symbolic, culturally redemptive. Something was Florence Lawrence,

Little Mary Pickford, "Broncho Billy" Anderson, Francis X. Bushman. But if you name your players, they'll start putting on airs and asking for raises. They won't feel like paper boxes anymore. So thought the patents men, the first bosses of the movies, named because of their monopolistic access to Thomas Edison's patents.

However, their upstart challengers, the so-called independents, saw actors' popularity as a gambit in the battle for an open market. So feisty independent Carl Laemmle coopts Biograph's Florence Lawrence, thus far billed only as "The Biograph Girl." Imagine the deal: Laemmle tells Lawrence, "We give you a raise, we give your husband a raise, we let you make whatever movies you want."

Lawrence likes this.

"And I got news for you—we're gonna call you Florence Lawrence."

"You don't have to call me Florence Lawrence," she replies. "I *am* Florence Lawrence."

No, that was the point: actors did have to be called, identified, made known. As the profits began to swell in direct response to these actors' films, as these actors pressed for a piece of the action, as the aggressive upstart moviemakers outbid the established firms for these actors' services, the trim, one-size-fits-all production of movies expanded, treating stories of some detail, relaxing the narrative tempo, giving the key personalities more room. Two reels good, seven reels better. When the patents men lost their monopoly in the courts through crucial antitrust decisions in 1914 and 1915, the First Era of Silent Film was over. Griffith, more than anyone, cut the path that the movies must take: the phenomenal success of *The Birth of a Nation* (1915), disarmed nickelodeon resistance to become the movies' first *national* achievement. The patents men, almost entirely upper-middle-class WASPs, had outlawed initiative in directors and reputation in actors. Their parvenu challengers, working-class and Jewish, overwhelmed them by encouraging individuality and fame. The individuality entitled the directors, gave movies drive. But the fame of the players gave movies penetration—character, you might say, with a human face.

So. A studio now, in the late 1910s, is among other things a collection of stars, of certain kinds of stars: for each studio emphasizes a different assortment. There is the Dangerous Man, ruthless and romantic. There's the Folk Hero, the Boudoir Dandy. There is the Queen of the Lot, majestically versatile, and the Sweetheart and the Sinful Woman. There are clowns. There are the Prestige People, from the stage—or, better, the English stage. Winning with a particular type led a studio to seek out more examples of that type, to win again but also to mitigate risk in cases of health emergency or box-office fatigue. Having, say, an arriving Boudoir Dandy in the wings tended to keep the reigning Boudoir Dandy on good behavior. Projects readied for a Sweetheart whose popularity had climaxed could be reassigned to a fresh Sweetheart with scarcely a change in production plans.

A studio is stars. But it was not too soon for sages to note a temporary quality to stardom. Most players had a vogue more than a career, with fast rise, short regime of riches and fame, then a stubbornly lengthy play-out of—shall we say—guest work at a minimum wage.

Consider the case of Theda Bara. Type: Sinful Woman. Subtype: Vamp. Studio: Fox. Bara was the most potent draw of the Vamp stars who prevailed during the first years of Silent Film's Second Era, during and just after World War I. The Vamp was an implacable man-eater, ruining not only her lovers but their dependents as well—invariably a wife and progeny but, with luck, a best friend and an invalid mother. Her motivation was, on the surface, money and power; at heart, she was pure evil. The aim of her devastation was devastation. Call the Vamp a symbol of the gathering outrage of oppressed women, an unleashing of barbarism in tune with wartime hysteria, or simply another Hollywood skin game. Whatever her basis, the Vamp became an imposing portrait in the movies' gallery of types, setting a pattern for Greta Garbo and Marlene Dietrich. Building on the flash success of *A Fool There Was* (1915), Bara raised up a sizable oeuvre, all for Fox, of thirty-nine features, mostly as the Vamp but textured here and there by Sweetheart apologies—*The Two Orphans* (1915), from the source that D. W. Griffith used for *Orphans of the Storm;* or *Romeo and Juliet* (1916). They made movies faster than they do today, and all this spanned a mere four years, after which Bara was thoroughly discarded.*

* Bara also set a pattern for Hollywood retirement, taking an aggressive part in the social scene and occasionally inquiring of a producer if he had, in the works, Anything Suitable. Pathetically, she maintained a listing in the casting directories almost until her death in 1955: "At liberty."

A studio is stars. Metro, before it merged with the Goldwyn and Mayer firms, ran on the power of Alla Nazimova, here (left, on stairs) in Camille *(1921), her last film before arrogance and ambition destroyed her career. And a studio is rising* stars*: Nazimova's Armand, Rudolph Valentino (right, center), had just made* The Four Horsemen of the Apoca-

lypse *and would soon go to Paramount to play The Sheik.*
June Mathis, Camille's scenarist, "discovered" Valentino
and would follow him to Paramount; Natacha Rambova,
who designed this modern-dress Camille, *would become*
Valentino's second wife.

Other stars might enjoy a longer vogue, or luck into a comeback, or hang on in the cheapjack quickies of some minor studio well off the boulevard, willing to pay a miniature fortune for a Name that hasn't yet entirely cooled off. Gary Cooper reigned for life, Katharine Hepburn made a spectacular comeback, Joan Crawford trashed herself. There are almost as many stories as there were stars. And studios might muster new versions of burned-out stars, likenesses; or competing versions of yet vital stars, revisions; or trade one star for another, swap you your Sweetheart for our Queen of the Lot. So when we think of a studio as a collection of stars, we must allow for countless variables—of movie history in general and certain eras in particular, of eternal themes and temporary amusements, of shifts of perception in "look" (from Theda Bara to Marlene Dietrich, for instance) and humor (from Bob Hope to Woody Allen) and heroism (from Douglas Fairbanks, Sr., to Jack Nicholson; even from Fairbanks, Sr., to Fairbanks, Jr.). The variables are controlled by the studio heads on one hand, supposing, and by the public on the other, reacting. In the end, stars are property, studio inventory, as much as the banquet glasses and glycerine. Or no, stars are not hirelings, objects. Stars are agenda. And who reviews the agenda?

The heads, the managers, the producers. So a studio also is its moguls—the chiefs and their drive for conquest and respect. Remember, once the Second Era sets in, the dreary WASPs of the Edison circle are out and the finagling peddlers are in, as we move from the East to Hollywood. There's a great deal of insecurity among these nouveau monarchs in their new kingdom, too much fear of upheaval and not enough belief in destiny. Laemmle, Zukor, and Fox have won, but they remain outlanders: foreigners in America, rambunctious irritants in somnolent Los Angeles, purveyors of enchanting material in an always surprisingly leery culture. Movies are revelation, and in Puritan America that is subversion. Therefore, the Hollywood moguls need more than mere money success. They need respectability, assimilation, esteem.

This is the generation of moguls who founded Hollywood and saw it through its Golden Age. Along with old hands Laemmle, Zukor, and Fox, L. B. Mayer, Irving Thalberg, Samuel Goldwyn, and Jack Warner became significant during the silent period, and just after sound came in Darryl Zanuck, David O. Selznick, and Harry

Cohn joined them. (One uses the verb in its Pickwickian sense, as moguls joined each other in a state of war tempered by conspiracy.) Thus our understanding of how the studios functioned must take into account the contradictory nature of the mogul, his ignoble treatment of artists inseparable from his apparently genuine love of movies, his rages inextricably linked to his wisdoms, his implacable egotism constantly humiliated by servile pandering to the national taste and the placating of various special-interest outrages. What the mogul must have is prestige.

Each mogul, however, reacts differently to the notion of a prestige star, a prestige director, a prestige picture. At different times, prestige lies in a florid director from the Continent, or in anyone British or named Barrymore, or even in the use of Technicolor. To Samuel Goldwyn, prestige was a screenplay by a New York playwright, to David Selznick an adaptation from Dickens. To Carl Laemmle a prestige picture was big, to Harry Cohn a prestige picture was big and long, and to Irving Thalberg a prestige picture was big, long, polished, brilliant, and edifying, with, if possible, Jean Hersholt in a touching cameo.

There is as well these moguls' contrasting views on the size that movies should aspire to, in length, in complexity of plot and character development, in pictorial splendor. We know, if a studio is a fixed budget, that the moguls who replaced the patents men understood that the budget must accommodate the public's expectations. As David Selznick saw it, only two kinds of movies make money—the very cheap and the very expensive. Much of studio history outlines a conflict between the two kinds. There's easy money; there's the big win. There's weepies and backstagers and westerns; or there's *Grand Hotel* and *The Ten Commandments.* The moguls generally try to enhance a schedule of bread-and-butter movies that more or less film themselves neatly and cheaply with a certain number of "specials"—often troublesome, certainly expensive, but sometimes incomparably profitable. The balance of ordinary films to spectacles varies, again, from studio to studio. Universal had so many gradations of expenditure that it could market Red Feathers, Bluebirds, Butterflies, Jewels, and—as Carl Laemmle worried and grouched—Super-Jewels. MGM, on the other hand, spread money throughout its system, upgrading many B programmers to an A level and delivering routine

A's with a sparkle that was almost—well, Super-Jewel. Even studios run on austerity programs might venture, as RKO did with *King Kong* and Columbia with *Lost Horizon*.

By 1922, silent film was ready for its Third (and final) Era. The First comprised the primitive stage, the Second the national acculturation. When exactly to chart the beginning of the mature, formidably artistic stage is debatable. But 1922 will serve, as a great year for influential films in realism (Erich von Stroheim's *Foolish Wives*), spectacle (Allan Dwan's *Robin Hood* with Douglas Fairbanks), conscientious transformation of a theatre masterpiece (Nazimova's own production of Ibsen's *A Doll's House*), and documentary (Robert Flaherty's *Nanook of the North*).

Studios now are virtually estates of talent, sprawling, dense, and diverse. Biograph was a debased building in a run-down urban neighborhood. Universal, Paramount, and MGM glitter in quasi-suburban settings behind entrances as promising as the turret of a castle, the offices, shops, and main stages clustering up front, and the backlot of street scenes, college malls, quaint village squares, meadow, forest, jungle, and a working railroad station spreading out over the back forty. The outlying studio ranches and the nearby convenience of ocean, wild country, and desert afford a variety of natural settings that even romantic, dangerous Fort Lee, New Jersey, could not. Moreover, the human contingent of the studios' backstage has grown remarkably. Whole troops of artisans and engineers contribute to the production process, where Biograph made do with a few men to build and paint sets, a basket of props, and a clump of all-purpose costumes.

Indeed, the designer, charged with creating the "look" of each film and, by synecdoche, the visual style of a studio's entire output, is one of Hollywood's significant technicians. The editing of film, too, has changed greatly from Griffith's first days. At Biograph, the cutters had only to splice takes together in correct order. Now, in the late 1920s, shooting has become so complex that a gifted editor can cultivate a film through selection of takes, juxtaposition of setups within a given scene, and timing of the cutaways and fades. No wonder MGM was celebrated for its polish: MGM made a point of hiring the best in every department. By contrast, Paramount's less consistently capable editing shop could demote an A picture to a B through clumsy selection.

A studio, then, is yet another thing: a level of expertise. A studio is a politics, too, depending on the way its moguls and directors and writers look at the world. One studio concentrates on revealing patterns of oppression and resistance in the class war. Another soothes the masses with glorifications of the received secular pieties of Falling in Love and Getting Ahead—at any rate, of Shutting Up and Fitting In. Film historians tend to neglect writers. But they offer a strategic variable in isolating the "sense" of a given studio. Playing the word-association game, we hear "Columbia" and snap out, "Frank Capra." But if we hear "Capra," we snap out "Robert Riskin"—Capra's writer and, in a way, Columbia's voice.

Most significant of all the studio staff was the combination of director and cameraman, totally transformed from the mountebank and shutterbug of the First Era. Filming, to those two primitives, was simply that: you assigned the roles and turned on the lights, and when something moved, you cranked. Of course the more stimulated directors, like Griffith, eventually began to experiment, compose, manipulate; and the development of increasingly sensitive film stock challenged the photographer's imagination as well as his acumen. Dependent upon, even answerable to, the various assistant departments, the director was at the same time their lord—but he was the photographer's collaborator, sometimes his victim. This was film in the Third Era, a science of disciplines made unpredictable by the happenstance of interpersonal relationships.

The most troublesome of these, doubtless, was that of the producer and the director, another critical variable of studio life. One of the most important lessons that Hollywood had learned was: the better the director, the better the film. True, *stars* sold movies. But the star system had proved infuriatingly undependable, some actors losing public favor by their third or fourth vehicle, while directors might produce on a high level for decades. The biggest stars kept driving up their fees and percentages and benefits, each new precedent encouraging the setting of the next. Directors were content with merely good pay for good work. Moreover, stars were good for only one kind of thing—the Folk Hero in his rustic romances; the Sinful Woman savoring, ruined by, and at length repenting of the fleshly life—while most directors were game for anything and therefore easier to keep employed.

Admittedly, directors could be as troublesome as any star. Marshall Neilan, for instance, was unreliable, intolerably irreverent on the subject (and in the presence) of studio honchos, and volubly anti-Semitic, a provocative quirk in a company town run by Jewish men. Erich von Stroheim, even more brilliant than Neilan, was apparently unable to bring a film in on time and within budget, insistently shooting far more footage than could possibly have been marketed.

Yet there was this. Somehow, in ways both patent and occult, the director stood at the very center of the filmmaking process. This may sound like a truism in this age of the auteur, but way back then film was spontaneous, natural, autotelic, not the self-regarding art we parse today. Film was simpler, almost do-it-yourself. If one person could dominate a project, it was obviously the director. Everything passed through him—technical problems, artistic choices, the enacting, staging, look, and tone of the work. Put simply, the director was the artistic administrator of his films.

This is why the *politique des auteurs* strikes a chord of response even in those who do not neglect the importance of writing and acting. If Ernst Lubitsch more or less conceived his projects and collaborated with his writers; and if Lubitsch's famous "touch" is so palpable in countless ways in his films, and if Lubitsch's writers and actors tended to work in different styles for other directors, we see Lubitsch as the primary "author" of his movies. But other directors did less conceiving and collaborating. They lacked a touch. They simply received a finished script, approved the studio's casting plans, accepted the help of the technical people, relied on the photographer, and shot. In such undertakings, the auteur may be someone other than the director, or nobody. The auteur of some of Joan Crawford's early MGM talkies may be Adrian, her costume designer; and the auteur of *Grand Hotel* is MGM's star system.

Nevertheless, there have been a certain number of auteur directors in every period of Hollywood's history, and their relationship to the rest of the business—their freedom to create: their authorization by the studio, so to say—is another crucial element in the identification of a studio's style. The studio that gives its directors the greatest leeway may well release the most original movies, while the studio that most narrowly limits its directors may release the dullest—unless that narrow studio counters originality with competing qualities. Opulence, perhaps, the glamour of beauty affirming its legends. Or, contrarily, antagonistically, the slang and push of the zesty writer, to give films a smash-and-grab realism to complement America's new city culture, which overtook the agrarian population's majority as of the 1920 census. Or, in rebellion against our evident destiny, we might have illustrations of the peace and tribal solidarity of the rural scene, with its elegy of ageless continuity.

As it happened, one studio did give its directors a free rein. Another limited them to the compounding of totemic images. Another dwelled, raging, in the city. A fourth put the blunt honesty of the land above all else. Each approach claimed specialists, and here, too, the director was basic: for he alone of all the studio help had to comprehend the work, must know not only how to make a given picture but *why* the picture must be made. That much even the smartest producer (except Irving Thalberg and David Selznick) couldn't have told him. Besides the director, only the audience knew.

We reach the end of the Third Era of Silent Film by 1929, the first year of regular sound production. There were still a great many part-talkies* and a few envois from the major stars, whose public would put up with silence out of loyalty. But by midyear virtually all major films are talkies. Silence is over. Now begins the great Age of the Studios, from 1929 to 1948, when a Supreme Court decision forced a divestiture of the studios' theatre chains, undermining the corporations' economic foundation and bringing about a gradual dissolution of the studio as I have defined it herein. Though most of the old studio names introduce today's pictures with the familiar logos, postwar Hollywood is a disjunct pervasion of free-lancers, the ateliers closed, the expertise disbanded, the relationships nullified. Each film project now must feel like the first film ever to its advocates, as they doggedly sell their ideas to the idiots who now control the holdings. Investment capital: this is all that remains of the old production centers. Front money. The old moguls were brutal and ignorant but they did establish mediums of creativity and kept them operating. What more could an artist ask of a capitalist?

* Hollywood switched over to sound so suddenly, but so fully, that at first there was a shortage of the ingredients necessary for the making of talkies, including listenable actors, sound equipment, and writers. Thus many silent films were "corrected" by the addition of an effects-and-music track, or by dialogue scenes cut in here and there. Basically silents with the hiccups, the part-talkies paradoxically energized the invasion of sound by making the few remaining authentic silents appear all the more backward.

Anyway, what is—was—a studio? A studio is a *place* governed by a *budget* set by a *mogul* who believes he can market certain kinds of *stars* who are presented by a *staff of experts* who hold certain *social, artistic,* and *political* aperçus in common. As we move into the heyday of the studios, nearly all of them are established. We log the oldest: Universal, Paramount, and Fox. The challengers: MGM, Warner Brothers, and Columbia. RKO arrives more or less simultaneously with sound, and the outstanding independents, Goldwyn and Selznick, complete the scene, Hollywoodland.

Where, I ask you, does a studio get its informing energies—from the mogul? His production cohort? His directors? Writers? Stars? What sort of films most swiftly reveal a studio's themes to us—the Big Ones? The genre programmers? The exceptional films, out of sync with the output? Why do some studios emphasize certain forms while others do everything? Do they do everything competently, individually? Why is Katharine Hepburn one thing at RKO and something very different at MGM, while Barbara Stanwyck holds firm from studio to studio? How did the intently self-willed Frank Capra get to the least enterprising of studios while many a hack thrived at the most director-conscious of studios? How can we speak of studio style when all studios imitated each other—or does MGM's attempt at a Warner Brothers work-or-starve backstager only reveal MGM's qualities all the more?

Curtain going up: on the theatre of theory and practice, artists and repertory, in the Hollywood studios.

Sunset Boulevard, *the most autobiographical film Hollywood ever made: silent sensation Gloria Swanson revels in
yet rages against the cult of beauty to William Holden, a
writer turned gigolo. Note that, in the movie, beauty will
murder the writer. Hollywood wants personality, not
wisdom.*

PARAMOUNT

The Sophisticate

"Beginnings are always difficult," murmurs a bracingly elegant, penetratingly British, and solemnly erotic gentleman in dinner clothes ordering supper for two in a Venetian hotel. The Baron. (So we learn.) Beginnings are difficult, yet the Baron's pursuit of his guest, the Countess (so he calls her), is practiced. He doesn't as much as blink when the Countess calls him a crook. Indeed, he calmly passes her the salt and calls her a thief. Then, after closing the window curtains, he reaches for her hand, draws her up from the table, takes her in his arms . . . and shakes her until the wallet that she just stole from him, and that he stole from someone else earlier that evening, falls to the floor. Reclaiming the wallet, the Baron holds out a chair for the Countess, and they return to their meal:

THE COUNTESS: I like you, Baron.

THE BARON: (fervently) I'm crazy about you. (He hands her a small object, from out of his pocket.) By the way: your pin.

THE COUNTESS: (with a self-mocking smile) Thank you, Baron.

THE BARON: Not at all, Countess. There's one very good stone in it.

THE COUNTESS: What time is it?

(He can't find his watch; she hands it to him with a smile of victory.)

It was five minutes slow, but I regulated it for you.

(They bow to each other, virtuoso unto virtuoso.)

THE BARON: (tenderly) I hope you don't mind if I keep your garter.

(Startled, she checks her leg: he *did* take it! Topped by the master, she gives way to a thrill as he produces the garter, kisses it, and puts it back in his pocket.)

THE COUNTESS: Darling!

(They kiss.)

So begins what may be the definitive Paramount movie, *Trouble in Paradise* (1932), written by Samson Raphaelson and directed by Ernst Lubitsch, with Herbert Marshall, Miriam Hopkins, and Kay Francis. Film buffs will immediately spot certain elements as uniquely Paramount. There are the three stars, for instance, at the time all Paramount contractees in their prime. There is Lubitsch, who landed at Warner Brothers when he first set up shop in America and ended at Fox, but who, like his contemporary Josef von Sternberg, typified the Paramount director as maximum leader of unique cinema. There is Raphaelson, closely identified with Lubitsch, who would retell the plot of some boulevardier romp popular in Budapest a spring or so before—in this case László Aladar's *The Honest Finder;* let Raphaelson plunk out a script, edit it with him, then march to the camera, the entire show in hand. There is the European accent of the project— British Marshall, German Lubitsch, the Venice and Paris of the setting. There is the background of the naughty or foolish or scheming rich: for thieves Marshall and Hopkins move in on naughty plutocrat Francis with dishonorable intentions on her safe, while Francis's foolish suitor Edward Everett Horton almost unmasks Marshall, and Francis's scheming business associate C. Aubrey Smith actually does. There is the wit of Raphaelson's script, the wit of Lubitsch's eye—the wit, even, in the very faces of Marshall, Hopkins, and Francis.

None of the three was an important talent. Marshall had a habit of acting with his neck, craning his sleepy head forward as if he were something less than spot on his lines and had to pick up his cues visually. Hopkins was too often a thoughtless actress and Francis little more than a mannequin. Yet here the three are erotically electric, Marshall going slowly but all the way, Hopkins on permanent arousal call, and Francis rapaciously charming. Three deep-dish slickers. Think: whom would MGM have cast in 1932? Robert Montgomery and Madge Evans as the thieves, Norma Shearer or Myrna Loy as the rich widow. There's swank there, but no bite.

Certainly MGM would never have permitted Montgomery to advise Shearer on her makeup, as Marshall does Francis. Having stolen her handbag (at the Opéra) in order to meet her by returning it, Marshall takes inventory of its contents as she looks on, bemused. Ah! here's a love letter from the absurd Charles Ruggles, another Paramount intimate, as useful in spoofing amorous male aggression as men like Marshall are in sifting its nuances. Marshall is willing to overlook Ruggles's dreary style and low grammar, "but the letter," Marshall insists, "has no mystery, no bouquet." Then there's Francis's lipstick, scarlet number 4. "With your skin," Marshall observes, "I prefer crimson." And her powder is too dark. Fascinated, defensive, and very pleasurably threatened, Francis says, "Do you realize I have light eyes?" "That's a matter of eye shadow," Marshall replies. "I can straighten that out in two seconds." Thus Paramount's blasé charmer. MGM likes heroes who have been around the block; Paramount likes heroes who have been around the world.

Most Paramount of all in *Trouble in Paradise* is the droll nature of its sexuality. It is comedy's mission to laugh at risible beaux, like Ruggles here or, in *Love Me Tonight* (1932), Charles Butterworth, who hopes to woo Jeanette MacDonald with his flute-playing. Toppling from her balcony, he lands unhurt: "But I fell flat on my flute!" Paramount, however, laughs as well at the chosen who deserve love, those with the mystery and bouquet. Lubitsch had been generally influential in Hollywood since his five Warner silents, all romantic comedies, and he particularly left his mark at Paramount, where he not only directed but produced. We expect a touch of Lubitsch in all Paramount boudoir satires, not just those by Lubitsch. But even before he came to America, Paramount had seeded a generic field in the marital comedies of Cecil B. DeMille, the Gloria Swanson series with titles such as *Don't Change Your Husband* (1919), *For Better, For Worse* (1919), *Male and Female* (1919), *Why Change Your Wife?* (1920), and *The Affairs of Anatol* (1921), the last after Arthur Schnitzler, one of the founding fathers of modern sex comedy.

Paramount is a studio with a venerable tradition in this line, then, and by 1932 the form is in glory, not only technically but thematically, too. We take for granted Lubitsch's agile camera, wryly pausing at a doorway to eavesdrop; or the gently radiant lighting in which even gray comes off as a pastel; or the confidence of format, so versatile it can turn a tale into an operetta yet lose none of its realism. But we never quite get used to Paramount's amused view of courtship, marriage, infidelity—of sex—as transactions of various kinds.

In *Trouble in Paradise,* theft is a form of seduction, not only in Marshall's opening dinner with Hopkins but in Marshall's ensuing relationship with Francis and in Hopkins's attempt to express her jealousy by robbing Francis herself. Better yet: at Paramount, seduction *is* theft, the essential transaction among the worldly. Less so in DeMille, most so in Lubitsch, and subtly and erratically so in Mitchell Leisen's Claudette Colbert–Fred MacMurray–Ray Milland comedies, true love is successful larceny. Romance dims, marriages fail when thieves run out of stuff to steal. What is the mystery, the bouquet? Boodle.

This is truly subversive. Few if any thought so when the films were new, however, for all three directors worked in aggressive, dazzling styles that obscured the content of their pictures. DeMille's flashbacks to ancient times might have alerted the sensitive viewer, for this constant projecting of a contemporary romantic situation into the brutal parallel of a conqueror and his victim suggests that passion is bloodlust—that the flowers and candy of today betoken feelings of such intensity that the very survival of civilization rests on our suppressing them. DeMille opens the original, silent *Manslaughter* (1922)*

---

* The 1930 talkie remake, also called *Manslaughter*, with Fredric March and Claudette Colbert under George Abbott's direction, is less well known.

at a roadhouse of jazz babies in riot. "Real rose-leaves! Real champagne!" the titles warn us. "Everything real but the men and women!" To Thomas Meighan, the local District Attorney, these decadents recall the "wasters" who destroyed Rome from within.

Instantly, DeMille cuts to ancient Rome at high orgy. *Manslaughter*'s heroine and Meighan's love interest, Leatrice Joy, holds court on a dais flanked by tigers, imperiously enjoying a gladiator match. DeMille will show her! A barbarian horde rides in, led by Meighan in a stupendous winged helmet.

In other words, Meighan *takes* Joy. In another part of Paramount's forest, Meighan versus Swanson in *Male and Female,* the flashback takes us to old Babylon, where a Meighan-resistant Swanson is sent to the royal zoo for a date with a lion. No kidding: DeMille based the shot on the Victorian print entitled "The Lion's Bride." Sex is theft.

But why would anyone notice DeMille's harping on this note of sexual extortion? There are too many distractions—DeMille's fleet pacing, his flourishing of the latest in *dolce vita* accessories, from evening clothes to bathtubs, and especially his pietistic moralizing. Thus *Manslaughter* puts everyone through the mill: Leatrice Joy's maid Lois Wilson is sent to prison for stealing a ring from milady (albeit to raise the medical bill for Wilson's ailing son). Joy herself commits the titular crime while trying to outrun a cop in a car chase. Meighan, breast heaving, prosecutes, sends Joy to join Wilson in prison, then hits the bottle and the skids. At length, all three reform, Meighan successfully running for governor. In Russia, they say, everything not expressly forbidden is allowed. In DeMille, everything not expressly allowed is forbidden—after we get to enjoy it vicariously.

DeMille made Paramount "safe" for the truly risqué, for sex play as deeply motivated as it was elaborately manipulated. Lubitsch honored the trope with a more delicate vitality and a richer morality—his thieves get away with the snatch. Leisen fell into step with a stronger sense of contemporaneity set off with wit. What is most essential to the Paramount style, however, is not the slyness of its sex comedy alone, but the studio's reliance on directorial initiative. Paramount gave sly directors latitude. As long as their films made money, DeMille, Lubitsch, and Leisen were encouraged to follow their personal lights, even granted first dibs on their assistants of choice, such as DeMille's scenarist and sometime lover Jeanie Macpherson, Lubitsch's writers Ernest Vajda and Samson Raphaelson, or Leisen's producer Arthur Hornblow, Jr. This in effect gave them their own production units, something very common in the freewheeling Hollywood of the Second Era but very rare during the Studio Age of the 1930s and '40s. Then, studio chiefs instilled discipline, cost-efficiency, and fear by keeping the cards eternally in shuffle. Paramount was always exceptional in this regard—so much so that a director actually became the studio's production chief: Lubitsch, from 1935 to 1936.

The reason for this respect for directors lies deep in Paramount's history, which is virtually synchronous with the history of Hollywood, and explains why this studio takes first place in this book. Selig got to Hollywood first of all the picturemakers, and Universal, of Paramount's longer-lived contemporaries, was founded earlier than Paramount. But Paramount became the leader of the business by 1917 or so. It was not only the most successful studio, but the most intently competitive one, ceaselessly attempting to force its advantage. Much of the early history of the movies may be seen in Paramount instigating and the rest of the industry resisting or imitating. Paramount's advantages were many, but two above all: Paramount had the stars and Paramount had the theatres.

The advantage of a studio's owning a chain of theatres is obvious: guaranteed exhibition for your production. Better yet, the corporation could pocket the profits instead of sharing them with free-lance theatre owners. Best of all, cornering the market in major theatres in metropolitan centers called attention to one's product, amortized publicity costs and got the most out of word-of-mouth report. Nothing helped a movie like a big marquee and lines of keyed-up patrons right in the middle of downtown. Of particular note in the matter of studio stylistics is the edge this gave Paramount in experimentation, in deviating from the confines of genre and cliché. Universal, with little access to the influential picture palaces of New York, Chicago, Kansas City, San Francisco, or Atlanta, was forced to release most of its films in small-town theatres or the urban "neighborhood" houses. Thus Universal addressed a public considerably less sophisticated than Paramount's. This made Universal conservative. Paramount was able to dare.

As with the big theatres, so with the big stars. Paramount rounded them up. This is utmost power but, as I've said, somewhat less than a sure thing. Stars could get too big, self-willed, and expensive. Stars might top out in popularity sooner than expected, failing to draw just when a studio was spending a fortune on them. They might even try to sneak off to another studio. Paramount has many such cases to draw on, in, respectively, Little Mary and Valentino, who ended up capitalizing and releasing their films themselves; in Nancy Carroll, well liked but never a great moneymaker (and we'll shortly see why); in Gary Cooper, who was just hitting his zenith when he got sore at the studio and signed with Goldwyn.

Nevertheless. Stars, along with an important theatre chain to support them, had become a basic element of moviemaking by Silent Film's Second Era, virtually the essence of the difference between the patents men's approach and the rest of Hollywood history. Paramount knew this because Adolph Zukor knew this, and Adolph Zukor *was* Paramount, founder, developer, and, more or less until his death in 1976 at the age of 103, maximum mogul. Zukor's first shot, in 1912, was Famous Players in Famous Plays, an arrestingly Broadway-conscious notion, especially in the light of Paramount's later fascination with stage performers. Zukor's stars would be Broadway's big names, their vehicles Broadway hits, familiarized throughout the land on barnstorming tours. Merging with the Jesse L. Lasky Feature Play Company in 1916, Zukor began to build: stars and theatres. He was quiet, ruthless, and *very* observant. More than anyone else in the business, perhaps, Zukor had reckoned the patterns of success and failure. He quickly realized that stars were not famous players but engaging personalities. He wondered how big a big star or a big picture could get. What does Hollywood need?

This is what Zukor decided:

1. A good picture is better when a star makes it.
2. A good picture with a star is best when a gifted director makes it.
3. Therefore: stardom is inseparable from gifted direction.

Hollywood needs both. It must be popular but it may be art. This theory, set into motion by Zukor, sustained Paramount throughout the Studio Age, when Zukor had become Paramount's gray eminence, the first name on the opening credits ("Adolph Zukor presents . . ."), but something of a tradition, a legend, a vote in the boardroom. Such men as B. P. Schulberg and Y. Frank Freeman bossed production on site. Yet Zukorism stimulated Paramount. Just as Warner Brothers was the studio of the writer (not out of respect, but because Warners' production moved too fast to allow for much rewriting) and MGM the studio of the star (as long as he or she followed orders), Paramount was the studio of the director. Not that Paramount worshipped its directors: just that it interfered with their work much less than other big studios did.

Directors, after all, are Hollywood's most disruptive force. Producers and actors are conservative, fearful of risk. Writers are headstrong, true, dangerously idealistic; but writers have no power in Hollywood. Anyway, the Hollywood habit of generating scripts through teams and editors, step by step, effectively silenced loud voices. It is the director, again, who holds exclusive rights as artisan of the popular.

But there is this, too, a dandy side effect Zukor had noted with his other insights: big directors are the only power capable of subduing big stars. Yes, a producer might threaten a troublesome star with unemployment, and a few egoistic agitators were indeed cast out of the industry. Yet these were exemplary punishments, to keep the others in line—no studio could afford to alienate or destroy even a portion of its contract list. A director, however, was of vital aid to a star; and the smart star knew it. Did not the great D.W., master of directors, the one who taught all the others everything they knew (or so it was thought) . . . did he not launch star after star? Little Mary, the Gish sisters, Mae Marsh, Blanche Sweet, Constance Talmadge, Richard Barthelmess, Henry B. Walthall, Robert Harron, all of whom eventually worked for Paramount, including Griffith himself.* Little Mary and her grim mother Charlotte Pickford would encircle tycoon Zukor in contract negotiations like wolves admiring a lamb; but such was the authority of a big director that Zukor was

---

* This is not even to mention the many historic names that stipple Griffith's casts: Pauline Starke, Bessie Love, Alma Rubens, Seena Owen, Noël Coward, Alfred Lunt, Erich von Stroheim, Donald Crisp, Lionel Barrymore, W. C. Fields, Owen Moore, George Walsh, silent Tarzan Elmo Lincoln, Eugene Pallette, Tyrone Power, Sr., Louis Wolheim, Joseph Schildkraut, Henry Hull, Neil Hamilton, Lupino Lane, as well as future directors Raoul Walsh, John Ford, and Tod Browning—and, in bits of *The Birth of a Nation* and *Intolerance*, the man who was to become one of Paramount's biggest stars, Wallace Reid.

able to force Little Mary to send a humble telegram to DeMille as they readied to collaborate on *A Romance of the Redwoods.* And Little Mary, by then, was the biggest of big stars, her vehicles so instrumental in selling a studio's line that when Zukor couldn't face another negotiating session, he offered her an evil fortune if she would take a five-year vacation and make no movies for anyone.

A humble telegram to DeMille! But was there any other kind? Here we delve into the origins of Paramount, in DeMille's famous pioneer filming in 1913 of the first of Jesse Lasky's Feature Plays (the line that, joined to Zukor's Famous Plays, emerged as Famous–Lasky: Paramount itself). The subject was *The Squaw Man,* a Broadway hit of 1905 with William Faversham as an English chap who nobly shoulders another's guilt and flees to the American West. (The villain of the original staging, by hap, was to introduce the movies' paragon of the "good" outlaw, William S. Hart.)

Apparently, all Lasky and DeMille started with was the stage star Dustin Farnum and the notion of presenting him in a film based on one of his Broadway hits. (Note that Lasky agreed with Zukor that established stage properties featuring a celebrated stage name would give their output prestige and squeeze.) DeMille passed up what would have been the logical choice, *The Virginian,* the play that gave Farnum his big break in 1904. It was, to boot, more endearing than *The Squaw Man,* like it a western but less plotty, more personalized.* But Farnum had played a tour of *The Squaw Man,* with a week in New York, only two years before DeMille approached him. Perhaps Farnum thought it the fresher property. Or perhaps DeMille preferred the cliché contrivances of the English-gentleman-out-West tale to *The Virginian*'s more inward conflicts of friendship and honor. Certainly, throughout his career, DeMille was better at telling than showing: at manipulating action than at talking to actors.

Anyway, Dustin Farnum did film *The Virginian* (1914) with DeMille, for *The Squaw Man*'s success set Lasky Feature Plays on its course of, at first, competition with and, latterly, collaboration with Zukor's plays-and-players scheme. For the first two years and some

---

* As witness *The Virginian*'s endurance in cinema and *The Squaw Man*'s retirement. DeMille remade *The Squaw Man* in 1918 and 1931, by which time it looked impossibly corny. *The Virginian* held up in 1929 (with Gary Cooper, Richard Arlen, and Walter Huston) and 1946 (with Joel McCrea, Sonny Tufts, and Brian Donlevy), and was even adapted as a television series, albeit vastly enervated.

Erich von Stroheim (far right, in white) musters his troops for The Wedding March *(1928). Given von Stroheim's auteurist panache, it's surprising that he directed only this title for director-oriented Paramount. Ironically, von Stroheim made his biggest hit,* The Merry Widow *(1925), for MGM, a studio of producers more than directors.*

fifteen features, DeMille adhered to the famous-plays-and-players formula, with a few famous novels thrown in. But after a while he began to film original ideas and de-emphasize the stage names in favor of the new generation of actors becoming famous not as players but as film stars. Bessie Barriscale headed *The Rose of the Rancho* (1914), a Frances Starr vehicle on Broadway; Blanche Sweet led *The Warrens of Virginia* (1915) and *The Captive* (1915). Theatre people were not actually dispensed with—Fannie Ward, Ina Claire, and Victor Moore went to work for DeMille in 1915, as did Geraldine Farrar, who was operatic rather than strictly thespian, but The Most Famous Player of them all. Nevertheless, we note that Ward's vehicle, *The Cheat* (1915), was conceived for the screen, not an adaptation, and that succeeding features not only affirmed the "original scenario" approach but increasingly concentrated on the personalities shaped not by the Anglophile, fourth-wall, staircase-entrance, well-made American theatre but by moviemaking. When DeMille began his collaboration with Gloria Swanson in 1919, he was working with an actress who had literally no stage experience whatever.

As we shall see, the era of the Famous Player was not entirely over at Paramount. What is important here is the revelation of an era of the director, of his ability to marshal his staff and pursue his vision with little or no superintendence by a front office. If it works, don't fix it: directors were the works, the craftsmen who framed the stars. Toward the end of the silent period, Hollywood generally closed in on the power of individuals, especially the stars and the directors. The libertarian days were over; the despots were ensconcing themselves. There was such trouble in paradise then that even director-conscious Paramount caught the germ, and suddenly hit on DeMille for his expansive budgets.

Yet DeMille was no spendthrift. Like David Selznick, he believed that either very cheap or very expensive films make money. And, like Selznick, DeMille was making very expensive films. Outraged that the studio that he had helped found was turning on him—was DeMille not Paramount's first, most chosen director?—he bowed out and went off to other pastures, most notably MGM. But there DeMille realized the difference between being the biggest tuna in a school of tuna (the Paramount context) and a tuna in a school of shark (MGM). DeMille came home.

And stayed there. Most of Hollywood's directors moved from place to place, as eras and taste and contract possibilities changed. Not DeMille. From his homecoming entry, *The Sign of the Cross* in 1932, to his last film, *The Ten Commandments* in 1956, DeMille remained at Paramount, his research, pre-production planning, shooting, and post-production occupying him for one year per picture, slowing down at the end to one every few years. Gloria Swanson, the entirely celluloid-derived star, might have said, "I am the movies." DeMille might have said, "I am Paramount."

How Paramount was he? He was so Paramount that in his Swanson films he in effect evolved the form that the incomparably more gifted Ernst Lubitsch was to refine into a classic Hollywood genre. He was so Paramount that even after he gave up sex comedy his films retained a sexiness that troubled prudes. He was so Paramount that the studio let him come and go through a special DeMille gate, for his unit alone. He was so Paramount that, to the end of his days, his pictures were always DeMille pictures, no matter who was in them, with his voice narrating (as if from On High) and his signature—"produced and directed by"—penetratingly displayed. Paramount might have said, "The director is the movies."

DeMille's Paramount talkies are an odd bunch, almost invariably historical epics but at first conflicts of religion in the ancient world, then conflicts of capitalist interests in pioneer America, then ancient holy wars again, as DeMille nears death and fears God. The films vary enormously in texture of pace and characterization and thematic pungency. *The Sign of the Cross,* pagans versus Christians in old Rome, with Fredric March caught between a pagan harlot and a Christian innocent, drags horribly. The Christians are as dull as a hymnal, their patriarchs bearing atrocious beards in the shape of Commandment Tablets. Yet the florid gloom of Charles Laughton's Nero and Claudette Colbert's lascivious Empress keep it game, not least when Colbert takes her famous milk bath, the liquid *just* topping her nipples. A confidante rushes in with unpleasant but at any rate romantic news. "Take off your clothes," Colbert snarls; "get in, and tell me all about it."

Nor does *Cleopatra* (1934) uphold DeMille's reputation. Colbert presses a little on the sultry, and her Marc Antony is Henry Wilcoxon, a hot Briton but more Briton than hot. He's tempestuously wooden. Yet, in the sequence in which Colbert seduces Wilcoxon on her burnished barge, DeMille shows talkie-goers why silent-film buffs feel superior. In one very long tracking shot, DeMille backs away from the splendid couple, up the length of the boat, past dancers and slaves, to the pounding of the drum that keeps the oarsmen in stroke, taken up on the sound track in a heavy symphony of Mediterranean pastiche that sounds (like DeMille himself) as shocked by sex as fascinated by it, still backing away as the dancers pose and the slaves grovel and silken curtains blow closed on the immortal hunger of Egypt and Rome as the barge glides on through the night . . . the purely visual inflamed by music: silent film.

Too much of DeMille, however, is uninspired, especially the later talkies. The insistent spectacle becomes strenuous, as if DeMille saw American history as a series of train wrecks and attacks by giant squid. At that, the parting of the Red Sea and the sculpting of the Tablets in the talkie *Ten Commandments* are less dazzling than their silent originals. Nor is DeMille able or willing to sustain the conflicted prurience of his youth, the fastidious voyeurism of the preacher who attends an orgy just to know what to preach against. He even loses his touch in simple romance at times. The sparring courtship of Wild Bill Hickock (Gary Cooper) and Calamity Jane (Jean Arthur) at the heart of *The Plainsman* (1937) has no grip; we get only sparring, no sense that the two are wild—literally wild—for each other. Yet just a year before, for Columbia and Frank Capra in *Mr. Deeds Goes to Town,* Cooper and Arthur made a persuasively involved couple.

All this said, we nevertheless see why DeMille remained a force in Hollywood, and why Paramount let him run his own unit and spend his big budgets. DeMille even held out for the precise editing that Paramount seldom administered even on A films. *Reap the Wild Wind* (1942), a saga of shipwrecks and salvaging in the antebellum South with Ray Milland, John Wayne, and Paulette Goddard, is easy to put down as "just another" DeMille spectacular, bigger and longer than most films, with a huge cast and Technicolor, still rare enough then to be thought eventful. Its logic of character is elemental: good guys and bad, wild women and haughty bluenoses, sentiments murmured and war cries bellowed as the men and the typical DeMillian Lusty Lady (Goddard) dash about the land battling for power, wealth, and love. (Raymond Massey is the exception here; he only wants power and wealth. You can always tell the villain in a DeMille film: he'll be the only guy who isn't in love.) "Sweeping" is the word for it. You can't look through a window without seeing half the South behind it. The movie lacks the more detailed antiquing of MGM's historical films, or the cynicism desperate for an ideal that we get from Capra's view of Americana. But it is fast and vital, and there are the odd DeMillian touches, as when Milland, his locks Byronically atumble, plays ventriloquist with his pet highland white Scottie, or when Goddard sings a scandalous sea chantey to shock a party of prudes.

In fact, DeMille at his best is not only fast, vital, colorful, and elemental but characterologically sound, even passionate—and almost genuinely epic. His talkie masterpiece—if a style of such coarsely overloaded grandeur may be said to claim one—is *Union Pacific* (1939). To a medley of old American ditties, the credits unfold on a length of railroad track, and the first scene takes us into the United States Congress just after the Civil War for a hot debate on whether or not to run the railroad to the West Coast. This is instant history, to say the least, but what is on DeMille's mind is not history but the taut triangle of good guy Joel McCrea, Lusty Lady Barbara Stanwyck (complete, here and there, with an Irish accent), and Robert Preston, McCrea's old war buddy, his rival for Stanwyck, and, for bite, the hired bravo of bad guy Brian Donlevy. Even at his best, DeMille is uneven, and just as we get a mixture of history true and false, of a worldview now compassionately democratic and now callously right-wing, of dialogue both sensible and ridiculous, so do we get a diverse quality of a portrayal. Self-starter Preston is fine and Donlevy confident. But McCrea needs Preston Sturges and Stanwyck wants Capra.

Technically, *Union Pacific* is stupendous, the back projections persuasive, the train wrecks (this one has two, but no squid) spectacular, and the narrative rhythm masterly. The violence is especially fetching, for the bad guys are more charming than usual for DeMille. As the principals ride west in a crowded car, a young Indian joyfully stunt-rides his horse alongside the train, and one of Donlevy's hoods shoots him for the fun of it. McCrea socks the murderer, and, as the fight spreads through the car, DeMille catches it in a riot of energy and detail that is, from shot to shot, amazingly terse yet intelligible. It's one of the outstanding set-piece brawls of its day, and, for a capper, McCrea knocks the culprit who started it all right off the train. DeMille sits with him in the wilderness, shooting over his shoulder as the train roars off and leaves him behind.

DeMille's lifetime tenure with Paramount indicates how strongly the studio felt about directors, even the rigidly self-willed directors who did things their own way. In fact, Paramount's top directors generally stand out for their distinct styles, their touch. Most other studios preferred directors whose pictures didn't look all that different from those of their colleagues. Throughout the studio era, fiercely individual directors tend to rove—Alfred Hitchcock, for instance, or Howard Hawks. Paramount seemed to welcome or at least tolerate individuality—from Lubitsch, Rouben Mamoulian, Josef von Sternberg, Mitchell Leisen, Preston Sturges, and Billy Wilder, among others, along with DeMille.

Perhaps this, too, relates to Paramount's seniority in the industry. It was the first truly big studio, head of Hollywood so long ago that, in 1916, when Zukor and Lasky merged and Paramount proper took shape, *The Birth of a Nation* was still in its original release. This is old, old Hollywood, still totally entrusted to the director. Thus Paramount must have absorbed a respect for the breed quite aside from Zukor's savvy about how expedient directors were in the showcasing of stars. As the greatest of studios, Paramount put a premium on turning out a number of pictorially splendid films as evidence of its greatness.

This was not simple bravado, but strategy. Paramount had a prestige to maintain. Zukor's devouring monopoly had driven his competitors to a do-or-die resistance. A group of exhibitors banded together in 1917 as First National, creating their own studio specifically to free them from dealings with Paramount. New moguls as sharp as Zukor were on the rise. Most dangerous of all, in 1919 the biggest stars founded *their* own studio, United Artists. Now Paramount must reaffirm itself, justify its eminence.

Let other studios go for prestige of big casts, spectacle, or roadshow specials. Paramount made its point through elegance, imagination, beauty, the vivacity of the visual. There is a difference between a merely sizable movie and a truly handsome one. Let's play word association again. To "Paramount" one might respond "society comedy," and, yes, this was Paramount's stock-in-trade, with that sly sex-is-theft innuendo that slithers through the eras from DeMille to Sturges. *Trouble in Paradise,* for instance: this is society comedy at the zenith, a world in which everything is handsomely ordered and brutal truths are eased into fey jokes. Translate all that into an aesthetics of the camera and you have Paramount in the 1920s—Allan Dwan, Herbert Brenon, Maurice Tourneur complementing the more direct DeMille with deftness of code, all the more telling for its delicacy and point.

This side of Paramount was most in evidence in silent days, when the visual was everything. Today, unfortunately, only buffs and historians have access—through preservation prints, stills, and the enthusiast's rapt nostalgia for a time and place he has never known—to what hasn't simply vanished forever. Perhaps Herbert Brenon's *A Kiss for Cinderella* typifies this side of Paramount, coming, in 1926, at what turned out to be the start of the climax of an epoch. That year, Warner Brothers released *Don Juan,* the first film with its own music-and-sound-effects track; the next year they issued *The Jazz Singer,* the first part-talkie. Great silents continued to appear: *Sunrise, The Last Command, The Wind.* But they marked a last heedful celebration of the doomed, and in 1929 all Hollywood spun over into sound. Having reached a superior evolutionary state, the movies hastily retrogressed.

Many great silent directors were inhibited by—even entirely at a loss with—sound. Herbert Brenon fell away so badly after 1929 that many checklists pass him up—neither Andrew Sarris's nor Richard Roud's encyclopedia of filmmakers mentions him. Yet he made some exponential films, both of Hollywood's version of the heroic world —the Ronald Colman *Beau Geste*—and of the American 1920s— *Dancing Mothers* and *The Great Gatsby*—all three for Paramount in 1926, the year of *A Kiss for Cinderella.* The source of the last-named is James M. Barrie's play about the London servant who dreams that she is Cinderella at the ball, and Paramount billed Barrie alone above the title, though the Cinderella, Betty Bronson, had won some notice the year before for Brenon's film of Barrie's *Peter Pan.* Brenon, however, gets two credits, for "A Herbert Brenon production" on the title card and, immediately after, a name credit as director. There is no question about who Paramount thinks is most answerable for the quality of the film.

The quality is high indeed. Brenon cagily keeps the camera work plain in the framing real-life scenes, treating Bronson's romance with a bobby (Tom Moore) in wartime London. Investigating Bronson's suspicious behavior, Moore visits her penny-a-tick doctor-tailor-minister shop to partake of baked potatoes with her gang of homeless kids.* After Bronson catches pneumonia dreaming of her Cinderella ball in the snow, Moore comes to her convalescent bed to propose marriage and look worried at the fade-out clinch, an arresting way to end a love story: the heroine may not recover.

It is the central fantasy sequence, the *Cinderella* of the film, that gives us Paramount at its most dazzling. We expect the Fairy God-mother (Esther Ralston) to change Bronson's rags into a gown in a wink; in fact, the after is a bit out of sync with the before, as Bronson's head moved between the shots. But the use of animated drawings to build the pumpkin and mice into the coach and horses is delivered with delightful precision. Then Brenon builds the sequence, as the streetlamps almost jump out of their joints bowing to Cinderella's coach, and the coach pulls through process shots to climb into the sky, past clouds and then stars as the theatre orchestra seconds Brenon's visual crescendo with a symphonic one, the sight and sound merging in a shot of pealing bells as Brenon takes us all into the ball itself.

This we see entirely through the cockney slavey's eyes; it is, after all, her dream. Brenon gives us demented clowns, frantic pages in busker kit, paper-bag dinners, dropped h's in the title cards—and of course "Prince Hard-to-Get" is bobby Tom Moore. "Let's loose the beauts," he says—twenty-four of them in spectacular gowns, rudely hustled off when they fail the slipper test. After Bronson takes the competition, the King announces, "There's an ice-cream cone for everybody!" An army of organ-grinders has appeared to play for the dance, and everyone goes into what looks like a fox-trot.

Then midnight strikes and the entire ballroom begins to spin.

Apparently through double exposure, Brenon sets Bronson in the

---

* One of the kids is German. Patriotic Bronson decorates her cradle with worsted cut to resemble barbed wire, and denies her the other children's paper hats with the British flag on top. Most Barrie heroines are a little nutty.

center of the screen in natural time and the rest of the cast in the background in slow motion, slowly revolving around her, unaware and uncaring as she dithers and despairs, as her dress devolves back into rags, as her pitiful dream dissolves, visual delirium. At last we see her cowering against a pillar as her four homeless kids, in their nightgowns, shield her from the bon ton. One of them hands the Prince her glass slipper. The slightly off-the-wall nature of the splendor is authentic Barrie, and Brenon has thus brought off not only a beautiful film, but a fair one.

Paramount welcomed directors of high style, even the eccentric ones, even the Europeans. Elsewhere in Hollywood, strangers were expected to assimilate the more straightforward, less keenly nuanced American approach. True, there was F. W. Murnau, brought to Fox from Berlin to make perhaps the most European movie ever produced in Hollywood, *Sunrise* (1927). But we think more often of William Dieterle, Fritz Lang, or Douglas Sirk, all of whom modified their approach for American audiences. We think of Mauritz Stiller, hired by MGM along with his protégée Greta Garbo, but mysteriously neglected once he got here—even separated from Garbo, taken off her films and replaced by company men. Crushed, Stiller went back to Sweden and died. But he did make three films for another studio before he left Hollywood. Which studio?

Paramount. So we are not surprised to find another intensely willful director and his protégée making a similar journey to Zukor's atelier, and bringing with them a Continental art of such gesticula-tive eroticism, such impishly grotesque sophistication, that even today it's hard to believe that Paramount let them make six films together within five years: *Morocco* (1930), *Dishonored* (1931), *Shanghai Express* (1932), *Blonde Venus* (1932), *The Scarlet Empress* (1934), *The Devil Is a Woman* (1935). Josef von Sternberg and Marlene Dietrich.

Von Sternberg had already worked for Paramount in late silent years. But his Dietrich cycle is set apart, unlike anything that either of them did on his own. There were key collaborators: photographers Lee Garmes and Bert Glennon, art director Hans Dreier, couturier Travis Banton (strongly guided by Dietrich herself), writer Jules Furthman (on three of the six), and the Paramount publicity depart-ment. But this certain oeuvre feels wholly von Sternberg's; seldom has a Hollywood output so supported the auteurist conception of an onlie begetter amid the assembly line of studio procedure. The series is, at once, typical Paramount and unique cinema, most Hollywood yet least Hollywood, mass entertainment arranged by one man about one woman.

Yes, Dietrich shifts position through the cycle. In the immediately preceding *The Blue Angel* (made in Berlin in 1929 but released in America, in an English version, just after *Morocco*), Dietrich is the destroyer, pure Vamp. So in *Morocco* she is a cynical romantic, born to love in doom; in *Dishonored* the same, with firing-squad finale; in *Shanghai Express* the same, with happy ending, albeit with Clive Brook; in *Blonde Venus* a housewife, toy of men; in *The Scarlet Empress* a ruler of men; and in *The Devil Is a Woman* back as Lady Irresistible, full cycle. Nevertheless, these are all the director's takes on the Vamp, all studies of Dietrich as von Sternberg's boon and nemesis. He cast his own double, Lionel Atwill, in *The Devil Is a Woman*— what studio but Paramount would have had a double of Josef von Sternberg under contract?—to rage at and woo Dietrich. "The most dangerous woman you'll ever meet," Atwill warns young Cesar Romero. The grandee's advice impresses Romero, but soon enough they're dueling over Dietrich. And she tells Atwill, "You've always mistaken your vanity for love."

The quotable lines, the quaint casting, Dietrich's bizarre song spots, the pervasive European atmosphere, the opulently exclusive lighting, plundering the view of everything but secrets—this is a world all its own. Yet it tells strongly of Paramount. Surely no other studio would have released *Morocco,* let alone five more such, with its resplendently dreary illumination of sexual hunger in places now as constricted as a closet, now as empty as a wilderness. No other studio would have allowed the heroine's nightclub number to manifest so bluntly the sex-is-theft paradigm, passing her among the customers bearing a basket of forbidden fruit. "What am I bid for my apples," Dietrich sings, "the fruit that made Adam so wise?" Another studio might have let Dietrich sing a second number in a man's tails and topper, but only Paramount's von Sternberg would have redoubled the stakes of their gender roulette by having Dietrich kiss a woman and throw a flower to Gary Cooper. Later, visiting Dietrich's room, Cooper picks up her fan and cools off, as they flirt, like a debutante in rut. Yet he was, at the time, the studio's most promising male star,

How different Marlene Dietrich and Gary Cooper seem in their Paramount days, as here, from the way they will later on at other studios. Her calculated sensuality will cool off somewhat, grow more natural and less exotic. His elegance will shift toward an outdoorsy virility.

somewhere between a Dangerous Man and a Folk Hero, more mysterious than MGM's Clark Gable and more versatile than Warner Brothers' James Cagney. At Paramount, Cooper would prove as comfortable with Ernst Lubitsch as with "Wild Bill" Wellman, simply indispensable. That Paramount could, first of all, so blithely put Cooper in von Sternberg's charge and, second, release *Morocco* without bowdlerizing retakes tells us how deeply erotic Paramount's famous elegance in fact was, how deftly it uncovers the trouble in paradise.

Morocco is in some ways the most extreme of Paramount's von Sternberg–Dietrich sextet, the one nearest to *The Blue Angel* not only in time but in its view of love as an endless humiliation of one's self-esteem. We see this, too, in DeMille's early society comedies, with Gloria Swanson and Wallace Reid, even in the more optimistic Lubitsch, when Jeanette MacDonald tries to make Maurice Chevalier her royal gigolo in *The Love Parade.* DeMille and Lubitsch do at least tie things up happily at the end. Von Sternberg prefers lovely doom. "What a charming evening we might have had," Warner Oland tells Dietrich in *Dishonored,* "if you had not been a spy and I a traitor." "Then," she replies, "we might never have met." "How true," Oland concedes; and shoots himself.

While pursuing his personal vision, von Sternberg collects and binds the elements of Paramount art, especially in the practice of making a story's emotions visually intelligible. Let us consider one of the von Sternberg–Dietrich sextet in detail. It almost doesn't matter which. They are of such quality and (despite incidental differences) consistency that commentators variously cite them—except the excessive *Dishonored*—as "the masterpiece." We might take *Shanghai Express* for its unusually classic format, the *Grand Hotel* trope of disparate types flung together to test, under pressure, their grace. We might try *The Scarlet Empress,* von Sternberg's version of Catherine the Great and, but for *The Blue Angel,* his most pictorially dynamic talkie. We might draft *The Devil Is a Woman,* the fulfillment of von Sternberg's skulking autobiographical romance—the fulfillment as well of his photographic precision, for it marked the first time that titles credited him as cinematographer. (He had in fact been serving as his own cameraman, but had to join the union to get a byline.) Dietrich herself prefers *The Devil Is a Woman*—because she looked so beautiful.

Let's use *Blonde Venus*, because only here did von Sternberg tackle a venerable Hollywood genre, the Sinful Woman weepie. (Fittingly, *Blonde Venus* is the only film of the cycle to be set, partly, in the United States, even if von Sternberg still makes it look like Europe.) Who but Paramount would have made a soaper—the most strictly conceived, inflexible form in the movies—as a directorial tour de force? Who but von Sternberg would have seen such possibilities behind the veil of cliché?

Thus: research scientist Herbert Marshall learns that "radium emendations" have given him a fatal disease.* Marshall can be cured in Germany, but can't afford the trip. So his wife, Dietrich, a former cabaret singer, returns to the nightclub scene, where she meets Cary Grant, who gives her the needed money for the traditional favors. Marshall is cured but humiliated, and he throws Dietrich out. She will never see her little boy again—the one male in the whole film whom Dietrich truly loves. She flees with the boy, Marshall and detectives in pursuit. Her family a shambles, Dietrich gives up her child and vanishes, surfacing in Paris as the cabaret toast of Europe and Cary Grant. At length, the child reconciles Marshall and Dietrich.

Cliché, cliché! The stiff husband, the worldly lover, the contrived happy ending are too familiar; and, while Marshall's ingratitude is hard to swallow (Dietrich only cheated on him to save his life), weepie plots often turned on the egomania of men. Even the connection with the cabaret world, something we associate with Dietrich rather than with weepies, is not out of place. In silent days, the more flamboyant weepie queens often were seen building a stage career after their love lives had shattered. So here's a tradition. But Paramount, through von Sternberg, infuses the trite concoction with a thousand unique effects, partly because Paramount had been doing unique for well over a decade by then and partly because von Sternberg, irritated by the studio's clear attempt to sanitize the Vamp he had created, indulged in scathing jokes about the American family. Note, for example, the breathless care with which Dietrich gives little Dickie Moore his bath, or the gargoyle mask Moore wears on the back of his head, making him something of a two-faced totem.

* "Presumably one," historian Charles Silver observes, "which causes him to give numerous tedious performances throughout the thirties." True, we see none of Marshall's *Trouble in Paradise* éclat in *Blonde Venus*. But that is presumably von Sternberg's doing. Back with Lubitsch (and Dietrich) in *Angel* (1937), Marshall revitalizes.

Nor are Dietrich's numbers anything like the nightclub spots in other studios' films, sanitized or not. After the homelife scenes with morbid Marshall and the turgidly impish Dickie, "Hot Voodoo" is refreshingly disturbing. First, a shot of a beaten drum, then chorus girls dressed as warriors in war-painted blackface swaying in to a hard-boiled, downtown beat, bearing shields and spears and leading a gorilla on a chain. Lumbering through the club, the ape pulls off its head—it's Dietrich—and dons a blond Afro. Now the song itself, delivered in the rabid velvet of the old, knowing Dietrich, *The Blue Angel*'s Lola-Lola who "can't help it." You want a hausfrau, America? von Sternberg asks. I'll give you a hausfrau: as Dietrich sings, "All night long, I don't know wight fwom wong," in her gorilla suit. Later, in her dressing room, making down, Dietrich trades cracks with a colleague known as "Taxi." "How much," asks Dietrich, "do you charge for the first mile?"

Most interesting is von Sternberg's handling of Dietrich's fall and rise. The fall is nightmarish as Dietrich throws a wad of bills at a beldame in a flophouse and staggers out on a wave of bitter laughter. The rise, to cabaret stardom, is matter-of-fact, so absolute of itself that von Sternberg doesn't give us a hint of how it happened. At Warner Brothers we would have had one of those synoptic montages of newspaper headlines and backstage vignettes. Von Sternberg contemptuously waves his hand, and presto! Dietrich takes Paris. Why should I bother? he says. Dietrich as a cabaret star isn't hard to believe. Dietrich as a *wife* is. And there's our hausfrau, in white tails and top hat, to sing "I Couldn't Be Annoyed" and pinch a chorus girl's cheek.

The production itself is dazzling. Not expensive: vivid. Everything is close, constricted, even the railroad yard where Marshall catches up with Dietrich and the boy. At MGM, Dietrich's Paris nightclub would have been as big as the Colosseum; Paramount shows us a place so small it seems to have buckled in on itself like an accordion. At Warner Brothers, during the film's central flight-and-chase, every city would look like every other city; all Warners has is the Ritz and the slums. Von Sternberg keys a sense of place into his films as if stock shots and real life didn't exist. His picture of the American South is as laden with milieu as anything in *Morocco* or *Shanghai Express*; one of Dietrich's hideouts appears to be an *art moderne* chicken coop. Even Hattie McDaniel, Dietrich's maid, seems a bit unraveled here.

And talk about sex-is-theft! Every principal in *Blonde Venus* is a thief of romance. Wife robs husband of his self-esteem, lover steals wife, wife steals child, husband steals him back. This is so insistent a theme at Paramount that after a while we see the Paramount elegance as a metaphysical euphemism for the Paramount eroticism: for a sophistication of earthiness, the glister barely covering the honesty. It cannot be coincidental that almost all Hollywood's big scandals, on and off screen, involved Paramount people: Wallace Reid's death through drug addiction; Fatty Arbuckle's rape-murder case; the William Desmond Taylor murder implicating Mary Miles Minter;* Clara Bow's messy suit against her secretary, who vindictively told all at the trial; the uproar over *The Story of Temple Drake* (1933), cautiously adapted from, but at times arrestingly faithful to, William Faulkner's *Sanctuary*; and, hard upon those heels, the eruption of Mae West. Except for Reid's sad end, all these scandals were of sexual content. Surely, in the often improvisational and impressionistic world of film, life involved in filming related to life as filmed. If Paramount was the studio of Famous Players, or Adolph Zukor, or Cecil B. DeMille, Little Mary, Gary Cooper, or of pictorial panache or society comedies, it was as well the studio most secure in erotic intensity. I underline this because, again, it is the director who compounds this element: in his editing of the screenplay, his coaching of the actors, and his manipulation of the visual matter. In what he allows.

Not that Paramount went out of its way to find directors gifted in the erotic. Paramount went out of its way to find gifted directors. As if Zukor's Famous Players syndrome were still in service, the studio hunted Broadway for new directing blood at the time of the transition to sound in 1928–29. After all, stage directors had experience in working with stage actors, and these were being brought to Hollywood by the trainload to handle that forbiddingly newfangled invention, speech.

Paramount had an advantage, too, in its Astoria studio, a short

---

* Till 1986, terming this murder unsolved was one of the Hollywood writer's most valid clichés. No more: King Vidor solved it. Or believed he did. See Sidney Kirkpatrick's book *A Cast of Killers*, but await Robert Giroux's promised rebuttal.

subway ride from midtown Manhattan. Rival firms had shut down their Eastern operations during the 1920s to keep all production under mogul supervision. How typical, then, that the directors' studio maintained a place three thousand miles from B. P. Schulberg, head of the Hollywood Paramount and something of a supervisor. Astoria was in the hands of the more accommodating William Le Baron (in the 1920s) and Walter Wanger (during the transition to talkies). "It was certainly not another Hollywood," Gloria Swanson recalled in her memoirs. "The place was full of free spirits, defectors, refugees, who were all trying to get away from Hollywood and its restrictions. There was a wonderful sense of revolution and innovation."

Better yet, Astoria was convenient for theatre people who couldn't or wouldn't travel to the Coast. Thus director Rouben Mamoulian could slide into film from Broadway by a kind of back door in *Applause* (1929), an unpretentious backstager with another Broadway name, Helen Morgan, as a burlesque star on the skids. Both Mamoulian and Morgan enjoyed a great year in 1927, he staging DuBose and Dorothy Heyward's adaptation of Heyward's novel *Porgy* for the Theatre Guild, she for her Julie in the original *Show Boat*. Mamoulian was noted for his resonant stage pictures and his "choreography" of sound effects, Morgan for her plangent fragility as a woman destroyed by bad men and luck. So the use of these two neophytes is not all that surprising. It already suggests a burlesque movie. Still, *Applause*'s producer, Wanger, took a bold chance. The movies had long been a veteran's world, where practiced directors, popular stars, and old-hand techies were the sure thing. Remember, at this time D. W. Griffith was still directing and Little Mary about to win a Best Actress Oscar. The founders still inhabited Hollywood. Newcomers, however inevitable (especially as stars, ever trading off light to draw the flighty public), meant upheaval.

But 1929 was a time of upheaval anyway: the first year of Absolute Sound. Significantly, Griffith's and Pickford's films that year were talkies, though Griffith couldn't get the hang of it and Little Mary, who could, didn't like it. Other old-timers had been dumped for various reasons, all of them Inadequacy in Sound. But who would be adequate?

Theatre people.

Thus Paramount enjoyed a special connection to Broadway, to

Mamoulian and Morgan. *Applause* was not enthusiastically received, in the event—drab characters, shady places, tragic ending, too realistic. But this very realism has made *Applause* an archive favorite, a historian's Super-Jewel. Mamoulian set out to play the wonder boy. His first shots of burlesque in action—cutting from backstage through the gallery to directly overhead in the flies, then close up on the tawdry girls and the crass audience—dazzle.* His experiments in dubbing two separate channels of sound into the standard single track enchanted a generation of directors, especially when Morgan gently sings "What Wouldn't I Do for That Man" to a photograph of her sleazebag boyfriend, and Mamoulian wipes a second scene onto the top half of the screen: the sleazebag and his doxie-on-the-side. As Morgan's blissful song continues, the other two converse, sound and sight. Then he leaves, walks down a hall, and opens the door on Morgan as Mamoulian wipes the screen whole again.

Another of Astoria's virtues was the possibility of location filming in Manhattan. *Applause* gives us a secondary romance between Morgan's daughter and her nice sailor boyfriend, and their dating takes us right onto the Brooklyn Bridge, then to the roof of an office tower to gaze down on the Woolworth Building and New York Harbor. During the scene, a plane happened by, and Mamoulian not only kept shooting but tilted up to show us this noise, this chance of life. It's real. So is the moment in which Morgan's boyfriend makes a brutal pass at the daughter, unnervingly real.

Again we find Paramount daring what most studios wouldn't, using New York talent not only for the theatre of sound but to borrow the honesty—the hard realism—of artists not yet softened by routine. The tryout paid off, too, for Mamoulian moved to Paramount's West Coast studio to create four more unique films, including the best of all versions of *Dr. Jekyll and Mr. Hyde* (1931) and *Love Me Tonight* (1932), the one musical not by Lubitsch to do what Lubitsch did as well as Lubitsch did it.

If Paramount was a great studio for directors, however, it was a

* *Applause* was shot late in 1929, after many of the worst of sound's problems had been licked, and the kinetic vitality of this opening sequence is thrilling after the often static or cumbersomely mobile production numbers of earlier musicals. The rackety camera had to be closed up in a booth to let clean sound onto the track; but then the camera couldn't move. Wonder boy Mamoulian simply filmed this scene silent, then dubbed in a "wild track"—i.e., laying sound over the picture without worrying about whose mouth is singing what note at which moment.

tricky one for actors. From one regime to another, the studio showed an astonishing lack of imagination in capitalizing on the talent at hand. By contrast, MGM's primary energy lay in the scouting, grooming, and developing of stars, each A film regarded as a vehicle for stardom, not—as at Paramount—a thing-in-itself. Paramount might easily have filmed, say, Eugene O'Neill's *Anna Christie* simply because it was a Famous Play, suitable for any number of women on the lot—Sylvia Sidney, perhaps, or Carole Lombard. MGM filmed *Anna Christie* specifically to ease Greta Garbo into talkies, through a role in which a Swedish accent would help rather than hinder. And MGM had to bestir itself somewhat to buy the property, for First National had filmed the play with Blanche Sweet in 1923, and Warner Brothers, which had taken over First National, now owned the rights. MGM was even willing to junk a film if it threatened to hurt an important career. After Joan Crawford tearfully begged L. B. Mayer to get her out of *Great Day!*, Mayer viewed the rushes, decided the movie would do *no* star good, and closed it down altogether.

Granted, MGM was outstanding in this regard. But no studio was as reckless as Paramount in the handling of its contractees. Fox and Warner Brothers each headed off difficulties by signing only the kind of performers who suited the films the studio was prepared to make. MGM chose the stars, then found appropriate vehicles. Fox and Warners had the vehicles, and so found appropriate stars. Paramount, however, would sign anybody and put him or her into anything.

This was partly the result of Zukor's expansion in the Second Era of Silent Film, when Paramount was turning out nearly one hundred twenty films a year.* It was also the result of Paramount's diversity: an eclectic line needs a varied personality pool. But it was as well the result of haste and sloppiness. Paramount ran on a treadmill—better, Paramount swirled like a firecracker, every part of it going off at once. This aided the directors; the producers were too busy maintaining tempo to do much hanging around the set or fussing over rushes. But this hurt the stars, for there was no Irving Thalberg or Darryl Zanuck promoting careers through the subtle gradation and

* By the Third Era, when features were running longer, the total fell to about seventy-five, still higher than any other studio's output. Even in talkie years, Paramount churned out about fifty-five to sixty pictures per annum—and this with its most famous director, DeMille, tying a horde of people up for a single entry. Compare this to MGM's schedule, which planned on one release per week—and never once made the whole fifty-two.

renewal of type that kept one reassuringly familiar yet refreshingly surprising: Norma Shearer as a Noël Coward screwball in *Private Lives* (1931) yielding to Norma Shearer as a Eugene O'Neill trage-dienne in the following *Strange Interlude* (1932); or Tyrone Power a tad too absurd as a French engineer in *Suez* (1938), so Tyrone Power most creditable in the next one, *Jesse James* (1939).

On the contrary, at Paramount you were underestimated, mis-perceived, or locked into type and ground into a truism. Zukor had seen stars blaze up and then flicker over the years; most gave out early. Movies, after all, were about beauty and sex—Zukor's were, anyway. So why expect longevity of an icon of energies that suit only the youthful? Yes, there was Little Mary and Doug, Chaplin and Keaton, the Talmadge girls, and Zukor's own Swanson, Queen of Paramount. Long careers at the top. But these were exceptions. The washouts numbered in the thousands. (And lo, within the first years of sound, all of these but Chaplin were out or dimming.) You could create a star. You could create a thousand stars. But you couldn't create an exception. Besides, when they got big they went independ-ent. Swanson actually turned down Zukor's offer of a flat million for one year's work—the biggest deal ever offered—to join United Artists.

The Paramount approach, then, favored chance and repetition rather than strategy and planning. The years overlapping silence offer many an instance—Evelyn Brent, scintillating in the von Sternberg films *Underworld* (1927), *The Last Command* (1928), and *The Drag Net* (1928) but lost in the hands of directors who couldn't place her; or Betty Bronson, enchanting in her two Barrie parts but then hustled into flapper roles and a Zane Grey western that broke her delicate hold on the public.

At least these women claimed some fine films. Nancy Carroll suffered a limelight based entirely on critics' sympathy for the gener-ally inane scripts assigned her. A vitally pretty girl with a neat, smooth style and a sweet voice (she even sang), Carroll looked like a winner. But no one wins in *Honey* (1930), a glum little musical in which impoverished Southern belle Carroll runs a boardinghouse. Or in *Personal Maid* (1931), a witless society comedy in which work-ing-class kid Carroll crashes the upper class to choose between Gene Raymond and Pat O'Brien. It should have worked, with Mary

Boland hot to dither as Raymond's screwball mother and the typical Paramount sass about the morals of the haut monde, where, as Carroll observes, "the men are handsome and polite and the women sleep in luxury." (Add adultery, divorce, a fabulous bathroom, and a classical orgy, and you'd have early DeMille.) But this comedy doesn't field a single joke. For long stretches, it doesn't even try to. Maybe it isn't a comedy; but it isn't much else, either. Worst of all is *The Woman Accused* (1933), this one a melodrama, based on a trick story concocted by ten different writers. Carroll is The Woman, acquitted of murder though she is in fact guilty, if sympathetically so. The clothes, at least, are a wow, not only on Carroll and co-star Cary Grant but on the extras, a notion of deep-pocket costuming that even MGM might have questioned. But by this time Carroll's career needed heavy acquitting itself, and this violent weepie couldn't deliver.

Paramount's odd take on the star system simply processed the names, pulled in so many different sorts of performer that it might exploit good luck when it struck. Sometimes the studio couldn't even do that. Carole Lombard's seven-year contract with Paramount took her from starlet to Major Name, yet her important films were made at other studios, on loan or post-contract, as a free-lancer. Paramount gave Lombard such memorable events as *It Pays to Advertise* (1931), with Skeets Gallagher and Norman Z. Foster, and *Up Pops the Devil* (1931), with Skeets Gallagher, Norman Z. Foster, and Stuart Erwin; one wonders why MGM even bothered making *Grand Hotel* with this kind of competition. Then there was *Bolero* (1934), Lombard forced to perform the indicated dance with George Raft, eventually seconded by *Rumba* (1935), again baiting the tomato in a ballroom with Raft. Even Monogram giggled at the silliness of *Rumba*, not unlike Stuart Erwin giggling at the silliness of Norman Z. Foster.

Twentieth Century (1934), you say? *My Man Godfrey* (1936)? *Nothing Sacred* (1937)? *Made For Each Other* (1939)? *To Be or Not to Be* (1942)? Columbia, Universal, Selznick, Selznick, and United Artists, respectively. Lombard never made a first-rater at her home studio. *No Man of Her Own* (1932), a consummately mediocre film about a librarian's reformation of a hood, is remembered because it's the sole film Lombard made with her later husband, Clark Gable, on loan to Paramount because MGM needed Fredric March. As a comic dynamo, sharp and vulnerably tough, Lombard not only had to find herself at

Wynne Gibson, another casualty of steeplechase casting, played leads and support in the first four years of the talkie. Here she visits the "Main Street, U.S.A." of Paramount's backlot, probably wondering whatever happened to Wynne Gibson.

other studios but develop as well. Paramount gave her nothing but the final "e" in her first name. And that was by accident.

On the other hand: Gary Cooper. It may be that other studios would have fudged this one by trying to force Cooper into some standard type. Cooper was *sui generis,* a one-man type: affable yet moody, a born cowboy who knew how to wear a suit, natural in his line readings yet just as natural saying nothing—a beautiful boy in the form of a serious man. After stunting and bits, Cooper got to the Goldwyn studios, but Goldwyn thought him impossible to cast, and let B. P. Schulberg bring him to Paramount. Of course, Schulberg found everyone impossible to cast—properly, that is: but Schulberg didn't mind. Tossing Cooper into Paramount's picture factory, he let the actor find himself, as most Paramount stars had to. Cooper lucked into a notable cameo in *Wings* (1927) as a gallant flyer, setting himself up for leads of comparable character in such films as *Beau Sabreur, Lilac Time* (on loan to First National), and *The Shopworn Angel*, all in 1928. Imaginative directors like William Wellman, Gregory La Cava, and Victor Fleming filled him out, and by the time he made his first all-out talkie, *The Virginian* (1929), Cooper was established. Established as a soldier or a cowboy. Typical Paramount. Cooper made *The Texan, Seven Days Leave, A Man from Wyoming, The Spoilers,* all in 1930, all soldiers and cowboys. The studio was running Cooper's one-man type into a one-man cliché, and working him so hard that he sometimes rushed from a day's work on one set to an evening's worth on another.

Then came von Sternberg and *Morocco*, with successive exposure to Rouben Mamoulian, Frank Borzage, and Lubitsch. Cooper was still expanding, perfecting his brooding cowboys and stricken soldiers while adding city dwellers, even Dandies. In Lubitsch's *Design for Living* (1933), Cooper played a Noël Coward part, not only by Coward but for. Thus Cooper became something like the essential Paramount star, in his treadmill industry, his exposure to brilliant directors, and his ability to cope with the society-comedy aspect that any long-term Paramount star must deal with. By the end of the 1930s, Cooper had got as much from the studio as he had given it, and left. Unlike Brent, Bronson, Carroll, and even Lombard, Cooper departed at his most bankable.

Claudette Colbert worked at the studio longer than Cooper, and in certain ways is even more basic as a Paramount contractee—even considering that many of her best roles came about on loan-out to other lots. Like so many Paramount draftees, Colbert won first notice on Broadway. She was not yet a Famous Player, but she holds the distinction of having created a lead in Eugene O'Neill's worst famous play, *Dynamo*, in 1929. O'Neill himself points up how well suited Colbert was to the movies when he complained that she distracted the audience by showing off her legs; but *Dynamo* needs every distraction it can get. Colbert was sexy and elegant, with a "common sense" inflection in her voice, a deadpan wryness. This was perfect Paramount material: attractive irony. Colbert was like an after-hours Nancy Carroll (whom Colbert somewhat resembled), and, having been raised bilingually, Colbert had the advantage of fluent French. Paramount, keeping its Continental eye on foreign markets, was the most avid of the studios in releasing foreign-language versions of its films in the "let's try anything!" chaos of the early talkie; for a few years, Paramount, too, spoke fluent French. Colbert not only filmed *The Big Pond* (1930) and *The Smiling Lieutenant* (1931), both with Maurice Chevalier, in English and French, but stepped in for Evelyn Brent (with Adolphe Menjou, another bilinguist, for Clive Brook) in *L'Enigmatique M. Parkes*, the French version of *Slightly Scarlet* (1930).

Nice work; but Colbert has become useful rather than indispensable. Chevalier tolerated support, not co-stars, and *Slightly Scarlet* was no winner in English, much less in a French version that few Americans had (or wanted) access to. Colbert was in danger of becoming a failed Nancy Carroll, for instance dwindling between those champion showboaters George M. Cohan and Jimmy Durante in *The Phantom President* (1932). Then, so legend has it, DeMille spots her on the lot, strides up, and asks, without preamble, if she'd like to play "the wickedest woman in the world." The reply is absolute Paramount:

COLBERT: I'd love it!

The woman was Poppaea, in *The Sign of the Cross*, followed two years later by DeMille's *Cleopatra*. Colbert does a good wicked, and even manages to persuade us that she is obsessively in love with, respectively, Fredric March (which can't have been fun) and Henry Wilcoxon (which can't have been easy—and the ghastly Julius Caesar of Warren William presses her other flank). More important,

Colbert was filling in between DeMilles with work in the films that would place her style: contemporary, urban-urbane, debonair. Society comedy, in short. *Three Cornered Moon* (1933) is very much in point here, a terrible film but excellent Colbert. The title itself has resonance for its reputation in exploring the "oddball family" trope that would soon become a convention of screwball comedy; and Mary Boland, ace Dizzy Dame, is the mother. But curious movie buffs, settling in for a find, quickly tire of the vapid script and Elliott Nugent's paceless direction. Boland's family isn't oddball as much as self-indulgent—except Colbert, who manages to steer a course of charm and wisdom even when the picture suddenly switches tone (as early-talkie Paramounts very often did) from unfunny comedy to watery melodrama.

Colbert was not as versatile as Paramount's silent Queen of the Lot, Gloria Swanson, who could play *anything* (including musicals). Stars virtually had to at reckless Paramount. At Warner Brothers, as we'll see, a rigid adherence to a few favorite genres kept specialist personalities at work in their specialties. At MGM, stars were made as comfortable as possible, seldom stretched in a challenge part. But at Paramount there was no time and no patience. Movies are the world: sooner or later, everything happens to everybody. So even as Colbert was revealing her unflappable erotic poise, she had to make her musical, *Torch Singer* (1933), handling four Ralph Rainger–Leo Robin songs without dubbing; had to don Puritan garb—even unto capes and eyes-cast-down-on-market-day aprons—for *Maid of Salem* (1937); and had to stand by as the studio handed a Queen of the Lot role, one of Swanson's great ones, to the latest discovery of the minute, Isa Miranda, in the remake of *Zaza* (1939). (In the event, Miranda did not work out, and Colbert took over.) This, perhaps, was Paramount stardom: always compromised one way or another. Today, of course, *Torch Singer* and *Maid of Salem* are largely forgotten, and we place Colbert in more appropriate roles in better films, savvy in her passions and decisive in her sensitivity as she wages gender war with Ray Milland, Fred MacMurray, or Gary Cooper under the guidance of Lubitsch and Leisen.

This is fit company. This is a career. Colbert stayed at Paramount from 1929 to 1945, long enough to seem more basic to its history than any other star. Yet the studio was all too ready to declare her defunct when she was in her prime—and she always looked absurdly young, anyway. Paramount's Queen of the Lot role in 1944, Liza Elliott in *Lady in the Dark*, went to Ginger Rogers, who wasn't even a Paramount contractee. I hear murmurs in the house—isn't *Lady in the Dark* a musical? Not after Paramount got hold of it.

Paramount was spendthrift in stars, but Paramount was never short of supply. On the contrary. "More stars than there are in heaven," MGM crowed in self-congratulation. No. MGM had as many. *Paramount* had more. Consider the very early 1930s, the time of *Trouble in Paradise.* Besides the above-mentioned Dietrich, Cooper, Chevalier and MacDonald, Lombard and Carroll, Paramount had under contract: Sylvia Sidney, Jean Arthur, Tallulah Bankhead, Ruth Chatterton, Wynne Gibson, and Fay Wray; Fredric March, Buddy Rogers, William Powell, Richard Dix, Adolphe Menjou, Jack Oakie, Phillips Holmes, George Raft, Cary Grant, Richard Arlen, and George Bancroft; as well as the former silent comic Harold Lloyd and the promising singer Bing Crosby. Some of these names have faded, some retain a nostalgic glow, and others are legendary. But all, at the time, were more or less hot business.

So let MGM pull out its *Grand Hotel* and *Dinner at Eight*, with their all-star guests. When Paramount planned a celebrity picnic, it, too, could light up the screen. At the dawn of talkies, the major studios put together fancy revues. Poor little Fox tried to sneak by without stars, Warner Brothers imported a load of New Yorkers, and Universal made it on spectacle. MGM deployed keen artillery in *The Hollywood Revue of 1929*: Lionel Barrymore directing John Gilbert and Norma Shearer in the Balcony Scene from *Romeo and Juliet*, in pure and jive versions; Joan Crawford conquering Major Nerves (this was in effect her talkie audition) in "Gotta Feelin' for You";* plus Buster Keaton, Marie Dressler, Jack Benny, Laurel and Hardy, debonair William Haines, dauntless but thin Nils Asther, golden-toned Conrad Nagel, and a backlot's worth of "Singin' in the Rain" for the finale.

Paramount aced MGM out, not only with more headliners but with better film. MGM's revue is defensively ingenious, a little too "now Marion Davies goes into her dance, and you didn't think she

---

* Was Crawford really so nervous that they had to print her like so, all astew, or was she helpfully and historically portraying talkie anxiety for us? Pirandello might know.

could.''* *Paramount on Parade* is more worldly—Chevalier and Lubitsch take part, for starters. Interesting, too, that Paramount put the whole thing in the care of Elsie Janis, a Broadway actor-manager with zip and smarts but no ties to Hollywood. While *The Hollywood Revue* goes for special effects in miniatures and double exposure, and Paramount shoots it straight, MGM ends the more stage-bound. Of all the big-star early-talkie revues, only *Paramount on Parade* was *movie* vaudeville, with a camera framing the action, not a proscenium and curtain.

All the better for Paramount: for, in truth, it could compete with MGM in imagination, not in density of glamour. Another all-star Paramount entry, *If I Had a Million* (1932), shows us why. Here's a neat idea for a Depression chaser: dying plutocrat Richard Bennett (the father, by the way, of Constance and Joan) decides to give certi-fied checks for a million dollars to names in the phone book. It could happen to you—and you not only get the money, but a chance to fulfill universal dreams. Clerk Charles Laughton blows a Bronx cheer at his boss. Prostitute Wynne Gibson checks into a deluxe hotel—alone. Charles Ruggles smashes a storeful of china. (He also buys a rabbit; but let's save that for another book.)

If I Had a Million is not all escapism. Prisoner Gene Raymond, on death row awaiting execution, thinks the check will get him a new trial and freedom. "It's all a mistake!" he screams as the guards drag him to the electric chair. Wanted forger George Raft, who can't set foot in a bank, trades his thus useless check for a bed in a flophouse; laughing, the proprietor burns it. Most disturbing of all, and most touching, is May Robson's segment, set in a home for old women. It's not a happy place, and at the slightest criticism the head gun reminds Robson that she is "free to go" anytime. We know—and Robson declares it, in case we don't—that the dispossessed are never free. There is a terrible moment, at mail call, when the inmates line up hopefully. Only one of them gets a letter; the camera pans the others' faces. A shocking and sorrowing sight. Worse yet, the letter is junk mail, a come-on for a man's hair restorer. One of the women asks if the recipient would kindly read it to her: someone else's mail is better than none. And we do get a reading, of one of those empty-brained but oh-so-comforting letters from one's daughter-in-law. Partway

---

* Afterward, you still don't. Davies kicks out a competent tap, but why is she doing it at all? Margaret Truman might know.

through this fantasy, the woman breaks down and rips the letter up, crying, "They never write to us anymore!" Luckily, Richard Bennett arrives just then to hand May Robson a check. Fade in on a renovated home, Robson's property now, run like a country club: except the former staff (including the men) are forced to do nothing all day but decline in rocking chairs.

For a sentimental sequence, it's grisly; it makes you want to die young. Such honesty is very Paramount. Warners or RKO might have dared that look at the dejected faces of the forgotten old people. But Warners wouldn't have bothered with the anthology genre, considered bad box-office and even somewhat arty; and RKO couldn't have fielded the talent. Alas, neither could Paramount—not in the MGM sense. The chemistry of the Garbo–Barrymore and Beery–Crawford encounters in *Grand Hotel* is extraordinary, whereas *If I Had a Million*'s episodic structure separates the talent, denies us the special pleasure of clocking novel interactions. At that, good as *If I Had a Million* is, it has not a single draw to rival those in *Grand Hotel*. Its only real stars are Gary Cooper and W. C. Fields, and in 1932 they were yet ahead of their days of command.

At least *If I Had a Million* is a neat film. What of *Alice in Wonderland* (1933), with half the Paramount lot in the character roles? There are some wonderful special effects reminiscent of *A Kiss for Cinderella*'s magic (including a cartoon for the poem on "The Walrus and the Carpenter") and possibly the most Hollywood-rich cast ever assembled. But it's a disaster. The worst thing about it is Ida Lupino: because she isn't in it. Paramount brought her over from England to play Alice, and she would have been superb. But the sluggish, sing-song Charlotte Henry ended up in the role, and drives the film right down the, uh, rabbit hole. Folklore tells that the movie fails because all the familiar stars are totally obscured behind Tenniel-inspired makeup jobs. In fact, most of them are readily discernible, but miscast. Edward Everett Horton's Mad Hatter isn't mad, just aimlessly manic. W. C. Fields's Humpty Dumpty is respectable Lewis Carroll but limp Fields. Cary Grant, as the Mock Turtle, has to sing. He shouldn't. One doesn't actually see Richard Arlen as the Cheshire Cat—Paramount uses an animated model. But it doesn't even sound like Richard Arlen. And why is this Zesty Sidekick playing the Cheshire Cat in the first place?

Some of *Alice* is fun. The usually imperious and self-righteous

Edna May Oliver, as the Red Queen, gets to play dizzy for once; smart casting. But for an all-star special, *Alice* is leaden. The idea is not just to hire stars but to *set* them, like jewels in a crown. Herbert Marshall's "There's one very good stone in it" to Miriam Hopkins in *Trouble in Paradise*'s sex-is-theft dinner rings all the more clear: Paramount's jewelry was often sloppily forged.

One thing the studio knew how to use was clowns—not just comedians but self-starting jesters with a unique style and a vaudevillian's nerve. Paramount stood out in Hollywood for its love of stage clowns, in fact. An echo of the Famous Players ploy? The Marx Brothers, W. C. Fields, Mae West, and George Burns and Gracie Allen, most notably, not only concentrated a jesters' energy at Paramount, but helped create a unique format for verbal comedy comparable to the silent rhythms set by Charlie Chaplin and Buster Keaton.

It begins, Famous Players–style, with the Marx Brothers' Broadway hits *The Cocoanuts* and *Animal Crackers*. Paramount filmed the first in 1929 while the second was still running, the boys commuting each day from Astoria to Broadway. This is not unusual, for 1929 was a gala year for the adapting of Broadway musicals, sometimes faithfully and sometimes very loosely. Paramount's *Cocoanuts* manages to be both. Of the original stage company, only Margaret Dumont joined the brothers, and most of Irving Berlin's score was dropped. Yet the studio followed the play's action, a spoof of Florida land-grabbing, and the score's remnants point to standard-issue musical comedy—a dance for a "trouser chorus" (young women dressed as hotel pages); "The Monkey Doodle-Doo," one of those big numbers that rave about the alleged latest dance craze without ever quite telling you how to do it; a Spanish-flavored number for the closing costume ball that (a little history here) introduced the overhead shot into the film musical. All the show's ballads vanished, so Berlin turned out a new one, "When My Dreams Come True." Directors Joseph Santley and Robert Florey field a free camera and the brothers keep the tempo in quickstep, Groucho merrily walking all over Dumont's lines. In short, fair Broadway and useful cinema.

Animal Crackers (1930) is much better because it is much freer. This time there's almost no music at all, except for Chico's piano and Harpo's harp. (He sneaks in a bit of piano, too.) Better, there is almost no story. Mrs. Rittenhouse (Dumont) is giving a house party and the

Paramount had so many players on payroll that grab-bag
casts like that of Alice in Wonderland were almost inevitable. We certainly can recognize Edward Everett Horton as
the Mad Hatter; but little Jackie Searle and Charles Ruggles
are quite translated as the Dormouse and the March Hare.
Charlotte Henry looks more involved in this still than she
does in the entire movie.

boys turn up to disrupt it. Yes, there's some plotty nonsense about a stolen painting. But, basically, locating the boys in the setting is itself the "story": what will the phoney professional, the Italian con man, and the randy scamp* do in (and, let's hope, to) Society? There are treasurable moments here, as when Chico unmasks a pretentious WASP art critic as the former "Abie the fish man," the poor parvenu begging for mercy as Chico and Harpo stamp around on an art nouveau staircase chanting (Harpo miming) "Abie the fish man, Abie the fish man!"

There is a truly classic bit when a police detective, taking Harpo's hand to congratulate him for going straight, shakes most of Mrs. Rittenhouse's silverware out of Harpo's coat. What is fetching about the scene is the absolute lack of reaction from the rest of the cast, assembled and silent. Knives and forks clatter to the floor as the detective continues shaking Harpo's hand, utterly ignoring the evidence of new crime. Yes, Harpo looks a little guilty. Yet he, too, just stands there. Only Groucho and Chico register what is happening, punctuating the sight gag with commentary. (Groucho: "I can't understand what's delaying that coffeepot." Then, when it appears: "Where's the cream?") This is comedy of the stage, where nothing is real. To take it from Broadway into film without naturalizing it, rationalizing it, is an act of either slavish theatre-worship or very generous imagination. Yet it works. Even Groucho's occasional direct address of the audience—and he looks us right in the eye— is forgivable in the context. Paramount treated the stage aside as fair game. Lubitsch had Maurice Chevalier try it in several films; at the end of *One Hour with You*, even Jeanette MacDonald dares it.

If *The Cocoanuts* is a filmed play, *Animal Crackers* is a movie made from a play. Most of the key characters came along with the brothers from Broadway, including not only Dumont, Abie the fish man, and Dumont's scheming social rival but the haughty butler (Robert Greig). He moved to Hollywood with the Marxes to stay on as Paramount's haughty butler in residence. (That's Greig's sneer filling the screen in the famous shot, looking up at Greig from the floor in *Love Me Tonight*, when Chevalier walks out of MacDonald's château.)

The Marxes' three remaining Paramounts developed *Animal*

* Zeppo, the fourth Marx Brother, was the square of the set, on hand, like the many nephews of Universal's Carl Laemmle, mainly to draw a salary and stay out of the way.

Crackers's format of a situational premise rather than a generic structure. Much as Chaplin would take, say, the pioneer Northwest as a starting point and end up with *The Gold Rush*, *Monkey Business* (1931) proposes the Marxes as stowaways on a ship, *Horse Feathers* (1932) takes them to college, and *Duck Soup* (1933) lands them in Middle Europe in time of war. *Monkey Business* and *Duck Soup* expand the elements of the unreasonably bizarre, auditioned in Harpo's handshaking bit with the Rittenhouse silver. However, now the tricks are turned around for film. Paramount has not only imported stage talent, but reinvented it. Other studios would assimilate it, use it—as we'll note when the brothers move to MGM. But the Marx Paramounts have moments no other studio would have filmed—*Duck Soup*'s "mirror" sequence, for instance: Harpo, disguised as Groucho, pretending to be Groucho's reflection. The bit is so obvious and so silly that laughing at it is pointless, wasteful. It isn't about anything; it *shouldn't* be funny. Besides, laughing will only encourage them. Paramount, strangely, is comfortable with the bizarre. And note that the entire scene is silent, a striking boycott for an early talkie.

There are yet more absurd scenes, like *Monkey Business*'s "passport" sequence, each stowaway brother trying to get off the boat with Maurice Chevalier's papers. Now, we know that none of them is Chevalier, and the ship's officers know it, too. *Chevalier* is Chevalier. Yet such is the pervasive lunacy of the Marxian world that each of the four gets a chance to prove he's Chevalier by singing "You Brought a New Kind of Love to Me," complete with straw boater, the studio orchestra obligingly slipping in. Zeppo actually has a go at an imitation. Chico and Groucho push the joke beyond the absurd by making no attempt whatever at the Chevalier style—Chico even sings in his gumba inflection. It is Harpo who goes over the top: he does a flawless Chevalier, doubly ridiculous because till this moment Harpo has been mute. Then his song runs down like a Victrola that needs winding, and he turns to show us a phonograph strapped to his back. *Even then* the officer in charge merely looks on, no more dubious than he had been all along. This fantasyland must cede to real life, however, or the film cannot end, and the officer tries to run Harpo off. Whereupon Harpo springs into the real work of the hour, grabbing the approval stamp and inking everything in reach, including the officer's bald head.

Monkey Business also offers a rare moment of the genuinely uncanny, in which the realism never finally subdues the fantasy. This is the scene in which Harpo, fleeing the authorities, blunders into a roomful of kids enjoying a Punch-and-Judy show. Hiding inside the little theatre, Harpo becomes a puppet himself, now throwing his face into a "gookie," now showing a mask on the back of his head (paving the way for Dickie Moore in *Blonde Venus* a year later). As the other puppets alternately badger and collude with him, Harpo bedevils his chaser and the ship's captain. When he kicks at the two men through the front curtains, they grab his leg and pull on it—but watch: Harpo himself comes out, helps them pull, and all fall down grasping a false leg. Now Harpo makes his escape in a kiddie car on a track as the children laugh and jeer. Yet who, I ask you, was working the puppets? We are left with the feeling that no one was, that it doesn't matter, that zany comedy does not equate the credible with the necessary.

The Marxes did not equate movie work with dedication. "One of them was always missing" is the first thought that seizes reminiscent participants. Nor did the Marxes seem to enjoy collaborating with Paramount's bolder directors. Yet we note that the better directors oversaw the development of the freewheeling form in which the Marxes thrived; and the best ever, Leo McCarey, directed their masterpiece, *Duck Soup*.

Paramount's other comics made some adaptation to the movies. Mae West fit right into the sex-is-theft, albeit with the boldest delivery yet. *"Suckers!"* she sneers at an all-male audience after presenting her cooch dance in *I'm No Angel* (1933). The sound of West is something new, and her fondness for Tenderloin settings and plain clothes on everyone but Mae inhibited Paramount's visual panache. Still, her storytelling itself was straightforward. Burns and Allen were even easier to handle. They could be plunked into anything as assistant zanies, playing doctor-and-nurse shtick in *International House* (1933), or as explorers filling out the island on which the juicy sophisticates are shipwrecked in *We're Not Dressing* (1934). Mary Boland and Charles Ruggles saw service as the befuddled rich, a type almost any Paramount movie could fit in somewhere.

But the Marxes had to find their form. Despite the contempt with which they treated the studio and its staff, they needed Paramount, not just to film their capers but to give them form without confinement. To cultivate lunacy. Yes, Paramount was the sexy studio. In *I'm No Angel*, a fortune-teller peers into a crystal ball and sees "a change of position." "Sitting," Mae asks, "or reclining?" Yes, Paramount was the studio of zany chic. In *We're Not Dressing*, as Ethel Merman and two tuxedos (Ray Milland in one) dole out the bridge hands, dummy Leon Errol pores over a pamphlet. "Oh!" he cries. "Here's a cocktail we've never tried!"

But, mainly, Paramount was the protean studio, accepting the shape of the material as it evolved. Sometimes a strong director assisted. Still, original jokers had a free run. W. C. Fields came to Paramount in 1932 as an odd-jobber, working his signature routines without impinging on the form of his films as wholes. Mayhap he'll juggle, or pull out his pool-playing skit. His roles are but one in a crowd of roles, like his Humpty Dumpty in the all-star *Alice in Wonderland.* A character is developing nonetheless, in the car owner who declares war on "road hogs" in *If I Had a Million*, using his check to buy a fleet of vehicles and literally smash aggressive drivers off the road; or in the Wrong-Way Corrigan pilot of *International House. Million* finds Fields naturalistic, a deputy for every American male who resents arrogant drivers. *International House* finds him fanciful, spouting one-liners and, despite murderous rivalry from Bela Lugosi, dallying with Peggy Hopkins Joyce. "And believe me," Fields tells her in his distracted growl, "I can dally!"

Soon enough Fields is a star, head of his own art and spreading his character through the action. He plays the victim of battering wives, asinine neighbors, and various enraged schmucks. Withal, he is something of a con man, yet with a tender streak, muttering platitudes and curiosa to hold the enemy at bay. He most notably gathers all this into one part on loan to MGM, as Mr. Micawber in *David Copperfield* (1935). Back at Paramount, however, Fields is making film his medium, blending the fanciful into the naturalistic, as in *Man on the Flying Trapeze* (1935). Burglars have broken into Fields's basement (one of them a shockingly youthful Walter Brennan). Fields's brutal wife Kathleen Howard urges him to investigate. It seems that the burglars, happening upon casks of Fields's home brew, have taken refreshment and burst into song. This itself is strange enough. Even stranger is the response upstairs, as Howard demands, coaxes,

Of all Paramount's vaudevillians, Mae West fit into narratives most easily—as, indeed, she had done on Broadway.
The Marxes, W. C. Fields, and Burns and Allen have to play
shtick, but West only has the odd song spot, as here in
Klondike Annie (1936): "I'm an Occidental Woman in an
Oriental Mood for Love." Then, too, as her own auteur,
West appealed to Paramount's trust in creative talent. West
not only wrote her scripts but kept a beady eye on the director except when she was off screen—which wasn't often.

reproaches, shudders, and storms while Fields thinks of every gimmick in the world to delay the business at hand. "There are burglars singing in the cellar!" cries Howard. "What are they singing?" asks Fields. He needs his socks, he needs his bathrobe, he swats a fly, he fusses in a drawer, he does a bit with a glove and some walnuts—all this to Howard's hectoring litany and, from the cellar, the strains of "On the Banks of the Wabash." At length, Fields finds a gun. No sooner has he assured Howard that it isn't loaded than the gun goes off, and Howard crumples on the bed. "Did I kill you?" Fields asks, wincing. At last he heads for the cellar. Burglars will be nicer to him than his relations.

Actually, daughter Mary Brian likes him, and his devotion to her unsettles his image as a curmudgeon. *Man on the Flying Trapeze* is something of a Cinderella tale, with the weak father as protagonist. And note the abstract sense of the title—not *The Man* in particular, but *Man* neat, a general assessment. There is something universal about the Fields figure. Like Mae West, he took a superintendent view of his films, writing the dialogue or at least mapping out the action. Thus he centered his shows on his view of life as a series of humiliations capped by the turning of the worm. In *The Old Fashioned Way* (1934), Fields endures a dinner next to the ingeniously hostile Baby Leroy. At last the other diners run to the window to see "one of them new-fangled horseless carriages." Fields looks about, hoists his trousers, and boots the kid in the ass. In *Man on the Flying Trapeze*, he decks stepson Grady Sutton to defend Mary Brian.

Best of all, in *It's a Gift* (1934), Fields actually tops the incessant Kathleen Howard. The film's central sequence is a classic: Fields trying to sleep on his back porch, attacked by every noise imaginable, even one implausible: a coconut pirouetting down six flights of stairs, crashing into a garbage can at each landing, then daintily turning to clop down the next flight. There is but one cure for the ills of agitated Middle America: California, whither Fields drags his family, Howard vigorously fuming all the way. Typically, Fields has been suckered into a dump. But a friend tips him off to some commercial development heading his way, and, sure enough, a real-estate sharpie tries to buy him out. Fields handles him coolly, holding out for top dollar as Howard rants and wails. "You're crazy," Fields tells the sharpie. "You're drunk!" sharpie retorts. Fields agrees. "But I'll be sober tomorrow and you'll be crazy for the rest of your life." And Fields nets a fortune.

He was difficult to work with and, despite a cult among the literati, not widely popular. Perhaps his character was a little too eccentrically universal for comfort, too much the worm, too late in turning. So Paramount held his vehicles to B budgets and finally slipped him unceremoniously into a Bing Crosby musical, *Mississippi* (1935), and another of those would-be all-star specials, *The Big Broadcast of 1938*. So Fields left Paramount.

Still, along with the Marx Brothers and Mae West, he contributed to a unique format for comedy, not a genre as much as an excuse: vaudeville running wild. At other studios, comedy was heavily plotted, securely scripted; and comics were actors playing characters. *The Awful Truth, Bringing Up Baby, Libeled Lady, My Man Godfrey*—this is Hollywood comedy in the 1930s. Next to these, Paramount's comic wing seems virtually surreal, a *Verfremdungseffekt* of shtick and routines. At times the films obey a near-realism, as in Leo McCarey's *Six of a Kind* (1934)—three pairs, rather: second-honeymooning Mary Boland and Charles Ruggles, traveling companions Burns and Allen, and boondocks sheriff and *hôtelière* W. C. Fields and Alison Skipworth. It's disappointing, perhaps because there's too much plot, not enough shtick. The spree never takes off. However, at other times Paramount's vaudeville runs riot, most successfully, and legendarily, in *Million Dollar Legs* (1932). Edward Cline, one of Fields's (and Buster Keaton's) most constant directors, was in charge. Yet this is not a Fields film, though Fields is in it. Anyway, no one's in charge. *Million Dollar Legs* is a Marx Brothers movie without the Marxes.

It has been compared to *Duck Soup* for their shared Ruritanian setting and political spoof. But *Duck Soup*, for all its capering, pursues a consistent line of attack at a headlong pace, from diplomatic contretemps through war to victory, all its principals closely interacting. *Million Dollar Legs*, on the other hand, runs like a whirlpool, flying around its subject (Klopstockia enters the Olympics) in a catalogue of comic styles. Jack Oakie does his slick-in-the-outback patter, girlfriend Susan Fleming plays deadpan crackpot, Lyda Roberti (as Mata Machree, "the woman no man can resist") lends her Broadway belt and timing, Klopstockian President Fields bustles around enacting a character, and spy Ben Turpin thinks he's in a silent.

Duck Soup's camera follows the Marxes relentlessly; at least one of them is in virtually every minute of the film. But *Million Dollar Legs* is filled with incidental quiddity. The Klopstockian national anthem is gibberish sung to the tune of "One Hour with You." Mata Machree's butler informs visitors that "Madame is only resisted from two to four in the afternoon." Madame herself reads her lines in a Scandinavian accent—on top of Roberti's natural Polish—and not till the film's end do we learn why. "Ay t'ank Ay go home now," Roberti announces: an allusion to the words Garbo spoke to L. B. Mayer when salary negotiations reached an impasse. The line became the talk of Hollywood because Garbo did go home, closed off communication, and threw MGM into a panic.

Million Dollar Legs will do anything for a laugh. The Klopstockian head of the opposition, Hugh Herbert, leading his cabinet through the woods, thinks someone's following them. He hears a birdcall. A spy! "No," says a crony. "It was a mockingbird." Herbert is relieved. Then he hears the same call. A mockingbird? "No," says a crony. "It was a spy."

Paramount's vaudeville comedy died out by 1940. All the specialists were at other studios by then, and only Fields had taken Paramount's libertarian program with him. We hear its echo, perhaps, in the wacky spontaneity and anti-realism of Paramount's *Road* series with Bing Crosby and Bob Hope in the 1940s, and even in the studio's Martin and Lewis vehicles in the 1950s, especially after Martin broke away and Lewis, still at Paramount, began directing himself. Lewis's sheep-in-sheep's-clothing clown gathers all his surroundings into himself much as Fields's Ambrose Wolfinger and The Great McGonigle did. In at least one film, *The Nutty Professor* (1963), now doing Jekyll and Hyde as a wolf in sheep's clothing, Lewis reclaimed the inspired lunacy of the classic Paramount vaudeville.

Bringing these performers to the screen, Paramount honored its Famous Players beginnings while preserving a vital piece of American theatre history. Still, the Marx Brothers and W. C. Fields are not key exemplars of the sexy elegance that Paramount made its trademark. A "Paramount star" has not mania but wit, not a fright wig or a juggling act but dinner clothes. Paramount was strong in Dandies and Debs, and disdained the gangster, western, and mystery thrillers that most studios delighted in. Made them, yes: but disdainfully. A studio that must pump output into an overextended theatre chain has to make everything, so Bulldog Drummond, Hopalong Cassidy, and other stock figures of the second feature were a part of the Paramount community, so to say. But they were, for the most part, strictly segregated among the B units. At Warner Brothers, stars were glorified in gangster pictures—James Cagney, Edward G. Robinson, Humphrey Bogart. MGM relished the notion of mixing its creamiest stars with a very dregs of character players in a thriller—William Powell and Myrna Loy versus a slew of colorful toughs in *The Thin Man*, for instance.

But Paramount liked stars who could bounce some soigné off each other, as if Lubitsch were doing all the contracting. Thus MGM's top man was Clark Gable while Paramount's was Fredric March, lighter, drier. Thus Warner's major costume-action star was Errol Flynn, while Paramount's was Gary Cooper, who looked at least as good in a suit as Flynn and didn't keep glancing at the vest as if wondering what it's supposed to do. Burrowing deep into Paramount's past, into the days of Griffith and Little Mary, we find that Paramount has Hollywood's biggest male star who isn't a clown or a cowboy, Wallace Reid. And Reid, too, was a Dandy, at ease anywhere but most useful when rich, suave, and mildly bored. *Too Many Millions* (1918) would be his problem, *The Love Burglar* (1919) his calling—sex is theft—and *Nice People* (1922) his crowd. As the top draw in the time when Paramount was literally a movie factory, Reid played everything—race-car driver, detective, logger, criminal, boxer, miner, even cowboy. He was big, handsome, and collegiate: "all-American" is the indicated phrase. Yet at heart he was . . . at *heart*. A romancer in adventurer's costumes. A Boudoir Dandy. This is the Paramount hero.

Briefly, in the late 1920s, the studio seemed to have discovered a tougher and sexier avatar in George Bancroft, anti-hero of underworld tales. Bancroft had menace, a quality in short supply at Paramount. But Bancroft was too ponderous to interest the public for long. It's very Paramount that, after Gary Cooper, the studio's most successful male to make the transition from silence to sound was Adolphe Menjou, so elegant that, to this day, no one believes he was born in Pittsburgh.

Paramount liked elegant heroes so much that it built a romantic fantasy around Noël Coward, *The Scoundrel* (1935). Another Astoria project, this was produced, written, and directed by Ben Hecht and Charles MacArthur under a special arrangement as an independent unit. Still, who but Paramount would have closed a deal with these metropolitan codgers, knowing that they would almost certainly concoct something like *The Scoundrel* if only for purposes of cultural flimflam? The clipped Coward delivery, the New York witticisms, the put-downs and malaise: "Marcel Proust!" a woman enthuses to Coward. "Don't you admire him?" "I'm very polite to him," comes the reply. But he's rough on mankind in general. Aghast at the suggestion of a stroll through Central Park, he cries—no, utters . . . nay, *clips,* "On Sunday? It's full of butlers!" And listen to him with ingénue Julie Haydon, who asks, sobbing piteously, "Don't you even love me anymore?" "That," Coward snaps back, "is an ungallant question that women always want answered gallantly."

Yet we are to believe that Coward is a womanizer, loveless himself but inspiring it in others. It's a bit of a stretch. He's at his most airily brittle here, surrounded by the riposte-but-don't-touch salon set, complete with a surprisingly camera-shy Alexander Woollcott. The establishing scenes of smart parties are extreme even by Paramount standards. MGM wouldn't have dared; it loves the power of New York. RKO loves the prestige, Warner Brothers the explosive hungers. But Paramount loves New York's nonconformity, the art of its style. So *The Scoundrel* makes sense in its schedule, even after it turns from grim comedy to spooky moralism. Coward dies in a plane crash, but must walk the earth (dripping seaweed; he leaves some in his office chair) till he finds one "who weeps for you." Haydon obliges. *The Scoundrel* is not a great film, but an illustrative one, for it wouldn't have existed if Paramount had not been invented.

As the 1930s wore on and Paramount, like other studios, finished disposing of its silent heroes (such as Bancroft, who made the mistake of hitting the Old Testament God, Adolph Zukor, for a raise when Bancroft was on the way down), it found itself with a new stable of Dandies. These could talk: Cary Grant, Ray Milland, Fred MacMurray. Grant, wasted till RKO's *Sylvia Scarlett* revealed his exuberance, was actually being readied as a Dangerous Man, smooth, hot, and mean. In the aforementioned Nancy Carroll vehicle, *The Woman Accused*, Grant must convince disreputable witness Jack LaRue to change his testimony to exonerate Carroll. Grant does this by beating LaRue savagely, at times in the face, with a rawhide whip. And certainly the more polished, though still intimidating Grant of Dietrich's *Blonde Venus* seconds the motion. But Grant departed Paramount in 1936, leaving the ultra-suede Milland and the rough-hewn MacMurray. Truth to tell, the closest thing the studio had to a Dangerous Man by then was Mae West. Or so she seems in *I'm No Angel*, when she euphemizes the swordsman's smoking-car credo into "Find 'em, fool 'em, and forget 'em." Anyway, West left the studio shortly after Grant.

Here's a formula that might take. Put Milland or MacMurray with Claudette Colbert in some more of those society comedies, with a little sex-is-theft now and again and contemporary settings to keep costs down, and Paramount has a worthy heir to its by then two decades old tradition of boudoir snafu. There was an important difference, though—an Americanization of place, characters, accent. Lubitsch's people had been largely replaced. Yes, Milland was as British as Herbert Marshall, and Colbert, like Maurice Chevalier, was born in Paris. But where Lubitsch had delighted in the Continental inflection, his successor Mitchell Leisen toned it away. Lubitsch shows us sex appeal in the way Marshall closes a bedroom door. Leisen shows us sex appeal in the way Fred MacMurray's shoulders fill out his coat.

During the years of the Leisen series, from 1935 to about 1944, all Hollywood purged much of the European flavor from its pictures. This is the period in which MGM tried to naturalize Garbo in a bathing suit, in *Two-Faced Woman*; in which Universal used John Wayne and Randolph Scott to knock the von Sternberg out of Marlene Dietrich; in which Chevalier went home. The rise of Nazi aggression closed off Hollywood's European market (except for Britain), the crucial profit margin for every studio's A output. Savvy held that a big movie broke even in America and earned money in Europe.

No more. But Leisen made another break with the studio's usage in society comedy, generally avoiding the ecstatically consumerist décor that DeMille had employed in his American society comedies. That side of Paramount was over, for Zukor's extensive theatre holdings had proved disastrous in the Depression, throwing the company into receivership. The visual excitement did not die, but budgets were tightened.

As it happens, Leisen had got his start as a designer, both of sets and costumes. Realism of home and attire is his forte, but his are largely middle-class subjects, so he often shows dull hallways leading to small apartments of throw-out furniture. Such was his influence that other directors working in Leisen's mode with Leisen's casts tended to absorb his look. Mark Sandrich's *Skylark* (1941) exceptionally provides a sprawling suburban ranch house and the latest mode in frocks. When we first see Colbert, she is in a ritzy boutique overhearing husband Ray Milland's friend Walter Abel picking out Colbert's anniversary gift because Milland couldn't be bothered. The gift, a bauble costing $2,100, tells us we are in Paramount's favorite haunt, the world of plenty. Back at the Millands', Sandrich savors the patio; and when Colbert goes night sailing with Brian Aherne, the camera watches the two glide past a huge ocean liner—to a swelling of the sound track—just for the plenteous beauty of it all.

But *Skylark*'s best scene descends into the New York subways, where only the people are plenty. Milland has been remonstrating with Colbert; to still his lecture, she takes the desperate step of intro ducing Paramount society comedy to public transportation. But then, as we'll see, Paramount is democratizing its society. Scenarist Allan Scott fills the train with picturesque kibitzers, a kind of urban foxhole: the pensive professor, the tough guy, the Jewish leftist, the opinionated housewife. "What would people on earth *be* without women?" she asks. "Scarce," replies the professor. "Mighty scarce."

Leisen's *Midnight* (1939) is probably the most celebrated of the series. It is certainly the most lavish—also the most colorful, a Cinderella story set in Paris with a huge spoof of a performance by John Barrymore and the unexpected Don Ameche supporting Colbert. But, like *Skylark*, *Midnight* misleads about the nature of the Leisen–Colbert school of contemporary romance. Wesley Ruggles's *The Bride Comes Home* (1935), back when the cycle was just revving up, is more typical. Of course Colbert is Of Family, but her father has just lost everything, which gives couturier Travis Banton so little to work with that at one point we find Colbert doing housework in a babushka. (The lady's game. As long as you remember to keep the camera off her right side, she'll wear anything.) Paramount being Paramount, there's got to be money in this somewhere, and Robert Young, a three-and-a-half millionaire, has it. But he's a thoughtless dumbbell, a little boy with a big wallet. Colbert prefers Fred Mac-

Murray, Young's bodyguard. "He starts fights," MacMurray explains, "and I finish them." Young also starts a men's magazine, with MacMurray as editor—and Colbert as editor's assistant, Mac-Murray putting Colbert through humiliating paces to make an example of this working-class heiress.

It's class war, then—but completely without drive, point. Warner Brothers teaches the politics of caste, MGM glamorizes the shopgirl's ambition, Columbia (in the Capra films) identifies the despot, the anarchist, the running dogs, the redemptive people's hero. Paramount just wants to get everybody into bed. Granted, in Leisen's *Hands Across the Table* (1935), MacMurray, spending the night at Carole Lombard's apartment (in Production Code twin rooms) is so wracked by temptation that he sneaks out. But Leisen films the scene with notable steam; we really feel that if MacMurray didn't leave, the Production Code would shatter like Moses' Tablets. At that, Leisen closes the sequence with Lombard entering MacMurray's empty room.

One wonders if any other studio would have tolerated Leisen's sensuality. Like Lubitsch, he can eroticize a relatively innocent script by his handling of actors and what his camera sees. Leisen's *Swing High, Swing Low* (1937) is not properly of this series, more melodramatic than comic and almost a musical. (Dorothy Lamour keeps dancing, or threatening to.) But it shows us how well Leisen handled sex, and why he justifies mention with the amazing Lubitsch.

After some establishing shots of the Panama Canal, MacMurray, in uniform, spots Lombard, sailing past. He pushes for a date. Lombard is not amused. "How about scramming," she adds, "so I can see some of the scenery down here?" and MacMurray replies, "I *am* the scenery down here." Lombard is thrilled and disgusted, a very typical state for a Hollywood heroine touching base with her co-star; it works as well for Margaret Sullavan and James Stewart, for Ginger Rogers and Fred Astaire, or for Norma Shearer and Clark Gable. Nothing special there. A bit later, however, in a bar where a demobilized MacMurray sits in on trumpet, Lombard is exclusively thrilled, and Leisen films it as a mating call, sweet and low with a hint of wild riffs to come. And when the pair hook up as a singer-trumpeter act, Leisen has them pose together as braided as a lanyard, she singing to his axe while resting in the crook of his arm, as sheltered as possessed.

Claudette Colbert looks wary, but she's going to choose reporter Fred MacMurray over British aristocrat Ray Milland, which is why we left him out of our still of The Gilded Lily *(1935), another of Paramount's triangular "society" romances.*

Paramount loves the sex that works because the romance works. This is why Mae West's comedies were never directed as romantic comedies, the essential Paramount genre. Mae believed that the sex works because sex works. "Diamonds," she said, and might have emphasized, "is my career." So Mae's films are bawdy but they aren't sexy, because Mae never connects with anyone emotionally. Worse yet, she had a habit of playing love scenes with men like Roger Pryor, Paul Cavanaugh, and Victor McLaglen. "Only connect!" the studio begs; and Mae replies, "Beulah, peel me a grape." (One wonders what she would have been like with MacMurray.) Leisen connects. There's a semi-forgotten, very sexy little gem of a movie called *No Time for Love* (1943), something of the capstone of the Leisen cycle, that gives us connection of such intensity that Lubitsch might have been shocked.

This is Colbert and MacMurray again: attraction in opposition. He's a sandhog, genially hostile to men and a pickup artist with women. She's a photojournalist, who accidentally gets him fired and guiltily signs him on as her assistant. This makes for a certain uproar among the effete cohort of her magazine. One of the boys calls Mac-Murray a "Viking"; MacMurray, unruffled, calls him "dollface." MacMurray has appetites and energy, which both alarms and intrigues Colbert. What could she possibly find in this two-bit couch pouncer? And his confidence, Leisen knows, does not impress her. She hopes. For instance: MacMurray uses his position to cop a date with showgirl June Havoc, borrows Colbert's car, and fails to return it till the next morning:

MacMurray: It was so late when I finished that—
Colbert: Finished what?
MacMurray: (grinning) Are you kidding?

Colbert eyebrows this away. But how, then, to explain her dream in which an old-time melodrama villain menaces her among the clouds till MacMurray, in Superman tights, flies in to the rescue?

We expect ambivalence from Leisen's heroines, the opposition in the attraction. But *No Time for Love* goes farther, to question the very nature of masculinity. Even Lubitsch never got to that. Leisen gives us a kaleidoscope of samples here, of various size, class, and culture; and he sees one thing common to all: vanity. The Colberts of the world are doomed to flatter the reckless self-love of men, whether they be publisher or sandhog, subtle or pushy, a dream or a drip. Leisen even confronts MacMurray with a caricature of himself, in a saphead muscleman stripped to briefs for a modeling shoot for Colbert's camera. Naturally, MacMurray and the body immediately get a feud going. MacMurray wins, felling his "rival" with light booms and a barbell. No doubt it never occurs to MacMurray that the preening muscle jerk is his own vanity peeled to a visual metaphor. No doubt: for, at the end, unreconstructed, MacMurray carries Colbert off caveman-style, and she couldn't be happier.

Unfortunately, the revelation that MacMurray is in fact no workingman but a college-trained technician gums up the works. It is meant to assuage our doubts. Okay, he's brutish, but he's smart. Except he hasn't really been smart, just brutish. Charming, yes— that's MacMurray's advantage over Ray Milland and the other Paramount Dandies: MacMurray has charm *and* shoulders. Still, Leisen has got us wondering just what mixture of self-confidence and intelligence does work in romance. An odd note for a romantic comedy to strike.

It's fitting that *No Time for Love* virtually closed down Paramount's tradition of society comedies. Bob Hope's vehicles and the *Road* series occupied the studio's comedy wing in the 1940s; and the democratic experience of wartime put the kibosh on conspicuous swank, certainly on $2,100 baubles and satiric adultery, two of Paramount's conventions in this genre since early DeMille. Yet, at the same time, a new wing had been opened up in the early 1940s, one that sometimes set the vaudevillians' strut into the society setting, and at other times seemed to create its own style out of new characters and settings. This new wing was Paramount in its strong directorial steerage, Paramount in its use of nonconformist wit and subjects. This new wing was the writer-director Preston Sturges.

Sturges, a screenwriter since 1930, was eclectically motivated. Single-handed, he dramatized Paramount in costume (*If I Were King*, 1938) and Paramount screwball (*Easy Living*, 1937); and, for Fox, *The Power and the Glory* (1933), the work that paved some of the way for *Citizen Kane*. There was Sturges gone deep and Sturges in frolic, Sturges practicing genre and Sturges mapping out new terrain. Sturges wrote so well that by the end of the 1930s he decided to become not only the author of the scripts but the auteur of the films, and told Paramount he'd take next to nothing if they'd let him direct his script for *The Great McGinty*. Paramount agreed and the film was a hit, initiating an oeuvre that, on form, gave us seven films in five years: *McGinty* (1940), *Christmas in July* (1940), *The Lady Eve* (1941), *Sullivan's Travels* (1941), *The Palm Beach Story* (1942), *The Miracle of Morgan's Creek* (1944), and *Hail the Conquering Hero* (1944).

Some of these fall right into parish grooves—the dinner clothes and sex-is-theft atmosphere of *The Lady Eve*, the randy society cartooning of *The Palm Beach Story*. We think back to hairdresser Jack Buchanan forcing himself on Jeanette MacDonald in a film that would of course be called *Monte Carlo* (1930)—the Riviera, the money, the chic. "That's what you get," MacDonald wails, "for being nice to your servants!" Paramount is still Paramount; Monte Carlo has been Americanized into Palm Beach.

But *Christmas in July* is working-class, plain to see; and the war-conscious pair of 1944 examine the small-town bourgeoisie. And two of Sturges's heroes are artists, McGinty a politician and Sullivan a movie director. However, Sturges's eccentric pacing recalls to us Paramount's nurturing of the self-willing director. Now Sturges sets up an interminable two-shot, now he's gamboling about at the gallop. His love scenes are funny, his curmudgeons (and he has plenty) tenderly wrathful. He casts Claudette Colbert in her usual role, Barbara Stanwyck as a heroine so predatory and self-assured that we wonder how many times Billy Wilder screened *The Lady Eve* before he began *Double Indemnity*. And, mind you, this is the heroine of a comedy.

Sturges may be the most perverse of all Paramount directors, more so even than von Sternberg. *Christmas in July* offers Dick Powell in his first role after having spent the Depression buoying everyone up with song at Warner Brothers. Suddenly, here, he's unbuoyant, grouchy, even cynical. "You gotta look out for yourself in this world," he tells his wife, Ellen Drew. "You gotta see the main chance and grab it." It's discombobulating, especially when Powell enters a motto contest sponsored by a coffee firm. This is hard-times comedy, so we have to root for Powell to win. But his slogan is, "If you can't sleep, it isn't the coffee, it's the bunk."

Sturges wants us to laugh at this pathetic version of grabbing the main chance, and, more perverse, lets Powell think he's the winner through some co-workers' practical joke of a telegram. Most perverse

yet, when Powell shows up to claim his check, the coffee manufac-
turer (Raymond Walburn) believes the telegram, too! Naturally,
Powell's own boss (Ernest Truex) is impressed by this young go-get-
ter's zeal, and the joke spirals outward, verging on sadism when
Powell buys out a store on credit, to gift his whole neighborhood.
Just wait till the whole thing explodes in his face, Sturges promises,
chuckling. As we squirm.

At length, the joke is exposed, and Sturges lets everyone get just
uncomfortable enough before he pulls his own practical joke. The
contest judges have been deadlocked throughout the action, and
finally they announce a winner:

Dick Powell.

Sturges has one last stunt to pull on us: he never gives us the relief
of seeing Powell and Drew learn that their phony good fortune is
genuine after all. The movie fades out on the saddened couple heading home, unaware that the one, true congratulatory telegram is on
its way. The last thing we see is a black cat.

There's love in Sturges's bite. He needs to believe in the classic
values as much as he likes to toy with them. Typical Paramount, he
knows about politics but doesn't really need them. Humanist more
than socialite, he likes to show a Capraesque world without an
Edward Arnold—*Christmas in July*'s bosses, Walburn and Truex, are
touchy but never vicious or power-hungry. Also typical Paramount,
Sturges loves to remind us that sex is the first pleasure. *The Miracle of
Morgan's Creek* gets its plot going when a serviceman out on a gang
date suggests everyone get married—that is, have sex by outsmarting
the Production Code. And all do; but Betty Hutton, the police chief's
daughter, gets pregnant and can't remember whom she married.
"Ratzkywatzky" is the closest she can come to his name. There's
another funny name in Morgan's Creek, hers: Kockenlocker. And,
speaking of outsmarting the Code, it's Hutton's kockenlocker (pardon me, but the joke is Sturges's, not mine) that gets the ball rolling
in the first place.

This devilish chuckle at the human need for, uh, recreation is
where Paramount and Sturges are most in harmony. In *The Palm
Beach Story*, Sturges is willing to present a good old-fashioned
romance in the marriage of Joel McCrea and Claudette Colbert on
the condition that Sturges can split them up so two millionaires can

chase them. True, Rudy Vallee woos Colbert daintily, his libido like a trust fund: you live on the interest, not the principal. But Vallee's sister Mary Astor goes for McCrea like Mad Margaret spotting a maypole. And here is another perverse resolution: Colbert and McCrea have reconciled, so whom can Vallee and Astor marry? They only want Colbert and McCrea. Sturges gives them just that, in a surprise ending as contrived as Gilbert and Sullivan's babies-switched-at-birth. It virtually *is* switched babies, for, out of nowhere, Colbert and McCrea each produce identical twins. Or no, not out of nowhere. I told you so, says Sturges . . . as we suddenly realize what was happening in the film's incomprehensible opening, a breakneck rumpus involving Colbert and McCrea: *those were the twins!*

This is Sturges's madcap side, harmonizing the Marx Brothers' anarchy and W. C. Fields's masochistic misanthropy in secure plotting while respecting their comic vitality. Surely Sturges would have been Sturges without these predecessors, but surely he is the richer for their instruction. As writer-director, he never quite denies their inspiration, though he has a dark, semi-realistic side they did not share. The travels of Sullivan, farcically trailed by an anxious suite of studio and household staff, eventually take him into the custody of law at its meanest, in a chain gang.

Coincidentally, *Sullivan's Travels* closely resembles a Paramount silent, *Beggars of Life* (1928),* directed by William Wellman, with Richard Arlen, Louise Brooks, and Wallace Beery. Joel McCrea, Sullivan, is a member of the leadership class, Arlen just a hobo; but both travel with an attractive young woman disguised as a man, her hair tucked into a floppy porkpie hat. (McCrea's companion is Veronica Lake, not entirely unlike Louise Brooks in spirit.) "Some beg for one thing and some for another," says Arlen by title card, sounding Wellman's theme. "Everyone wants something he doesn't have." This is Sturges's theme, too. Sullivan, a director of comedy, wants Serious Prestige. He wants his audience to think, an innovative idea for a Paramounter. This is the studio of entrancing pictures. You don't think; you watch. Oddly, just as Sturges's Sullivan wants to experience life among the unprotected, *Beggars of Life* is a rare excursion of Paramount into a world in which everyone is homeless and

---

* This was Paramount's first part-talkie, released to theatres that could handle it with a music track and a few dialogue scenes. Apparently only the silent survives.

the social code comprises aggression against the defenseless. Trouble in paradise? How about trouble in a hobo camp when Brooks's disguise is exposed and Arlen has to face down a crowd of men who would as soon rape her as eat pie? Even Beery, who falls in with Arlen and Brooks as a comrade, keeps trying to take Brooks by force. But Sturges, at his darkest, still has a lighter take on the world, and Sullivan, reinvigorated by his fellow convicts' self-redemptive laughter at a cartoon, is restored to his studio.

Sturges's era as writer-director, the 1940s, was the heyday of film noir. This very slightly expressionistic form is a director's medium; naturally Paramount excelled. It had another writer on the lot who, like Sturges, wanted to direct, Billy Wilder. Teamed with Charles Brackett, Wilder as scenarist had logged almost as various a catalogue as Sturges—*Champagne Waltz* (1937), a Gladys Swarthout musical; *Midnight*, in the Leisen series; *Hold Back the Dawn* (1941), a weepie with Charles Boyer and Olivia de Havilland. As director, however, he actuated an acerbic, gloomy worldview in which men are hustlers and women cheats: one of film noir's most identifying opinions.

There is no precise definition of noir; or there are several, which scrambles the precision. But this is one genre that, like the western, does not admit of studio peculiarities, of stylistic variations from one company to another. Even so, it was Warner Brothers that pointed the way in its crime films, especially those tending to nighttime settings of deserted streets or great, empty meeting places, with a stable of picturesque or freakish secondary characters and nightmarish accents in the lighting and camera work. By the time Warners produced *The Maltese Falcon*, in 1941, the form was jelling, especially in the treacherously seductive Mary Astor. Wilder introduced a crucial new element: the criminals are not professionals but middle-class people tempted by greed and sex. In what may be the exemplary noir masterpiece, *Double Indemnity* (1944), Wilder proposes Fred MacMurray as an insurance salesman, Barbara Stanwyck to lure MacMurray into killing her husband for the insurance payoff, and Edward G. Robinson, as MacMurray's boss, to expose them. The film is not only brilliantly but infuriatingly suspenseful, for by giving us two of Hollywood's most likable actors as the two murderers, Wilder throws us on their side, making Robinson and justice not the forces we root for but the things we fear.

Thus noir takes crime into the American home, through the agency of Fred MacMurray, Colbert's and Lombard's boyfriend, and Barbara Stanwyck—a Capra heroine, no less! MacMurray understood the casting ploy well enough to refuse the part, but then George Raft also turned it down. Raft had a history of rejecting great parts—Sam Spade in *The Maltese Falcon* was one of them—and now Wilder was able to persuade MacMurray to play a killer. In the event, the film gave him more attention than all his Leisens put together.

Double Indemnity is loaded with generic credentials—the Los Angeles location shooting, the tough comebacks and double meanings of pulp fiction, the flashback voice-over narration, MacMurray's address of Stanwyck as "baby": "I'm crazy about you, baby," but also "Goodbye, baby" as he shoots her. Two progenitors of noir dialect turn up in the credits, Raymond Chandler as Wilder's collaborator and James M. Cain as their plot source. John F. Seitz, the cinematographer, was to light and frame several noir classics. Looking back historically, we approve the purity of form and excellence of delivery.

At the time, the studio was unhappy at the prospect of such steamy criminality. But by 1950, when Wilder made *Sunset Boulevard*, noir was in, and the studio not only enthused at the idea of a silent-movie queen binging on solipsistic nostalgia into madness and murder, but let Wilder give it the documentary witness of Paramount's former Queen of the Lot, Gloria Swanson. We even journey to the studio itself, where Swanson approaches a gently incredulous Cecil DeMille about effectuating her comeback as Salome.

Wilder pushed noir beyond the limits of popularity in *Ace in the Hole* (1951), in which reporter Kirk Douglas plays up a story about a man trapped in a cave for personal advancement, corrupting local officials and sabotaging the rescue operation. The trapped man dies. I define films noirs as pictures so darkly lit that people like me can't take legible notes; but *Ace in the Hole* is furiously bright. It is as if Wilder meant to expose human selfishness, for once, not in noir's glamorously morbid darkness but in the bum clarity of daylight. *Double Indemnity* had a fair man in Robinson, and *Sunset Boulevard*'s William Holden does no worse than hire out as a gigolo. But every principal in *Ace in the Hole* is a creep except the man in the cave. Even Jan Sterling, his wife, sees his captivity simply as her escape, a chance to hit the road. "Honey," she tells Kirk Douglas, "you like those rocks just as much as I do!" Most horrifying of all are the nonentities who swarm to the site like tourists doing Pompeii, waiting out the rescue in their trailers, mouthing observations to journalists, enjoying the amusement park thrown up overnight complete with Ferris wheel, and, in one spectacular long shot, dashing off an arriving train in gleeful hordes. Wilder gives us virtually the opposite of Capra's Americana, in which the general mass of people leans to eccentricity but responds to good instincts. In *Ace in the Hole*, everyone's an idiot or a monster.

All credit to Paramount for making the film. But what the studio wanted from noir was sex and mystery. *Ace in the Hole* is open, mean, and honest—and there's no love in it, not even for Douglas. Luckily, the studio had already discovered a fetching boy-meets-girl noir combination in Alan Ladd and Veronica Lake. Their three noir duets,* *This Gun for Hire* (1942), *The Glass Key* (1942), and *The Blue Dahlia* (1946), complemented Wilder's noirs with a more sensual, less social construction. Moreover, *This Gun for Hire* gave Paramount its first genuine Dangerous Man in Ladd's killer, the physically and emotionally scarred Raven.

Paramount had more or less introduced the Dangerous Man in George Bancroft, the good-bad hero of Paramount's underworld cycle in the late 1920s and early 1930s. The studio found a few successors to Bancroft: in George Raft, Fred MacMurray, Sterling Hayden, and Kirk Douglas. But none of them is quite of the type. The Dangerous Man is the talkies' reponse to the silents' Great Lover, more naturalistic, less florid, very contemporary in style. Think of the leap from Rudolph Valentino to Clark Gable—this is Great Lover ceding to Dangerous Man. This new version of the romantic hero may appear in period costumes, but never attempts antique manners—Gable, for instance, as Fletcher Christian or Rhett Butler, not making a move that couldn't have been made on an American street corner in the 1930s, not even putting on a British or Southern accent. The Dangerous Man is sexy and tough, often an outlaw but honorable once you get through to him. Darryl Zanuck outlined the type well: "Women love bums."

This is a peculiar hero, not as elegant as Tyrone Power or Errol

* The fourth and last Ladd–Lake teaming, *Saigon* (1948), is a pedestrian thriller with touches of noir at most.

Flynn, but with a kind of no-nonsense gallantry. Above all, he is virile, bold, menacing. Under the charm, he's all balls. Raft, a dreary personality, was out of the running however many Bancroft roles he played, and MacMurray's menace was compromised by a streak of the Dandy. Hayden, a promising talent, didn't luck into a telling vehicle till he left the studio, and Douglas's walking-the-blade dynamics tend to hype an already explosive character.

However, something about the petite, baby-faced Ladd registered menace in the camera, which gave him a blend of lovability and ferocity that absolutely placed him in the type. Lake was his complement, for her icy heat conveyed the dark side of the noir heroine while allowing her to play nice with Ladd. *He* is the corrupt character when they meet in *This Gun for Hire*, coldly trying to gun her down after she helped him sneak through a dragnet. It's a mean moment. Only his reformation—through her sympathy—and his foiling a money boss collaborating with the Japanese redeem him in our eyes.

Lake's part in Raven's salvation importantly debilitates a noir archetype, the Treacherous Woman. We meet this figure throughout the noir arena, not invariably but in most of the key films: Stanwyck and Swanson in the aforementioned Wilders, of course; also Ava Gardner in Universal's *The Killers*, Rita Hayworth in Columbia's *Gilda*, Claire Trevor in RKO's *Born to Kill*, Joan Bennett in Universal's *Scarlet Street*, Jane Greer in RKO's *Out of the Past*. Suckering men not only for profit but because it gives her a tingly feeling inside, the Treacherous Woman was instrumental in combining noir's most basic components, crime and sex. Woman is the lure that instigates the crime, the wanton who destabilizes the social contract, then the renegade who piles deception upon disorder.

As the director's studio, Paramount responded to the possibilities. Thus *Double Indemnity*: not only the film with the most spectacular wanton-renegade in all noir, but the earliest of the masterpieces in noir's heyday. Other studios brought out their classics after Paramount set the style. However, as the sexy studio, Paramount was not altogether comfortable with the Treacherous Woman. Love is supposed to be benison. So the Ladd–Lake partnership put romance back into noir. Let the man commit the crimes; that's a man's job. Woman must be supportive. Mysterious, okay. Tough-talking, fine. But above all: lovable.

This in itself makes their three noirs noteworthy, for other noir women, if not wholly foul, are wholly sweet. Just as well—for Ladd and Lake's films are not in themselves first-rate. *This Gun for Hire* has an amusing freak in bad guy Laird Cregar, nattily, effeminately huge, with a fondness for peppermints. *The Glass Key* has William Bendix's sadistic beating of Ladd, culminating in Ladd's escape and headlong fall through a skylight onto a family at table, thrillingly surveyed in tightly edited quick shots and one last overhead view as Ladd breaks up the breakfast. *The Blue Dahlia*, a whodunit, boasts a script by Raymond Chandler, though his original choice of murderer, a serviceman, was vetoed as insulting to veterans, and his "buddies heading for the nearest bar" fade-out replaced by more of the Ladd–Lake romance. Colorful films: not good ones.

What is good, like it or not, are Ladd and Lake. Many do not like it. The two can't act, can't simulate acting, have so little energy that they're little more than present. Yes, these are the forgeries of stardom. But their tense charm stays with you. "She's audience-proof!" is one man's comment on entertainer Lake in *This Gun for Hire*. "Gets 'em bug-eyed!" Indeed, her magic-act-in-song is a knockout, with the special effects, real magic, that few films of the time displayed. We begin to see why old-time buffs are bored with movies today. Acting has improved, but the actors are . . . actors. Lake is cold voodoo. Ladd, too, is cold, even after *This Gun*'s trench coat gives way to *The Glass Key*'s suits, even when, in 1949, Paramount made its second version of *The Great Gatsby* and exploded the hero's mysterious past with an establishing montage of gangster action, Ladd right in there with nothing on his face whatever. But his cool sears, in the glimmer of a smile when Raven pulls his trigger, in his dogged refusal to let Bendix's beating stop him, even slow him down. Too bad Lake and Ladd never worked with Billy Wilder; that would have been noir deluxe.

But then Wilder liked energy and actors—Stanwyck, Swanson, MacMurray, Douglas. Lake and Ladd lack the guts of noir, the hunger. Yet Paramount could turn out decent noir without anyone special in view, proving how much a director's medium both noir and Paramount are.

William Dieterle—another of the unspectacular but gifted directors who go unsung while utterly unendowed directors like Edgar

Ulmer are made festival—gives us a taste of Paramount's less pretentious noir style in *Dark City* (1950). This was Charlton Heston's first Hollywood feature, as a Dangerous Man whose partners in a rigged, big-stakes poker game are killed one by one. We get the crummy streets, the New York and Vegas, the eccentric assistants, the oddly peering camera—but only love, no sex, no Treacherous Woman. Dieterle, originally Wilhelm, believes more in Goethe's *Ewig-Weibliche* than in Barbara Stanwyck. Dieterle gives us two women, both nice, Heston's friend Lizabeth Scott and an innocent clue to who'sdoingit, Viveca Lindfors. It's a fine piece, not great film but a very efficient secondary production. This may typify Paramount as much as *Double Indemnity* does: even the routine is interesting.

Of all Hollywood's genres, in fact, Paramount failed in only one: the musical. Early in talkies, of course, the studio distinguished itself here, for Lubitsch was doing musicals. But in 1932, after *One Hour with You* and Mamoulian's *Love Me Tonight*, Paramount renounced leadership. Not only did it lose its distinction, even decent routine eluded it.

All the major song-or-dance stars except Bing Crosby were at other studios;* Paramount seemed to be making up for the shortage by varying Crosby's vehicles far more than MGM did Eleanor Powell's or Universal did Deanna Durbin's. Odd that it worked, for Crosby was a limited blessing. He was no actor, couldn't dance, and didn't look good in anything but his Sunday cardigan and golf hat. Crosby was little more than a singer, but a delightful one, touches of blues and scat inflecting his easygoing style.

Melody and personality, then, carried Crosby through his diverse oeuvre. Some Crosbys are full-scale musicals, with production numbers and singing co-stars; some are straight films incidentally dittied. There was Crosby in modern dress and Crosby in costume, as the peaceful presenter of three Rodgers and Hart ballads and a little Stephen Foster, for instance, in *Mississippi*. Though he loses his Southern fiancée for refusing to fight an unnecessary duel, he brawls with a heckler who won't let him sing, and when the smoke clears, the heckler is dead and Bing may take stage as "The Singing Killer." It sounds beyond him. But a double handles the fight scene, the rest

* Unless one counts Betty Hutton, not really a major star and not as consistently musical as Crosby.

of the cast reacts to his reputation, and Bing sings the songs. It works.

Unquestionably, Crosby is more comfortable in regular clothes —so much so that he shows up wearing his own in a period piece, *Birth of the Blues* (1941). The scene plot is New Orleans in the early 1900s, and, sure enough, there's Brian Donlevy in some picturesque haberdashery and Mary Martin in a lacy gown. Then Bing strolls in, looking as if he's ready for his golf game with Bob Hope.

Crosby's character varies along with the genres. He is most natural when mildly dauntless, as the Crichton figure in *We're Not Dressing*, hopelessly outclassed by Carole Lombard's weight of presence but compensating for it in the songs. Interestingly, when Crosby does a brother picture with Fred MacMurray and little Donald O'Connor, *Sing, You Sinners* (1938), it is Crosby, not MacMurray, who plays the wastrel brother, flunking out of jobs and stealing MacMurray's girl. Director Wesley Ruggles guides Crosby well—or, rather, doesn't guide him—to preserve the natural quality that carries him along. But Crosby was really at his best when facing off solid musical-comedy talent, people who speak his language. What can he do with *Mississippi*'s Joan Bennett except deliver his Rodgers and Hart? But with Ethel Merman and Charles Ruggles in *Anything Goes* (1936) Crosby is sharp, on his steel.

A very successful series, pleasurably unpretentious. However, these were more Crosby films than musicals—there was no essentially musical staff to develop them, as there was at RKO for the Astaire–Rogers dance musicals or at Warner Brothers for the Busby Berkeley backstagers. In fact, Paramount had no musical unit to speak of. More often than not, it derived its musicals by imitation, following other studios' leads as the cycles were revealed.

Thus we note, for instance, the MacDonald–Eddy operetta, from MGM. A typical Paramount copy is *All the King's Horses* (1935), doughy of action and dumpy of score where MGM's series has tempo and melody; and aren't Carl Brisson and Mary Ellis a little too Ruritanian even for a Ruritanian operetta? MGM's Eddy may be wooden and MacDonald something of a pageant, but Brisson and Ellis suggest something that pranced out of a hollow tree.

We note the Fox Alice Faye backstager, with Faye herself (on loan), *Every Night at Eight* (1935), so Fox that when Faye gets onto a yacht, all the socialites are loathsome and stupid—no Mary Boland, no Charles Butterworth, forgivably zany. We note the "great" MGM musical bio: *The Great Victor Herbert* (1939), not, in fact, a bio but a "star is born" romance for Mary Martin and Allan Jones, with Herbert (Walter Connolly) beaming and sputtering and conducting in the background. The movie looks expensive and was well researched, with a lot of unusual Herbert along with the hits, even whole scenes of *The Rose of Algeria*, one of Herbert's best, neglected scores. There's one unusual bit, when Martin and Jones court on bicycles to the words of a specially constructed Herbert medley; and young Susanna Foster sings a fine "Kiss Me Again." But MGM's ability to hang number after number upon a phony "life" is beyond Paramount; it just doesn't believe in this kind of thing.

We note the big-band musical, too, in *Second Chorus* (1940). Here, at least, Paramount holds its own. It's *apparently* awful, with Fred Astaire and Burgess Meredith as collegiate trumpeters, no one but Paulette Goddard for Astaire to dance with, and Artie Shaw in a dramatic part. But if you write books like this one, you have to see films like *Second Chorus* more than once, and they grow on you. Astaire is always welcome, Meredith at least can act, and Shaw is, for an amateur, acceptable. We get Charles Butterworth, still quaintly bizarre after all these years, but having traded in his *Love Me Tonight* flute for the flat-back mandolin. Sponsoring a Big Concert for Shaw and Astaire, he reminds us that the rich can be nice—exploitable, anyway. And, by the way, Goddard manages to keep up with Astaire in "I Ain't Hep to That Step, But I'll Dig It." She has better legs than Grable, too.

We also note the classical-music musical, an unremitting horror misleadingly entitled *There's Magic in Music* (1941). Not this time, there isn't. Other studios had Lawrence Tibbett, Grace Moore, Lily Pons, Lauritz Melchior, even Jascha Heifetz. Paramount itself had Gladys Swarthout. *There's Magic in Music* has Interlochen Music Camp, whither Susanna Foster, as the slang-spewing burlesque attraction Tootles Laverne, hies herself on the lam. Foster is a diva of burlesque; her act consists of singing the Shadow Song from Meyerbeer's *Dinorah* while stripping. (It's nothing much: she drops a veil here and there. It's the kind of thing you could bring Mendelssohn to.) Foster is only an excuse to take us on a tour of Interlochen, though Paramount does add a putting-on-the-show plot, just in case we get *extremely bored* meeting all these fervent *twelve-year-old violin-*

ists, solemnly tow-haired *Finnish conductors*, and other corny prodigies. This is not to mention the ghastly B-unit editing that Paramount suffered, agreeing with David Selznick that very cheap pictures make money. This movie has but two boons: a rare film appearance by then Met mezzo (and later Broadway operetta artiste) Irra Petina, as herself and, alas, not vocalizing; and Foster's scooping of Bette Davis by eight years on the line "What a dump!" as Foster gets her first glimpse of her Interlochen Music Camp cabin.

Looking back to the Lubitsch classics, we despair. All the things that made *The Love Parade, Monte Carlo,* and the others special are so quickly gone. As long as Paramount was doing imitative musicals, why didn't they imitate Lubitsch?

Take *One Hour with You*. Consider its sexy vitality: in the way Maurice Chevalier and wife Jeanette MacDonald carry on, so hot they seem adulterous, or in the way Lubitsch caps "What a Little Thing Like a Wedding Ring Can Do" with a loving, lingering look at the marriage bed.

Consider its wit: as when Chevalier first meets neglected husband Roland Young. Chevalier introduces himself as "Dr. Bertier. Physician." Young responds with "Professor Olivier. Ancient History." Then, looking at a painting of his blonde young wife, Young says, "When I married her, she was a brunette. Now you can't believe a word she says."

Consider its delight in devious excess, setting up the central dinner-party sequence, when the web of cheating and spying must draw taut. As Chevalier and MacDonald duel over the setting of the place cards, Charles Ruggles, dressed as Romeo, learns that the party is not, as his butler had told him, a costume affair. Ruggles confronts the butler. "Ah, Monsieur," says he, with an impenitent smirk, "I did so want to see you in tights."

There is sheer expertise of form, in the coy "rhymed dialogue," virtually spoken songs; in the use of pantomime keyed to music; in the way the title song is passed from person to person at the party, its lyrics and tone changing as spy turns cheat and vice versa. There is the confident use of décor, neither insistent nor modest, but appropriate, correct. Paramount doesn't have to pile on the class in the visuals because the actors already have it: through direction, script, themselves.

Why did the studio turn from this to *Every Night at Eight* and *Sec-*

ond Chorus? Perhaps it is simply that the musical is not a medium for directors and writers, the two talents Paramount was rich in. The musical is a performer's medium, and the performers, for the most part, were elsewhere. One wonders if the Lubitsch–Mamoulian series would have come off half as well without Chevalier and MacDonald, virtually the studio's only musical stars at the time. Anyway, were these musical films as much as they were Lubitsch and Mamoulian films, even given that Rodgers and Hart wrote so originally for *Love Me Tonight* that some scenes are as musical as opera? Were these not simply more exquisitely evolved samples of Paramount's typical society comedy?

In truth, much of Paramount's sexy vitality, wit, devious excess, and even technical expertise was drained out—not only of the musical but of Paramount altogether—during the reinvigoration of the Production Code in 1934, the democratization of subjects and style during World War II, and the divestiture that forced all the studios to separate production and distribution from exhibition. As we'll see, this in effect ends the studio approach to filmmaking, disconnects tradition. By 1950, a furiously devolved financial structure forces the studio to retrench and undo, and soon afterward we find little in Paramount's output that relates to its work in the Golden Age. Hope, Crosby, and DeMille remain till the middle of the decade. There's a whiff of Famous Players in Famous Plays in Shirley Booth's preserving her Broadway Lola in *Come Back, Little Sheba* (1952), even in the filming of *Li'l Abner* (1959) almost exactly as it looked on stage. We sense a chaste revival of the Paramount society comedy in *Breakfast at Tiffany's* (1961). We note a fluttering of that *Verfremdungseffekt* of Lubitsch and the vaudevillians, the direct address of the audience, in Joseph Anthony's *The Matchmaker* (1958). Shirley Booth, in the title role as Dolly Levi ("born Gallagher"), even dares an anachronistic reference to "You people who go to the movies" as she looks right at us—this in a story set in the 1880s. And is that not a recollection of Paramount's love of visual fantasy in the delightfully fake miniature of a train chugging against an old-fashioned lithograph as *The Matchmaker* travels from Yonkers to New York?

In the end, though, it is the end—of what Paramount meant as a studio. The movies of course survive, as does Paramount, at least in name. But now there is true trouble in paradise; now is Hollywood a dark city.

MGM invented the backstage musical in 1929, in The
Broadway Melody, *but Warner Brothers reinvented it in
1933, in* 42nd Street. *So MGM made* Dancing Lady *that
same year as a kind of 42nd Melody, with a big-number
finale in the Busby Berkeley manner. Admire Joan Crawford and Fred Astaire, center.*

METRO GOLDWYN MAYER

The Supreme

Paramount was the director's studio. MGM belonged to the producer. The difference lies in the characters of the two presiding moguls, Adolph Zukor and Louis B. Mayer. Zukor was the deal maker, out of reach in the Eastern boardrooms. He didn't produce: he presented, in name only. Zukor hired junior executives to turn out the films while he conceived the mergers, the bond issues, the certificates of bank. Mayer, on the contrary, was the honcho in situ. He was a presence, a factor, strolling the lot with overwhelming camaraderie, receiving staff in his magisterial office, making decisions about movies—specific movies, right there on the turf—alternately wheedling and threatening dubious actors, sizing up his Christian directors and trading *so, nu?* philosophy with his Jewish "supervisors." Directors were Them and supervisors were Us.

A supervisor was a producer. Or, rather, a producer *supervises*. He takes charge and keeps everyone in line so the firm can make some smart money. At that crazy Paramount, they let directors drag it out, dream up special effects, make a big mess all over the lot. At that schmudl little Warner Brothers, with the Rin-Tin-Tin and the Al Jolson, they're so afraid of spending three cents to make an actress look like a princess that their films seem to be dreck you should wrap your garbage in. And look what they got for a princess—Bette Davis! Universal is so lost in the dark ages, when you go to a Universal, you're surprised it's a movie—you thought maybe they're going to do *Uncle Tom's Cabin* with the real bloodhounds, remember? On a stage? At Metro, it looks nice, it looks big, it looks pretty. And you know how we keep it nice, big, and pretty?

We watch those sons-of-directors and arrogant ham stars every step of the way.

The rage of Mayer. The conservative zealotry, the dire ooze of his blackmail, the unctuous sentimentality masking the tyranny. His themes were God, country, and mom's chicken soup; his equals were such as William Randolph Hearst and Franklin Roosevelt; and the man he hated to love was Irving Thalberg, a fellow producer and, unlike Mayer, a genius at moviemaking. Thalberg was the ideas behind MGM; Thalberg *produced*. Mayer supervised.

Like Paramount, MGM must be regarded in its historical context. Paramount was Old Hollywood, out of the days when Griffith, Little Mary, Marshall Neilan, and Lillian Gish ran the business. Why shouldn't they run it? They were the movies. MGM came along twelve years and—counting Paramount's output alone—about fifteen hundred films after Zukor. Hollywood had changed vastly. The pioneer stuff was over; the industry was wising up. In fact, MGM was formed by a combine in search of (1) picture material to fill theatres, and (2) a Savonarola to run the factory. Or no: a Tiberius to run the factory, for cinema was beauty and love and presumption. But this Tiberius was a Savonarola who thought the human comedy containable.

It starts when exhibitor Marcus Loew is looking for a studio to control. He buys Metro, the first "M" of the future MGM. But

Metro, a typical studio of the Second Era, is a chaos of headstrong directors and spoiled actors. Moreover, it's logistically a bit limited. Luckily, the Goldwyn studio is in chaos, too, mainly because Goldwyn is no longer heading it, forced out by a partner. Why not combine Metro and Goldwyn? Something should come of it; if nothing else, Loew's, Inc., will have the benefit of Goldwyn's lavish studio, originally Inceville, after Griffith's contemporary Thomas Ince. Thus we achieve Metro–Goldwyn. (Note the new status of the producer: the firm retains the name "Goldwyn" even though the man himself, to all intents of the deal, did not exist.) Now, who will manage Loew's new studio? The present Metro and Goldwyn chiefs are inadequate. Ah, here's L. B. Mayer, who runs a tiny studio all his own. An iron hand in an iron glove. Metro–Goldwyn–Mayer. He'll do.

And he did; but see what he learned. For instance, *Ben-Hur* (1925). This was a Goldwyn project, one of the spectacles that Hollywood was emphasizing at the time. Perhaps to outspectacle the industry, Goldwyn's scenarist June Mathis decided to film in Italy, the cradle of cinema spectacle when Griffith was still doling out two-reelers at Biograph. But the Italian labor pool proved impedient, hoping to prolong the paytime, and scuffles between Fascists and anti-Fascists further slowed the work. Worse yet, the rushes trickling back to America were highly unpromising. Yes, the film was big, but it wasn't good, a Super-Jewel with the manners of a B programmer. Meanwhile, Goldwyn slipped into Metro–Goldwyn–Mayer, and Mayer's sage advice was "Use plenty of camels!"

On second thought, Mayer and his supervisors did better than that. They replaced the director and most of the leads, including the Ben-Hur. This was George Walsh, a minor star who had spent the Second Era playing amiable action-hero parts for Fox, a second-string George O'Brien. Walsh had moved to Goldwyn and, given the limited acting stable there, was a likely choice for Ben-Hur. But the addition of Metro's roster gave the reorganization of the film some leeway in heroes, and Ramon Novarro took over. Because the production had received so much publicity, Walsh's career was badly hurt. Even more of the blame fell on Mathis, technically the on-site authority. Mathis had been more an artist than a company person. *Ben-Hur*'s problem, clearly, was disastrous working conditions, but to

MGM the problem seemed to be lack of supervision. The entire company was shipped home to work under the eyes of, and to answer to, studio chiefs.

Even artists working in the studio had to be watched—Erich von Stroheim, for instance. His *Greed* (1924) was another Goldwyn project under June Mathis inherited by MGM. Filming Frank Norris's *McTeague*, von Stroheim didn't adapt Norris's novel: he literally filmed it, for nine months, using the novel as his script and ending up with forty-two reels, a seven-hour movie. "It was masterful in many ways, and parts of it were riveting," recalls Irene Mayer Selznick, one of the few who saw the original version. "But it was an exhausting experience." How had von Stroheim been allowed to film an epic of such impractical length? To MGM, the problem seemed again to be lack of supervision.

Why was *Ben-Hur* allowed to linger in Italy under adverse labor problems? How could von Stroheim pursue, unchecked, his outrageous idealism? From L. B. Mayer's standpoint, these were mistakes that, under supervision, would never have occurred. Mistakes don't just happen; mistakes are made, especially by studios that don't examine their artists. As parents must guide their children, so must studios guide a June Mathis and a von Stroheim, who blithely make movies as if this were still the pioneer days. That was fine for the helter-skelter of Old Hollywood, when you could make a feature in a week for pennies. But we're talking Third Era now; we're doing nice, big, pretty, and, above all, *expensive*.

Consider: Griffith's *Intolerance*, a very sizable movie, cost less than a million dollars in 1916. *Ben-Hur*, of comparable dimension, went into production only eight years later and cost four million. This was an astounding figure for the day, so out of line that the film was a tremendous success yet never paid off. Yes, the Italian adventure had run up the bill. Yes, whoever had negotiated rights to the property had blundered in signing away 50 percent of the gross. Still, *Ben-Hur* was mismanaged—or, rather, not managed at all.

It was clear to Mayer that his new company was going to have to break with Hollywood tradition. Metro and Goldwyn, founded on the old habits, would be reinvented as Metro–Goldwyn–Mayer, would treat its employees as employees. Not only would they be supervised; they must show company loyalty. Heretofore, Holly-

wood had been an entanglement of coteries, of comrades and protégés—like this same June Mathis, who guided Rudolph Valentino
to stardom and had the gall to hit her own company, Metro, for a
raise in his salary. She wanted a hundred a week more, Metro offered
fifty—and when Valentino huffed over to Paramount, Mathis went
with him! When she left Paramount for Goldwyn, von Stroheim
came *this* close to directing *Ben-Hur*. Terrific. When he finally called
that one a wrap, it would have been the biggest hit of 1999. And how
about the director Rex Ingram, so contemptuous of Hollywood that
he moved to France to run his own unit like an exiled king, luxuriating among sycophants? Ingram's another one of that gang, a confed-
erate of von Stroheim in the cutting of *Greed* and desperately eager to
take over the direction of *Ben-Hur* when Charles Brabin was fired
along with George Walsh. They're all in it together. It's a conspiracy
of artists, a rebellion inadvertently subsidized by the authorities.

No more. Under Mayer, MGM was the authoritarian studio, a
place of moguls. Thus the new corporation, officially founded in
mid-1924, instituted an important break with the movies' oldest tradition: that of the independent director serving as source and overseer
of the art, Griffith-style. At MGM, filmmaking was an assembly line
of departments, each answerable to a producer, each producer
answerable to the head of production, and the head answerable to
Mayer. MGM's stars, moreover, would be nothing like the merry
players of the old days, culling their favorite directors, idea men, and
supporting players into mini-studios, choosing their properties, cutting their films. MGM would choose, cull, cut. The directors would
direct, the writers write, the actors act—all separate, all supervised.

To enforce discipline, Mayer made deterrent examples of a few
resisters. Mae Murray, an impossible silly poodle of a star, became *so*
impossible that she wasn't worth her grosses; Mayer not only dumped
her but more or less ran her out of Hollywood on an industry-wide
ban.* John Gilbert was another of Mayer's victims, one of Hollywood's biggest stars and thus a prize cautionary tale for the whole
town to hear, as a series of utterly terrible pictures blasted Gilbert's
hold on the box office. Because sound killed so many silent careers

---

*When Murray finally tried a comeback, she had to make do at a quickie lot. She also got into
two RKO B films, because her friend Lowell Sherman directed them; but then RKO was
brand-new and disdained the informal alignments of establishment Hollywood.

and because Gilbert was the ultimate silent star, romantically demonstrative rather than naturalistic, legend holds that Gilbert was undone by his unmanly tenor. No. Gilbert was undone by Mayer for personal reasons—and because Gilbert's million-dollar contract had been negotiated by Nicholas Schenck, of MGM's New York office.

This Eastern interloping grated on Mayer, who was determined to consolidate power on the supervisor level, starring himself as absolute supervisor. His grandstand coup—earlier than the Gilbert episode, back in the late 1920s, when MGM was but a few years old —involved another star with a New York contract, Lillian Gish. If Murray was a tempestuous diva and Gilbert arrogant, Gish was something far more threatening, a wise and self-willed talent, the compleat moviemaker. She was part of The History, not only the essential D. W. Griffith star but a founder of Old Hollywood. Virtually her own producer, a collaborator with her directors and writers, an expert in design and photography, she was bigger than Mayer. She must be contained.

Granted, Gish not only made films to please herself, she made fine films, commercially successful ones. But in her gently reasonable way she insisted on artistic control, and had that control written into her fancy Eastern contract—and all Hollywood knew it. More than once, as Gish recalls in her autobiography, Mayer literally threatened to ruin her if she didn't learn how to take orders. But where Mae Murray was banned from the screen and John Gilbert was encouraged to destroy himself with alcohol and despair, Gish simply departed Hollywood for the more liberal atmosphere of the New York theatre world. She had had enough.

Writers like Mathis, directors like von Stroheim, and actors like Gish would not be tolerated at MGM. No free spirits: *team spirit*. We see this most immediately in MGM's directors, especially compared with the highly original men who thrived at Paramount. MGM preferred company men who could play ball—for instance, W. S. Van Dyke, nicknamed "One Take" for his speed on the set. Yet note that Van Dyke's films were consistently successful, many of them prime projects—*The Thin Man* and its sequels, the key MacDonald-Eddy pairings, *San Francisco*. The bulk of MGM's directors observe the pattern, as secure technicians who respect a studio style rather than create their own, and we are constantly surprised, viewing some classic, at the lack of resonance in the director's name—Sidney Franklin, Richard Thorpe, Harry Beaumont, Sam Wood, Robert Z. Leonard, Jack Conway.

Not that MGM never used a brilliant or high-strung director. King Vidor, one of MGM's contract directors in the late silent and very early sound eras, is responsible for one of the most purely director-authored movies ever made in Hollywood, *The Crowd* (1928). And there were drop-ins from other studios. Ernst Lubitsch directed four films at MGM, *The Student Prince* (1927), *The Merry Widow* (1934), *Ninotchka* (1939), and *The Shop Around the Corner* (1940).

Even Paramount's not most typical but most constant director, Cecil B. DeMille, did time at MGM. However, his lavish musical *Madam Satan* (1930) does not ring of Paramount, except in its society-comedy milieu. (The plot is brazenly taken from *Die Fledermaus*, even unto the wife's flirtation with her unknowing husband at a costume ball.) The film is a famous disaster, DeMille so out of his element technically—this is his only musical—that the establishing scenes of Reginald Denny and Kay Johnson's ailing marriage and Denny's clandestine visit to Lillian Roth's apartment drag horribly. Nor is DeMille successful with the MGM players, accustomed to directors who minister, counsel, suggest. DeMille knew how to display actors, not talk them into their roles. They're actors, aren't they? They're paid to act; so let them. Denny hammers home double-meaning lines meant to be thrown away, and Johnson needs to move or make a face every time she speaks. The last third of the film livens up as the full cast assembles for the big ball aboard a dirigible, with lots of song and dance and, for a DeMillian disaster climax, the destruction of this party of decadents by a bolt of lightning. One thing DeMille knows how to film is a special effect; as the party drops back to New York by parachute, DeMille shoots from above to catch the packs popping open, and a back-projected process shot of parachutes raining down behind the principals is very authentic.

DeMille's inability—or refusal—to coach actors sets off what may be the essential talent of the MGM director, his treatment of the stars. Where Paramount got its inspiration from the director and Warner Brothers from the sheer energy of its gangsters, reporters, and show people, MGM communicated through the charisma of its stars. We occasionally notice a certain flourish of the visual, even from mere journeymen, as when Roy Del Ruth welcomes Virginia Bruce into *Born to Dance* (1936) with a camera so gladsome it swirls along with the music. Generally, however, MGM's directors are intent on enhancing character.

Clarence Brown may be Metro's most typical director, then, almost invariably assigned to star vehicles, especially those of the Big Three: Greta Garbo, Joan Crawford, and Norma Shearer. In a studio that plumed itself on its women stars, this was heavy responsibility, and Brown gets heavy credit—the title card of *Anna Christie* (1930) reads "Greta Garbo in Clarence Brown's production of," with the standard "directed by" coming later on. And the film is no small challenge, for, respecting its Broadway source, it is extremely intimate, a story with but four people and a few ordinary locations. The emphasis is on character—the prostitute trying to reform, her sailor boyfriend, her naïve father, and his slatternly girlfriend. In fact, after a few quick shots establishing the New York waterfront on a foggy night, Brown moves to a saloon and stays there, in two nearly empty rooms, for thirty minutes—a third of the running time. Of course, Brown has two of Hollywood's most extraordinary faces to puzzle out, Garbo's and Marie Dressler's. It's quite a duo, the world's most beautiful woman and the world's funniest, the naturalistic primitive versus the vaudeville ham, their lines drawn from the then Great American Playwright.

Brown must have worked most carefully with Garbo, anxious over her sound debut, at that in a language she wasn't comfortable in.* But he also troubled to tone down Dressler, who, at her most liberated, could come off as an octopus doing a drag act. For once, Dressler really listens to the lines, even dabbles in portraiture. Luckily, Brown does not exorcise her joke-shop *joie de vivre.* Garbo, new in town, asks Dressler—a lifelong waterfront rat—if she's familiar with the neighborhood. "Oh," says Dressler, doing a little of this and a little of that, "off and on."

Brown is handy, too, at giving us a little movie with our play. For a sequence in an amusement park, he sets up a few unusual camera

---

*Garbo also made *Anna Christie* in German, a language she was comfortable in, and is said to have responded warmly to the advice of Jacques Feyder, who directed the otherwise all-German cast. However, the German *Anna* was made after, not simultaneously with, the English, so the *Anna* we usually see gives us Brown's, not Feyder's, Garbo.

angles to catch the hurdy-gurdy of the place, and a view of a renewed Garbo floating down the East River on her father's barge allows for a superb panorama of the metropolitan skyline, the Woolworth Building made prominent for a touch of the antique. The city, of course, is back-projected stock footage, and looks it—but the clearness of detail is telling, more vivid than what other studios could produce even five or six years after.

Perhaps what MGM was rich in, among directors, was the inspired hack, less than a Lubitsch or a von Sternberg but more ingenious than a factotum. Victor Fleming, for instance. His versatility confounds the auteurists—he does adventures, weepies, comedies, musicals. *A Guy Named Joe* and *The Wizard of Oz*. Had he no themes? He had one: to stay employed. Given, say, Jean Harlow and Mary Astor to fight over Clark Gable, Harlow openly and Astor guiltily (because she's married to nice Gene Raymond), Fleming has nothing to worry about. There's a Southeast Asian rubber plantation for color of setting complete with monsoon and tiger; and the actors know what to pull off.

This is *Red Dust* (1932), a film that more or less takes care of itself, what with Harlow calling Astor "the Duchess" and Gable "Big Boy," with Gable nursing Raymond through malaria and having to endure the kid's gushy admiration as well as his wife's skulking lust, with Gable mixing sex chemistry (with Harlow), romance chemistry (with Astor), and hero chemistry (with everyone else). By the time Metro's platoons of writers, local color arrangers, weather makers, and special-effects operators put in their contributions, all under producer Hunt Stromberg's eye, Fleming has little more to do than call, "Roll 'em."

Tortilla Flat (1942), however, was Fleming's challenge, a film that must be taken care of. First of all, there's the source, John Steinbeck's loving look at the wastrels of Hispanic Monterey. The book's charm lies in Steinbeck's parable-like narration, and his ear for the lingo, and the way he builds episodes into a cultural panorama. How to transfer this to film? Metro could backlot its way through *Red Dust*—forests and rivers are no problem. But where in Culver City, aside from some intermittent background footage, is the look of northern California, the amiable waterfront of the fishing boats and canneries, the mission, the shabby little houses and lots and dirt roads? And who on the

Is MGM hotter than Paramount? Jean Harlow says yes, to
Clark Gable in Red Dust.

contract list suits the folk of Steinbeck's Monterey? Spencer Tracy? Frank Morgan? Maybe they'll borrow the Jewish New Yorker John Garfield from Warners for some genuine *paisano* smarts, and of course that Mexicali rose Hedy Lamarr can play his girlfriend.

In fact, this *is* the cast that MGM gave Fleming. They seem all the more out of place next to the truly Hispanic bit players. And yes, except for a touch of location footage, the look is very soundstage. However, John Lee Mahin and Benjamin Glazer wrote with great fidelity to the original, even preserving the sense of trival ritual that Steinbeck observed; and Fleming makes it work. It can't have been easy. Tracy, as el honcho of the group, is absurdly miscast. Garfield, though affecting, is unlikely as the good-timer whose *mañana* philosophy is ruined by love of Lamarr. And John Qualen, throwing off risible *caramba* inflections in a mustache as big as a sombrero, is fighting the memory of his poignant Muley, the "old graveyard ghost" of an Oakie, bulldozed off his land in Fox's *The Grapes of Wrath* just two years before.

Yet Fleming can create a Steinbeckian atmosphere, as in a delightful scene in which the gang gets drunk and sings to Garfield's guitar. We sense that such moments of carefree fraternity are all that these people have to live for, the only thing doing in their part of Monterey besides cutting squid and growing old. Fleming also conveys the childlike rapture of the vision of St. Francis that appears to Frank Morgan as a filthy, dog-loving scavenger known as The Pirate. The visitation occurs in a forest, and through a process shot Fleming films it as a spill of light in a cathedral of redwoods. In short, where Fleming's *Tortilla Flat* is worthy, it is so *despite* MGM, a triumph of spirit over star-system casting.

This suggests the resourcefulness of the better Metro directors, different from that of the Paramount directors, who could do wonders with a story but, often, nothing for a personality star. Josef von Sternberg stands out for his styling of Marlene Dietrich; at MGM, such idealizations were routine. "People have the odd idea that the director is a kind of lion tamer," George Cukor observed. "Actresses say, 'No, no, no, I will not do zat,' and then you say, 'You *will* do zat' and all that absurd thing." Cukor was expert in gauging the range of talent, the possibilities of personality. Given the evocative power of Metro's designers and cinematographers and writers, all intent on instructing our adoration of redemptive personalities, Cukor was a witch doctor. His art was voodoo.

He holds a magnificent record, counting essential films of Katharine Hepburn, Greta Garbo, Judy Garland, Spencer Tracy, Cary Grant, and John Barrymore, as well as the impossibly star-stuffed *Dinner at Eight*, wherein Cukor must blend the natural Jean Harlow with the huff-and-puff Wallace Beery, the uncharacteristically underplaying Lionel Barrymore with the overwhelming Marie Dressler. Then there's *David Copperfield*, working something like two dozen principals into a Dickensian panorama while making sure W. C. Fields doesn't slip in his juggling act; and *Romeo and Juliet*, Shakespeare with and without actors.

Cukor eventually became known as a "woman's director." But this is the man who discerned the comedy latent in Tracy and Grant, who exhorted a sliding John Barrymore to reaffirm his professionalism, who coached Fredric March, James Stewart, Charles Boyer, James Mason, even Aldo Ray to important performances. The "woman's director" typing began when David Selznick fired Cukor from *Gone With the Wind* at Clark Gable's insistence, supposedly because Gable was unnerved by the speed with which Cukor had established rapport with Vivien Leigh and Olivia de Havilland. We are meant to visualize Gable saying, "No, no, no, I will not do zat" —or at least being neglected as Leigh does zat and de Havilland does zis. According to Cukor—as he finally revealed in the last interview he gave before he died—Gable had him fired because Cukor recalled Gable's days as a hustler along Hollywood's gay circuit in the lean time when Gable first got to Hollywood. Now that Gable was King, he wanted all that put by; and Cukor was a memento. So Victor Fleming took over the film, Fleming being ostensibly the "man's director" to counter Cukor's feminizing. However, we have another reading of the case, from someone who is virtually an oracle on matters concerning production at both MGM and Selznick International: Irene Mayer Selznick, daughter of L.B. and wife to David. As she saw it, "George's work was simply not up to David's expectations." Perhaps the project was too big for him. *Gone With the Wind* is grander than its personalities, for all the trouble Selznick had in settling on a Scarlett. *Gone With the Wind* is history, an epic, an *action* film. Fleming had the power for it, the ruthless grasp; it may well be that Cukor did not.

Still, Cukor was not only a fine performers' coach, but a wonderful creator of environment. What Brown can do with Garbo, and what Fleming can do with Steinbeck, Cukor can do with all sorts of actors and settings. Take *Camille* (1936), often called Garbo's greatest picture. It is also Laura Hope Crews's—the perennial Aunt Pittypat at last given some meat to bite on as a greedy hanger-on. "Someone bring the cheese!" she wheezes as the party moves along. The picture is as well Lenore Ulric's—a great David Belasco star in a rare historical preservation. But surely *Camille* is, above all, Cukor's greatest picture, for the way he brings the Parisian demimonde to life, far more persuasively than one would have thought possible after the 1934 reinforcement of the Production Code.

This is a guiltily rhapsodic film, an infuriatingly honest film, a deviously discreet film: it depends on your mood the day you screen it. Certain moments never shift effect—the way Garbo's signature morbidity is made merry when Robert Taylor says, "No one has ever loved you as I love you!" and Garbo replies, casually laughing, "That may be true, but what can I do about it?" The way protégeur Henry Daniell stolidly answers Garbo's request for money, lets her kiss him and cry "Thank you! Thank you!" . . . and suddenly slaps her. The way Rex O'Malley matter-of-factly interprets Gaston as a gay sidekick, and is the only person in the movie to understand and love and never exploit or betray Garbo.

And there is Garbo's performance. "You watch carefully what she's doing," Cukor advises. "You make suggestions, but you let the impulse come out of her . . . Oh, I had something to do with it— exactly what I really can't say." Something, certainly. For, compared with Garbo's Anna Christie, her Camille is liberated, nuanced. But what makes her seem so comfortable is the inductively Continental milieu. For once at MGM, we believe that a movie takes place abroad. There is none of Fleming's soundstage Monterey or Culver City *paisanos*. Cukor gives us Paris.

But Thalberg gave us *Camille*. Seeing the film today, one thinks the picture could not have been made without Cukor, not in this form. MGM says form is adaptable; the picture could not have been made without Garbo and Irving Thalberg, Mayer's chief of production and, in person, *Camille*'s producer. Thalberg died during shooting, and the studio felt the loss so heavily that it made *Camille*'s Los Angeles premiere a veritable regatta wake, opening up the corral for celebrity demonstration, and even getting Garbo herself to show—a real achievement, as Garbo delighted in deterrent omissions, such as not showing up just when she was most expected.

But then all Hollywood, not just Garbo, was obliged to Thalberg. It was Thalberg who laid down the standards by which Hollywood measured prestige. He got his start at Universal—as everyone there did—simply by coming into contact with Uncle Carl Laemmle. Short, slight, and gentlemanly in a business of tough guys, Thalberg often failed to impress new associates. He simply wasn't what a mogul, so far, was. Yet he was running Universal before he was old enough to vote. When Uncle Carl got stubborn about paying Thalberg what he was worth, Thalberg joined Mayer's outfit, and moved with him when Metro-Goldwyn became Metro-Goldwyn-Mayer. Till 1933, when overwork forced him to renounce his studio satrapy, take a long vacation, and return to vastly reduced activity, Thalberg largely originated, cast, inspired, edited, and re-edited every film that came out of MGM. As this studio's most influential man, Thalberg became the most influential man in Hollywood—for, as we shall see, MGM wrested industry leadership from Paramount by 1930 or '31.

The most influential man in Hollywood. As the sword cuts with two edges, so is Thalberg's lesson either admirable or a shabby ostentation, depending on one's viewpoint. Some say his "prestige" amounts to the grafting of Broadway onto Hollywood, one pompous glamour piled on another, the insecure parvenu borrowing the glitz of veteran swank. They say Thalberg always went for the emptiness of big rather than the penetration of honest. They say his refusal to put his name on the credits of his pictures was not modesty (I like David Thomson's phrase—"accountancy propriety") but arrogance multiplied to the sublime. They call the picture of Thalberg viewing the rushes of every MGM film an impractical practicality, that no one with Thalberg's agenda could have spared the time.

Those who find Thalberg admirable, or at least a better influence than most of his fellow moguls, would counter that pompous glamour, especially as shaped by Thalberg, was one of the things Hollywood did best in these years. The candor of Warner Brothers' Depression parables is very taking, and the Lubitsch effect at Paramount is a glory of the Studio Age. But we must remember that by far the bulk of Hollywood's output, in the days of what the Russians would call *Thalbergshchina*, was pure snake oil.

*History likes Thalberg for spending money on art, even
unto letting King Vidor take* The Crowd *to New York for
verisimilitude of setting. James Murray at right.*

Thalberg refined it. He respected good direction—it was Thalberg who brought Lubitsch to MGM, for instance, and Thalberg who put von Stroheim in charge of *The Merry Widow* even after their set-tos at Universal, and at Metro over *Greed*. He even respected certain directors' right to attempt the uncommercially novel—not only King Vidor's *The Crowd* (1928) but Tod Browning's *Freaks* (1932), so heedless of MGM's image as Glamour City that it benignly views the mutilation of luscious Olga Baclanova into a "chicken woman." (After the first release, Mayer recalled the prints and had the MGM logo cut off.) Most important of all, it was Thalberg who propounded the notion that a successful studio could make a worthy film or two every year without expecting a profit—and the tone of voice in which he spoke pronounced "could" as "should." This notion, inimical to the very basis of the studio system from Biograph on, actually held firm at MGM after Thalberg's death, enabling Mervyn LeRoy to produce one of Hollywood's greatest films, *The Wizard of Oz* (1939), despite a prohibitive budget.

As for Thalberg's obsession with Broadway, this is undebatable. But what is this disdain, this terror of theatre properties and talents, on the part of certain writers on Hollywood's past? Is there something more noble in a weepie, a backstager, or a film noir (each form more or less peculiar to American cinema) than in Thalberg's desire to film a Broadway hit? Anyway, Hollywood before and after Thalberg drew insistently on stage talent, adapting plays and stealing writers and performers and techies. Famous Players in Famous Plays, remember? So why blame Thalberg? Some would say that it was Hollywood's great accomplishment in these years to preserve the work of fabled thespians, not only Paramount's vaudevillians but the Barrymores, Jeanne Eagels, Nazimova,* Gertrude Lawrence, Al Jolson,

*Nazimova is mostly remembered today for her Bagdad West dissipations—séances and orgies, her recklessly bizarre *Salome* film with an all-gay cast, her swimming pool in the shape of the Black Sea. Back before there was a Hollywood, however, Nazimova was playing leads at the Moscow Art Theatre under Stanislafsky and Nyemirovich-Danchenko, then startling Broadway with the textured realism of her portrayals. She was so prominent that she had her own theatre. Another dissipation: doing the grande dame at some party in about 1920, Nazimova snubbed Thalberg, taking the *enfant dirigeur* of Universal for an underling. Years later, her film career a shambles, she applied to MGM for a contract in talkies: and there was Thalberg. Nazimova didn't recall the encounter; Thalberg had hoarded the recollection. "Never, Madame," he told her, smiling, his eyes on ice. "Not as long as I am here." Ironically enough, in her Hollywood heyday Nazimova had been Metro's Queen of the Lot before Mayer and Thalberg had come along. Yet more ironically, when Nazimova returned to Hollywood, it was at Metro, in *Escape* (1940)—and Thalberg's widow was on hand in the same film, just two titles short of *her* more or less enforced departure from Metro, and film.

Fanny Brice, Eddie Cantor, Marilyn Miller, Mrs. Patrick Campbell, and a great many others, some defending their legend and others dispelling it, but all giving us a taste of what they were like on stage. This is archival footage. At that, Thalberg was less fanatic about securing Broadwayites than other producers, if this be virtue. Paramount, Warner Brothers, and RKO were nearly shanghaiing people in Times Square. Thalberg held out for the top stuff—O'Neill and Coward, the Lunts and Helen Hayes; and Katharine Cornell, who put on her *Candida* face and said no; and Edward G. Robinson, the stage player made a star by the movies. But Robinson was so unnerved by Thalberg's predatory determination that he ran out of his office and threw up.

What, in the end, was Thalberg's idolodulia?* Let us decide the case of Thalberg in *Grand Hotel* (1932), his and MGM's and perhaps all Hollywood's most typical film, the exception that proves the rule. Hot people in a good story: this is the Studio Age formula for movies. And this is *Grand Hotel*—but dressed up beyond what studios other than MGM found affordable. Just as Thalberg seemed to know in advance what would be prestigious and unprofitable (like *The Crowd*), so did he know what would be extremely profitable, and thus all the more prestigious, for Hollywood respects, above all, a hit. *Grand Hotel* was the year's top-grossing title and, virtually therefore, copped the Best Picture Oscar.

Grand Hotel gives us Thalberg the showman rather than Thalberg the idealist. *The Crowd* is a starless picture with a working-class background and no pre-sold source in fiction or theatre: Thalberg's approval of the project was pure idealism, for it had nothing to idolize.† *Grand Hotel*, however, gives us people of grace and wealth, power and beauty. A ballerina! A jewel thief! And a stenographer who gets to shuffle off to Paris on the arm of a man who is not only rich but terminally ill! Better yet, we meet them in a dazzling art deco pal-

---

*This word needs reviving, given the direction our times have taken. I quote the shorter Oxford English Dictionary, Volume V, p. 953: "veneration of an inferior kind given to idols or images." The only critical instance of such I can cite in Thalberg is his sponsorship of Norma Shearer. Everybody's got something.

†Indeed, this is just what *The Crowd* is about: the lack of glamour and romance in everyday life. Viewing the slum apartment, the stuffy office crammed with nameless men, the big empty bridge from which the dully pleasant hero is ready to jump, we realize that the only stars life knows are movie actors. A notably depressing film for Thalberg to have made—or did he make it precisely to tell us why we must idolize, why we need Hollywood and especially MGM? For where does Vidor take us for a slightly upbeat fade-out? To a movie theatre.

ace in a European capital, lured by the fanfare of an international stage hit. Thalberg the showman, the juggler of legends. Imagine—five strangers of utterly different backgrounds, each facing the crisis of his life, are thrown together in the public and private rooms of the Grand Hotel. In Berlin, Max Reinhardt kept the multi-scened tale moving on a revolving stage; the New York production limped from set to set with stage waits that disconcerted the human-comedy panorama. Obviously, here was fiction that could also be a play but was born to be a movie, and MGM had smartly bought the rights to Vicki Baum's tale so early on that the studio helped back the New York production: as if Thalberg were insisting on a Broadway hit to give his film éclat.

Of course, the movie's éclat really resides in the stunt of teaming six stars, four of them among the biggest names in Hollywood— Garbo, John Barrymore, Joan Crawford, Wallace Beery, and, less spectacularly, Lionel Barrymore and Lewis Stone. (We also have Jean Hersholt in, yes, a touching cameo, as a hotel clerk awaiting news of his wife's delivery of a baby.) Such charismatic stuffing of the screen had never been tried before. But then no studio had filmed a story as layered as this. Stone's part—that of a doctor with a hideous scar covering half his face—is little more than atmospheric decoration, like a hip-bath or an elephant's-foot umbrella stand. The other five principals carry the story. Each is very slightly limned with a past and a future, rather than with true character development, so these are not ensemble but star parts, running on the energy of the proprietary personality rather than on enlightenment of writing. Broadway's *Grand Hotel* got along on an admirable but not especially personable cast— Eugenie Leontovich in Garbo's role, Henry Hull as the smooth thief, Sam Jaffe as the deferential Kringelein. But then Broadway does not require the copiously brilliant personalities that swallow the camera. Theatre people needn't fill a stage the way Hollywood people filled a screen. It's not that the audiences were different: the expectations were.

It was moviegoers' expectations, of course, that Thalberg was in the business of stroking. All-star films, like the musical revues of 1929–30 and Paramount's *If I Had a Million*, were episodic anthologies. Thalberg proposed not to exhibit the charisma but multiply it —bouncing John Barrymore's plangent dash against Garbo's instinctive sorcery, countering Beery's unctuous and Lionel's unapologetic hambola with Crawford's expedient bravado. Just the sight of the names of Garbo and Crawford together on a marquee was a measure of MGM's throwing arm in star power—as Thalberg intended it to be. In Old Hollywood, when Little Mary and Chaplin were young, the biggest names almost never co-starred. Their films were solos with chorus. By the Third Era, this had largely changed, largely because MGM thought the possibilities in a poster reading "John Gilbert and Greta Garbo in *Love*" were too awesome not to pursue. Jamming Garbo and John Barrymore together, then, was not unorthodox; and adding Lionel and Beery would not shake the earth. But to bill a second woman star was unheard-of benison. Total the names: this is enough personal magnetism to fill three A-prime pictures.

With such grandeur of personality at his disposal, Thalberg decided not to open the play's action beyond the confines of the hotel. The film would be big enough in sheer character. Besides, MGM's art director Cedric Gibbons would fill the eye with another of his art deco pleasure domes, a series that had the film industry gaping and imitating since *Our Dancing Daughters* (1928). This film made Crawford a star, but she shared attention with an early-middle Neverland of cookie-cutter furniture, automobile-hood-ornament bric-a-brac, pleated walls, and church-tower windows. By the time of DeMille's *Madam Satan*, the style was peaking. Gibbons veritably deifies the facetiae of art deco in the zeppelin party, especially in a "ballet mécanique" and little rocket cars for the waitresses to ride on.

But this was the climax. As *Grand Hotel* was filmed, the rage was settling down and Gibbons's main work lay in designing the hotel itself, rather than its accessories. In one notable shot, we gaze down through the center of the building in loose focus, past six circular tiers of rooms and hallway, looking over the central lobby far below. It's a Jazz Age Tower of Babel. And what Gibbons didn't visualize, Adrian would, gowning the women so spectacularly that one generally misses the first few lines while taking in the fashions. Even Crawford's dress, that of a stenographer on the job—a black number trimmed with lace that insouciantly emphasizes her bust—seems designed to suggest the working girl and celebrate her Cinderella transformation at once. We see why Adrian had to work for Metro, why Metro had to employ Adrian, why style and personality were, at this studio, synonymous. Both must be lavish; you are what you wear.

No wonder Metro laid more importance on a film's look than on its director. No wonder the studio's key technician was a cinematographer, William Daniels. All a director could do was induct a performer into his story. Daniels could purify you, vivify you in MGM's extreme lighting range, running from rash white to an almost blinding black. It took time. It slowed production and upped the costs. But by the time Daniels was through, you came off as if you had a portrait somewhere in a closet, aging for you. If *Grand Hotel* is an MGM special, it is also a state-of-the-art demonstration piece, in its passionate view of star charisma. No wonder Adrian left MGM when Garbo did. "Glamour," he explained, "is over."

Glamour was in its heyday at the time of *Grand Hotel*, though of course Thalberg never thought to secure the glamour of first-rate direction. Why bother, with all these self-creating talents, from Garbo and John Barrymore to Gibbons and Daniels? What might we have had if Lubitsch or Cukor had taken charge? Thalberg hired Edmund Goulding, a free-lancer known for women's pictures—he had directed both Garbo and Crawford before, and would go on to lead three of Bette Davis's prime weepies at Warner Brothers. Goulding was also known to be slow and sloppy on the set, and some of his cut-ins don't match the master shots—a surprising gaffe for a biggest studio's biggest event.

Analysts praise the bracingly cinematic opening, as Hollywood shows Broadway how to check into a grand hotel. We track through Gibbons's lobby, take in the direly subterranean Stone as he renders universal wisdom like the leader of a Greek chorus. A hotel full of people, new ones every day, yet "nothing ever happens." Cut to the switchboard girls, and we see how much is happening. One by one, characters take to the phones to reveal a troupe of individuals deep in *agon*. Businessman Beery *must* pull off the deal, Garbo's maid informs Garbo's manager that her mistress has lost the will to dance, jewel thief John Barrymore reveals the do-or-die nature of his latest scam, and so on.

Yes, it's very cinematic, but it's straight from the script of Baum's play. Hollywood, much less Goulding, isn't showing Broadway anything, except that movie stars are bigger than theatre people. In fact, *Grand Hotel*'s screenplay is credited to William Drake, who is no screenwriter but simply the man who translated Baum's German into

English for the Broadway mounting. Five other writers, uncredited, emended Drake in Metro's characteristic too-many-cooks approach to composition, as layered as the mound that Schliemann found at Troy. Yet many of the most resonant lines originate with Baum, such as Crawford's so very Crawfordian comment that caviar tastes like herring. (The shopgirl princess: she has access to the high life but retains her earthy honesty.) Even Garbo's resounding "I want to be alone" was first uttered by Eugenie Leontovich.

Too bad Garbo and Crawford never appear together, except in the famous PR shot of the seven stars lined up in the lobby (the six Names plus Jean Hersholt, dignified rather than touching; but just wait). Too bad Goulding couldn't give Garbo much help in realizing Grusinskaya, the ballerina whose moribund art revives at John Barrymore's kiss. One of Hollywood's most reproachable conventions is the casting of movie stars as artists. At MGM alone we find Kirk Douglas as a painter, Robert Walker as Brahms, and, least credible of all, Joan Crawford as a musical-comedy diva, dancing with the deftness of a Tyrannosaurus rex. We keep forgetting that Hollywood's less pretentious backstagers are still delightful because they give us musical performers *as* musical performers. Eleanor Powell plays a dancer because she is one; Judy Garland is a singer; Mickey Rooney is an all-purpose juvenile.

But now we have Garbo as a ballerina, complete with tutu. The year before, in *Mata Hari*, she let a double do most of her dancing, little more than an Oriental box step, at that.* If anyone not a ballerina could suggest one, it is Garbo; but even Garbo cannot. The physique is wrong—we can't picture her in a performance of *The Sleeping Beauty*, can scarcely imagine her attending one. Her portrayal is nonetheless an ingenious failure, conveying the character's volatile shifts of mood forcefully, almost athletically, spinning like an angel on the head of a pin. In the dark, Garbo curls up as if she were withering, only to expand, quivering, in the light. This *is* a dancer. Her dalliance with Barrymore is entrancing, all the more so because she is obviously stimulated by the rare chance to play with one of the out-

---

*Garbo does lead a floor full of people in *Two-Faced Woman* (1941), her last film, doing the chica-choca with Robert Alton; and be it said that she is competent and delightful. However, most of us can creditably mooch around on a public dance floor; it takes a soul born to dance to get through a creditable *Sleeping Beauty*.

standing thespians of the day. Barrymore himself was fifty, and past his greatness (or past the willingness to trouble to exercise his greatness). But he extended himself here before subsiding in caricatures and spoofs; and Daniels gave Barrymore the same loving attention he gave Garbo. "How do they light you?" he asked Barrymore, assuming that, like most veterans, he carried a mental file of flattering filters and deferential angles. No file.

"Well, then," says Daniels, "how would you like to look?"

Ah. "I would like to look," says Barrymore, "like Jackie Cooper's grandson."

An odd wing on *Grand Hotel* is the wayward character of its Continental flavoring. Garbo is naturally exotic, Barrymore is transatlantically suave, and Hersholt always came off as Heidi's grandfather no matter what he was playing. But Crawford makes no attempt to be anything but Crawford (if perfected by Goulding), and Beery, bizarrely enough, not only attempts to impersonate a coarsely proper Middle European bourgeois, but incorporates the accent. As everyone plays with everyone else—except Garbo and Crawford—the tone somewhat scrambles, though Metro retains the original German names, each a key to the character's personality. Grusinskaya ("Georgian") is not only a typical ballerina's stage name but a reference to the gloomily jumpy temper of Stalin's homeland. Crawford's Flaemmchen, aptly, is "Little Flame," and Beery's Herr von Preysing is a pun on "Lord of Praise." Who is Hersholt, you ask—Hersholt on whom everything depends? He is Senf: "Mustard." Just in case all this doesn't quite bind it all up Continentally enough, the sound track ladles out a medley of Rachmaninof, Johann Strauss, and "Wien, Wien, nur du allein."

So? What's so prestigious? *Grand Hotel* has stars, glamour, and polish, that's all. That's all MGM wanted. What more is there? "Diamonds is my career," says Mae West. MGM's is stars. Glamour is what stars are for, or you end up with Jimmy Cagney and Joan Blondell doing prison pictures for the rest of your life. Polish insures that the glamour does not falter. Thalberg must have been doing something right, for in the early 1930s, when Depression woes caught up with the box office, every major studio lost money except MGM.

No wonder Thalberg was arrogant. His refusal to put his name on the pictures he produced may not have stemmed from perverse modesty as much as from the belief that he more or less produced every Metro picture, and must thus sign all or none of them. He was so caught up in the nuts and bolts of moviemaking that, no matter how he planned his day, he could never keep an appointment on time. His waiting room was a kind of *Grand Hotel*, with eye-filling groups of stars waiting for their chance. In fact, Thalberg did view the rushes of all MGM productions, a feat of sorts but, as simple math reveals, quite possible. MGM made about fifty films a year, at an average running time of ninety minutes. Allowing for scenes that were filmed but cut before release, and for retakes, this means that Thalberg had perhaps two hours of footage to screen per week.

Of course, Thalberg put in yet more time advising his staff on improvements, on evening out that polish. This is a kind of in-group prestige, a producer's pride of ownership. The other two outstanding producers, Samuel Goldwyn and David O. Selznick, similarly plumed themselves on the finish of their work, on not just the money but the effort spent. And Thalberg expected as much of his staff. Once, at a preview of a film produced by Hunt Stromberg, Thalberg spotted an error in storytelling—someone who had been established as being *here* suddenly turned up *there* at the same time. Thalberg turned around in his seat to stare at Stromberg, sitting just behind him. Thalberg stared, and Thalberg stared, and Thalberg stared at Stromberg in the darkness of the crowded theatre, just staring at that loafer till Stromberg cried out, "For God's sake, Irving, I'm *sorry,* all right?"

The previewing of films to test audience reaction—and, if necessary, spice up needy fare with retakes—was a Hollywood convention. Thalberg promoted it to an unvarying ritual at Metro, and the retakes themselves became a convention. Unfortunately, dragging actors back to old sets after they had started on another picture sometimes led to visual or verbal discontinuity, to a lapse in the matchups or a virtually parenthetical explosion of dialogue that explained some rash turn of plot but threw a scene's tone out of control. In theory, the films were being rationalized; in effect, they were being agitated. Worse yet was Thalberg's habit of taking at face value the comments that he read on the preview cards. Was he really making his prestige pictures for any lunkhead or burrito waitress who happened to venture an opinion? Why did he preview the Lunts' *The Guardsman* (1931) for San Diego yokels? How could he dare read their worthless ratings to the Lunts? Lynn nearly handed Thalberg his head for it; and that preview experience may be one reason why the Lunts never returned to Hollywood, no matter how much money Thalberg offered them.

Digging more deeply into this Thalbergian polish, we find some odd rough spots. *The Champ* (1931), for instance. This is no fast-buck programmer. King Vidor directed and top scenarist Frances Marion wrote the tale of bum boxer Wallace Beery on the way back up through the love of his kid Jackie Cooper. Intemperate sentimentality made the film popular, but technically it is atrocious, as sloppy as a Monogram. If Thalberg passed this film in rushes, there is more to Thalberg's sense of Metro perfection than his legend is letting out. Flubbed lines and "accidental spontaneity" abound. The camera setups look as if Norma Shearer lit them for a Joan Crawford picture. The script is a shambles, some scenes not ending but dwindling away. And where's all that budget that MGM put out? Beery gives Cooper a pony, which Cooper nauseatingly calls Little Champ—but at least this leads us to a big racing sequence. At last, production values. But the stock racing footage is simply clamped onto the film, not placed within it. Then Little Champ takes a tumble. As Cooper runs out of the stands, Vidor pulls back for a long shot—and we're stunned to see that it wasn't stock footage at all. The raceway, the hundreds of extras, the horses—this disreputable chaos is actual MGM celluloid, "a King Vidor production," and, I am dazed to report, a nominee for a Best Picture Oscar.

If Thalberg's institutionalizing of Metro polish is a sometime thing, his sense of form was not. At Paramount, a film could find its own structure and tone; at MGM, everything had been done before. Why invent forms when the existing ones work? We feel this most palpably with the Marx Brothers, who went to Metro after they left Paramount—for suddenly their helter-skelter is mapped, centered, reproved; their films have been turned into musicals with love plots; and, worst of all, the anarchical nature of their comix has been turned around so that now the Marx Brothers are salubrious and even sentimental.

Groucho is still a back-alley hustler passing himself off as various eminences. But Chico is now a confidant of thwarted young love and Harpo his well-meaning assistant, no more the Dionysian zany who can be counted on never to be counted on. (Zeppo is gone, so we get something out of the deal.) It's a commonplace to rail at the Marxes' MGM love stuff, but the problem is not that Kitty Carlisle and Allan Jones are in *A Night at the Opera* (1935), but that Thalberg forced the brothers to believe in Kitty Carlisle and Allan Jones; or make believe in them.

After all, there are touches of romance in the Paramounts, usually involving Zeppo and probably taking in footage that Paramount snipped as being meaningless in the Marxian world. But if Paramount *had* given us more of Zeppo and an ingenue, with a duet or two, it wouldn't have hurt the films, because Groucho, Chico, and Harpo would have been otherwise engaged. What's chilling about the MGMs is, for instance, the scene in *A Night at the Opera* in which Groucho has to comfort Carlisle, who has sailed for America thinking Jones is back in Italy. Jones is in fact on board as a stowaway, and Groucho knows it, and Thalberg has him trying to be understanding, trying to care about love. This isn't in Groucho's repertory. No less irritating is Thalberg's attempt to link the piano-playing Chico with tenor Jones through a shared conservatory background. Oh, come on. Chico is no virtuoso. He's a parlor star, strictly by ear. What's wrong with *A Night at the Opera* is not the subplot lovers, but this intimidation of the Marxian vaudeville.

Like most people in Hollywood, the brothers didn't like Thalberg, but needed him. They had washed out at Paramount: *Duck Soup*, classic though it would become, had bombed. With an output of one film a year and a single salary to split, the brothers were in emergency—and, again like most, they were impressed with the way Thalberg serenely seemed to know Exactly What to Do. In a twice-told tale, they expressed their opinion of his oversubscribed appointment book by breaking into his office to strip nude and roast potatoes in the fireplace. Good for them. But Thalberg was offering big money and major production. To get it, the boys had to submit to Thalberg's "well-made" formulae.

A Marx Brothers movie is a series of sketches on a theme. But a Thalberg movie is a story clearly told. Not only does he lumber the Marxes with young lovers, but he organizes the adventure around a plot—their first, really, since *The Cocoanuts*—and assigns the boys set roles in that plot. Concomitantly, we lose the wonderfully surreal aspect of the Paramount Marxes, the jesting that is physically possible but socially improbable. Thalberg's trouble is credibility; he thinks movies are real.

What's odd about all this is that *A Night at the Opera*, the brothers' first MGM, is second in their canon only to *Duck Soup*. (Some prefer it.) This proves that even Thalberg could not, finally, contain the boys, and that, perhaps not inadvertently, he had given them the sweetest challenge to their anarchic energy in utilizing opera as a background. Nothing is more alien to the Marxes than opera, with its piss-proud tenors and society divas. Nothing more surely deserves the Marxian treatment. There is a touching key turned here, too, in Metro's inclusion of dear Margaret Dumont from the Paramounts, a woman born to play the pretentious grand-opera maven, basking in her box. As *Animal Crackers*' house-party hostess or *Duck Soup*'s patriot, Dumont was useful. Here she is essential—the woman virtually *is* an opera, with her gala physique and florid demeanor. Without Dumont, one wonders how far MGM would have been willing to go in the desecration of opera. For this film is no mere spoof; it *wars* on opera. And MGM, as we shall see, has something of an opera fetish. But Dumont's role, as the lady bountiful of the opera season, moves the naturalism into the picturesque by the effusiveness of her grandeur, aided by Sig Ruman's copiously Middle European impresario and Walter Woolf King's nasty tenor.

In such company, we need take only Carlisle and Jones seriously, for this isn't real opera. At Metro, real opera is Lauritz Melchior singing Flotow and Verdi in *This Time for Keeps* (1947) or Kathryn Grayson singing Lakmé's Bell Song in *It Happened in Brooklyn* (1947), or Jeanette MacDonald and Nelson Eddy, in *Maytime* (1937), leading a full cast in *Tsaritsa*—a fake opera, run up out of warring bits of Tchaikofsky. But it looks stuffy; that's real enough. As it happens, *A Night at the Opera*'s shooting script closed with a rather mild send-up, but in the final version the brothers literally take *Il Trovatore* apart. It was L. B. Mayer, a former junk dealer and now one of the highest-salaried men in the country, who maintained Metro's opera lobby, and he must have been shocked by these goings-on. No doubt he took solace in the climactic triumph of Carlisle and Jones in the Miserere

Before MGM and after: Jeanette MacDonald looks sexy at Paramount in the early 1930s, playing to the seductive Maurice Chevalier; then, later in the decade at MGM (over-leaf), we turn the page and a corner of film history to find a rigid diva playing to the arduous Nelson Eddy.

Admire the MGM MacDonald, here in The Firefly *(1937).*
She is not universally popular. Noël Coward, viewing the
MacDonald–Eddy version of Coward's Bitter Sweet *(1940),*
said it was "like watching an affair between a mad rocking-
horse and a rawhide suitcase." (See page 161 for more on the
renovated MacDonald.)

—Carlisle, for you opera buffs, daring the traditional interpolated high options on the repeat of "Di te scordarmi" that had fallen out of fashion by 1935 and today startle even the cognoscenti (though Montserrat Caballé retains them, when permitted).

All this may suggest that the Marxes thrived at MGM, either despite or because of Thalberg's principles. In fact, while all five of their Paramounts remain vital, the Marxes' five MGMs steadily deteriorate. *A Day at the Races* (1937), seldom inspired, is at least lively. But *At the Circus* (1939) lacks the excruciated logic of *Opera*'s famous Stateroom Scene (in which body piles on body till the room literally explodes) or *Races*' "tootsie-frootsie" bit (in which Chico takes Groucho in one of the most confounding shell games on record), and the music is not as good as *Opera*'s "Alone" or *Races*' "All God's Chillun Got Rhythm." *Go West* (1940) is the unthinkable in Marx films: unfunny. And *The Big Store* (1941) finds the brothers demoted to a B-unit staff and a so-so budget, virtually supporting Tony Martin and Virginia Grey.

Thalberg didn't necessarily stifle individualist talent. But one did have to fit into the Metro structure. Virtually no one created at Metro except the producers—seldom the directors, even less often the performers (with the occasional autotelic exception such as Lon Chaney or Garbo), and never the writers. In MGM's cautiously grinding mesh of departmental cogs, the eight best writers put together told less of a story than William Daniels. What Daniels did, no one else could do. But any writer could lay out a script, given MGM's corrective revisions—one team for plot, one for construction, one for character, one for gags, and so on. If one doesn't put it across, another will.

A terrible berth for a writer. Most writers choose their work to avoid collaboration and workplace *Angst*; Thalberg instituted them. There would be none of Paramount's Lubitsch–Raphaelson understandings, no Billy Wilder–Charles Brackett partnerships free of interference. There would be no independence. MGM's supervisor system worked so well that, even after 1933 when Thalberg stepped back to run only his unit, the system functioned on inertia right through the 1950s.

This is a system with few heroes. Buffs of the musical rally around Arthur Freed for his generosity in trusting the talent he hired, and even Thalberg has his backers. But writers especially flocked to MGM for the rich wages and hated MGM for the extensive revisions. The classic case in point is F. Scott Fitzgerald's *Three Comrades* (1938), from Erich Maria Remarque's novel of Germany in the first years after the Armistice. Barring the European atmosphere, which MGM had no intention of suggesting in the first place, this was choice meat for Fitzgerald, a circle of youthful friends adoring the magical woman at their center. Yet the film's producer, Joseph Mankiewicz, assigned Fitzgerald a hack collaborator for revisions and rewrote the script himself. Mankiewicz had been a screenwriter, and was a cultured man—not just for a producer but for anyone. A very cultured man. Still, posterity has denounced him for harassing poor Fitzgerald and denying us an all-out Fitzgeraldian experience in his only screenplay actually to go into production and bear his name on the credits.

However, Fitzgerald's original text has been published. To follow it as one watches the movie is to acquit Mankiewicz of artistic vandalism. Fitzgerald's text is voluminous, giving too much of minor characters and too little of the principals. Words, words: yet little is conveyed. Nor does Fitzgerald have any grip on what Hollywood wants, what movies do. We are always heartened when someone tries to break through the rigid factory philosophy with something original—but when Robert Taylor first calls Margaret Sullavan, Fitzgerald gives us a winged angel at a switchboard connecting us with St. Peter, who says, "cackling, 'I think she's in.' " Is this Fitzgerald's spoof of Hollywood romance? An attempt to purify his love plot? A touch of comedy in an otherwise rather somber piece? It would seem boldly arch even in Lubitsch at his most Paramount, and certainly did not suit a naturalistic film such as *Three Comrades*. It is the only violently incorrect moment in Fitzgerald's script, but the rest of it isn't all that correct.

The film was a hit, despite Mankiewicz's staying with the heroine's death. But only Margaret Sullavan registers truly, Frank Borzage's direction being serviceable, Robert Young and Franchot Tone being competent, and Sullavan's vis-à-vis Robert Taylor being Robert Taylor. The finished script, credited to Fitzgerald and E. E. Paramore and greatly emended by Mankiewicz, works well but never touches eloquence, neither in Fitzgerald's lines nor anyone else's. At least Mankiewicz did let Borzage shoot Fitzgerald's finale of the ghosts of the dead Sullavan and Young walking with surviving comrades Taylor and Tone into the horizon; and Mankiewicz resisted attempts by Hitler's diplomatic functionaries to change the apparently Nazi villains into Communists. Granted, the Nazis are not identified by party and lack the armbands and brown shirts. How absurd, for a film released in 1938! Whom did Metro think it was protecting?

What, in fact, did Metro stand for, besides the producer's power and the star's appeal? Metro stood for prestige at any cost. Yea, cost *is* prestige. So Metro stood for "production values" generally and splendid pictures specifically, upgrading B's to a semi-A level, punching up routine A's, emphasizing super A's as a studio hallmark, and constantly experimenting in the Big One.

Dangerous territory. D. W. Griffith made history with *The Birth of a Nation*, a Big One. He put his entire career into debts he never quite got free of just a year later with *Intolerance*, a Big One. Paramount, Fox, and Universal ran through the silent years on the unspoken promise that no matter how much they might spend on an A, a spectacle, a Super-Jewel, they would avoid the Big One. Big Ones can make you; but Big Ones break you. A Big One broke Charles Ray, a Folk Hero of the Second Era. *Tremendous* star. Tiring of his amiably rustic vehicles, Ray financed a breakout special, *The Courtship of Miles Standish* (1923), and went over like the *Titanic*. Ray never recovered, winding up in small parts in talkies, even as an extra.

Big Ones break you—so the studio that regularly turns out Big Ones must be the elite studio. The secure studio. The studio of industry leadership. The more money it spent, the more money it made. Other studios, however eager to imitate, could not risk the capital. Mayer and Thalberg had instituted the budget-as-an-art-form before the rest of Hollywood was aware of the ploy, and by then it was 1932 or so, when Metro was the Grand Hotel and every other studio was losing money. Without a challenger, MGM got more elite, more secure, and stayed the leader, the Hollywood studio as its own self-fulfilling prophecy.

It's interesting to slip back to the very first Metro–Goldwyn–Mayer release: "Louis B. Mayer presents Victor Seastrom's production of" *He Who Gets Slapped* (1924). What profile does the studio present here? How does it want to be perceived? First, there's the demonstration of class in the source, Leonid Andryeyef's play, a Theatre Guild hit in New York in 1922. Second, there is, surprisingly, not a Clarence Brown or a Sidney Franklin but a Major Director in Victor Seastrom, who was clearly encouraged to film it as he called it, without interference. In fact, between Andryeyef and Seastrom, and given the European setting, we have only the MGM logo lion to tell us what studio we are in. Yes, there's Cedric Gibbons already ensconced in the designer's chair, and the three principals are names cherished by students of house style—Lon Chaney as He, Norma Shearer as the circus bareback rider He loves, and John Gilbert as the rider *she* loves, to Chaney's suicidal despair. However, Gibbons's work here gives no hint of the MGM of *Our Dancing Daughters* or *Grand Hotel*, not to mention *Andy Hardy's Blonde Trouble* (1944) or *Callaway Went Thataway* (1951). Seastrom endows the film with so many images of the circus arena—every important act has an audience, romance makes men white-faced buffoons, and villainy may be paid off by a rampaging lion—that the director serves as his own designer. And none of the leads is starred: all three names stand below the title. Chaney had just won renown for *The Hunchback of Notre Dame*, the last title in his Universal contract (whereupon MGM snapped him up), and Shearer and Gilbert would of course rise to great fame at Metro. But Seastrom is this film's star.

He Who Gets Slapped is one of the glories of the Third Era of Silent Film, the equal of Fox's *Sunrise* and the better of almost all else. It's art, like it or not, in Seastrom's punctuational theme pictures, such as the repeated shots of Chaney as a laughing clown holding a spinning globe; or in one shot of the circus in full cry, looking out from backstage at the performers and public, that blends realism with expressionistic character development. The title's He is a learned man, cheated and cuckolded, slapped before his colleagues by swindling Marc McDermott and called "Fool! Clown!" by his own wife. And so Chaney becomes: "The World's Quaintest Clown," the titles announce, a pathetic jester who is slapped as his audience howls in delight. Seastrom's staging of the act is one of the most stunning instances of naturalistic surrealism in all film, as a huge troupe of white clowns dance into the ring led by a child clown, all playing fake instruments and bearing colossal books to usher in Chaney, deadpan on stilts. Now He is to be slapped in his comic ritual—but Seastrom suddenly turns the circus ring into the academic rotunda where Chaney was decisively humiliated. And here's McDermott at the circus, laughing along with the rest. In a last struggle with his self-esteem, Chaney attempts to tell the crowd what McDermott represents, denounce the villain. But Chaney's fellow clowns, sensing the burlesque lilt of the moment and not Chaney's terror, slap him, gag him and slap him, restrain him and slap him, destroy him. The crowd goes wild with joy. Only Chaney and we know what he feels.

"What is death—?" the last titles read, in the picturesque compositor's style of the day. "What is life—? What is love—?" An unusually grave work for MGM, where such questions were usually asked not by writers but by the stars. The movie is atypical in form, too, like *Sunrise* a weepie seen from a man's viewpoint—an odd flotation for the studio that was to be known for its women stars. Where's the star power, the glamorizing, distilling, *producing* of personalities?

Perhaps Metro determined to beat Paramount at Paramount's game. *He Who Gets Slapped* does look different from Third Era Paramount silents in the lighting, with that high-key MGM look that so beautifully interpreted black-and-white registration. But Seastrom's sumptuous visuals suggest an attempt to challenge the studio that was, in 1924, running Hollywood—and that attempt is pure MGM: in the defiant offer to wrest leadership from the reigning house. Eight years later, *Grand Hotel* seems much more appropriate than *He Who Gets Slapped* as an MGM movie, perhaps *the* MGM movie, with the director toned down and the stars scrupulously set forth. But then by 1932 Metro was no longer bothering to defy its rivals; it no longer had any.

As the studio of Big Ones, MGM controlled a far greater range of characters than the kinds that show up in *Grand Hotel*; its grandeur is typical Metro but not, shall we say, absolute Metro. There is the "common man" MGM, street-smart and flashy, in a film such as *San Francisco* (1936). This is most MGM yet, far more characteristic than *He Who Gets Slapped* or *Grand Hotel*: in the vitally self-effacing direction of W. S. Van Dyke, tight and sure but uncommentative; in the blatantly American atmosphere, historic but with a contemporary twang; in the determined centering of interest on the bonding of

*Victor Seastrom's "What is life?" clowns examine Lon
Chaney's expression; is it grin or grimace?*

Clark Gable and Jeanette MacDonald, the studio's shameless adoration of Gable's amoral (but redeemable) Blackie Norton tempered by dutiful appreciation of MacDonald's chastity and opera singing. The opera is not just tucked in but heard at length—though we feel Mac-Donald endears herself more keenly in her proto-swing version of the title song, as if MGM knew it can only put over the prestige of opera if it supplies a little totsy to soothe the common denominator in us. As if we pay for the jazz with the classical, forfeit Gable's lawlessness to MacDonald's motherly tact. (Assisting is Spencer Tracy's tough-guy priest, who forms the no-win third of a triangle, the better to frame MacDonald's desirability and Gable's overwhelming attractiveness.) One other MGM element in *San Francisco* is the amount of money the studio could spend on the disaster finale. Again, money makes money: by upping a love triangle into a two-hour music-and-place spectacle, MGM swamps the theatre competition for that month and shows up handsomely at the Oscars, with nominations, most notably, for Best Picture, Director, and Actor (Tracy). *San Francisco* would have won Best Picture, too, but for an even bigger MGM entry, *The Great Ziegfeld*.

The big MGMs weren't always lavish; sometimes they were just long. This is in itself a statement of prestige, as length has always been touchy in Hollywood. D. W. Griffith was thought rebellious simply for exceeding the two-reel limit; and DeMille regarded it as a mark of rank to run his features a half hour over the regulation ninety minutes. Indeed, as A's hugged the ninety-minute mark and B's wrapped up at from sixty to seventy-five, the running times of significance must lie on the far side of ninety. One had to move delicately, however, for exhibitors had settled on the ninety-minute feature as the ideal working element in a full-scale presentation. Ninety minutes plus a live show was your top-dollar attraction; ninety plus a comic short, a cartoon, a newsreel, and a trailer was your first-run, picture-palace special; and ninety plus a shorter second feature was your neighborhood bargain. Now, *there's* a slick system. Two and a half to three hours from lineup to exit, and everybody's happy.

Unless a studio made longer pictures—worse yet, longer pictures that everybody wanted to see, which threw the timings off at every kind of theatre, from the Roxy to the nabes. One way out was the "road show," the reserved-seat, two-a-day exhibition that treated a movie as if it were theatre. The road show was prestigious because theatre was prestigious; giving *The Birth of a Nation* the road-show treatment helped acculturate it as upscale fare simply because real people saw it in a real auditorium (as opposed to proles piling into a nickelodeon). However, the road show threw off the velvet schedule of A and B releases that Hollywood had evolved. In a business in which a film must take in its domestic grosses inside of a week, timing is crucial. Thus the road show generally turns up only at times of upheaval in the movies' history: at the transition from First to Second Eras, when the conservative patents men crashed to doom and Hollywood was settled; in 1929, when the wonder of the talkie, the musical, and two-strip Technicolor combined to pull tremendous audiences into theatres; in the 1950s, when wide-screen spectacles were emphasized to withstand television; or in the late 1960s, when *The Sound of Music*'s incredible grosses led producers to capitalize musicals of such overweening expense that they must earn out or destroy one of Hollywood's most basic genres.

Just as MGM played aces beyond rivalry in *Grand Hotel*'s agglomeration of stars, so did it up the stakes by making its Big Ones long ones. Long, before 1929, meant spectacle, something out of the ordinary. MGM instituted long as something ordinary . . . for MGM. A running time of 110 minutes became almost routine, and when MGM got to *Mutiny on the Bounty* (1935), it released a 132-minute film, as if any decent shipboard melodrama with Charles Laughton and Clark Gable would run over two hours. And *Bounty* was no road-show spectacle—scarcely a spectacle at all, though we get a full-undress native pageant in Tahiti and a superb montage of fast takes in the *Bounty*'s launching at Portsmouth, with sailors mounting masts, Laughton surveying, sails rolling out, and excitement, anxiety, and enthusiasm all scrambling about each other.

One didn't have to make spectacles to be the studio of big pictures, then. Prestige has many aspects. MGM could even adopt material born for the B programmer and turn it out *osmotically* big, through exposure to the Metro system. Edgar Rice Burroughs's *Tarzan*, for instance, fair game for various exploitation firms and a Universal serial in silent days, seems an unlikely subject for MGM, the studio of stars and Adrian gowns and art deco love seats. What Metro star would play Tarzan, Jane, a white hunter, an African native?

What will Adrian say when he sees all the trees and aardvarks? True, we scent production values in the arcane jungle, the deadpan veld, the exotic animals loafing and skulking and charging. Still, what do you want—Clark Gable and Norma Shearer in Clarence Brown's production of *Tarzan*?

It was not Brown, of course, but one of Metro's "man's world" directors, W. S. Van Dyke, who pulled it off, mainly because Van Dyke had taken a unit to Africa for *Trader Horn* (1931) and wisely logged a good deal of extra footage just in case. However, Gable was considered for Tarzan, as he was then still a newcomer to Hollywood and to Metro. No one knew what he would be good for, and at least he was big and bold. In fact, MGM had no one under contract remotely sturdy enough, for Tarzan isn't a resident Hollywood type. Fox's George O'Brien might have done, but MGM seems to have wanted someone as yet unfamiliar, untyped, perhaps even totally unencountered. Cyril Hume, who was laying out the scenario, found their man in former Olympic swimming champion Johnny Weissmuller, who happened to be disporting himself in the pool of Hume's hotel. Weissmuller had a powerful build enlightened by the swimmer's natural grace, just the physique Metro had despaired of finding. The man was handsome, too, with an almost feminine turn of feature that would photograph as darkly mysterious. Twenty-seven years old then, Weissmuller had already tried and failed to crash the movies, logging but a single appearance, as a near-nude model in the Ziegfeldian tableaux of Paramount's *Glorifying the American Girl* in 1929. This wasn't even a Hollywood job. Paramount filmed it in Astoria to include not only authentic Ziegfeldians Eddie Cantor and Helen Morgan but a raft of New York types, taking in Mayor and Mrs. James J. Walker, Texas Guinan, an Algonquin wag or two, and our own Adolph Zukor, still scheming to rule the world.

So there was Weissmuller and there was Hume, and MGM has solved its casting problem. Building on Van Dyke's African footage —not just as scenery but cagily brought into the action through back projection—and adroitly deploying the stuntmen, MGM spent its usual time and money and turned *Tarzan the Ape Man* (1932) into a huge international hit. The rudimentary plot, in which C. Aubrey Smith searches for the elephants' burial ground, can't have contributed much. Nor is the dialogue anything to remember. (Though it is amusing to read, on the credits, "screenplay by Ivor Novello," a sort of Noël Coward, handed the job because the few creatures in the film who actually speak are supposed to be crusty Britons.) What put *Tarzan* over was the pictorial novelty of the setting, the sharp attack of the action scenes, and the overtly erotic character of Tarzan's meeting with Jane, Maureen O'Sullivan. "Mothered by an ape," the posters moaned, "he knew only the law of the jungle—*to seize what he wanted!*" In truth, the cat-and-mouse foreplay of Weissmuller's first date with O'Sullivan, a dip in a river, is very sexy, O'Sullivan countering Weissmuller's increasingly aggressive approach with a fetching innocence. From the look on their faces as he carries her up into the trees for the fade-out, it appears that they're not going to spend the afternoon doing clever things with coconut shells and tapa.

Now, here's prestige: rather than jump the fad and ride it till it flags, Metro held off releasing a second *Tarzan* picture for two years, meanwhile keeping its exotic leading man off the screen. This was expensive unemployment, as Weissmuller was on full salary whether filming or not. It was feared that if the jungle lord materialized in any form other than his unique one, he would compromise his mystery. Strange to say, however much MGM identified Weissmuller with Tarzan, it never gave him star billing. Both he and O'Sullivan are cited below the title on *Tarzan and His Mate* (1934), the first sequel and generally thought to be the glory of the six MGM Weissmuller–O'Sullivan *Tarzan*s.

The studio's art honcho Cedric Gibbons is the film's nominal director, but almost all the footage is the work of Jack Conway, who took over when the master of art deco found himself out of his element in the ways of the jungle. MGM's first *Tarzan* had been expensive, but on this one the studio went all out, confident that it had a major cycle in hand. The film has hardly begun when Neil Hamilton's safari is attacked by a hostile tribe, and the tension scarcely lets up thereafter. The panicky fleeing of Hamilton's bearers, the implacable brutality of the raiding natives, the circling and dodging and retreating are brilliantly handled; and just as Hamilton's people reach safety on a mountain, giant apes hurl rocks on them. MGM's *Tarzan*s not only deal with mayhem but revel in it, even lyricize it: shots of bearers tumbling from the heights are shockingly beautiful. The constant vine-swinging has not lost its airy delight, despite the clear use of doubles and process shooting. It's even more effective on this second trip, especially when Tarzan swings Jane in trapeze style, to be caught by Cheetah, the family chimp.

The plot, again, is nothing; it's the effects that tell. Weissmuller's underwater battle with a crocodile is so thrilling that MGM revived it in several of the later issues, and Van Dyke's old footage of a charging rhino is ingeniously blended with Conway's Jane and Cheetah to present real danger. There is quite some surprise, too, when Cheetah dies protecting Jane—isn't the home team exempt from casualties? (Tarzan furiously rides the rhino to the ground and slays it, as we keen for Cheetah.) One thing is missing—the profuse eroticism of the first *Tarzan*. But the couple is more or less married now; anyway, the Production Code had been reactivated. Instead, we get more of the comic aspect of Tarzan's outback naïveté, not least when he stalks a gramophone playing dance-band music. Because Burroughs's tales had not enjoyed lavish productions before MGM took them up, we have the sense of seeing cliché not quoted but created, as when Weissmuller leads in more elephants than there are in heaven to stop the white hunters from despoiling the burial ground of its ivory.

MGM held to the two-year hiatuses and Weissmuller's concentration on this one part. However, by *Tarzan Finds a Son!* (1939), the grosses were falling, especially with the European market closed off. Then, too, Weissmuller was thirty-five and spreading, his features dense and his mystery clotting; and O'Sullivan, who had worked constantly between *Tarzan*s, was tired of running around looking like a tropical bag lady. There was some novelty in the addition of little Johnny Sheffield as Boy, but the action sequences had become reminiscent. The rhino charge from *Tarzan and His Mate* turns up again here. What, no water buffalo? The studio pushed out a few last *Tarzan*s in short order on tight budgets and closed the office.

It's interesting that the studio that most depended on the star system to put its product over would take such trouble with a series without a star. Admitting the chemistry between Weissmuller and O'Sullivan, and between them and Sheffield, we find little or no charisma in the *Tarzan* players, no performer stuff. C. Aubrey Smith, in the first entry, is always fun. But after that it's Henry Wilcoxon here and Benita Hume there.

Obviously, MGM's craft extended beyond an art-for-stars'-sake craftiness. The historians' commonplace for this is "gloss," as if Metro were a shoeshine parlor. It was partly gloss. It was also care taken, money risked, experts hired and respected. It was Thalberg's belief—and therefore Mayer's—that quality tends to pay off. It was spending the time, above all.

MGM could move quickly when it wanted to. *Grand Hotel* was very nearly thrown together, the shooting launched just as the thirteen-month Broadway run was ending, the wrap called after six weeks. Previews and retakes took another five weeks, and the film opened in New York just two weeks later. Generally, however, the studio maintained an even tempo, as if adopting the *Largo maestoso* of Thalberg's waiting room. Well made is well thought out. As Aljean Harmetz reveals in *The Making of The Wizard of Oz*, the studio could throw an astonishing amount of highly skilled artisans into one unit, tying them up for, in this case, five months of shooting alone, not counting the pre-production. This involved not only the development of the script, which began with Noel Langley's treatment, first text, and three revisions, and went on to take in wholesale renovations by Florence Ryerson and Edgar Allan Woolf, Langley's revisions of their revisions, and dabs by various kibitzers; not only Harold Arlen and E. Y. Harburg's composition of the score, not to mention Herbert Stothart's symphonic accompaniment; not only the costuming of a scarecrow, a tin woodman, a Bowery lion, good and bad witches, Munchkins, fighting trees, and flying monkeys; not only the designing of a considerable amount of fairyland; not only the technical trial and error necessary to render a tornado, the good witch's floating arrivals and departures, the bad witch's materializations and broomstick rides, the flight of a hundred monkeys ... not only achieving all this, but first taking the time to conceive the project artistically and uniquely.

No wonder morale was so good at MGM in Mayer's day. His employees knew they were at the top studio, which is good for the soul. They weren't being whipped along a treadmill, which is good for the life span. And they were contributing to extraordinary films, which is good for the self-esteem. It is safe to say that no other studio would have put the kind of effort that MGM did into *The Wizard of Oz* (1939). And note again that the studio did not hedge the wager with celebrity pull, nor even limit the casting to the contract list, enlisting the wicked witch and the lion from the free-lance directory and replacing a felled tin woodman on a loan-out from Fox. Granted, the original intention was to borrow Shirley Temple for the heroine; now there was pull. But when the studio couldn't get her, it didn't waver. It simply put a likely MGM contractee in the part—the key part, remember, in one of the biggest Big Ones till that time. Given the kind of show MGM put on, and given its wisdom in casting, it cannot be coincidental that *The Wizard of Oz* was the film that made Judy Garland a star.

Thus the MGM energy revealed choice talent as easily as it exploited it. The studio's vast machinery gave its stars more leverage than those in other studios had in the celebration of self, the proclaiming of type. Paradoxically, the stronger the stars got, the more efficient the machinery grew in illuminating the selves locked inside the types. Thus once a Clark Gable or Joan Crawford survived the break-in period and lucked into work valid enough to lead the studio to claim its option, the actor had only to land that key part to set the machinery into motion. Directors, photographers, writers, designers, PR people, and, above all, the producers would collaborate to honor the type with a fetching edge of self. No other studio so keenly enhanced its players. Paramount didn't have the patience. Warner Brothers didn't have the money. Fox and Universal didn't have the versatility. RKO, new at the game, lacked the others' experiential hard-knocks savvy. At these studios, a pungent personality might be diluted, coarsened, staled. Metro made fewer mistakes. It's unlikely that Mayer's people would have blundered with Nancy Carroll as Paramount did, or have let Gary Cooper slip out of reach through lack of confidence in his pictures. Taking it from the other side, it was Metro that refreshed Katharine Hepburn's ailing career—for, much as we may love her earlier RKOs, most of them did so-so or poor business.

There are many other such instances, as MGM's elated tact sifts through and compounds (Thalbergs, you might say) its treasures. Hollywood had plenty of shopgirl heroines—Nancy Carroll was to have been one of the notable ones. But neither she nor the others were as handsomely defined as Joan Crawford. And what other Dangerous Man compared to Gable? What Vamp to Garbo? The biggest movie stars enjoyed a romance with the American people as represen-

Some studios merely hired stars; the sharper ones exhibited stars. But MGM demonstrated stars—as, here, Garbo.

tatives of some glorious essential character, we often hear; it is less seldom ventured that MGM, most artificial of the studios, claimed by far the greatest share of these characters in its years of primacy in the first three decades of the talkies. Its artifice must have been very persuasive.

Perhaps this is because MGM did not need to prepare *Grand Hotel* caviar every other month to keep its stars glowing. Daily hash was good enough—if "well made"—because the stars had been so carefully rendered in advance. *China Seas* (1935) is illustrative here, as a ramshackle melodrama pasted together with clichés so hoary D. W. Griffith's grandmother fell out of her cradle jeering at them. The director, Tay Garnett, is a typical MGM pro, competent and uninflected, the dialogue just stands there, and the exotic possibilities of a boat run from Hong Kong to Singapore caught Gibbons's art department on a snooze day. What makes the film go is the stars—Clark Gable as the good-guy captain, Wallace Beery as the front man for a gang of pirates, Jean Harlow and Rosalind Russell as the tramp and the lady, Gable to choose between them.

Not that there's great acting here. Gable and Harlow simply play type, Russell has little to work with, and Beery, never a convincing thespian, is so loose that we can scarcely credit the danger he represents, even when the pirates put a "Malay boot" on Gable to torture him into disclosing the whereabouts of a cargo of gold. The best line delivery is that of Hattie McDaniel, Harlow's maid, on receiving the hand-me-down of a tight beaded dress. McDaniel is thrilled—she's had her eye on that number for some time—then reflective. "I might," she admits, "have to have it taken out a smidgeon."

If the stars aren't acting, how do they make *China Seas* go? By reference: to what MGM has shown of them in better pictures. It is as if we aren't dealing with portrayers but with invented abstractions, symbolism with a human face. The film goes because Gable is heroic, Harlow an erring hot lady, and Beery a brute; and because we believe that such people exist, and that erring ladies may abet brutes but will ultimately favor the hero, who defeats the brute. Hokum, yes. But we view it cross-contextually, combining reflections of Gable's amused tolerance of Harlow in *Red Dust* with Harlow's charming exploitation of Beery in *Dinner at Eight*, meanwhile thinking back to the three stars in *The Secret Six* (1931), playing the same mutual perspective in a city setting. It's like the serial publications of Dickens and Thackeray: the fascination of the whole redeems the weakness of an entry here and there.

Because MGM had such a large contract roster, so much charisma on call, it grew expert in multiplying this serial chemistry in teams. If William Powell and Myrna Loy in *The Thin Man* (1934), why not Powell and Loy in *Escapade*, an elegant complement to Powell and Harlow in *Reckless* (1935), scandal right out of the tabloids, "the Libby Holman case," so they said. But Loy, overworked, slipped off on vacation, so it's Powell and Luise Rainer in *Escapade* (1935), and that's a hit. So while waiting for Powell and Loy to resume, why not Powell and Rainer in *The Great Ziegfeld* (1936), so big it has room for Powell and Virginia Bruce and Powell and Myrna Loy as well?

Sometimes we have the feeling that Metro is marking history with its teams, inadvertently laying down archival celluloid. Thus the three teamings of Clark Gable and Norma Shearer reveal their separate rises in cross-section. In *A Free Soul* (1931), Shearer is the Lady in need of a jolt, which Gable, then almost strictly a thug, is ready to apply, though she's the star and he merely a comer billed well below the title. ("A new man," she murmurs. "A new life." This is sound prophecy.) By *Strange Interlude*, Shearer is moving into her Distinguished Lady of the Theatre phase, in a role written by Eugene O'Neill and first played by Lynn Fontanne; Gable is broadening his arena, more the leading man now than the local hood. But he isn't comfortable in this line of work, and they take separate roads, he to his newspapermen and gamblers, she to her Jane Cowl and Katharine Cornell parts, her Shakespeare, her Queen of France, bearing The Most Prestigious Feathered Headdress Yet Seen in the Western World, at that in a two-and-a-half-hour Big One that has everything in it *but* Jean Hersholt: *Marie Antoinette* (1938).

By the time Gable and Shearer meet again, in *Idiot's Delight* (1939), they are a match, two industry kingpins so well established that it's no longer What They Do but Who They Are. These are Lunt and Fontanne parts, but you'd never know it from the film, as Shearer combines the look of Fontanne with the histrionic subtlety of Le Pétomane, and Gable does Gable. Nevertheless: Lunt and Fontanne aren't what MGM movies are about, as Lunt and Fontanne themselves discovered while making *The Guardsman*. They were too good not to be interesting, but they were not movie stars, and Metro —Thalberg himself, planning the cut of the trimming velvet—could not therefore *install* them. In film, the Lunts were of no reference. No reference whatsoever.

In fact, we begin to notice that, despite Thalberg's theatre culture, MGM works best with actors who are not strongly theatre-trained. Garbo, Lillian Gish, Loy, Crawford, Shearer, John Gilbert, and Ramon Novarro were naturals; Gable had logged more experience manning an oil rigger than speaking lines; and Robert Montgomery, William Powell, James Stewart, and Robert Taylor had barely skimmed the stage before coming to Hollywood. Marie Dressler was a longtime veteran, Franchot Tone and Spencer Tracy were heading for theatre celebrity when they got into movies, Eleanor Powell had already made it to Broadway fame, and of course the Barrymores bore a dynastic tradition and—John, at least—immense thespian reputation. But most of the convinced troupers, the ones who played film with an ear cocked to casting news back in the real place, New York, tended to work for other studios. Paramount, we know, kept a studio in the East to cultivate stage talent, and RKO, as we shall see, was similarly alert to noises made along Broadway. Even Warner Brothers keyed its scouting exclusively to the New York stage, where it not only collected hundreds of sink-or-swim contractees (James Cagney and Joan Blondell, for instance, snapped up on Al Jolson's recommendation along with the rights to a play Jolson owned), but shopped for its Prestige Kings John Barrymore, George Arliss, and Paul Muni. Even Ruby Keeler, billed fourth on her debut in *42nd Street*, had been, though briefly, a Ziegfeld star.

At MGM, however, talent and seasoning mattered less than look and grit, not to mention how well one complemented the other lookers. We see the rise of a star in the Gable–Crawford–Montgomery triangle of *Forsaking All Others* (1934), which becomes Montgomery–Crawford–Tone immediately afterward in *No More Ladies* (1935), whereupon an established star slides into third place for Montgomery–Crawford–Powell in *The Last of Mrs. Cheyney* (1937). Montgomery, it seems, does some sharp complementing. Even more telling is the triangle made of Gable and Tracy as fixed points, the woman as variable—baroque Jeanette MacDonald in *San Francisco*, game Myrna Loy in *Test Pilot* (1938), and, on loan from Paramount, sweet Claudette Colbert (giving us her taboo right side in one shot—knuckling under to Metro's dictatorial power?) in *Boom Town* (1940). The studio even indulges us in a foursome, in *Libeled Lady* (1936): Powell–Loy and Tracy–Harlow. No other lot could pull off this kind of thing as sheer business as usual. As if gloating, Metro kicks off the credits with a shot of the four stars merrily strolling arm in arm. Look what we've got on our turf! Paramount's Leisen comedies could trade Milland–Colbert for MacMurray–Colbert, or try a Milland–Colbert–Mac-Murray, or borrow Jean Arthur from Columbia. But this was the extent of its latitude, and the less eclectic Warners and Fox were even more confined. This, then, was the grasp of MGM's star power: vitality of combination.

There were generically practical teamings that turned out to be chemical, such as Judy Garland and Mickey Rooney for musicals. There were perilous teamings that could illuminate or dim you—we think of Laurence Olivier, his Hollywood career put on ice for five years when Garbo froze him out of early shooting on *Queen Christina* (1933). She forced the studio to replace him with John Gilbert, her former lover and, by a nice bite of history, the Great Lover against whose magic a young and rising Garbo herself had been tested, on her third American picture, *Flesh and the Devil* (1927).

There was the absolute rightness of teaming, not only special but culturally almost inevitable, like the Tracy–Hepburn series of the 1940s, celebrated for the breezy interlock of their repartee and the sophistication of their collaborators, including director George Cukor and writers Donald Ogden Stewart, Ruth Gordon, and Garson Kanin. After the gaudily sensitive artiste of the RKOs, Tracy's Kate is shockingly straightforward. He simplified her! the fans cry in wonder. But it is little remarked that she in turn inflected him, brought out his latent whimsey. She didn't just lose her mannerisms; she lent him a few. In *Adam's Rib* (1949), as married lawyers, they call each other "Pinky," as fey a touch as anything in the RKO *Alice Adams* or *Morning Glory*. As they put dinner together, he flourishes a bottle crying, "Chutney! Chutney! Chutney!"—sounding like Sylvia Scarlett doing an imitation of Cary Grant.

By far MGM's most indispensable pairing was that of Gable and Crawford, two junk-class kids who commanded more respect than everyone in the society columns put together. Hollywood was full of such anomalies, especially in the silent era, when the revelation of the class in one's speech was protected. Warners exploited the urban vernacular; Fox dined out on rustic dialect. MGM had almost everyone speaking the King's English. We take this in stride when William Powell, most dapper of Dandies, flips a British *yu* into words like "sue." It's fancy; Powell's a fancy guy. But it's absurd to hear Gable in his gangster roles employing the grammar of a librarian, prudently avoiding the false adverb "good" when he means "well" or observing the rule governing subject-verb agreement in or-nor phrases. And Crawford's clipped pronunciation is unnatural in any part; even elocution teachers aren't that clear.

It was MGM that spoofed this Pygmalion effect, ironically enough, in *Singin' in the Rain* (1952), as Jean Hagen's diction coach (Kathleen Freeman) hammers away on the dos and don'ts of speaking English right on the set, oblivious of the turmoil around her. Hagen typifies the slum kids who made it in silents on looks and guts. Sound revealed their lack of class—rather, their background in the "wrong" one, impedient to purposes of fantasy. We should know our stars in full kit, not as they were. The framework of a bio, some chance data, perhaps the citing of a favorite dessert . . . just enough to tantalize. This is a spur to the imagination. The truth can hurt. Yes, over in Burbank at earthy Warner Brothers, stars showed themselves plain. You could tell where they came from, could even assume that they had breakfasted on an egg cream and a "nickel a shtickl." RKO maintained a come-as-you-are wing to lend their New York pictures aroma and tone (think of *Stage Door*), and even Paramount did nothing to educate Clara Bow for talkies, though she was one of the most thoroughly Brooklyn of performers in word and deed. Most studios, then, didn't particularly mythologize or obscure its stars.

MGM did. We have countless instances: in Mayer's sending his goddesses home to change if they showed up *anywhere* and for *anything* out of totemic wrap; in front-office advice to stars dating incorrectly or unfamously; in a number of interfering managements of police cases to avert or redirect a scandal. Metro officers often paid or lawyered off prosecution, even indulged in benign neglect of certain controversies in order to screen out worse ones. And what to do with the million-dollar Tarzan, Johnny Weissmuller? How to preserve the illusion of the jungle Lochinvar in a man who was married, dully

—Metro thought—at that? No sooner had Weissmuller divorced his wife than he became fiercely involved with Lupe Velez. (Fierce, it's sad to say, was the only kind of involvement Velez knew. She was so tempestuous she packed a stiletto.) What was the point of keeping Weissmuller expensively offscreen between *Tarzans*, keeping him inviolable of conjecture, if he was going to make the papers for his bouts with Velez? MGM's honchos must have loved Garbo's PR blackout. Sure, it gave them headaches at first. However, once the press realized that after all the types and subtypes and four-picture wonders and showboaters and fakes, they finally had something unique—that they could speculate about her endlessly and never use her up—everyone not only respected but enforced Garbo's seclusion. It was good for business.

Gable and Crawford were best for business, as Metro's pet proles: up from nowhere through minor stage work* to the clammy principles of glamorizing, including glamorous marriages with fellow actors. Crawford smartly partitioned hers, taking first Douglas Fairbanks, Jr., son of Pickfair and virtually the Prince of Hollywood, taking next Franchot Tone, intellectual, lightly political, and lo, a Metro contractee himself. Gable, after several liaisons with older women who smoothed out his rough edges, did even better, taking Carole Lombard, one of Hollywood's official princesses.

Both Crawford and Gable bore unglamorous secrets, her stag film and his hustling. But these were efficiently guarded and, anyway, too disreputable to print until recently. It's notable, though, that MGM's two most lavish proletarians were—well, lavish as few proletarians are. Workingmen don't look like MGM's Clark Gable; they look the way Gable did before MGM, with crooked teeth and stupid ears. Working women don't come up with those smashingly right-on-it ripostes with which the onscreen Crawford slashes at lovers and villains alike; working women sound like Warner Brothers' Joan Blondell, with her "Oh yeah?" Or Ruby Keeler tooting, "Gee, that's swell!" In fact, no one of any class looks or sounds or carries himself

---

*Crawford's stage career consisted of chorus hoofing. But Gable actually played leads, some with divas who cast their juveniles in anticipation of sampling their couch technique; and once in a significant historical event, Sophie Treadwell's *Machinal* (1928), one of Broadway's most successful experiments in expressionism, based in part on the Ruth Snyder–Judd Gray murder case. Gable, billed by type (like all Treadwell's characters) as A Man, plays the heroine's adulterous boyfriend, featured in two big scenes.

like Gable and Crawford, and that too was part of the MGM style, the MGM prestige, the MGM glamour. MGM's films weren't just prettier than Warners' and more expensive than Paramount's and wittier than Universal's. MGM's films perfected the human comedy, cleaned everybody up so splendidly that William Daniels's backlighting gave them halos.

Possessed (1931), the third Gable–Crawford teaming and the first important one, carefully framed around their escalating popularity, proposes Crawford as a factory worker who uses sex to break into the high life and Gable as a lawyer entering politics. "There are only two kinds of people," Crawford observes at the start, "the ones in and the ones out." It is MGM's notion that Crawford is both kinds, in enough to hook up with Gable but out enough for his enemies to use her against him. Joan, loyal and loving, must now pretend to dump Gable for his own good. "*Common!* That's what I am!" she rages at him, reveling in it. And common she was, most uncommonly so. Thus, where MGM is at its most naturalistic it is in fact least naturalistic, developing a religion of sex and ambition with sexy, ambitious people who have been purified of their reality.

The Gable–Crawford partnership was so potent it ran through MGM's 1930s like a theme song, even a hymn. They made eight films together, each a remake of the preceding ones, and they would have made even more if the studio could have figured out something else for them to do besides hurdle the social barriers on behalf of romance. Their respective social positions vary, at least, whereby the films derive a slight comparison of texture. In *Dance, Fools, Dance* (1931), their first picture together, he is a ruthless gangster, she an impoverished heiress. Though they do not really work out a romance (Crawford ends up with the ruthful Lester Vail), we sense the erotic menace each spots in the other, the "if it's so bad, how come it feels so good?" sensuality that bonds these two throughout their Metro years. Then, in *Laughing Sinners* (1931), he's of the Salvation Army, she of the clip-joint cabaret, an absolute reversal of *Dance, Fools, Dance*. In *Chained* (1934), however, she's back among the high and mighty and he's a cattle rancher.

Attempts to alter the style emphasize the style all the more. *Dancing Lady* (1933), a backstage musical with Gable as the director and Crawford as the up-from-burlesque would-be Broadway star, is actually just another Gable–Crawford film with a bunch of musical numbers stuffed in at the end; and *Love on the Run* (1936), an attempt at runaway-heiress screwball comedy, only reminds us that Gable is most comfortable playing newspapermen and that Crawford has no sense of humor. A Gable–Crawford film is: roughneck smoothie jousts with luncheonette tragedienne, and it always works because, under all that Metro finish, that's exactly what those two were.

Surprising to report, this studio that essentialized duo and trio teamings was for a long while known as "the woman's studio," not only for a preponderance of woman stars but for a certain address of the woman moviegoer in the camera's point of view. How is this possible, with all these Gables and Tracys and Taylors and Montgomerys taking the lead?

It isn't possible. MGM was no more a woman's studio than any other studio was—except in its early years, when its big draws were flamboyant women like Mae Murray and conventional women like Alice Terry, along with Lon Chaney and two Great Lovers, John Gilbert and Ramon Novarro. When Mayer and Thalberg took over, MGM had no Gable to test the self-control of Norma Shearer, the irresistibility of Garbo, the aggressiveness of Crawford—or, later, the homemaking of Loy, the reserve of Garson. There were no Tracys to tame or Montgomerys to delight their co-stars. Neither Gilbert nor Novarro registered with truly virile power, and Chaney, who did, seldom played romantic roles. (As in *He Who Gets Slapped*, he generally loves from afar.) So MGM's most telling stars in the late 1920s were, indeed, women. Shearer could run through the uptown of the male roster within a year, then find herself partnered with Lew Cody or Conrad Nagel. Garbo, who had the pick of the lot, overpowered even John Gilbert in great loving; and Crawford, at her wildest in *Rose Marie* (1928), had nothing but James Murray to play against, which tends to hobble one's wild.

By the talkie years, the studio was actively working against its reputation, signing up solid men to match the women. But no one could match Garbo—here was the most resonant exemplar of "the woman's studio," all forces poised to make the most of the diva, and no male in sight big enough to enchant her, not even Gable. Nils Asther, Ramon Novarro, Robert Taylor? *Des petits déjeuners*, and Garbo gorges. *Grand Hotel*'s John Barrymore complements rather

The MGM male before Gable: Nils Asther in The Single
Standard *(1929)*, one of Garbo's last silents. Like John Gilbert and Ramon Novarro, Asther is light, a poetic rather
than a rugged hero, in the Valentino manner. Perhaps MGM
was trying to make up for its oversight in losing Valentino to
Paramount: he had come to prominence at Metro before the
amalgamation into MGM.

than confronts her, *Anna Karenina*'s Fredric March, unable to cope, walks through his role, and the Great Gilbert, making his comeback in *Queen Christina*, is a dazed shadow of stardom, shaking like a beaten dog. Garbo's co-stars conventionally do reverence to her momentous intangibility, but when Gilbert tells her, "You're an illusion—you'll vanish before my eyes," it's Gilbert we worry about. Garbo isn't a phantom; she's a sensory overload. *Gilbert's* the temporary party here, all the more so because he no longer looks remotely like the man who drove her into raptures in the late 1920s. Only Melvyn Douglas acquits himself, in *Ninotchka* (1939): and *Ninotchka* is a comedy, as foreign to Garbo as beau Paris is to Soviet Ninotchka. Suave Douglas naturally has the edge.

Except for *Grand Hotel*, Garbo's films are not only centered on but nearly confined to her, as if they all grew out of Rouben Mamoulian's famous last shot of *Queen Christina*, the Face enigmatically reflecting. So these films, at least, are women's films, even if Garbo spends most of *Queen Christina* as a man, striding about in tunic, pants, and boots, bragging about her sexual exploits, swearing to "die a bachelor," and kissing a woman on the lips.* And, like all studios, MGM made weepies, the woman's form. MGM even managed, at times, to fork the narrative attack in other genres to trade off between male and female points of view, yielding stories without a clear protagonist.

We note this particularly in the Gable–Crawford teamings. In *Dancing Lady*, she is so surely the principal that Gable was unhappy making the film, and looks tired when he doesn't look bored. (His refusal to play in a comparable setup, again with Crawford, led MGM to punish him with a loan-out to shabby Columbia, where *It Happened One Night* finally put him over as Hollywood's top male star.) By 1940, however, with *Gone With the Wind* behind him, Gable could not realistically support anyone, and *Strange Cargo* veers with difficulty in order to justify her story while telling his. At length, all the leads end up drifting in a boat with an unnervingly heavenly character (Ian Hunter); Gable and Crawford keep eying him as if he's Orestes, she's Electra, and Sophocles has just introduced the Third Actor. Certain regions of the country were sufficiently impressed by

---

*Note the Paramount influence. Mamoulian, on loan to Metro, had just finished spelling von Sternberg in the extrapolation of Marlene Dietrich, on *Song of Songs* (1933).

Hunter's Grace to ban the film as blasphemous. But at least Crawford copped top billing.

Norma Shearer, in her prime, held out for this most telling prestige as a rule. On *Escape* (1940), she even gets a credit for her hairstylist. Like Crawford and Garbo, she generally dominated her terrain. *Escape*, incredibly, is a thriller in the form of a woman's picture, for while the plot concerns Robert Taylor's attempt to take his mother Alla Nazimova out of Nazi Germany, the feelings of the film are all Shearer's—her sympathy for Taylor, her fear of getting involved in the espionage (conquered after fifty seconds of reunion between mother and son), her serene bravery in facing down arch-Nazi Conrad Veidt. Give MGM credit, two years after *Three Comrades'* hedging about Fascism, for delivering a real sense of the horror of life in Hitler's Germany. We *see* nothing worse than a Nazi glaring murderously at Taylor after they bump shoulders. But the air of terror is fully rendered. First baiting Taylor brutally, Veidt then taunts him for not defending himself. He, Conrad Veidt, would do so even in a strange country.

TAYLOR: (coolly) That's easy to say. Come over to *my* backyard someday and find out.

VEIDT: I'll do that.

A moment for the men. All the rest of *Escape* is for women, to admire not only Shearer and Taylor but Nazimova, superb as an actress fingered for execution for having harbored Jewish refugees in America. Thus we have a suspense film about mother love and Shearer love— an action film that runs on emotions more than on plot.

This tendency to build so many films around women does not reflect a "woman's studio" temperament as much as the experience of having organized its forms at a time, the late 1920s, when the studio had three Queens of the Lot—Garbo, Shearer, and Crawford. By definition, this is a paradox, for the Queen takes first choice of parts, first call on everybody's favorite director, cameraman, and designer, first demand of male co-stars, first billing above the title, and is the last to set foot on the set on the first day of shooting, the awaited diva. Nonetheless, all three women had claim on the rank. Garbo commanded immense prestige and an extremely lucrative foreign market. Shearer had Thalberg's ear. But Crawford had Mayer's, and was the most popular of the three in America.

It was something of a tie, then, or rather a judgment that can't be called, because it never quite came to a head. This was mainly because the three played very different kinds of roles, and thus never had to fight for a plum project. Queens of other lots, unique in their splendor, had to be versatile, to encompass the range of prima donna roles that happened the studio's way. Think of Warner Brothers' Bette Davis, tense in *Jezebel*, pathetically dying in *Dark Victory*, bracingly querulous in *The Private Lives of Elizabeth and Essex*, a very wicked lady in *The Letter*, then regally prim, the schoolmarm as saint, in *The Corn Is Green*.

MGM's Queens split the assignments, each claiming her special territory. Garbo's roles were too exotic for the two Americans, and if Shearer's Great Dame parts were too limpid for Crawford, Crawford's whores were too vehement for Shearer. (Imagine Shearer as Rose Marie, Crawford in *Smilin' Through*.)* At various times, we glimpse one or the others in an act of competition, as when Garbo refuses to be put through the all-star paces of *The Hollywood Revue of 1929* while Shearer and Crawford check in; getting your studio to exempt you from a lot-wide jamboree is a Queen's arrogance. Later in the decade, we have Shearer limiting her appearances to one film a year; only the Queen could afford such tight-fisted charisma. Crawford's great stunt as Queen actually involved two lots, when she left Metro for Warner Brothers, waited two years, and blitzed the business as a dark lady of noir in *Mildred Pierce*, winning her Oscar and bumping off Bette Davis, Warners' Queen till that moment.

Metro did everything it could to keep each of the three Queens from feeling threatened by the others. It was a cinch with Garbo, as she inhabited a more or less private world, anyway. With the more disputatious Shearer and Crawford, Thalberg was discreet; he may well have launched Shearer on her cavalcade of thespian tours de force specifically to allot Shearer's old Lusty Lady parts to Crawford. But art imitates life, and at length the two Queens faced off in *The Women* (1939), with Shearer as Queen of Marriage and Crawford as the Usurper. It was a hot set. On the first day of shooting, Rosalind

*Crawford did play a Shearer part, in *Paid* (1930), another of the Broadway artiste roles Shearer specialized in—Jane Cowl had originated it in New York. Shearer bowed out of the production when she became pregnant. Lucky Joan: it was her first chance at a solid dramatic part, and placed the dance-hall *Sturm und Drang* that would characterize her from then on.

Protean Joan Crawford gives us (above) the lavish prole and (overleaf) the dangerous sophisticate.

Crawford was the shopgirl; but Crawford was a princess.

Russell, who knew this film would put her over, was in costume and makeup and ready to roll, but, out on the street, Shearer and Crawford were circling the stage house in their cars, each refusing to light till the other one did.

Metro was enough of a woman's studio to have a fourth Queen, Marion Davies. But here was a supplemental monarch, in that Davies reigned at William Randolph Hearst's Cosmopolitan Pictures, which had set up shop within Metro's walls. Call Davies a Metro Queen of the Lot by morganatic decree: she had the prestige but few of the rights. Davies is unlike any other Queen also in that she had no field of specialty. She played everything from costume romance and melodrama to comedy and musicals, but other than her sassy imitations of her colleagues, Davies's one forte is summed up by Hearst's pet Louella Parsons in her tireless rave "Marion never looked lovelier."

Lovely Davies certainly was, and apparently a madcap in real life. Yet on screen she seems dutiful, even tentative. She is hardly the tomato-baiting imposter that Orson Welles and Herman Mankiewicz may or may not have made of her in *Citizen Kane*, and in moments of rough-'em-up spoof Davies gives us a glimpse of something unusual. But she doesn't connect with her stardom the way Garbo, Shearer, and Crawford did, never appears to *need* it. In the musical *Going Hollywood* (1933), Davies plays a French teacher in a musty, hidebound girls' school run by crabby beldames. Hearing Bing Crosby on the radio changes her life. She defies the headmistress and packs her bags to seek out "music, life, love," not to mention Crosby. It's a good start for a pleasantly silly film, but Davies puts no urgency into the scene. To Davies, all lines are equal. Yes, yes, yes, I *will* do zat. Now I'm a French teacher and I'm seeking music, life, love. Only in Raoul Walsh's rapturous close-ups of Davies dreaming of Crosby do we get a sense of why Hearst was so devoted to his doll.

We know why MGM was devoted to Davies. Her pictures were expensive propositions even for MGM, and, as Davies preferred partying to shooting, they took two or three times their fair term and tied up important male stars—often just as their fame was breaking, when they needed more attractive vehicles than these Davies extravaganzas. But the Hearst connection yielded another kind of MGM prestige: power. If Thalberg reveled in his glosses on Broadway,

Mayer reveled in the authority of being close to Hearst. Cosmopolitan had first pitched camp inside the gates of Paramount, but Zukor tired of locking horns with a fellow magnate, and Hearst took Davies to the Goldwyn studio, where there was no Queen to rival Davies and no mogul to speak of, Goldwyn having already departed. Came then the Metro merger, and Mayer assuaged Hearst's doubts with a timely proposition: Davies will be separate-but-equal Queen and Hearst will put his newspaper empire at the service of MGM. It was costly, but it produced awesome publicity. It worked well, too, for Davies was so busy playing the young cutie that she could neither threaten nor envy Garbo, Shearer, and Crawford. (Crawford, the only one of the four who verbalized feelings of competition, rooted all her complaints in Shearer.) But lo, Hearst was miffed when Thalberg reserved *The Barretts of Wimpole Street* for Shearer, and irate when Thalberg announced *Marie Antoinette* for her, too. Hearst reckoned these as Davies parts. Thalberg, however, was not about to humiliate his aesthetic of the well-made movie with the erratic Davies. Away Cosmopolitan went, to—of all places—Warner Brothers.

MGM had an abundance of Queens, for there was Myrna Loy as well, so legitimate a pretender that when the fans voted for a King and Queen of Hollywood, they chose Clark Gable and Loy. But this points up Loy's identity: as consort rather than ruler. Loy was the perfect complement, the ideal sweetheart-wife, the essential co-star. Even in the 1940s, after the late Thalberg's influence had waned and the Big Three had departed, Loy remained secondary in her unique way while Greer Garson became Queen as The English Lady (though Irish), more respectable than Thalberg's sexy divas, more to Mayer's taste—the Mayer Garbo, one might say.

The voters who picked Gable as King chose well, for his appeal characterized not only MGM's star system but that of all Hollywood, as the exponential Dangerous Man. Here was the best prestige possible in the business, a winner who couldn't lose—except in *Parnell* (1937), and only because he flouted Dangerous Man convention and blundered onto an unflattering page of history. For twenty years, with a break for war service, Gable styled a type less influential than overpowering, and his era—the Studio Age, the golden days of talkies—saw the dissolution of the Great Lover as much because Gable reinvigorated the type as because dialogue ridiculed it.

The Great Lover was above all a romanticist—as was silent film. Spoken dialogue, in the naturalistic survey of the talkie, made lyricism perilous. Suddenly, those sweeping gestures and agitated faces seemed absurd. Then too, the Great Lover was not adept in action parts. John Gilbert went to war in *The Big Parade* (1925), yes; Novarro was Ben-Hur. But these were exceptional outings, while Gable's Dangerous Man was as natural in a fight as in love. Thus he could be used to incite not only women stars' sensuality but men stars' virility. No wonder he was so crucial to MGM's system of teamings. In the text of *Machinal*, Sophie Treadwell describes the character Gable played as "pleasing, common, vigorous." *Exactly* right; and Spencer Tracy analyzes further in *San Francisco*, warning Jeanette MacDonald, "He's as unscrupulous with women as he is ruthless with men."

There were few authentic-seeming roughnecks in the Studio Age—Charles Bickford, James Cagney, Fred MacMurray at times (the Paramount style generally smoothed out male aggression), Aldo Ray. Gable belongs on the list primarily, as he was bigger and smoother than the rest of the pack. Those who know him say his magnetism was yet more taking in life than on screen. He was taller than he photographed, surer than his scripts made him, not as articulate but tougher. Loremasters delight in quoting Carole Lombard's put-downs of Gable's virility, but Lombard was an iconoclast who couldn't resist the satirically belittling oxymoron—great Gable as ungreat lover. It's doubtful that she meant these remarks literally. Heaven knows Joan Crawford didn't see him so, and Crawford knew him well. And in *Hold Your Man* (1933), Jean Harlow is found reclining on a couch the morning after a fade-out, looking at Gable in a dazed bliss that surely had wives pondering and husbands muttering all the way home.*

From that moment on—from any number of such moments since Gable had arrived at Metro in 1931—Gable's studio was a man's studio, taking his point of view and looking for other stars to second him. Gable freed Metro to exploit sex as well as romance. In silents, Metro was eloquently sensual. But in talkies the studio lost its grip on

---

*A historians' cliché holds that women adored Gable and men admired him. But there must have been a lot of schmudls whose married life was disrupted by the example of Gable. All women could adore him, but inferior men, who could laugh away Valentino and even John Gilbert, must have been given pause. Would someone like to do a monograph on this?

the erotic. Gilbert dissolved in runny pictures, Novarro's tenor lacked punch, and Conrad Nagel spoke well but just didn't ignite women's dreams. In Gable, Metro had a kind of complement to Garbo, a sure thing in love. And that's what made Hollywood.

An arresting interior contradiction here: MGM eventually became known as "the family studio," celebrating the righteousness of the hunter-cook alliance—sex as marriage. Even better: marriage as the haven that makes sex unnecessary. This other MGM occurs as a result not of Production Code pressure but of the passing of Thalberg in 1936, when Mayer became more active in the hiring and developing of talent, the acquisition of properties, even the thrust of narrative. Thalberg's grip on studio enterprise did not give way on his death; all Hollywood, not just Metro, had been trying to imitate him. But Mayer had never entirely approved of the pronounced sexual vitality of Thalberg's films, much less of Thalberg's reputation as The Man Who Made MGM. The smart money at the studio followed Mayer's reactionary lead, and perhaps we find the line separating Thalberg's from Mayer's MGM in the "there's no place like home" mentality of *The Wizard of Oz*—which, nevertheless, troubles to show us that home is boring. There's no place like *Oz*.

Thalberg's Metro was a kind of Oz, a big parade of laughing sinners: music, life, love. Mayer's Metro is a kind of home respecting Our Father, loving Dear Mother, admiring Big Brother, razzing Sis, and understanding Kid Brother. Mayer's ideal cast: Lewis Stone, Mary Astor, Van Johnson, Lucille Bremer, Butch Jenkins. Ah, but life is not an MGM movie. Astor, for one, hit the headlines when her husband's divorce suit brought her ribald diary into testimony and it turned out that George S. Kaufman had more than wit up his sleeve.

It might have been an episode in a Thalberg movie. What contempt that man must have had for bourgeois values—in Queen Christina's celibacy, or Mata Hari's sadistic refusal to bed Ramon Novarro till he puts out the votive light given him by his mother. Look at the family life of Anna Karenina, wherein Our Father, Basil Rathbone, is a rigid beast living on jealousy of his son and for revenge on his wife. "It isn't me you love," Garbo moans. "It's your career and your appearances." After throwing her out of the house, Rathbone tells son Freddie Bartholomew that Garbo is dead. The movie's sympathy lies with an adulteress.

Granted, this is not a Thalberg picture. David Selznick produced it. But it fits into the Garbo file as Thalberg organized it. Remember, Thalberg was virtually story editor for all MGM films until 1933, and his recipe kept the stew simmering for some years thereafter. Think of *The Crowd*, of the despair of the workingman, lonely even amid his family. Think of Charles Laughton's psychotic relationship with his daughter in *The Barretts of Wimpole Street*. Think of the violence that Thalberg saw in sex, the woman-slapping Gable—slapping Mrs. Thalberg, in fact, and still at it ten years later in *Boom Town* (1940). He tells wife Claudette Colbert that he'll lick her if she strays. And she's thrilled! "I'll save it," Gable growls, "till you need it." Ten years after *that,* in *To Please a Lady* (1950), he meets Barbara Stanwyck, trades insults, makes a face, and pops her one. Is this guy a lover or a boxer?

Gable was so perdurably characterized during Thalberg's reign that Mayer did not try to reform him, though he did take some of the ginger out of his hedonism in the PR tag line of *Adventure* (1945): "Gable's back and Garson's got him!" But Mayer was energetically purifying other parts of the forest. By the late 1930s, even, we notice what might be called the Mayer Touch sneaking in. Taking the lead from Warner Brothers, MGM gave us *The Last Gangster* (1937), with Edward G. Robinson as a smugly snarling crime boss sent to Alcatraz while his wife (Rosa Stradner) carries their child. Ostensibly, the film follows Robinson's attempt, on release from prison, to reinstate his authority in his gang. Emotionally, however, the film veers over to Stradner's point of view, with sweet music and a doting camera to celebrate the birth of her baby boy; with a shot of her bathing him that is simply irrelevant; with a scene, in the prison visiting room, where Robinson adores his infant heir and ignores Stradner. Manipulating the lighting and musical punctuation to make us feel as hurt as Stradner does, MGM seems unsure whether this is a gangster picture or a weepie.

At Warner Brothers, the gangster routinely treated women as objects—mother as fetish, moll as whore, wife as breeder. But an MGM husband and father was expected to sentimentalize his responsibilities. When Robinson neglects his wife for his son, he commits an act more fatal than any miscalculation he made as Little Caesar. Given Mayer's scale of values, the withholding husband is renouncing his right to participate in the human comedy. Outlaw is bad enough, but mean husband? This Mayer cannot countenance.

Eventually, Robinson does try to redeem himself. While seeking revenge on his turncoat gang, he befriends his now adolescent son. Still, there is no place for him, no family to reclaim. Stradner has married James Stewart to raise the boy without knowledge of his real father. A felon shoots Robinson down in the street, and we fade out on a keepsake his son had given him, his Lincoln Award medal, reading "For Outstanding Achievement." Thus Metro reminds us that Robinson left nothing behind him: no family.

Neglect of spouse is not Mayer's worst sin; sexual browsing is. The studio hits Vivien Leigh especially hard for prostitution in *Waterloo Bridge* (1940). She was busy keeping herself true for fiancé Robert Taylor, but her money ran out and she believed him dead, so she turned to the streets and the railway station around Waterloo Bridge. Meeting the troop trains to pick up a soldier she runs into . . . Robert Taylor, thrilled that she's there to meet him and, not too surprisingly, failing to catch the significance of the circumspect version of hooker chic that Metro puts on her. *Waterloo Bridge* is filled with absurdities. Taylor is supposed to be a Scot, yet doesn't attempt an accent in a film filled with true Brits; and when he goes to see ballerina Leigh dance with a small company in a vaudeville theatre, we get a spiffy auditorium, a gigantic stage, and a soupy medley of *Swan Lake* tunes though the décor suggests ancient Greece.

The worst of it is Metro's obdurate morality. Taylor takes Leigh up to Scotland to meet his family, and she charms the lot of them. But her terrible secret haunts her; streetwalking has made her unworthy. She flees, throwing happiness away. Surely this is suffering enough? No: she must die. Distracted in despair, she steps in front of a car on —what poetic justice!—Waterloo Bridge.

A home-wrecker is even more reprehensible than a prostitute, though Joan Crawford survives in *The Women*. Still, we are made to feel the *horror* of adultery, the agony that the straying husband causes Norma Shearer, the sociopathic glee of the intruding Crawford. Opening on a troop of upper-middle sophisticates dishing and loafing in a space-age beauty parlor, director George Cukor speeds us to a view of Shearer and daughter Virginia Weidler, noble by comparison. We find them horseback riding, taking photographs, loving mutty dogs, and engaging in loving roughhouse. They're virtually men; Shearer even bites on a pipe. Later, she says, "Stephen and I are equals." No wonder. Is Cukor saying that the admirable women are masculine? But Crawford is about as ballsy here as a woman could get, yet she's the biggest villain in MGM history. *Home-wrecker!* We think back to Paramount's *One Hour with You* and its merry circle of adulterers. We think of Maurice Chevalier singing to us of his adventure with the embracingly risqué Mitzi—"Now, I ask you, what would you do?" We'd give in. He shrugs. "That's what I did, too!"

But this is sex-as-theft. MGM gives us the sacrament of marriage, the purity of trust, the clarity of child-raising. MGM gives us the wisdom of mothers, when Shearer's (*The Women*) mother advises her, "Keep still." Women must bear their hurt silently "to keep our men." (And note that Shearer's mother, Lucile Watson, also plays Robert Taylor's mother in *Waterloo Bridge*: oracle in residence.) MGM especially gives us the inviolable sharing, the mutual respect of American marital bonding—the Loy Effect, so to say. Another of The Women, Mary Boland, discoursing on the many husbands she has known and even had, tells Shearer, "I bet you picked *yours* for character." Shearer is startled, but agrees. That's what married life depends on, excellence of morals.

However much movie buffs may call *Grand Hotel* or *San Francisco* or *The Wizard of Oz* typical MGMs, this family-portraiture side of its output is very central to its post-Thalberg period. It explains, for instance, why MGM could not compete in film noir. The form's love of middle-class evil must have horrified Mayer; even an out-and-out noir source such as James M. Cain's *The Postman Always Rings Twice* yielded, in MGM's hands, one of the few noir titles (1946) notable for sunny lighting, fear of sex, and disgust with crime, virtually a Walt Disney noir. At times, MGM's domestic scene produces a great film —*Meet Me in St. Louis* (1944), for example, a most evocative nostalgia. At other times, the idealization of the American family comes off as agitprop, as in one of Mayer's favorite films, *The Human Comedy* (1943).

Directed by Clarence Brown and based on a story by William Saroyan, *The Human Comedy* stands to MGM's 1940s as something like *Dinner at Eight* stands to its 1930s, in cast, tone, design, theme.

MGM has reached its second generation, and in place of Marie Dressler, the Barrymores, Jean Harlow, and Wallace Beery, we get Mickey Rooney, Van Johnson, James Craig, Marsha Hunt, Fay Bainter, and Donna Reed. Only Frank Morgan is on hand from the old days, and he, typically, is an outsider in the tale, as an old drunken bachelor. In the world of *The Human Comedy*, the elect believe in temperance and relatives.

The setting is contemporary, in the San Joaquin Valley, mostly among members of the Macauley family. We open with the atrocious Butch Jenkins, his freckles as big as polka dots, contemplating a groundhog and waving at trains. Ah, the mysteries of life—the passing of the seasons (note groundhog as emcee of spring), the passing of man's temporal vanity (machinery breaks down but nature is endless). Later, Brown catches Jenkins at home, lying on the floor and staring at his mother, Fay Bainter, through the strings of her harp to ask life's major questions. Where is brother Van Johnson? (Away at war.) Where is Father? (Dead.) What is death? What is love? When are we going to rerelease *Grand Hotel* and get some real cinema going? By the time Bainter finishes cluing Jenkins into the epic cycle of love and death, the child is asleep; and he's not the only one.

The movie wakes up a considerable bit to look in on the rites of growing up—kids stealing apricots from a tree as the owner looks on in delight, a schoolboy's first crush and rivalry, soldiers picking up girls. (Amusingly, the three soldiers are Barry Nelson, Don DeFore, and Robert Mitchum.) And Brown's survey takes in some notable moments, as when telegram delivery boy Mickey Rooney, yet another of Bainter's sons, brings an annunciation of death to a Hispanic woman who can't read. Would Rooney oblige her? It's her son, of course, a casualty of war, and after Rooney stumbles through it, the poor woman takes it with a sadly dead-on calm, offers Rooney candy, sits on a rocker, and sings a lullaby as she weeps. Brown cuts to a young woman rocking a baby: life in the presence of death. Here, at least, this strange film lives up to the grand scale of its theme. It is not natural, not even falsely natural in the ease with which Dressler and Lionel Barrymore fence in discordant styles of shtick in *Dinner at Eight*, or in the touchingly overplayed dynamics of John Barrymore's death scene, a great actor declined into ham rising to greatness to play a ham. *The Human Comedy* is contrived in a contrived way. But some of it is quite genuinely felt, and this telegram scene is a prime instance. It is not readily forgotten.

Like religion, Golden Age movies help us deal with the fact of death, with the inevitability of the death of loved ones. *The Human Comedy* clearly intends to execute this office. It is filled with death. The late father Macauley narrates in voice-over and converses, as a ghost, with Bainter. Frank Morgan dies on the job, leaving Rooney to take down another telegram from the War Department—brother Van Johnson is dead. But life is as inevitable as death, and the film ends with Johnson's orphaned war buddy visiting the Macauleys to —we sense—take Johnson's place. Ghosts of father and big brother look on as Rooney brings the new Macauley into the house. "The end," observes the father, "is always a beginning." And so the movie . . . begins.

Mayer thought *The Human Comedy* as fine a picture as could be made. But his favorite project in all MGM was the *Andy Hardy* series, fifteen films made from 1937 to 1946, with one last try in 1958. Here we encounter Mayer's MGM at its ground-zero. The Hardys of Carvel, Idaho, are dreary white Protestants who make one feel good to be single, Jewish, or an axe murderer. No small-town cliché is neglected—the man-to-man father-son talks that, no matter what the subject, are always about their mutual affection; the chic Eastern girlfriend versus the loyal mid-American one; the mother thrown into terror by a telegram (and who can blame her, after *The Human Comedy*?); the maiden aunt who hangs on at the edges of things, answering the doorbell and making sensitive remarks at dinner; the patronizing view of adolescent interest in cars and copping a hot date for the prom; the noble Judge Hardy bucking township consensus on a controversial issue. This series isn't just corny and simplistic. It's insidious hogwash. It's blackmail. It's lies. Even a touching cameo by Jean Hersholt couldn't save it, though at least Judy Garland turns up in three of the films. Protagonist Mickey Rooney does a nice job with a stupid character. But does Mayer really think that American teenage boys should be saying "Gosh all hemlock"? Unbeknownst to Mayer, a more typical American teenage boy, and a Metro contractee, Jackie Cooper, was playing stud to Joan Crawford at the time. And is Lewis Stone Mayer's idea of the ideal, or even average, American father? That dourly self-righteous fat cat? A *judge*? How many of you, boys and girls, had a judge for a father? This series would have been better, I submit, with my own father, a college football hero, an OSS spy in World War II, a swank golfer, and a terrific guy. Moreover, he can speak fluent Polish and Russian and get ghetto kids to turn off their radios. Now, that's an American father.

The Hardy series began as something of an encore to MGM's successful filming of Eugene O'Neill's *Ah, Wilderness!* (1935), with substantial carryovers in casting—Lionel Barrymore as Our Father, Spring Byington as Dear Mother, Eric Linden as Big Brother, Rooney as Kid Brother, and Cecilia Parker as Sis. When the essentially unimportant picture jumped the box office, MGM proposed a sequel. Family series were a Hollywood convention—Fox had the Joneses and Universal, later, would carry the Kettles. Why not launch another? Switching to the cast that would more or less maintain the cycle, Metro upped the *Hardy* budget to promote the programmers as primary features. Interesting: here we find neither the Metro prestige nor its star system or polish, yet the *Hardy* series left its impression upon a generation. As Adrian might have said, Thalberg is over.

The *Hardy* era falls into the age of another key Metro form, "the MGM musical." This is usually reckoned around the Freed Unit— producer Arthur Freed's gang of writers, musicians, designers, choreographers, and directors—and thus runs from 1939, when Freed assisted Mervyn LeRoy on the production of *The Wizard of Oz*, into the late 1950s. On the contrary. MGM's musical wing is as old as the talkie. The first all-sound film, right at the start of 1929, was an MGM musical, *The Broadway Melody*.

This is an almost forgotten movie, datum more than a classic. It bears on this chapter, however, as an instance of how this pridefully superior studio tackled technical problems facing all Hollywood. Sound was the thing, and the musical, sound's most typical novelty, must be instituted. But what is a musical? Hollywood supposed that it was closely connected with New York, with its jive and juice and crabby sentimentality, as if song-and-dance were something that naturally occurs at the junction of Broadway and Forty-second Street. But how does one capture this feeling? By buying the rights to Broadway musicals, setting them up on sound stages, and turning the cameras? What about casting? Silent stars were having trouble just trying to talk, let alone sing. And there's all that difficulty with the microphones—won't the musical's inherent mobility make recording even harder? And when the singers do record . . . how do you explain where the orchestral accompaniment comes from? What if they're in a forest? A boat on a lake? On stage, anything goes, but movies are real.

The Broadway Melody was a Thalberg project—had to be, given its decisive potential. So once again we have the benefit of Hollywood's all-knowing, all-seeing genius. Sure, the first musical in Hollywood's history* will borrow its energy and point from Broadway. But why film a show, take art at second hand? Why not *tell about* Broadway in a backstager? There will be no problem about working in the songs and the accompanying band, for theatre people are always performing or rehearsing. As for casting, we'll bring Charles King over from New York; he sings and struts. We'll let Metro's own Anita Page play the girl he loves; she doesn't sing but with her looks she doesn't have to. And, as Page's sister who loves King in vain, we'll use Bessie Love, a Hollywood veteran and a natural strutter.

This appears to contradict Thalberg's belief in star power. But in *The Broadway Melody* it's the form itself that stars, the studio's ease in shaping and developing it. The 1929 original has been overshadowed by MGM's more elaborate *Broadway Melody* "sequels" of the middle and late 1930s with Eleanor Powell, also by Warner Brothers' Busby Berkeley backstagers, which reinvested MGM's format with an explosive realism. However, *The Broadway Melody* gave film an imperishable gift: the pre-recording of musical numbers.

Thalberg didn't like the rushes of an onstage scene, "The Wedding of the Painted Doll," and had it reshot. But hold. As the song's vocal is a voice-over by an unseen tenor, why drag the orchestra back to the soundstage? Why not simply play back the music, already tracked, as the dancers do their stuff? Then lightning struck. Why not let singers record their numbers first and, in filming, mime to the

---

*Depending on how one defines "musical." There had been silent musicals like von Stroheim's *The Merry Widow*, with a pit orchestra churning out the Lehár tunes; and Warners' part-talkies *The Jazz Singer* and *My Man* preceded *The Broadway Melody*. As vehicles for, respectively, Al Jolson and Fanny Brice, each offers five or six songs. However, this is all the music they offer —no one else in the cast takes part in the song-and-dance. *The Broadway Melody* was the first film in which musical elements ran through the action, the cast generally sharing in the responsibilities of the entertainment. That's what I call a musical.

pre-recorded track? Even the Warner Brothers, fathers of sound, had gone through the pain of recording and filming Jolson's and Brice's numbers on the spot, with the noisy camera frozen in its sound-proofed shack and the treacherous mike picking up hiccups in Pasadena. Thalberg freed the Hollywood musical from the tyranny of sound.

One thing MGM borrowed from Warner Brothers: the big number. Early musicals tended to adhere to Broadway conventions in musical staging—not in camera work, necessarily (remember those overhead shots in *The Cocoanuts*), but in choreography and production. After Busby Berkeley pushed open the "stage" in the title number of *42nd Street*, the Hollywood musical ceased trying to duplicate Broadway and began conceiving song-and-dance cinematically.

There is no big number in this sense in *The Broadway Melody*; everything is stage-possible, so to speak. One song, "Love Boat," doesn't move at all: a tableau. But Joan Crawford's big backstager, *Dancing Lady*, adopted the Berkeleyesque cinema Broadway; and the big numbers in Eleanor Powell's films emphasized grandeur of dimension: in the battleship finale of *Born to Dance* (1936); in "Your Broadway and My Broadway" in *The Broadway Melody of 1938* (1937), with its principals and chorus in white and black (Powell in black tails) trucking on a tiered stage before a huge *moderne* rendering of Manhattan skyscrapers and marquees; in the gigantic drums Powell dances on in *Rosalie* (1937).

Metro's finesse extended to technique as well, as in *Going Hollywood*'s title number. Marion Davies, Bing Crosby, and a horde of extras converge at Grand Central Station as Bing, slapping on a beret, boards the Twentieth Century Limited to zip off to movie fame. A big number is indicated, and, as always in the mid-1930s, the Albertina Rasch dancers are on hand to dress the Metro scene. But the dancers scarcely dance. What we see are travelers, reporters, and fans pushing and running in time to the music, with just a hint of display motion when a few ballerinas ride around on a luggage van. The number gets its momentum from a constant shifting of the picture, art deco zigzags shaping the dissolves. This is virtually a choreography of editing.

The MGM musical also maintained a classical connection, in the employment of opera singers as stars. This runs right through

Metro's history—or, rather, L. B. Mayer's. One thing must be said of this controversial mogul: he alone of his generation of studio chiefs genuinely liked good music. Others, such as David Selznick, just didn't get it. A few, like Samuel Goldwyn and Joe Pasternak, thought it commercially useful and an emblem of status. Mayer liked its classy wholesomeness, no doubt, but he responded to the melodies as well —and someone at the studio had ear enough to hire the most dynamic singers, not only the personable ones, good for film, but the stimulating ones, good for music. Lawrence Tibbett and Grace Moore, who got to Metro in the first years of sound, stand among America's most vivacious musicians, and though Tibbett's vogue fizzled quickly and Moore was not to make her mark in film till she tried Columbia in 1934, Metro kept the opera roster active. Ramon Novarro fell into operetta when his career ran into trouble, but his soft-grained tone was a disappointment after Tibbett's gala thunder. The studio snapped back by acquiring Jeanette MacDonald, another very outgiving singer. However, note the change in character from the Paramount MacDonald to the Metro MacDonald. From Lubitsch to Mayer. From woman to bride.

Lubitsch himself broke MacDonald in at Metro, with Chevalier (and such eccentrically Lubitschian support as Edward Everett Horton, Donald Meek, and Sterling Holloway), on *The Merry Widow* in 1934. It's a delightfully sexy occasion, a Thalberg project but so Paramount in style that we realize that Lubitsch put a great deal more on his projects than a mere "touch." Take this exchange of Chevalier and MacDonald at a table in Maxim's:

MACDONALD: Let go of my hand.

CHEVALIER: Stop kicking me.

MACDONALD: Stop pinching me.

(Two beats)

MACDONALD: Give me back my shoe.

The dialogue itself directly recalls *Trouble in Paradise*'s sex-is-theft dinner of thieves. More Lubitsch yet is the visual, for the camera merrily hovers on a two-shot framed entirely above the table: we watch the flirtation without being permitted to see it. Then Chevalier notices a Turk eying MacDonald and angrily escorts him out of the restaurant. For a capper, utter Lubitsch, Chevalier puts the Turk in a hansom cab and tells the driver, "Constantinople."

*The MGM musical before the Freed Unit, in its three basic
forms. First, the backstager:* Broadway Melody of 1940
*(above). Eleanor Powell and Fred Astaire prepare to film
their classic "Begin the Beguine" duet, perhaps the key
moment in the whole* Broadway Melody *series—though, if
Powell was the "Broadway Melody Girl," Astaire had spent
the Broadway Melody years over at RKO. Next (right), we
come to MGM's dance musical:* Rosalie. *Dance film was an
MGM genre even before Gene Kelly signed on. Somewhere
in there is Eleanor Powell, not to mention the Albertina
Rasch dancers, another MGM genre, like Kelly, imported
from Broadway. We should perhaps note a typical MGM*

(continued on page 160)

touch in the slight sense of overproduction in the presenta-
tion of the dance numbers. Above, the third MGM musical
genre, the operetta: New Moon *(1940). Built around estab-*
lished opera stars like Lawrence Tibbett or legit Broadway
singers like (as here) Jeanette MacDonald, the series eventu-
ally took to creating its own stars, such as Howard Keel,
Jane Powell, and Kathryn Grayson. Note New Moon's
elaborate décor. Broadway Melody *is a sharp, spare New*
York and the very size of Rosalie *is a vulgarity. But*
how tastefully thoughtful of MGM to paint the inside of
MacDonald's piano.

Once out of Lubitsch's care, however, the MGM MacDonald turned into steel froth, losing the slithery tact of her Chevalier days for a family-show aplomb, squeaky and haughty at once, that makes one wonder if she glows in the dark. It doesn't help that Nelson Eddy behaves like a stick of zwieback. This is MGM plugging the clammy, clean Hollywood that few but Mayer ever wanted. Only the music saves these films. The two stars sing the hell out of Victor Herbert, Rudolf Friml, Sigmund Romberg, Noël Coward, and Richard Rodgers. We could have done a lot worse.

The MacDonald–Eddy series juiced out in the early 1940s, but the opera wing held on, in Kathryn Grayson, Lauritz Melchior, Helen Traubel, Mario Lanza, Jane Powell. Now they sing opera, now they sing pop: reputation lies not in the repertory but in the voice. Just as MacDonald's most typical Metro bit was her Enchanting of the Population Through Her Way with a Song, Powell in *Athena* (1954) entrances stuffy Edmund Purdom and his Japanese houseboy with her coloratura. But Powell is a California weirdo—a health nut, and this was before the national acculturation of tofu and sprouts. Powell offers to mulch Purdom's peach trees, and asks for "wax paper, watermelon rinds, and fishheads." Purdom's fiancée smugly asks, "Wouldn't you rather have a cocktail?"

Athena is a strange movie; it seems to disapprove of everyone in it. Powell's physical-culture-minded family turn out to be brusque (grandfather Louis Calhern) or dim (grandmother Evelyn Varden) or mean (Powell's muscle-boy brothers). They're no better than Purdom's coterie, just healthier. Then Powell, at a party, dips into "Chacun le sait" from Donizetti's *La Fille du Régiment*—in the original French—and suddenly we know what MGM approves of in *Athena*.

Nevertheless, it is the Freed Unit that carries the heavy reputation among MGM's musicals. In his introduction to the two-volume *Cinema: A Critical Dictionary*, Richard Roud calls Freed's productions "the most glorious string of musicals in the history of the cinema." Granted, this string includes *Meet Me in St. Louis, Summer Holiday, Easter Parade, Singin' in the Rain,* and *Gigi.* But it also includes asininely virginal reductions of three of Broadway's steamiest shows, in *Panama Hattie, DuBarry Was a Lady,* and *Kismet*; a number of really tawdry films like *Take Me Out to the Ball Game, Pagan Love Song, Royal*

Wedding, and *The Belle of New York*; the irredeemably vulgar *Ziegfeld Follies*; and two cretinous songwriter bios, *Till the Clouds Roll By* and *Words and Music,* that not only fabricate virtually every detail of plot but debauch the work of, respectively, Rodgers and Hart and Jerome Kern in jarringly unstylish arrangements, reaching an apex in Frank Sinatra's singing of "Ol' Man River."* Does Roud really think this series superior to RKO's Astaire and Rogers films, or Paramount's Chevalier–MacDonalds, or Warners' Berkeley backstagers?

Apparently many analysts do, possibly because these musicals were the best that Hollywood was turning out in the years when these writers were growing up and getting their first taste of the exhilaration of musical comedy, of its energy and innocent wisdom and even passion. Whether because of geographical or cultural barrier, they had no access to the more sophisticated musicals of Broadway, and made their formative contact with this inspiring form in Freed's company. It would seem that the critic's acumen has never displaced this youthful enthusiasm—and that, as lifelong movie buffs, they never became more than cursorily acquainted with the theatre. One senses in their writing a very vague awareness of the complex technical development of American musical storytelling, a glancing familiarity with such as Oscar Hammerstein II, Agnes de Mille, or E. Y. Harburg but an endless fascination for Stanley Donen, Hermes Pan, and Ann Miller. Freed's backers cite his team's experimental dexterity as if Broadway had produced no *Show Boat, Of Thee I Sing, Music in the Air, Jubilee, Lady in the Dark,* or *Oklahoma!*—not to mention Hollywood's own achievements in the 1930s.

The Freed Unit showed its strength not in originality as much as in the freedom with which its artisans made use of tools invented by their predecessors. Freed's were state-of-the-art musicals, seldom experimental. Still, the best ones truly exploited this freedom, exceptional in the history of MGM and its regime of the producer. Freed, who spent the 1930s at the studio as lyricist to composer Nacio Herb Brown,[†] greatly respected the creative impulse, and not only lavished

*It's a commonplace that all Hollywood's backstage bios are phony. Wrong. A few are as vile as these two—Warners' Cole Porter piece, *Night and Day,* or *So This Is Love* (1953), in which Kathryn Grayson gutlessly impersonates the gutsy Grace Moore. But a Metro entry, *The Great Ziegfeld* (1936), gives us a taste of the showman's style and authentic duplications of his stars (Fanny Brice plays Fanny Brice); and Warners' *Yankee Doodle Dandy* (1942) revives the vaudeville and Broadway of George M. Cohan with dazzling accuracy.

[†]It is worth noting that, as songwriters, Freed and Brown worked in the most simplistic style

nurturing enthusiasm on his staff but supported them when studio heads threatened to interfere.

Freed's films impress with their diversity. RKO's dance musicals, Lubitsch's operettas, and Warners' backstagers were genuine series in their homogeneity of format. Freed's people bounced from fantasy to naturalism, antique Americana to modern-dress Europe, the Broadway adaptation to the Hollywood conception. A few elements are basic to the Unit: a constant drawing on the great Broadway songwriters, from Cohan and Berlin and Gershwin and Porter to Arlen and Bernstein and Lerner and Loewe; a pronounced use of dance; absolute habilitation of the "story" song (which characters simply burst into, rather than set up in a performing context, as they had to in the contemporary musicals made at Fox and Warner Brothers); and regulars Judy Garland, Gene Kelly, and Fred Astaire, as well as the Freed staffers.

However, the material itself varies as at no other studio at any time from Edison to the collapse of the Golden Age. One never quite gets a bead on Freed's series *as* a series; one must consult the whole abacus. Freed offers the unusual, for instance, in the fable-like *Cabin in the Sky* (1943). Yes, Freed took the property from Broadway, and, besides shredding and emending the score, turned a fantasy into a dream (as in *The Wizard of Oz*). Still, one wonders if any other producer would have bothered filming an all-black show that was an artistic success but lost money; indeed, Freed flourishes its credentials in the credits: "The Broadway musical play." Further praise to Freed for giving Lena Horne her best role in films and retaining the stupendous Ethel Waters from Broadway—her best role in films, too. The original was a bit gamey for Metro, yet Freed retains the spirit, as when Eddie "Rochester" Anderson asks Waters for a song, "the one you sang the first time we—" *"Joe!"* cries Waters. This is, after all, L. B. Mayer's MGM, so limited in openness of spirit that *Cabin*'s cast had to take lunch in the private dining room of L.B. himself till he could countermand some official's racism and integrate the studio commissary.

---

possible, Freed going for trite rhymes and images ("You were meant for me" followed by "I was meant for you" in *The Broadway Melody*'s big love song) and Brown observing primary chords and basic rhythm. Yet far from resenting his artistic superiors, Freed worshipped their genius. Among producers, a very unusual man.

Freed offers, secondly, first-rate composition of script and score, for instance in *Meet Me in St. Louis*, by no less than seven writers, the songs by Hugh Martin and Ralph Blane. Even before the project is handed to the director, Freed's people have the makings of a superb show—and a Mayer-era picture of family life, moreover, without the dowdy clichés of the *Andy Hardy* films or the insufferable racial patronization of *The Human Comedy*'s picnic scene. Even obvious points of sentimentalistic reference are reinvented here, drolly naturalized, as in the sweetly macabre character of the Smiths' youngest daughter (Margaret O'Brien), now adding another little corpse to her doll graveyard out in the backyard, now boldly throwing flour in the face of the neighborhood ogre for a ritual Halloween prank. The script establishes O'Brien's ghoulish whimsey so well that by the time she is called upon to perform an unbearably disarming number with Judy Garland at a party, or break into hysterics after "Have Yourself a Merry Little Christmas," these essentially show-biz set pieces seem reasonable, even lifelike. In a less well written movie, such moments, however well performed, would feel false and manipulative on repeated viewing. One reason why *Meet Me in St. Louis* is a classic is that repeated viewings endear these scenes—because the script, as written, makes them not only pleasing but necessary.

Another facet of Freed's production is the decorative vivacity—the emphasis on Technicolor, certainly, but also the adventurous nature of the view, as in *Ziegfeld Follies*' prologue of animated puppets or *Yolanda and the Thief*'s almost Daliesque dream ballets. Most splendid of all, surely, is *The Pirate* (1948), a Garland–Kelly teaming with a Cole Porter score and a Caribbean setting. Vincente Minnelli directed all three of these exemplary films—*Cabin in the Sky, St. Louis,* and *The Pirate*. But *The Pirate*, far more than the other two, reminds us that Minnelli began, on Broadway, as a designer. This film is a riot of sights, colors, eccentricities of costume, and brandishings of poster art, from Garland's tam-o'-shanter and her friends' competitive hat style of early-middle Carmen Miranda, in the opening scene, to the Trinidadian tank tops and S & M biceps rings that Kelly runs around in later on. "You fill the eye," the local viceroy tells Kelly at his hanging. So many of these bloodthirsty pirates look, he says, "like bookkeepers."

There are no bookkeepers in *The Pirate*—the whole enchanting movie fills the eye. Every shot is inflected, tinted, shaped—a hotel bed of wicker weaving, a dominoed tunic, balconies with double shutters (wood, then cane); Kelly entering the film on a ship's cargo crane and flying up a rope one-handed (the other bears a torch) to let out the pirate Macoco's savage screech; Kelly trying to mesmerize Garland with a spinning mirror and accidentally hypnotizing Walter Slezak, Garland's fiancé and lo, the real Macoco. This saves Kelly from the noose and subverts the Mayer Effect in that it is Slezak who has been jawing off about the peace and safety of the home throughout the film and Slezak who is the thief and killer.* And note that while *The Pirate*'s script is sound and at times very funny, Porter is way off form here. It is, at heart, the look of the film that drives it, its atmosphere that gives it . . . atmosphere.

To appreciate the Freed Unit at its best, we must consider the collapsed state of the film musical in this era. Most studios had given up on all but second-feature genre stuff, and Fox's Betty Grable series, for all its dash, had none of Freed's variety. Let's look at two coeval top-of-the-line Technicolor musicals side by side, Paramount's *Lady in the Dark* (1944) and Freed's *Good News* (1947), both adaptations from Broadway. *Good News*, a conventional college show, is older— Metro had filmed it in 1930 in a fairly responsible version. *Lady in the Dark*, dating from 1941, is highly unconventional, less a musical than a play with three operatic dream sequences and one song. (*Lady*'s novelty shocked from its first moments, for the curtain rose as if on a straight play, without an overture or curtain music. As the Kurt Weill–Ira Gershwin score was the talk of the town, audiences were pleasantly bamboozled.) The two shows bear another crucial difference. *Good News* calls for some half-dozen song-and-dance principals; a little talent and a little more energy carry them through. *Lady in the Dark* calls for a star, and a unique one; it was written for Gertrude Lawrence, possibly *the* unique musical star Broadway ever had, and was so built around her that when her contract ran out the show closed, though still doing good business—and it has never been revived.

---

*Kelly comes through here, too, in an inadvertent defiance of MGM's love of nice grammar and corrected accents. Listen carefully when Kelly says the word "first" and you'll hear a good solid urban-Irish "foist." This is also one of the few Kelly films in which he does not play most of his scenes in an audience-eating grin.

Freed's *Good News* is nicely cast, though with Peter Lawford, June Allyson, Pat Marshall, Joan McCracken, and Ray McDonald it counts more Metro-contract personalities than true song-and-dancers. It does, however, have some great dance numbers (by Robert Alton) and retains a goodly amount of the original score (more, in fact, than the 1930 film did), cunningly rewriting or expanding them to help nudge the story along. "Lucky in Love," for instance, an up-tempo ballad duet in the stage show, becomes an ensemble number on a sorority-house porch. All the principals chime in, each with characteristic lyrics and business, McCracken dodging one swain and teasing another, Marshall shooting Lawford down with the French word *"incorrigible"*—thus setting up some plot development when Allyson coaches Lawford in French. And *that* yields a new number written by Freedians Roger Edens, Betty Comden, and Adolph Green, "The French Lesson." We see the Unit ingeniously at work, respecting its source while improving it according to new standards of composition.

Paramount's *Lady in the Dark* not only humiliates its source, but isn't even a good example of what it tried to be instead—a Mitchell Leisen sex comedy with music. The setting, in the offices of a fashion magazine, recalls *No Time for Love*, Ray Milland plays the approach-avoidance love match that Claudette Colbert so often dueled with, and Leisen himself directs. But Weill and Gershwin are so cruelly dismantled that the show's most famous song, "My Ship," is more quoted than sung; and Ginger Rogers is no Gertrude Lawrence. Consider: the protagonist is a woman who believes herself dreary and plain. In dreams she sees herself as dynamic and glamorous, the toast of sophisticates. Thus the show's limiting of the song-and-dance to the dreams—only there can the show explode into the all-basic effervescence of American musical comedy, the bracing show-biz audacity that shows us how it feels to be excitingly attractive. Paramount does give us some spectacular décor in the dreams, but no effervescence, no audacity. The rather ordinary *Good News* gives us more sheer excitement in any given ten minutes than the whole of *Lady in the Dark* does in one hundred.

This, then, is the Freed Unit at its best—unusual forms, excellence of composition, visual opulence, and a dependable, even brilliant level of performance. But the Unit at its worst is vulgar and lifeless—*Show Boat* (1951), say, so big yet so empty, big with multitudes yet empty of feeling. Captain Andy's unpretentious little river theatre arrives with what looks like a cast of thousands aboard (and of course everyone's got a tambourine). Yet such key moments as the forced departure of Ava Gardner and Robert Sterling because she is part-black go for nothing.

Or take *Brigadoon* (1954), frequently excoriated for the studio phoniness of its lochs and glens. A budget cutback held director Minnelli from shooting in Scotland, but that doesn't excuse the manufactured heather and the all too artfully tumbled rocks. Authentic location shooting would have been even more difficult on *The Wizard of Oz*, but that didn't stop Metro from designing a persuasive alternate in Culver City. Even worse than the décor is the idiot simpering of the Brigadoon townspeople, including a load of children who jump and point at nothing or stand frozen, looking on with sightless eyes like body snatchers. At the end of "Down on MacConnachy Square," the whole crowd takes the fade-out leaping and waving like Munchkins seeing Dorothy off—and listen carefully to hear, I swear to God, a brief clip of the 1939 Munchkin squeals spliced into *Brigadoon*'s sound track. All right, it's market day and Brigadoon has survived another magical century. But this is grotesque.

Perhaps the Freed Unit was feeling the pinch that all Hollywood felt in the 1950s, the loss of company-town euphoria that accompanied the collapse of the studio system. Metro did not achieve reorganization until 1959, but it began shrinking its contract list at about 1950, even dropping the King, Clark Gable, to his fury. Still, Freed or Freed-influenced personnel produced *Singin' in the Rain* (1952), *Seven Brides for Seven Brothers* (1954), and *Gigi* (1958), respectively upholding the Freed zing and artistry and decorative elegance. But Freed dropped many a dud on us in the 1950s, especially the most overpraised item in his canon, *The Bandwagon* (1953).

A host of theatre veterans made this one—authors Comden and Green, director Minnelli, choreographer Michael Kidd, and set designer Oliver Smith, using the songs of Arthur Schwartz and Howard Dietz. So why is this the only backstager in which it feels as if they're putting on a movie rather than a show? Jack Buchanan plays a sort of Noël Coward, an all-purpose entertainer. Why do we meet him enacting Oedipus Rex? Song-and-dance men don't play Sophocles. Out of town with a flop show, Fred Astaire, Nanette Fabray, and Oscar Levant join "the kids" at a party. Very *politique*. But this never happens. Out of town, the honchos don't party with the kids. The flop musical, an adaptation of *Faust,* is thrown out and that good old Hollywood standby, the revue of entirely unconnected numbers, is put together overnight. That isn't possible. And why does the marquee of the theatre in which the gang plays New York read "New York Opening Tonight" in lights? Are we supposed to believe that New Yorkers need a theatre marquee to tell them where they are? The misrepresentation of backstage life is so insistent that the tiniest details smell bad, as when Astaire jives about the great theatre past on a studio mock-up of Forty-second Street that looks like the alleyway of a convent. Wow, there's the Selwyn, Astaire cries, where Noël and Gertie played *Private Lives.* No, *Private Lives* played the Times Square Theatre, just east of the Selwyn. And lo, Fred goes on, there's the New Amsterdam, where Astaire had a hit for "a year and a half." I presume Comden and Green are referring to *The Band Wagon* itself, the only show that took Astaire into Ziegfeld's flagship house. It ran for 260 performances, about seven months.

Worse than this enthusiastic misrepresentation of Broadway is the attack on the ambitious musicals that had been making history before this film was made. Comden and Green, unreconstructed farceurs till very late in their career, picture the audience leaving the New Haven tryout of Buchanan's *Faust* musical in a trance. That's how bad it was. Because it was serious. What are Comden and Green saying? That musicals shouldn't be serious? That *Show Boat, Lady in the Dark, Carousel,* and *The King and I* are a bad idea? Or no—that pretentiously serious shows are. Bold shows. *Faust* musicals. Art. Like—to jump ahead in time—*The Golden Apple, Candide, Fiddler on the Roof, Follies, Pacific Overtures.* What do Comden and Green think a musical should be? Jack Buchanan and Oscar Levant? (No: the show *A Doll's Life* [1982], a beautifully written [by Comden, Green, and Larry Grossman] and staged [by Hal Prince] amplification of Ibsen that was savaged by critics with a *Bandwagon* mentality.)

The Bandwagon isn't the worst of "the MGM musical." For just as the studio had developed its own musical genres with Eleanor Powell's backstagers and the MacDonald–Eddy operettas, so were there other MGM musicals during the Freed years. Viewing them tells us how far the studio had fallen from the prestige and glamour that counted so heavily during Thalberg's reign and that Freed, for the most part, upheld. There is a certain authority implicit in Freed's bringing Astaire and Garland together, at the top of their form, in *Easter Parade* (1948), backing them up with some seventeen Berlin songs; and a festive enchantment in watching how keenly they blend. If Ginger Rogers gave Astaire someone to romance and Eleanor Powell gave him someone to dance with, Garland brings out his gladness of talent. Seldom did he seem so happy to perform.

But what authority or enchantment is there in *Torch Song* (1953), a backstager as ersatz as *The Bandwagon*? At least Freed's film has Astaire, Nanette Fabray, and Cyd Charisse; this one has Joan Crawford, unbelievably, as a gala musical-comedy star. Never was a "singer" so dubbed, never a "dancer" so perfunctory, never an "actress" so dreadfully intent. Autobiographical details unnerve us— the checks for sponging relatives, the careful love of fans, the furious, self-ratifying strength of will. This is Metro trashing its past, shaming the glamour.

Yet more revealing is Joe Pasternak's production of *The Opposite Sex* (1956), a remake of *The Women* with all the best lines and business cleaned away to make room for atrociously overproduced numbers. (One begins with the plucking of twelve pink double basses.) Even the color is garish, everything tending to Vegas lounge-act green. Bringing the men into the picture is a novelty . . . but Leslie Nielsen and Jeff Richards? The women are even less telling—and remember, the original had Norma Shearer, Rosalind Russell, Joan Crawford, Paulette Goddard, Mary Boland, and Marjorie Main, among others. Dolores Gray misses entirely the mitigating dizziness of Russell's bitchery; Gray just bitches. Joan Collins has none of the menacing hot that Crawford brought to the tramp role, and Agnes Moorehead gets nothing out of a role that made Boland immortal. June Allyson is pleasant enough, but Shearer—even without a man to play to—made us feel how desperately important marriage can be to a woman. Allyson has but one good moment, in her confrontation with Collins. "When Stephen doesn't like what I wear," Collins purrs, "I take it off." And Allyson cracks her a good one right across the face.

With the general collapse of the studio setup, it was the Freed Unit that played MGM's last cards of power and polish. Ironically enough, Freed's influence was not far-reaching, for other studios couldn't find fit counterparts for his artisans. Nor, surely, would they have wanted to sponsor a virtually independent unit that might turn out *Meet Me in St. Louis* one year but *Yolanda and the Thief* the next.

When Paramount decided to release a musical in the MGM style, it didn't imitate the Freed approach but simply brought Freed's staff to Paramount—director Stanley Donen, producer Roger Edens, orchestrator Conrad Salinger, conductor Adolph Deutsch, star Fred Astaire . . . even vocal arranger Kay Thompson, who also plays a sizable part (her only good one in a very spotty film career). The film was *Funny Face* (1957), somewhat akin to *The Bandwagon* in its use of an old show's title, its star, and its songwriters' catalogue in general —this time it's the Gershwins—but otherwise running up an original.

Funny Face, then, was not typical of Hollywood but of Freed: exceptional to Hollywood. This kind of musical had even become exceptional to MGM. Thalberg was dead, Mayer was out, and in the 1950s the studio they built mostly made humdrum, noisy, stupid films. There were grisly remakes of classics that, like *The Opposite Sex*, suggested that the day of classics was over. Yet there was Freed, at his summit in *Gigi* as late as in 1958 and planning, well into the 1960s, to make *Say It with Music*, a celebration of Irving Berlin. New blood was running the show now; the project never came off. And that was the end of Metro–Goldwyn–Mayer as a style. The studio had outlived its founding mannerists.

Not by long.

The smallest of the studios that mattered stood at Sunset and
La Brea in West Hollywood. Above, the genius of the place,
in City Lights *(1931).*

SMALL STUDIOS

The Independent

So much of Golden Age Hollywood history is written by ana-
lysts of big talent and big power that we lose sight of the panorama of
the movies. We lore up on Lubitsch, relishing the way he makes a
Paramount at MGM in *The Merry Widow*. We parse Griffith, who
spans the ages from Biograph's two-reelers to the talkies. We shake
our heads at Adolph Zukor's encircling of the theatre circuits, at L. B.
Mayer's pedantic sentimentalism. We begin to think entirely in
terms of the exceptional.

This is not Hollywood history. This is the index of what we
admire today. The nation went to a wider range of films as it assimilated the cinema—as it helped the business establish patterns of char-

acter typing and narrative bias that were to last for the better part of a century. Yet the curious may screen *The Great Train Robbery* (1903) and a Griffith Biograph—*The New York Hat* (1912), say, with martyred Little Mary and wise Lionel Barrymore and the Gish sisters as merry villagers—and, okay, that's the First Era of Silent Film: on to *The Birth of a Nation*. Two Eras later, we catch a Douglas Fairbanks adventure and a Lillian Gish MGM and it's on to talkies.

But this was the age in which America adopted cinema as its first entertainment, killing vaudeville, hobbling radio, and placing the theatre in jeopardy. Decisive art was churned out here; the studio factories changed the world. Yet whole chapters of the epic are missing. A warehouse fire destroyed the bulk of the first two decades of the Fox archives; this includes the early work of John Ford.

So, as we consider the respective styles of Paramount and Warner Brothers, MGM and RKO, Fox and Universal, we must remember that these were simply the overwhelming outgrowths of an industry founded on small operations. We know how American Biograph worked, because Griffith started at Biograph and Griffith bears scrutiny. However, few if any historians have a word to say about Biograph's patents colleague Vitagraph; yet Vitagraph lasted till 1925, when it was subsumed by Warner Brothers. Vitagraph must have been doing something right. Even First National, the only studio strong enough to challenge Paramount on Paramount's terms of star and theatre-chain power, is seldom mentioned—because, again, Warner Brothers took it over; and who needs another silent output to worry about? Bury it. So Colleen Moore, First National's Queen of the Lot and one of the biggest stars of the 1920s, is passed over and Louise Brooks gets credit for the flapper bangs that Moore originated.

The main reason for this haphazard scanning of the studio system in silent years is silence itself. Only the elite aficionado bothers even to wonder how dumb art made such eloquent history; and most of that art is lost in the first place. Where there wasn't a warehouse fire there is vault rot. Here's another sad story. Talkies cost more than silents, not only in terms of equipment and restaffing the firm but in the extra time involved in writing the scripts and smoothing out the technology. The added costs threw many small units out of business, and most of those that held on went under in 1931, 1932, and 1933, when the Depression economy caught up with movie attendance.

The small studios that did survive tell us one thing about Hollywood moviemaking: the most obvious difference between disrepute and prestige lies in one's budget. For the "Poverty Row" lots dealt largely in the forms and characters that the big lots favored, only on a vastly smaller scale—one so small that the poverty A's can scarcely compete with the big-lot B's. In this labor-intensive industry, a squeezed budget promises failures in quality at every step of production, virtually every setup of the camera. It didn't matter much in the western, a basic product of the quickie lot, or in the super-hero serials run up strictly for the kiddie matinee. But the "cheap and quick" approach seems passing strange in films designed to compete with the major studios in, say, Monogram's *Jane Eyre* or Majestic's *The Scarlet Letter*, both in 1934, just after RKO's *Little Women* and just before MGM's *A Tale of Two Cities*. Moreover, RKO has Cukor and Hepburn, MGM Ronald Colman's Sydney Carton and some epic crowd scenes of Revolutionary Paris. The obvious difference is size of budget, yes. But the essential difference is time, because time liberates talent.

Truly, the westerns and serials were dreadful, but they played to an audience of such low expectations that the westerns' cliché-bound plots and the serials' monkey-doodle nonsense were forgivable, perhaps even attractive. The small lots' more ambitious fare baffles, because it so consistently lacks ambition. At times, the small studios seem to be following practices laid down deep in the past, as in these adaptations of classic lit, a staple of the two-reeler days. At other times, the small studios imitate their big brothers, as in their exploitation of diminishing stars abandoned by the majors but still good for one last waltz. Mae Murray attempted her comeback at Tiffany after L. B. Mayer put his kibosh on her; Kay Francis washed up her fading career at Monogram; and it was Colleen Moore who played Hester Prynne in Majestic's *The Scarlet Letter*.

By far the most appetitive of the small lots was Republic, especially in knockoffs of the big-lot formats. Republic, under mogul Herbert J. Yates, was where Louise Brooks made a western with John Wayne; where Ramon Novarro, to his eternal discomfort, starred in a spoof of the Great Lover he himself had personified in his glory at MGM, in *The Sheik Steps Out* (1937). Republic was where Gene Autry and Roy Rogers built their careers as singing cowboys, not to mention lovely, skating Vera Hruba Ralston (Mrs. Yates), something of a Sonja Henie without acting ability, if you get my drift.

Republic eventually absorbed most of the smaller studios, and expanded its budget to become something of a minor major, though it continued to release the children's serials and weekend westerns that would have embarrassed the big lots. Then too, Republic's more important features often showed the makeshift nature of quickie moviemaking. Even when Yates extended himself to hire people the public had heard of lately for something akin to a big-lot entry, his pictures never quite connect. It's not that Republic is too imitative; it's that Republic isn't imitative enough. These movies keep forgetting how they're supposed to work.

Manhattan Merry-Go-Round (1937) is typical, something like the revuish backstagers that Fox was turning out then. Hollywood's prejudices may navigate along budgetary lines—the more you spend, the greater you are—but now we learn that prestige needs more than money, more than the time that money can buy. *Manhattan Merry-Go-Round* is atrocious. It's not a juicy laff riot of gaffes and spills, just risibly incompetent. The director, Charles F. Riesner, was a longtime B-unit specialist at MGM. (He got hold of real stars but once, in *The Hollywood Revue of 1929*, as Crawford, Shearer, Gilbert, Keaton, and company, busy on other pictures, had to film their guest spots at night, when Clarence Brown and Jack Conway had gone home and Riesner stayed on to oblige.) The cast is not wholly unrespectable— Phil Regan, Leo Carrillo, Ann Dvorak, with various guest check-ins from the likes of Ted Lewis, Cab Calloway, and Kay Thompson. The plot premise is workable: gangster Carrillo takes over a recording studio and sends his thugs out to drag in talent while singer Regan and secretary Dvorak do a romance.

At Fox, with Gregory Ratoff, Rudy Vallee, and Alice Faye, plus the usual Fox olio specialties, it would have run on sheer energy. But Republic has no energy; and every choice is wrong. Joe Di Maggio turns up for no reason other than to cue in World Series footage, which he remarks on in stilted voice-over. Carrillo, who usually played a "Nick the Greek" sort at the big studios, goes Italian here, complete with an old-country mother who slaps him around. Yet Carrillo makes no attempt to disguise his Hispanic accent. Tamara Geva, a ballet dancer who didn't sing, plays an opera singer (who

The thrill of Republic! Here's Vera Hruba Ralston in
Murder in the Music Hall *(1946), and you can see how*
thrilled they all are to be in on it. Rumor hath it that Vera
Hruba went to her genius of the place, mogul Herbert Yates,
and begged him to raise Music Hall's *budget by ten or*
twelve dollars so she could star in a real spectacle. Note Vera
Hruba's skates.

doesn't dance). Surely this is not the stuff a musical is made of, especially when obvious line flubs are printed, or when MGM's use of *Les Huguenots*' first-act finale, drafted earlier that year for Jeanette MacDonald in *Maytime*, is violated with a cheap copy for a heavily dubbed Geva.

How can one film make so many mistakes? If there were life on Mars, and diplomatic exchanges were made, and a party of earthlings flew up to officiate at a Martian Film Festival, and if the Martians had hospitably filmed an *hommage* to the late-1930s Fox backstager, they might have come up with something like *Manhattan Merry-Go-Round*. Like Mars itself, it is on one hand rather near, and on the other a great long distance away. Sometimes the difference is not only budget and time but craft.

Nevertheless. Through husbanding his resources, Yates built up Republic's budget during Hollywood's boom war years, till he could hire John Ford to direct Republic's own John Wayne, the excellent Maureen O'Hara, and a dazzling assemblage of Dublin's Abbey Theatre Players in *The Quiet Man* (1952). This is a superb film and—as Hollywood gasps—the Oscar winner for Best Direction. Republic is no longer strictly a quickie hostel. There's Fred MacMurray and Victor McLaglen beside the somewhat inevitable Vera Hruba Ralston* in *Fair Wind to Java* (1953), cheesy-looking and idiotically written but at least a working of a genre instead of—as is *Manhattan Merry-Go-Round*—a unique fiasco. And Nicholas Ray's *Johnny Guitar* (1954) claims a cult, as a sort of western's western with a cast drawn from the great on the downswing, the never-quite-starred, and miscellaneous schmengies: Joan Crawford, Sterling Hayden, Scott Brady, Mercedes McCambridge, Ward Bond, Ernest Borgnine, and John Carradine. It just doesn't sound like garbage; and it isn't. It's a great deal more securely run than *Fair Wind to Java* but lacks the genius of *The Quiet Man*. A fair effort: typical of a studio that rose from quickie obscurity but did not truly tip into the majors.

One quickie lot did—Columbia. And it did so because the essential difference between the majors and the minors was not money, time, or craft, but talent. Talent has craft, talent makes time, talent finds money. Some analysts might say that money, in Hollywood,

---

*Ralston might be called Republic's Queen of the Lot if only because of her marriage to mogul Yates. However, quickie lots lack the acting challenges and production enhancements that provision a Queen's regime.

was talent. Not true. The reason for Columbia's graduation from quickie to major was a director who worked for peanuts in order to command his films autonomously. This was Frank Capra, destined to be one of Hollywood's greatest self-defining creators. One would call him absolute auteur but for Robert Riskin, who wrote what Capra filmed; and plot and dialogue matter in Capra as much as iconography of character—whereas in von Sternberg or Ford, iconography of character is everything.

Columbia's mogul, Harry Cohn, was something of a self-defining talent himself. Almost all moguls were difficult in one way or another, but Cohn seemed to relish being the rudest and meanest, a cheat of cheats.* Columbia began in the Third Era of Silent Film, like most of the post-Edison studios run by a Jewish businessman who had fallen into cinema through respect of the potential profits rather than through a love of movies. But no other major-studio-to-be started as small as Columbia did. Zukor of Paramount began assembling important stars, skillful directors, and theatre chains from day one; Universal opened up the biggest lot in Hollywood within five years of its founding as the little patents-baiting IMP Company; Metro and Goldwyn were both major firms before the merger into MGM; William Fox set out to build his empire much as Zukor did; and RKO was from the first a studio with a strong sense of destiny. Only Warner Brothers started as unpretentiously as Columbia, and even Warners sought out a few important stars (such as John Barrymore) or events (such as the Vitaphone "talking" picture) with which to distinguish itself—not to mention its absorption of rival studios.

Columbia, uniquely, started small and, for a time, stayed small. It was worse than small: cheap, dingy, and heartless. "A riffraff of a place," Frank Capra noted when he first saw it. But Cohn had a belief in independence rare in this supervisor-heavy industry: no supervision. He himself answered to no money bosses in the East (as even L. B. Mayer had to) and let his staff make their pictures with the freedom the pioneers of Old Hollywood had enjoyed. Just do it, says Cohn, and if it makes money you can do another one, and if it loses money you're fired.

Cohn's laissez-faire gave Columbia fluidity, with the power to

---

*In a famous filmtown joke, the death of this most hated of moguls calls up the most heavily attended funeral of the age. Thousands of his employees and colleagues have come—not to mourn him. As the jest tells, "They wanted to make sure he was dead."

expand the budget from utter meanness to deep-pocket production to rival the majors. Like most quickie lots, Columbia was always ready to grab a name at marked-down prices—John Gilbert made his last film, *The Captain Hates the Sea* (1934), at Columbia, two years before his death. And Cohn's sharp business sense allowed him even greater leeway, in the hiring of still-prominent stars whose scenes would be "bunched"—shot consecutively, out of order—to allow Cohn to pay the star off after one or two weeks' work instead of pumping out his salary through the run of shooting. Better yet, Cohn bunched the budget around his bankable protégés, giving their films respectable productions while holding the rest to the usual small outlay. Thus Columbia rose to greatness on the strength of Frank Capra in the 1930s, then on Rita Hayworth in the 1940s.

Looking at early Columbias, it's hard to envision the studio power that would eventually produce *Death of a Salesman* (1951), *From Here to Eternity* (1953), or *Picnic* (1956). These are adaptations of titles in theatre and fiction, films with important stars, propositions of some expense. Dropping in on *Platinum Blonde* (1931), a Capra–Riskin collaboration with Loretta Young, Robert Williams, and Jean Harlow, we find a true quickie, saved only by Riskin's ear and Capra's ingenuity. The plot had already served many a silent, though it suggests the screwball comedies of the 1930s—playboy embarrasses his fancy family with a showgirl girlfriend; fast-talking reporter exposes story, romances playboy's sister. What's wrong with this movie is its cast. None of the leads is apt in the no-rehearsal, just-do-it pace of quickie shooting. Young is hopeless. Harlow, well ahead of the days when MGM's troubleshooting directors and photographers would develop her gifts, is a distinctly artificial heiress, not least when ushering the reporter into the "liberry." This reporter is supposed to be a cynosure—women falling all over him and men crowding around his restaurant table. But in Williams we get a pear-shaped goon whose idea of spontaneity is to say "Huh" in about eighteen different inflections, mostly during other people's lines.

The use of leading men of uncomely charisma is a historical quickie problem—think of the John Agars and Whit Bissells of the post–Studio Age. Poor visual and aural proofreading is another of the quickie's faux pas—Harlow's "liberry" in *Platinum Blonde*, or the telegram in Capra's *The Miracle Woman* (1931) addressed to New York's Bleeker Street; it should be *Bleecker.* On the other hand, *The Miracle Woman* shows a very promising Capra, especially in his work with Barbara Stanwyck as the eponymous heroine, the daughter of a minister driven to death trying to put the spirit of Christ into Sunday Christians. In a kind of revenge, Stanwyck takes over the family concern as a big-money revivalist, her meetings a clear reference to the theatrical Foursquare Gospel of Aimee Semple McPherson. Veteran Capra-watchers will note the director's characteristic approach-avoidance response to leadership cults; his populism needs a powerful hero yet fears a hero's power. More relevant to this chapter is Capra's growing narrative confidence, his rapport with Stanwyck and even with the far less gifted David Manners. We get a few pictorial flourishes here, too, particularly in a marvelous scene in which Manners entertains Stanwyck with toys, a clown that plays "The Farmer in the Dell" on a xylophone and a dancing black man worked by hand. Pausing to frame Manners's and Stanwyck's relaxed intimacy, Capra cuts to a wild party of Stanwyck's cynical associates, prancing in costumes—including a clown and dancer to match the toys.

The turning point, for Capra but also for Columbia and Harry Cohn, was *It Happened One Night* (1934). The very presence here of Clark Gable and Claudette Colbert throws us off our hunt, glamorizes the quickie lot. Surely it can't have been all *that* riffraff with these two on hand. On the contrary—this was Poverty Row at its direst: except when Cohn's wonder boy Capra was directing. At that, Capra had yet to produce the zany elegies on the American spirit, the *Deeds–Smith–John Doe* cycle that was to make him notable and culminate, after he left Columbia and went independent, in *It's a Wonderful Life.*

It Happened One Night was to have been just another Capra quickie, like *Platinum Blonde* or *The Miracle Woman.* But Gable had been acting up, and MGM sent him to Columbia on what we might call admonitory loan-out. Colbert was on vacation from Paramount; Capra wheedled, bribed, and bunched her into the schedule. The film's classic status began at the ensuing Oscar banquet, when the film, Capra, Riskin, Gable, and Colbert all won Oscars. This was Hollywood's first grand sweep, full house, and it not only convinced

Cohn to diversify his exchequer to compete with the majors* but helped found screwball comedy, a substantial sub-repertory of which was produced at Columbia: *Twentieth Century* (1934), *Theodora Goes Wild* (1936), *Mr. Deeds Goes to Town* (1936), *The Awful Truth* (1937), *Holiday* (1938), *You Can't Take It with You* (1938), *His Girl Friday* (1940), and *Too Many Husbands* (1940).

In fact, counting only the key screwball films—those most seminal or definitive—Columbia was virtually the studio of screwball. Interestingly, its nearest rival in the form, RKO (with such influential entries as *The Animal Kingdom, Down to Their Last Yacht, Bringing Up Baby,* and *My Favorite Wife*), was also smaller than most of the majors. A few even smaller lots donated important titles: Pathé's *Holiday* (the one Columbia remade with Katharine Hepburn and Cary Grant), Roach's *Topper*, and Selznick's *Nothing Sacred*.

None of the big studios really extended itself in screwball, despite their relatively sizable production schedules. Again keeping to key films: Universal left only *My Man Godfrey*, and MGM, though it honored the genre's picturesque characters and farcical plotting in, respectively, *The Thin Man* and *Libeled Lady*, did not truly encompass the form till *The Philadelphia Story* in 1940, after the screwball era had peaked. Fox and Warner Brothers never got the hang of the form. Paramount, with *Design for Living* (on the bohemian life), *Three Cornered Moon* (in a house of crazy relatives), and *Easy Living* (a working girl solves a rich family's problems), touched on important elements of the genre. But otherwise Paramount sublimated screwball in the Leisen and Sturges comedies. This was, in its essence, Columbia's game.

Unlike the backstage musical, the western, or the monster horror, screwball comedy isn't immediately self-defining by setting or characters. It is allotropic, made of so many parts that there is no absolute screwballer as *42nd Street* is the absolute backstager, *She Wore a Yellow Ribbon* the absolute cavalry-post western, or *Frankenstein* the absolute monster picture. Screwball is usually a contemporary court-

*Taking the five top Oscars at once is quite some feat, but for a Poverty Row lot to do it was a marvel. None of the other minors had copped as much as a single nomination, other than in the short subject. Consider, too, that the Oscar year of *It Happened One Night* also gave Columbia seven nominations for Grace Moore's vehicle, *One Night of Love*, including citations for Best Film, Best Director, and Best Actress and a special award for adventurous sound-recording technique. After all this, Columbia was a major whether Cohn liked it or not. He liked it.

ship tale with a witty script that favors the fashionable classes and instructs us to enjoy life in our own way rather than observe rules on love and work laid down by others. This outline bends, in one film or another, to crucial variations: to a confrontation of leadership and working classes, or of an ambitious worker and a playhound; to the romance of two strangers or the reunion of a divorced couple; to a fondness for the idle rich or an exposure of them; even to developing the "enjoy life" theme into a philosophy of outright rebellion against the existing social contract.

Elements of screwball informed literally hundreds of Hollywood comedies, from about 1932 to 1943, so the form stayed elastic and vital. It is instantly recognizable, yes: by its contradictions, exceptions, mutations. There were screwball musicals, screwball mysteries, screwball melodramas, even—in *Mr. Deeds Goes to Town*—a screwball noir. Some screwballers were definitive yet unique, like Roach's *Topper*, one of the form's most potent advocates of the easy life among the reckless rich but unusual because its advocates die in a car crash and spend half the film as ghosts. Some screwballers were almost wholly imitative, like Roach's *Merrily We Live*, embarrassingly derivative of Universal's *My Man Godfrey*. Perhaps the first decisive statements of the aesthetic were made in *Holiday* and *The Animal Kingdom*, in 1930 and 1932 respectively. Both, significantly, were based on plays by Philip Barry, whose favorite theme was the conflict between quasi-bohemian vitality and stuffy conformism among the rich. (That is, among those who have the social advantage of being able to choose their framing culture.) This conflict, the basis of screwball, had to be redecorated before screwball could be called complete, for Barry lacks the energy, the mobility (his plays hold their ground in a single set), and even the oddball assistants we love in *Bringing Up Baby* and *You Can't Take It with You*. But his milieu and theme generated the new form—even if Barry's rich were a little too gravely articulate for the movie public, who preferred the comic plutocrat, like the millionaire in *City Lights* who when drunk befriends Charlie Chaplin and when sober throws him aside; or, in talkies, the Mary Boland–Alice Brady Dizzy Dame.

Here is where Columbia comes in, for Howard Hawks's *Twentieth Century* offered an alternate pattern to Barry's. Forget the rich. Instead, let's pit a wild theatre director against his former protégée, now a movie star. We thus retain the conflict of the unruly (the theatre) against the drab (industry-town Hollywood), with the added fun of the colorful backstage atmosphere. (Note again the Broadway input, as Hawks's film was closely based on Ben Hecht and Charles MacArthur's adaptation of a script by Bruce Millholland.) The casting of *Twentieth Century* is significant. Instead of the somewhat dignified Ann Harding and Leslie Howard of the Barry films, Hawks gives us John Barrymore in one of his most athletically facetious performances and Carole Lombard breaking through to stardom as a rambunctious comedienne. Barrymore, waving his cane, his hair atumble, alternately wheedling or railing at his staff ("I close the iron door on you!") and covering his stage with unintelligible chalk marks till the wood vanishes from sight, glamorizes the eccentric. Lombard complements him beautifully: she fears the eccentric, so adopts it out of self-defense. "I'm no Trilby!" she cries at Barrymore's aides. Oh yes, she is: just then Barrymore stalks in, hatted and caped as the Svengali he played for Warner Brothers three years before.

We get a few other eccentric characters, all carried over from the play—a nerd with a compulsive urge to plant stickers reading "Repent" everywhere he goes, and two extraordinarily bearded men from Oberammergau who want Barrymore to produce their next Passion Play. But Hawks adds a great deal of his own. Eluding the law disguised as a Southern colonel, Barrymore hams the bit outrageously, virtually daring a sheriff to spot him. It's a wonderful moment. Even better, when Barrymore gets out of his costume, bits of makeup fluff adhere to his nose, turning the treacherous impresario into what he already is: Pinocchio.

Hawks's farcical tempo, too, expanded screwball's modus operandi. Such gems of the form as *Easy Living, Bringing Up Baby,* and *The Palm Beach Story* depend on pacing and surprise. But it was Capra more than Hawks who helped Columbia lay down an emotional blueprint for screwball. Barry's juxtaposition of the spiritually swank and the merely well-heeled appealed to Capra. But he reset the theme in his politicized world of the takers and givers. We see Capra working up to this in *Platinum Blonde*'s romance of heiress and reporter; but *It Happened One Night* sculpts the material more precisely, and in a much better movie. *It Happened One Night* virtually launched the era of High Screwball, for it was not only widely popular—in Europe, many thought it the most American movie they had ever seen—but brought all the genre's parts into play: the contemporary setting, the class opposition (when Gable shows Colbert how to dunk a dough- nut) harmonized in the mutuality of shared adventure (when Colbert shows Gable how to flag down a car), the learning how to relax (best seen in the informal group singing of "The Man on the Flying Tra- peze" on the big bus ride at the film's sociocultural center), and the rebelliousness (of Colbert, against her father). One element is miss- ing: the eccentricity. But Capra alludes to it, when Colbert's father, Walter Connolly, increasingly impressed by Gable, asks if he loves Colbert. *"Yes!"* Gable angrily admits. "But don't hold that against me. I'm a little screwy myself."

Why did screwball comedy find its most formative home at Columbia? Perhaps, for once, the tight budget proved a blessing. Screwball is by nature small in scope. The writer and director help far more than stars or production values. Then too, screwball needs spontaneity, for it is about spontaneity—about throwing off received cultural inhibitions. Spontaneity is one thing Columbia had, espe- cially from Capra and Hawks. Take *His Girl Friday*, Hawks's reworking of *The Front Page* from a buddy picture into a romance. (Ace reporter Hildebrand Johnson turns into Hildegarde Johnson, united by the nickname "Hildy.") Seldom does a film speed past the ear with such vigor. The eye, too, is busy—but one screens the pic- ture two or three times just to hear the lines. The first film version of the Hecht–MacArthur play, an independent production released by United Artists (1931), was supposed to have introduced the track- meet tempo of Broadway farce into the movies. But that original *Front Page* is not as much fast-spoken as fast-filmed: it isn't the actors who race, it's the camera.

The play takes place in a single set, the pressroom of Chicago's Criminal Courts Building. The 1931 *Front Page*, almost a literal film- ing of the playscript, seldom ventures out of that room. So director Lewis Milestone keeps the view restless, thus to find a cinematic equivalent for Broadway's one-set, fourth-wall, quicksilver farce. Constantly circling his characters, panning them, then lunging away, Milestone creates a bracingly exhausting movie, one that happens quickly because the frame never stands still.

Hawks opens up the action considerably. He is twenty-five minutes into the film before we reach the poker scene that launches the play. We see a newspaper office, a jailhouse, a bar, streets. (We also see those crazy Columbia women's fashions, bad enough in the Grace Moore opera musicals but dazzlingly terrible here. Rosalind Russell walks in in a striped tailored suit with a matching hat shaped to look like those children's birthday-party favors that explode when you pull their string.) Mainly, we hear once again that insistent advice that the free and even dangerous life (for instance, with Cary Grant) is better for you than a safe dull one (especially with Ralph Bellamy, screwball's favorite paper penguin).

Perhaps screwball worked so well at Columbia because it is a basically unruly and even subversive form. The small studio itself was disorderly by Hollywood standards, cheap where the big studios had decided on reasonable budgets as the entrance fee for membership in the industry. It was Capra, of course, who made the most subversive screwball comedy, once again bought from Broadway but once again reinvented as a study in class war: *You Can't Take It with You*.

See how Capra turns a George S. Kaufman and Moss Hart farce about an eccentric family into a Little People parable. First of all, he casts Edward Arnold, James Stewart, and Jean Arthur, the all-basic Capraesque Devouring Tycoon, Folk Hero, and Swell Kid. Next, Capra builds up Arnold's part in opposition to the Grandpa Vanderhof of Lionel Barrymore—opening not on apparent protagonist Vanderhof but on Arnold, ruthlessly grouching, monopolizing, and destroying fellow businessman H. B. Warner. (Is it a coincidence that Warner's most famous role was Christ in DeMille's *King of Kings*?) It is Barrymore who comes into Arnold's story—not, as in the play, the reverse—when Arnold tries to buy a block of real estate and Barrymore is the only holdout.

The screwball nature of Kaufman and Hart's Vanderhof family, the core of the play's entertainment, is irrelevant in Capra's world, where it's the heroes who are daffy. That is, independent. For society always regards originality as aberrant. So Capra concentrates his liberating technique on his two lovers, Stewart (Arnold's son) and Arthur (Barrymore's granddaughter). A gang of kids intrudes on their love scene in Central Park, demanding a dime for an exhibition of the big apple. (The kids, by the way, are astonishing dancers.) Thus instructed in cutting loose, Stewart and Arthur disrupt the cool of a posh restaurant by claiming to have seen rats. Delicious chaos follows; one grande dame actually mounts a chair.

It is not enough for the heroes to signal their coming out by trashing the solemnity of the fat-cat salon. We must have a clear spelling-out of the issues that divide Edward Arnold from the rest of us. In a prison sequence that the play only alluded to, we see Barrymore play "Polly Wolly Doodle" on the harmonica as the rabble dance and Edward Arnold glowers. He throws down his cigar; twenty men leap to nab it. Arnold calls them scum, and Barrymore, really roused, rips into Arnold enough to hurt him with the most Capraesque of insults: he has *no friends*. But the Fascist has feelings. He is even redeemable (as Arnold never is in his other Capra films), not a successful Arnold, it turns out, as much as a failed Barrymore. We close with the real-estate deal withdrawn and Arnold and Barrymore duetting on harmonica.

It was Capra, as Columbia's main man, who talked Harry Cohn into making the first Big One to come out of Gower Gulch, *Lost Horizon* (1937). In the three years since *It Happened One Night*, the studio's A product had been significantly upgraded, and now it seemed that Cohn need take but one giant step more to turn out a Really Big One: based on a best-selling novel by a well-known writer, employing in Ronald Colman a prestige star at the top of his form and asking price, calling for all sorts of elaborate effects and shots of thousands, and with a running time of 137 minutes.*

We can see why Capra wanted to make the movie. Here, in the midst of his quest for a clarified Americana in which Folk Heroes Gary Cooper and James Stewart take on Wall Street Fascist Edward Arnold, is a society that was never ruined. A society so pure it needs no clarification. Now we know what paradise is: life without Edward Arnold.

But why did Cohn want to make the movie? It was so expensive that even considerable success would fail to recoup the investment; indeed, *Lost Horizon* lost money. Perhaps there is a mysterious pressure in Hollywood that forces out the small operation. The eco-

---

*Subsequent releases cut down the footage, the better to fit the film into the average theatre's business day, and the television print currently in use is twenty minutes shorter than the original. In 1986, a restored print was assembled with cuttings from here and there, with stills and "personality portraits" filling in over the dialogue track for a few still-missing moments, in the manner of the restored Garland–Cukor *A Star Is Born*.

*Columbia's unique developments: screwball and little-peo-
ple Americana. Above, Irene Dunne interposes herself
between ex-husband Cary Grant and his socialite fiancée,
Molly Lamont, in* The Awful Truth. *Dunne and Grant
emphasize the Columbia screwballer's vivacity of co-star
teamings, which included not only such promisingly con-
cordant couples as Barrymore and Lombard, Hepburn and
Grant, and Stewart and Arthur; but also the surprisingly har-*

monious Cooper and Arthur, Grant and Russell, and Arthur and MacMurray; and even one improbably delightful couple, Gable and Colbert. Above, the world of Capra, as Fascist Edward Arnold uses police power to silence the second-coming Gary Cooper in Meet John Doe *(1941)*. Detractors carp at Capra's sentimentality, but his films teem with brutality as well. He must terrorize us with the threat of totalism in order to exhilarate us at its defeat.

nomics of moviemaking have favored the overwhelming competitor, which is why Lewis Selznick died the death and Adolph Zukor lived to break a hundred. The star system, the craze for prestige, the strategy of the Big One—all this forces the large studio to expand, the small studio to go under. Cohn's Columbia, then, was somewhere between the two possibilities in the early 1930s, when Capra was getting the studio major attention—it was Capra's quickies that nabbed Columbia its first Oscar nominations. But winning awards counts; getting nominated doesn't. It may sound neat to frame it thus, but Columbia had to make *It Happened One Night* in order to complete its transformation from riffraff to member of the club; and Columbia had to go on to *Lost Horizon* to maintain its standing.

This is, in synecdoche, the history of Hollywood, out of the Eastern brownstones into the sprawling Western lots; down with the two-reelers and up with the seven-reelers, the Big Ones, the Epics; try the all-star cast, color, stereophonic sound, CinemaScope. It becomes a rule that small is impractical over the long haul. Small is where you start.

So the Studio Age made life difficult for the small concern, especially for the independent artist who free-lanced to keep control of his work. The silent years generally made room for such people within a studio setup, but the example of MGM closed that option down. Buster Keaton is a classic instance of the independent destroyed by studio rule. Unlike Chaplin, Keaton elected to throw in with a major—MGM, in fact—and found his delicate genius harassed by supervisors. He was unable to turn out his pictures now: he had to satisfy Them. Within a few years, he had slid from stardom to support of lesser talents, and quickly fell into obscurity and despair.

Chaplin had his own studio and, with Little Mary and Doug and D.W., his own firm, United Artists. This is often thought of as a studio, but UA was one only in the modern sense of a releasing organization, a logo without a lot. UA did in fact have that most basic of studio parts, a production factory. But in the main UA didn't make films as much as distribute them.* This in itself was of vital impor-

*United Artists' curious output includes one of the most unusual musicals ever filmed, *Hallelujah, I'm a Bum* (1933), which may be defined as a Jolson film, a Lewis Milestone film, or a Rodgers–Hart film, depending on whether you believe in the star system, the auteur theory, or the black-and-white of composition. In fact, this is one of Jolson's least self-serving parts, and, excellent though Milestone is, the bulk of his work was done by the real storytellers, Rodgers, Hart, and scenarist S. N. Behrman, who wrote what is virtually an opera.

tance to any production company not berthed with a studio, for how else was any major proprietor to get his films into theatres? The quickie lots, churning out their programmers and serials, were contentedly locked into their "neighborhood" network. But any producer who made movies competitive with those of MGM, Paramount, or Warner Brothers faced their domination of the important screens. United Artists was their way in, and as such implemented exhibition for two versions of the most unexpected concept in the movie lot: the one-man studio. One man was Samuel Goldwyn; the other was David O. Selznick.

Goldwyn, of course, was Old Hollywood, as Jesse Lasky's partner on Cecil B. DeMille's first expedition west, then as the founder of the Goldwyn Studio—so far back that he was no longer connected to it when it merged with Metro and Mayer. Of course Goldwyn came right back with a second Goldwyn Studio, in 1923; and he was, without question, the master of a realm. He had actors under contracts, specialists in house—Gregg Toland, Orson Welles's cinematographer on the most thoroughly *photographed* movie of the Studio Age, *Citizen Kane*, was a Goldwyn employee.

So the mogul had a locale of production, a *studio* in the most practical sense. Still, he was the only thing in it. This star, that director, this story editor, that musician . . . these were Goldwyn pictures, Goldwyn signing his name at the very end of the credits, upending a long-honored Hollywood rule that the director gets the outstanding staff billing. "I made *Wuthering Heights*," Goldwyn supposedly told someone. "William Wyler only directed it." An inarticulate and uncultured man, Goldwyn determined that he would be known by his taste and vision, his passion for excellence. He had to be independent because only by himself could he promote unique projects.

Yet Goldwyn's output was largely programmer material handsomely displayed, the B movie as A feature. Goldwyn had neither taste nor vision; Goldwyn had money. What distinguished him from most producers was his obstinacy. He would scrap half a million dollars' worth of footage if the rushes offended him, though he never could say just what it was that he didn't like. He would drag all or most of a Broadway cast to Hollywood for the film adaptation, just because it *was* the Broadway cast, enough said, don't give me some argument. If he let an actor slip through his fingers and another studio signed him, Goldwyn wouldn't rest till he snapped that actor back up, even if it took a decade—as, with Gary Cooper, it nearly did. Goldwyn was obsessed with Florenz Ziegfeld, the only show-biz impresario of the day to make his name a common noun. Goldwyn tried to model his fame on Ziegfeld's—hiring a PR man to tout "the Goldwyn Touch" to rival Ziegfeld's, maintaining a chorus line dubbed "the Goldwyn Girls," employing Ziegfeld's top writer William Anthony McGuire, mounting *The Goldwyn Follies* (1938), even transporting a Ziegfeld hit from the New Amsterdam Theatre to Hollywood virtually complete to the last buskin—Eddie Cantor in Samuel Goldwyn's *Whoopee!* (1930)*—and then making his *own* Cantor musicals, one a year through 1936. Obstinate.

Goldwyn must have been extremely unsure of himself culturally, to judge by his sedulous hiring of Eastern writers, the more famous the better. As far back as 1919, Goldwyn promulgated the Eminent Authors project, through which novelists would approve adaptations of their work and even contribute original scripts. Goldwyn pursued this literary aplomb in talkie years, hiring such noted playwrights as Sidney Howard, Elmer Rice, Maxwell Anderson, Lillian Hellman, Rachel Crothers, Frederick Lonsdale, Ben Hecht and Charles MacArthur, Robert E. Sherwood, Preston Sturges, S. N. Behrman, and John Howard Lawson. Goldwyn even commissioned work from Maurice Maeterlinck, the Belgian playwright associated with the "Theatre of the Unexpressed"—an ineffable aesthetic not at all suited to film. According to legend, Maeterlinck, ensconced in a Goldwyn office, charged with the eructation of scenarios, decides to outline his novel *La Vie des Abeilles* (The Life of the Bees). Comes the day when Goldwyn peruses Maeterlinck's file and reads the outlines. A secretary hears a scream from Goldwyn's office, rushes in, and finds her boss staggering around the room in a daze. The frightened secretary helps him into a chair and fusses for a glass of water, a fan, the sal volatile. Whatever can be the matter?

Waving at Maeterlinck's typescript, Goldwyn gasps, "The hero is a bee!"

There is something pathetic in Goldwyn's tantrums and malapropisms and pointless largesse—who else would remake a film

---

*The movie *Whoopee!* enjoyed a change of choreographer, cuts in and additions to its score, and the loss of Ruth Etting, but is otherwise a near-duplication of the stage show, right down to the stage waits for the laughs.

Goldwyn not only filmed Ziegfeld's musical; he made a series of runoffs, all founded on Whoopee!*'s star (Eddie Cantor),* Whoopee!*'s setting (Cantor in an exotic place), the black-face number, the ladies of the chorus (the Goldwyn Girls), the bully, and the subsidiary love plot. Here's* Roman Scandals *(1933), which takes in the stage* Whoopee!*'s singing star (Ruth Etting) and the movie* Whoopee!*'s choreographer (Busby Berkeley). Goldwyn the (second greatest) Glorifier.*

before its first release? At least Zukor and Mayer and Cohn were direct. At least Thalberg was influential. At least Laemmle had been, in youth, a rebel. At least Zanuck really liked movies. And each of them knew what he wanted from a movie, and if he wasn't getting it he would ask for it in English. (Laemmle spoke German, but so did everyone else at Universal.) Goldwyn was forever looking for artists who could translate his stumbling suggestions into specifics—forever looking because sooner or later he offended everybody.

In a way, Goldwyn did have a vision: of himself as the greatest of producers. Let Irving Thalberg of Metro–*Goldwyn*–Mayer (ha!) turn out well-made films. Goldwyn's would be *perfectly* made. Beautiful pictures, expensive, everybody eminent. Goldwyn was a tragic hero, the only businessman in Hollywood who realized that cinema is art. But what is art? Trying to bridge the gap between what he knew and what might be accomplished, Goldwyn would contract Ronald Colman. He's swank, he's handsome, he's a Brit. That's Goldwyn's idea of prestige. No wonder he let Gary Cooper wander off to Paramount —he's raw, he's too sexy, he's a cowboy. Goldwyn didn't understand American charm. And when the irascible Goldwyn alienated Colman, the producer simply hired a replacement, David Niven. He's dull, he's talentless—but he's a Brit and he has the same mustache.

Some of the heart dropped out of the Goldwyn studio when Colman departed. There, now, was a consummate Brit, prestigious beyond qualification. With Colman in a film, Goldwyn told himself, a film was art. *Bulldog Drummond* (1929), for instance. Here's Colman breaking the sound barrier with such unstressed poise that he became one of the few silent stars not to survive the talkie but to predominate in it. His wryly stalwart detective considerably refines H. C. McNiele's original, a precursor of James Bond in his ruthlessness and Mike Hammer in his ruffianly politics. But then the whole film is smooth, smooth. Where, a few years hence, Fred Astaire will cheek a pompous men's club salon by going into his dance, Colman does it— in the film's first scene—by marching through the room whistling.

Ah, the eloquence of the talkie; this was Goldwyn's first. It has the odd empty spaces, repetitious lines, and erratic sonics of 1929, but is generally quite well crafted, even personable. Joan Bennett plays the heroine in distress, Lawrence Grant the vicious villain, Lilyan Tashman his abradant moll, and Claud Allister Drummond's silly-ass sidekick, Algy. A tasty brew in all. When a veiled, almost certainly beautiful stranger (Bennett, of course), arrives for a meeting with Colman, Algy dithers at Colman's butler in the next room. Algy spots a hole in the wall:

ALGY: (astounded) There's a hole!

BUTLER: It's a peephole.

ALGY: (delighted) Let's peep!

The whole thing is so quick and colorful, and so nicely essentialized in Colman's elegance, that one scarcely notices that the film is vacant fun. One can say little more for the weighty-seeming *Arrowsmith* (1931), not only with Colman but Helen Hayes as well; and Sidney Howard wrote and John Ford directed it. Simply the act of transcribing an Important Novel makes for Important Film, by Hollywood reasoning. And these brand names! Sinclair Lewis's book may not defend the reputation of one of the few Americans to win the Nobel Prize in Literature, but its moralism has force and fairness. The film has neither. The film has . . . Ronald Colman and Helen Hayes. Maybe Goldwyn did know what art is: art is class.

Class is what made the Goldwyn Studio—or, rather, the striving to achieve class by renting it. Thus the parade of Eminent Authors, not to mention Goldwyn's own draft of Famous Players in Famous Plays. Goldwyn was so impressed by the swank of Broadway that he made a habit of hiring the original supporting or even bit players when he filmed. *Whoopee!*'s reconstruction of the New York cast extends to one of the chorus girls. This is obstinate.

At least Goldwyn's fascination for the authenticity of the stage led him to preserve Marjorie Main's short but very telling role in *Dead End* (1937), from Sidney Kingsley's realistic look at life on the eastern end of Manhattan's Fifty-third Street, where a teeming slum abuts the river palaces of the rich. Lillian Hellman respected Kingsley's text, cleaning up here and there. She chastened the scene in which some punks* "cockalize" a pantywaist by pulling off his clothes and rubbing dirt into his genitals, startling even on Broadway, and pro-

---

*Huntz Hall, Leo Gorcey, Bobby Jordan, Billy Halop, Gabriel Dell, and Bernard Punsley. In short, the "Dead End Kids," who, like Main, stayed on to forge Hollywood careers. Typically, the kids made their best features for Warner Brothers, the studio best equipped to handle their gritty style. Also typically—considering small-studio procedures—when their vogue waned the boys moved to Monogram (as the "East Side Kids") to churn out programmers.

moted Kingsley's spokesman from a cripple named Gimpty into Joel
McCrea, Goldwyn's revenge on Gary Cooper for getting away.

Main's role, however, was let stand, especially the astonishing
scene in which her son (Humphrey Bogart), a public enemy on the
lam, attempts to see her again. The sequence lasts little more than a
minute, yet it was the talk of Broadway in 1935 and the most memorable event in a colorful movie. As William Wyler filmed it, Main
enters the picture as a small figure dragging up the street in the bottom left of the frame, Bogart in the foreground. They hold the
encounter itself inside a tenement hallway, Main above Bogart on the
stairs. "You no-good tramp," she calls her son in a strangely
unnuanced whine. She slaps him. "You dog. You dirty yella dog,
you. Don't call me Mom. You ain't no son a mine."

Now Wyler moves up the stairs ahead of her as she climbs. "Go
away," she tells the stunned Bogart in her hollow mewling, "and
leave us alone."

Famous Players in Famous Plays by Eminent Authors: outdoing
Goldwyn's old pals Lasky and Zukor. They only had Famous Players
in Famous Plays. Yet Goldwyn had a string of writers emend Lillian
Hellman's adaptation of her own *The Little Foxes* (1941), and director
Wyler expanded the show to take in the atmosphere of a small
Southern town, roving about in the opening to introduce each principal in his element—the breakfast table, the workplace, the street.
Ten minutes of cinematic exposition before Wyler catches up to the
play's first scene, the big dinner party of Southern family and Northern capitalist. Again, five of the original New York players were
brought out—not only to soothe Goldwyn's prestige anxiety, but
because a small lot can't afford to foster the variegated contract roster
that Paramount or MGM could. Snatching his players right off the
stage saved Goldwyn the trouble of sifting Hollywood's ranks and
possibly having to shell out extra for an actor under contract to
another studio. Oddly, the only truly notable *Little Foxes* creator,
Tallulah Bankhead, was passed over. (Or not that oddly: she had suffered a spate of dreary weepies at Paramount earlier in the decade and
was considered bad box-office.) Bette Davis played not only Bankhead's part but her interpretation, in a hairdo as tiered as a wedding
cake.

Taking into account the run of Goldwyn's repertory—the Ronald Colman–Vilma Banky silent romances, the weepies like *Stella*

Dallas (1925; remade in 1937), the musical vehicles for Cantor and Danny Kaye—the serious Broadway stuff was largely a front. More typical of the Goldwyn style, if style he had, is *The Hurricane* (1937). John Ford directed this combination of South Sea island romance and disaster movie, but the most significant names are no doubt Dorothy Lamour, in her greatest role (as faithful Marama); Jon Hall, in his (as audacious Terangi); Omar Kiyam, who designed their sarongs; and James Basevi, who handled the special effects of the climactic storm. Or take *The Adventures of Marco Polo* (1938), with Gary Cooper absurdly miscast and costumed to look like a cross between Robin Hood and Henry Wadsworth Longfellow. In fact, the whole movie is absurd, an American road picture shoved into the thirteenth century.

Historically, everyone's favorite Goldwyn blunder is *Nana* (1934), the film that introduced Anna Sten to America. We get a surer sense of the Goldwyn style in the year in which Sten was groomed and readied while Goldwyn beat the drum for his one-woman Garbo and Dietrich, obstinately rivaling the class of MGM and Paramount. This is Zola, this is quality, Goldwyn tells himself. This is art. But much of Zola's naturalism has been painted over; and naturalism was Zola's ideology. What remains, after the firing of George Fitzmaurice two-thirds of the way through shooting and his replacement by Dorothy Arzner, is a trim and picturesque Hollywood version of life in the Paris streets and cabarets. (At its best, it looks forward to the Cukor–Garbo *Camille*.) The cast includes veteran stage star Richard Bennett, briskly crotchety as the impresario who discovers Sten (did he model his portrayal on Goldwyn?), the credits offer cameos of the players mounted like daguerrotypes in hinged boxes, and Rodgers and Hart contributed "That's Love" for Nana's stage act. These may well be Goldwyn Touches. But the most telling Touch of all is Sten herself, lovely and not uninteresting but not fluent enough in English to carry off the part. Her line readings are often screwy, her gestures curious. She has—here it is again—no charm. She is tentative in "That's Love," yet she wows Paris. She also wowed Radio City Music Hall's box office on the day *Nana* opened, for Goldwyn's barrage of publicity drew a good-sized town's worth of the curious. Then word of mouth caught up with Anna Sten. Ridiculous, says Goldwyn, looking over the accounts. This is art.

The studio resolutely reissued Sten, revived, reintroduced her.

Zola was not art enough, it seems. Let there be Tolstoy, then! After all, Sten is half-Russian. So be it: *We Live Again* (1934), from *Resurrection* and with Mamoulian directing—Mamoulian directed Dietrich and Garbo, didn't he? *We Live Again* died. So we'll Americanize her: *The Wedding Night* (1935), with Gary Cooper. You can't get more American than that. It bombed. Methinks Goldwyn was insisting too much.

Obstinate.

A paradox of Hollywood's one-man studios is their lack of unity. Harry Cohn had Columbia literally under his thumb, yet we sense no line of repertory in his output. Paramount has a worldview and an aesthetic, Thalberg and Mayer each held distinct ideas on what made a movie. But Cohn is opportunistic, cranking out product till he hits upon a winner and then capitalizing on it—first Capra, so Columbia is doing Folk Hero satire; then Hayworth, so Columbia is doing dance musicals.

Goldwyn manifests a comparable miscellany, clouded by his struggle for respect as an artist. He shares with Thalberg and Mayer the realization that spending money earns money, and with Lasky the aperçu that Broadway is hot stuff, and with Zukor the grudging admission that better directors make better pictures. But what was Goldwyn committed to? Was it grandeur of soul and a keen sense of what a postwar America would feel like that led him to *The Best Years of Our Lives* (1946)? Nothing in the film particularly suggests the Goldwyn of earlier films, yet it is regarded as the ultimate Goldwyn picture—and did, finally, as one of the few universally admired films of the day, give him the prestige he demanded. And note that he made it without Broadway's help. Playwright Robert E. Sherwood wrote the screenplay, but his source was not theatre: MacKinlay Kantor had laid out the story at Goldwyn's commission, for some reason in the form of an epic poem. Of the leads only Fredric March was a thespian, and as much a Hollywood star as a Broadway actor. *The Best Years of Our Lives*, then, is all movie, and a Big One, three hours long on a Serious Theme. Yea, Goldwyn earned praise.

Still, what *was* Goldwyn? What of him is in this movie that was not more truly put there by Kantor, Sherwood, or director William Wyler? Why does Goldwyn make these films? Was it vision that compelled him to make *Porgy and Bess* (1959)—his last film, at the age

United Artists isn't treated heavily in this book, but as the major distribution arm of the independent producer it served many major figures: not only Goldwyn, Selznick, and Zanuck (when he formed Twentieth Century Pictures), but its four founding auteurs, Chaplin, Griffith, Little Mary, and Douglas Fairbanks, seen here in the triumphant climax of The Thief of Bagdad *(1924).*

of seventy-seven—when Hollywood thought it too way-out, when black pride denounced it as racially demeaning, when the budget broke five million dollars after a fire swept through the Catfish Row set and the costume storage? (Goldwyn imperturbably said, "So go replace it!") In 1959, George Gershwin's much-maligned opera was on its way to becoming an American classic. Yet not till the 1976 Houston Grand Opera revival was it officially declared Unimpeachable. Did Goldwyn know he was urging history on? Was Goldwyn simply daring the undoable to show the world what Goldwyn was?

If so, Goldwyn had an example in his colleague David O. Selznick, the third mogul of the important one-man studios, and the one who most demonstrates the power—the size, really—of the small operation. We see Selznick in relief when we set him next to Goldwyn, for the two had little in common. Selznick, first of all, was a very secure man, especially in the matter of his cultural polish. He was also articulate (to a fault: see *Memo from: David O. Selznick*) about what he wanted from film. And where Goldwyn was a founder of Old Hollywood, Selznick was its scion, the first second-generation mogul as the son of Lewis Selznick and the son-in-law of L. B. Mayer. David O. had no interest in Broadway or the day's Eminent Authors. His god was literature, especially Dickens. However, he did agree with Goldwyn (and not with Cohn) that a film's auteur was its producer. We think of Goldwyn's "*I* made *Wuthering Heights*" when we find Selznick firing John Huston from *A Farewell to Arms* (1957) because Selznick had, he explained, "asked for a first violinist and instead got a conductor."

That's shocking; but Selznick was not Hollywood's only arrogant mogul. Can anyone name a mogul who wasn't arrogant? Possibly arrogance comes with the job, with the day-to-day marshaling of egomaniacal performers, smug writers, and self-willing directors into a team. Anyway, show business has never respected anything but arrogance in its honchos. And Selznick's arrogance, unlike that of, say, Mayer or Cohn, was that of a man sure of his vision and judgment—his talent . . . even his Touch. Here was one one-man studio that was really run by one man.

Goldwyn started out as a boss. Selznick, a boss's son, started out at the bottom of the top, as a reader in MGM's story department. He moved on to Paramount and RKO, now as producer. And at RKO, in *What Price Hollywood* (1932), we get a take on Selznick's view of himself as the inheritor of a history, a man destined for the cinema. More than any other mogul, Selznick romanticized his profession. Other moviemakers loved power; Selznick loved having the power to make movies.

There had been plenty of Hollywood sagas before *What Price Hollywood*, even back in the First Era. They are a varied lot. By far the popular approach was a loving spoof wrapped around the tale of a small-town girl who crashes the business. MGM's *Show People* (1928), with Marion Davies, is the most enduring, if only for the heavy glamour of catching Metro stars at work and sport. However, First National's *Ella Cinders* (1926), with Colleen Moore, is more typical of the genre in its unpretentious farce and romance. We get a glimpse of the difficulties of breaking in and hanging on. Then the heroine's small-town boyfriend pops up to snap her into his arms and take her home. Finis.

Selznick determined to seek out a truer Hollywood, looking beyond the glamour to get more than a glimpse of the difficulties. Most moguls seem not to have questioned their stars' entitlement to stardom. When studios happened upon marketable charisma, they marketed it. Talent and craft were what directors and designers had. Stars had stardom. But Selznick, who did not vastly prize talent in his directors or writers, appears to have given considerable thought to what qualities make a star.

Selznick made a few stars himself (most notably Vivien Leigh, Ingrid Bergman, and Jennifer Jones), and wherever possible hired the most imposing stars of the day—Marie Dressler, Jean Harlow, the Barrymores, Clark Gable, Myrna Loy, Robert Montgomery, Helen Hayes, Joan Crawford, Wallace Beery, William Powell, Garbo, Fredric March, Ronald Colman, Marlene Dietrich, Janet Gaynor, Carole Lombard, James Stewart, Leslie Howard, and Joan Fontaine appeared in Selznick films, some more than once, within a span of seven years. Maybe Selznick was less interested in what a star is than in what creates one: what the public discovers about the world through the fantasy of stardom. Selznick was swept up in a dream of the movies; why not capture that dream in a movie, pressing on the fantasy to peer into the reality? For Selznick's peculiar dream was a dark wonder, dating back to Old Hollywood's destruction of the senior Selznick, forced out by his competitors.

The best thing about *What Price Hollywood* is George Cukor's direction, for if he had indifferent material to work with in script and cast, the film is laden with atmosphere, a Cukor hallmark. He opens on the glamour, with hopeful Constance Bennett mooning over a fan magazine. Taken with a photograph of Clark Gable and Garbo embracing in Metro's *Susan Lenox: Her Fall and Rise*, Bennett bends the magazine in half so she can cuddle up with Gable and imitate Garbo saying, "I loovfe you."

However, Cukor quickly shows us the quirks that sting the glamour. The mogul, Gregory Ratoff, has a surprisingly Jewish inflection; till then it was a convention that producers in Hollywood's Hollywood always appeared to be WASPs. The director who backs Bennett, Lowell Sherman, gives a rather swish reading. Is he supposed to be gay? Sherman reportedly modeled his portrayal on John Barrymore; and Gene Fowler, Barrymore's pal and one of the numerous collaborators on *What Price Hollywood*'s script, dropped in a few Barrymore-isms.* But we see Sherman only conducting Bennett through the dream factory, no more; the real Barrymore would have bedded or at least married her. And while Bennett does become a star, she pays a heavy personal freight: an anguished, alcoholic Sherman kills himself, and Bennett's big romance, played by Neil Hamilton, becomes fed up with Hollywood and walks out on her. As for the glory of stardom, there is the restless public to contend with. "They make you," Ratoff explains, "and they break you."

RKO, perennially strapped for seed money, narrowed Selznick's range. This was not the studio to buy up the hot properties and stars he needed. So he went back to MGM, perhaps as part of Mayer's plan to unseat or at least de-emphasize Thalberg with a contending boy wonder. Selznick had married Mayer's daughter Irene, so there was derisive commentary on Selznick's new job—surprising in that Hollywood had long observed such network procedures. Besides, Selznick was exactly the man for the job, as he proved forthwith.

Metro's view of moviemaking, with its star power, producer's input, and decorative enhancements, corresponded to Selznick's. True, he had no sympathy for that Metro staple, the musical—he consigned all but one of *Dancing Lady*'s numbers to a medley finale, and on *Reckless* (1935) cut almost all of a Jerome Kern–Oscar Ham-

---

*Barrymore repaid the homage, in Selznick and Cukor's company, on *Dinner at Eight* at Metro the year after. His beautifully observed ham actor, Larry Renault, was—so he told Cukor—"a combination of Maurice Costello, Lowell Sherman, and me."

merstein score. But Selznick outThalberged Thalberg on two all-star specials, *Dinner at Eight* and *Night Flight*, his first pictures at the studio, in 1933. This is coming on strong, with more stars and better directors (Cukor and Brown) than *Grand Hotel*. The heralding on *Dinner at Eight*'s posters of a "twelve star triumph!" exaggerates a little when the count includes such as Karen Morley and Madge Evans. (Jean Hersholt's cameo, for once, is on the surly side.) But *Dinner at Eight* has, along with that Metro glamour, irony and vivacity that make it, for many, *Grand Hotel*'s superior. *Grand Hotel* is so *serious* about itself. *Dinner at Eight* enjoys its moments of la-di-da—even ends on one, in Marie Dressler's famous exchange with Jean Harlow, the cut direct.

We grow yet closer to a sense of the Selznick style in *David Copperfield* (1935), especially when we spot Selznick's screen credit following director Cukor's—not the usual procedure at any studio but (of course) Samuel Goldwyn's. The large cast of principals includes no real stars; Lionel Barrymore's role is smallish and W. C. Fields is a bigger draw today than he was then. But we note an inspiring fidelity to Dickens in casting and in the carrying over of the novel's descriptive details. This is Selznick's commitment to the classics, not for shallow prestige but out of love and respect. As with von Stroheim and *Greed*, Selznick doesn't turn the book into a film: he wants to film the book. So there are Peggotty's buttons ripping off and Peggotty throwing her apron over her head to laugh; there's Barkis, willin'; and the "lone, lorn cre'tur" Mrs. Gummidge, just as the reader imagines them. And the Murdstones (Basil Rathbone and Violet Kemble-Cooper) actually look like brother and sister; and grown-up David (Frank Lawton) looks like a mature Freddie Bartholomew, who plays David as a child.

Beyond all this, *David Copperfield* is a treasurable film, again thanks to Cukor's appreciation of the temper of his subject's culture. There is but one false moment, when Fields flees his creditors over the rooftops and we get not the expected back projection of London but a flat photograph of St. Paul's dome. Still, the great moments and colorful portrayals illuminate the source, as in Cukor's dashing look at his young hero and a playmate running on a jetty as the ocean lunges at them from below, or when the evil Murdstones arrive to take David away and Aunt Betsy Trotwood (Edna May Oliver) throws them out of her house. She had cut her sister off when she

The authenticity of Selznick: MGM's David Copperfield, *almost as much a verification as a Boz cartoon: Mr. Murdstone (Basil Rathbone), Peggotty (Jessie Ralph), David (Freddie Bartholomew), and David's mother (Elizabeth Allan).*

gave birth to David instead of a girl; now the crusty old lady redeems her cruelty. The Murdstones gone, Bartholomew pathetically thanks Oliver, and her mortified embrace is priceless—the rigidly unloving person suffering love. This is not only good Hollywood, but good Dickens.

We note as well that *David Copperfield* runs a bit over two hours, typical of the Metro Big One but also of the Big Ones Selznick would soon risk his standing on. Selznick was a Big One himself, and could not stomach being an employee for long. In 1935, on the site of the old Thomas Ince studios, Selznick founded Selznick International Pictures. Now unencumbered, releasing through United Artists and making pictures for no one but himself, Selznick returns to *What Price Hollywood*. That RKO movie framed the anxieties of stardom but not its fulfillment, its rhapsody. We never even found out if Constance Bennett had the talent—the entitlement—to get where she did.

So Selznick makes *A Star Is Born* (1937), smartly conflating the Lowell Sherman and Neil Hamilton roles into one weary actor who not only coaches Janet Gaynor to stardom but falls in love with her as well. This is neater, more romantic—more tragic, too, when the actor's dour fatigue leads him to suicide. The satire is better trained this time, too, though Adolphe Menjou's mogul returns us to the absurd notion that somewhere in Hollywood a dapper, urbane, and compassionate man was running a studio. Most important, Selznick now gives us a heroine we can root for. Gaynor is no more an actor than Bennett, true—but the thespian gift is not necessarily part of movie stardom. The point is that where Bennett simply had the desire to be an actor, Gaynor needs it, wills it, fights for it. Like Selznick, she thinks stardom means something.

Some of the films that issued from Selznick's personal atelier affirm Selznick's stylistics, especially in the frequent use of Technicolor from 1936 to 1939, when color was extremely rare and thus prestigious; in the constant copping of Radio City Music Hall for his premieres, the most gala booking in the East; and in the emphasis on the classics, in *Little Lord Fauntleroy* (1936), *The Prisoner of Zenda* (1937), and *The Adventures of Tom Sawyer* (1938).* But all this is mere

*Ben Hecht once told Selznick, "The trouble with you, David, is that you did all your reading before you were twelve."

preparation for Selznick's Big One to top all Big Ones, wherein Selznick demonstrates his entitlement as Prince of Moguls: *Gone With the Wind*.

As Selznick came into his seniority six years into the Studio Age, and didn't release *Gone With the Wind* till four years later, he had plenty of standards to top. Goldwyn's pitiably ersatz Touch, Carl Laemmle's sluggish operation at Universal City, and Warner Brothers' tautly produced output were of little moment here; we're talking Big Ones. RKO, though highly motivated (even, at its best, avant-garde), was no challenge; this was basically a little studio acting big. RKO had distinguished itself commercially with *King Kong*, one of the biggest of the early talkies for the astonishing verisimilitude of its fantasy. But Selznick had signed *King Kong* as producer.* Anyway, it is a first rule of the mogul that you are only as big as your *next* Big One, not your last. You cannot coast.

Selznick's rivals, clearly, were Paramount and MGM, the old master and the upstart. Paramount was a challenge as an entity, as a studio rather than a competitive mogul, for by the late 1930s Paramount was running on inertia, not on any one man's vision. MGM was different, with its Mayer, its Thalberg (the late, after 1936), and its . . . Selznick, for he, too, had graced the MGM lot. He had himself to beat out as well. Paramount was the place where Hollywood was made, MGM the place where Hollywood was perfected. So ran industry consensus in the mid-1930s.

So. How to trump tradition and glamour at once? How to outromance all Hollywood?

This suggests that Selznick deliberately set out to make the biggest film in Hollywood history, founded his own studio, shopped out the property, put the show together, and gloated. I think that is exactly what Selznick did. He did not found Selznick International precisely to make a monster, seems to have hesitated to buy Margaret Mitchell's novel because of its size, and ultimately signed over distribution rights to MGM (to get Clark Gable), thus compromising his prestige with the larger firm's intrusive imprint. So. Yes. But at some point in the game Selznick, the one-man studio, realized what he had in his hands. It was *the* Big One, because much of literate America had read it, because Selznick would typically keep as close to the

---

* Selznick was in fact no more than *King Kong*'s budgetary counselor. This was one film whose auteur was the special-effects team.

You could tell when Selznick didn't care about his pictures by listening to the dialogue. Selznick edited classics and costume romances to the last comma, but The Garden of Allah *(1936) is twaddle, though it was Selznick's first splash in Technicolor. The birdcage is symbolic: Charles Boyer (left) has fled a monastery and broken his vows with Marlene Dietrich, though he will return to ascetic captivity at the end. At Paramount, a Boyer would have stayed with Dietrich or been destroyed, but he would never have left her for a monastery. She must be losing her touch.*

source as possible, because the film would be the longest ever released, and because the publicity it would generate must put him into legend. Selznick would make something new in the talkie: the film everyone had to see.

Something new in the talkie—not in the movies. There had been one other Big One this Big, a film everyone had to see, way back in Old Hollywood: *The Birth of a Nation*. The difference between Griffith's and Selznick's two epics illustrates differences between Griffith's and Selznick's eras—in Griffith's use of his stock company and Selznick's collection of stars; Griffith's revolutionary marshaling of middle-class audiences where Selznick had only to invite them in; Griffith's technical innovations as opposed to Selznick's state-of-the-art; Griffith's addressing of sectional passions while Selznick majestically exhibits a bygone Americana.

However, the similarities between the two films overrun such details. *The Birth of a Nation* was, till *Gone With the Wind*, the outstanding title in movie history. People who hadn't seen it spoke of it with reverence, and in the number of paid admissions it was thought to have exceeded all other titles. Forget those lists of "top-grossing" films, slanted to favor the constant rise in admission prices. Going by population count, and percentage of the population attending specific titles, *The Birth of a Nation* was the most successful movie in American history.

Until *Gone With the Wind*. Selznick had instinctively put himself up against not a mogul—none was big enough—but against a director, *the* director, in fact: the biggest person in American cinema who was not an actor. And notice that while we think of *The Birth of a Nation* as D. W. Griffith's, no one speaks of "Victor Fleming's *Gone With the Wind*"—no one who expects to be taken seriously. One might better call it Margaret Mitchell's *Gone With the Wind*, or William Makepeace Thackeray's, for Mitchell seems to have derived her characters from *Vanity Fair*.*

---

*Scarlett is Becky Sharp, Rhett Butler is Rawdon Crawley (with touches of Dobbin's sardonicism), Charles Hamilton is Amelia's brother Jos, and Amelia and George Osborne are Melanie and Ashley. There is no Miss Crawley (unless Aunt Pittypat is taken as a satiric inversion), no Marquis of Steyne (unless we count Rhett's demonic impulses). But the similarities are persuasive, with the Napoleonic Wars and the Civil War as historical parallels—and even Mitchell's ending is foreshadowed in Thackeray, though Rawdon's disgusted abandonment of his wife is, however decisive, not climactic.

But surely Selznick intended it to be Mitchell's *Gone With the Wind*, just as *David Copperfield* and *A Tale of Two Cities* at Metro had been Dickens's. Selznick plumed himself on fidelity to text, not because so many readers demanded that their favorite novel be so honored—what lobby could Dickens claim?—but because Selznick believed that The Novelist Is Right. A good novelist, anyway. Mitchell was no Dickens, but she told a compelling tale. That was a talent that Selznick, even above the age of twelve, had to respect.

In this, Selznick seems comparable to Goldwyn and his worshipful theatricals. But plenty of long novels had become movies before. No long novel had produced a movie nearly four hours long—not even *Anthony Adverse*, comparably proportioned but, in Warner Brothers' hands, reduced to a Big One so modest it might almost be a trailer for the book. Selznick's authenticity of text was worship beyond even history's call. In truth, Selznick contrasts with Goldwyn in the former's good taste. One makes authentic adaptations of deserving material, not of anything that happens to be a novel or a play. Moreover, it's difficult to imagine Goldwyn trading his logo away for a star, no matter who. Selznick must have fought quite some battle with himself over that; but he must also have decided that Clark Gable was the inevitable Rhett Butler, and so closed the deal. More than Harry Cohn and Samuel Goldwyn, and perhaps more than any other mogul, Selznick truly loved making the greatest of great movies . . . because they're there.

Making *Gone With the Wind* forced his ambitions. What do you do for an encore? One notices in Selznick a tendency to make the Big One a regular event after *Gone With the Wind*. *Rebecca* (1940), though not physically huge, has the éclat of Alfred Hitchcock's Hollywood debut and another no-fail novel as source (and Selznick, supervising the director's composition of the script, made sure that Daphne du Maurier, and not Hitchcock, remained the source in every detail.) Selznick and Goldwyn touch base on the civilian war movie, Selznick in *Since You Went Away* (1944) and Goldwyn in *The Best Years of Our Lives* (1946), both coincidentally timing out at 172 minutes. Big Ones. Selznick wins out in star power, Goldwyn in honesty. So it's back to untamed passions, Technicolor, extravaganza: *Duel in the Sun* (1946). This is *Gone With the Wind*'s follow-up in (1) a historical American setting, (2) a heroine caught between a tough man and a nice man, (3) the heroine's boldness, (4) the tough man's Dangerous Man heroics, (5) size and length, (6) Butterfly McQueen on hand in her *Gone With the Wind* part, and (7) the Griffith complex, extending to the hiring of Biograph veterans Lillian Gish and Lionel Barrymore. *Gone With the Wind* was something new in Hollywood, a precedent in Big Ones. *Duel in the Sun* was something newer, a multi-million-dollar B movie.*

This teaches us the folly of the one-man studio, especially when it fixes on a particular star. As Goldwyn had his Anna Sten (and Arthur Freed his Lucille Bremer, and L. B. Mayer his Ginny Simms, and Darryl Zanuck his Bella Darvi), so Selznick had his Jennifer Jones. Something about *Duel in the Sun* tells us that we are present not to investigate the playing out of an Indian legend (as we are inveigled to do in Orson Welles's opening voice-over), nor to mediate in the rivalry of brothers nice (Joseph Cotten) and nasty (Gregory Peck), but to worship the charisma of Jones as a wanton maid of mixed blood.

Sorry, no. It's Dance: 10, Looks: 10 for Tilly Losch as Jones's mother, highlighted in the cantina ballet of the opening sequence; but Jones is Acting: 2, and that only if we give Selznick's Comanche glass shots a 3. We're talking No Charisma. And note that, like Goldwyn, Selznick went all the way around Robin's barn with his discovery, where Metro's Freed and Mayer, bowing to system, held their protégées to appearances of limited exposure. Simms never carried a major lead, and Bremer did so but once—at that in a Fred Astaire musical, *Yolanda and the Thief*.

Selznick went on to *A Farewell to Arms* (1957), again with Jones, but less extravagantly now, a Big One designed to Cost Less. Another adaptation from classic literature, another precedent to shatter (if only the memory of Paramount's version with Gary Cooper and Helen Hayes), another very long movie. It was Selznick's last. He had made his point: the small studio needn't defer to the major, might even instruct it. Harry Cohn's Columbia rose by falling in line with the leadership studios. Sam Goldwyn pitched his lot as a noncon-forming conformist, of the moguls' ilk but too titanic, he hoped, to

---

*Too many of today's movie buffs know this road-show spectacle by a slashed television print, in debased color and with much explanatory and atmospheric footage cut. The original, however, is even more incomprehensible.

One thing Duel in the Sun *had that* Gone With the Wind *lacked: a rota of reverberant names. Except for Clark Gable,* Gone With the Wind *made stars.* Duel in the Sun *collected them, along with promising newcomers: (left to right) Harry Carey, Joan Tetzel, Charles Bickford, Walter Huston, Cotten, Jones, Peck, Barrymore, Gish, Scott McKay, Otto Kruger. Herbert Marshall and Tilly Losch were in it, too.*

conduct the assembly-line salesmanship of the other studios. Even Paramount turned out dreary westerns; even MGM made programmers. Goldwyn had to be unique, every release an A.

But Selznick made The Great American Movie. And made it by himself, the conductor. That his symphony ran flat after a while should not defame his achievement. There are no second acts in American lives, F. Scott Fitzgerald tells us; and Selznick's was a very American life, a Little Lord Gatsby Also Rises. The theme is talent. Or maybe the theme is belief: maybe those who truly love movies make the best (and worst) ones.

Selznick's querulous enthusiasm sets him apart. Only Irving Thalberg and Darryl Zanuck knew as much about moviemaking as Selznick did, and Selznick showboated them both on the ultimate Big One.

What price Selznick?—so to speak.

The Queen of the Lot in her prime: Now, Voyager *(1942)*.

WARNER BROTHERS

The Slicker

Hear this city music: car pulls up at a filling station at night, guy gets out, lights go black inside the station, we hear "Get back in there—put 'em up!"—three gunshots, guy returns, gets in the car, and it roars away. A fast wipe, and we get a clock, somebody pulling the minute hand back—setting up a phony alibi, see? Pull back, and we're in a diner, two guys there. The guys in the car. Holdup artists. Nice-looking guy and an ugly runt. The runt shows his pal a newspaper story about Diamond Pete Montana. "*He* don't waste his time on cheap gas stations!" Game is to *be* somebody. Big man, coming into your stuff, see? The nice-looking guy isn't sure about that. He could maybe get ahead on his dancing. Smoothie ballroom type, him in tails and his partner in— "Women!" the runt snarls. *"Dancing!* Where's it get you?" He doesn't need no dancing: "I figure on making *other* people dance."

Little Caesar (1931) is prime early Warner Brothers, all the parts in place—the urban setting, as clearly cross-sectioned by class as a real American city, from the fancy-dress nightclub to the ghastly flophouse; the urban noises, bulled up with slang and improvisational grammar; the urban faces, boldly featured, possibly of first-generation Americans or even immigrants, fast to react, uncomely but somehow compelling; the urban politics, restless and competitive, based not on ideology but on who gets what. And the whole damn show moves fast—like urban life, with a shock at every turn of the corner. Just a few seconds after *Little Caesar*'s diner scene, we find the runt applying for a berth in Sam Vettori's gang. Within a minute, Vettori has given the runt a nickname, from Caesar Enrico Bandello to "Little Caesar," all set.

The movie is fast, cheap, and furious; and it was made fast, too. Study the Warners shooting scripts—no other studio shows as much discrepancy between what was written and what was shot. This suggests spontaneity; in fact, the actors didn't have time to memorize their lines. Jack Warner said, "I don't want it good, I want it Tuesday." The speed of production was carried over into editing. *Little Caesar*'s diner sequence, as filmed, included the runt's second tampering with the clock hands, moving them back up to complete the establishment of the alibi for the time of the filling-station holdup, just before a cop comes in, questions him and his partner, and takes the diner man's word that they were otherwise engaged at the moment of crime. Editing stripped all this out, though many spectators are puzzled by the clock business. Warners' thinking was that pace, suspense, involvement carry one along more fluently than details and explanations. Besides, as the cheapest of the big studios, Warners had a lot of assembly-line packaging to cover up somehow. Keep it moving, and nobody will think he's been had.

Warner Brothers is the outstanding Hollywood studio: as the only major lot that was run on a quickie lot's budget. There was no patient glamorizing of stars, scarcely any glamorizing at all. The Warners style is hit-and-run, modern-dress smarts laced with a touch of sentiment but a grab of honesty. The look is close, plain, flat, not versions of places (as at Paramount and MGM), just places. *Little Caesar* gives us a diner, a hideout, a few clubs, offices and halls, apartments, and, above all, city streets. The lighting is clear and unbiased, with none of the lustrous riffs that William Daniels would do on a Garbo. The décor is . . . let's call it terse.

One thing above all marks the Warners output, especially in the late 1920s and 1930s: the cynicism of the sociopolitically disinherited. Whether gangster or secretary, entertainer or reporter, detective or killer's girlfriend, Warners' people are the heroes of the city, always aware that *Little Caesar*'s "be somebody" implies that most of the population is nobody. As if bearing witness to the congenital politics of the underclass, Warners' people speak neither Paramount's High Middle Salon nor MGM's Lexicon Transatlantic, but City Lingo. "You and me can do business," says Little Caesar. And "The food don't leave nothing to be desired." And "That skirt can go hang."

It's an odd format for a key office in an establishment industry to sound. But then the Warner Brothers were Hollywood underdogs themselves. Like Zukor, Lasky, Mayer, Thalberg, Goldwyn, Selznick, and almost all the other moguls, the Warners were Jewish and working-class; unlike the others, they did not quickly force themselves to the top, but hung on in secondary rank, letting the audacious majors battle for the big bookings, the press coverage, the prestige. Warner Brothers was the first big studio that did without the first two and, for a time, didn't believe in the last. Didn't need it. Prestige? Just keep the films cheap and they'll pay off. If the negative cost is low enough, *nothing* can fail. Almost nothing will succeed in any important way, either; but this studio will pay off on an aggregate of small profits rather than big gambles.

This tight-budget philosophy held Warners back from amassing a competitive roster of stars. The odd fancy name was extravagantly brought in from Broadway—John Barrymore in the 1920s, George Arliss in the early 1930s. But the studio's first bread-and-butter talents were a dog and a child, Rin-Tin-Tin and Wesley Barry, very cheap and mildly profitable on a regular basis. The Brothers Warner noted another money-saving possibility: the remake. Warners' titles were constantly in process, to be rewritten, recast, refilmed. However, their reputation for remaking has been exaggerated, mainly because they were open about it while other studios were cagey. In fact, all

Hollywood studios regularly "remade" films in the sense that every-one stole from himself and everyone else and that periods of cycle (of gangster movies, backstage musicals with Berkeleyesque numbers, film noir, and so on) particularly excited imitation. Why, Warners reasoned, pay out money for new properties that were essentially copies of old properties? Why not simply revise and reshoot the old property that you already own?

Save money to make money. A cheap studio, a quickie lot. Yet Warner Brothers made audacious history that affected all Holly-wood—a neat stunt for a minor lot. Paramount's most influential act was the sexualizing of the screen. MGM's was the disinvestiture of the director in favor of the star system as ruled by producers. Warners' was yet more far-reaching. Warner Brothers instituted the talkie.

This is a familiar story, the novelty of the pre-recorded orchestra and sound effects built right into the showing* of the otherwise silent *Don Juan* (1926); gaining strength and interest with a few song-and-dialogue sequences in *The Jazz Singer* (1927); followed by the part-talkies of 1928 as all Hollywood samples the trend; then the first all-sound pictures in 1929, as audio technicians become the new wiz-ards of film and most of Old Hollywood is thrown into retirement. Oddly, for all its head start in the treacherous science of the talkie, Warners did not handle it noticeably better than other studios. Per-haps it made its plunge too frantically, for this was a decisively expensive undertaking for a low-budget studio, virtually do or die.

At first, Warners exploited its advantage rather than developed it. In *Lights of New York* (1928), typically a cheap gangster picture, all action freezes as a pair of goons plot a caper as if struggling with a foreign language:

HAWK: I planted the stuff in Eddie's shop.
SAM: Yeah?
HAWK: And the dicks'll be there at ten o'clock.
SAM: Uh-huh.
HAWK: But they must not find (pause) Eddie.

---

*The music-and-effects was an intrinsic part of *Don Juan*'s exhibition but not literally a sound track, for Warners first used the cumbersome sound-on-disc method (Vitaphone) rather than the more practical sound-on-film approach (Movietone) pioneered by William Fox and eventually adopted for all talkies.

No studio could get by without a prestige star, and silent-era Warners had John Barrymore, here in Don Juan, *which launched Warners' prestige stunt: sound.*

(Long pause)

Don't you understand?

(Very long pause)

SAM: What, you mean . . . ?

(Very, very long pause)

HAWK: Take him . . . for . . . a ride.

(Another very long pause, as the concept sinks in)

SAM: Ohhhhhhhhhhhhhhhhhhhhhhhhhh.

The slang is there, and the emphasis on plain sets, and the shadier figures of city life. But where's the Warners restlessness, the city pace? *Lights of New York* succeeded despite itself, for audiences were fascinated by sound in any form in 1928. But once the other studios declared the talkie war of 1929, Warners lost its advantage in constant miscalculation, making movies as tentative as the dialogue of *Lights of New York*. *The Desert Song*, a quite faithful replica of the Broadway show, moves too slowly. *The Show of Shows*, an overstuffed musical revue, follows a pleasant song with an incomprehensible comedy sketch and drags out its production numbers so recklessly that a "sister number," a succession of real-life sister acts involving complete changes of décor and song for each pair, runs to five or six couples. *Noah's Ark* employed DeMille's moralistic-parable-with-flashback-commentary format just after the form had suffered permanent eclipse.

It would seem that the jump from little studio to big studio over-taxed the lot. In 1928, Warner Brothers absorbed First National Pictures, the studio founded to combat Adolph Zukor and a more complex outfit than the Warners were used to running. With Darryl Zanuck running the old Warners lot on Sunset Boulevard and Hal Wallis in charge of First National's lot in Burbank (whither the entire Warners operation moved upon consolidation, in late 1930), Warner Brothers underwent an expansion as frantic as it was determined.

Thus the miscalculations—thus also the sudden revelation of the Warners we are used to, the crash-paced city stories with the naturalism and grip that the romantic *Desert Song*, dizzy *Show of Shows*, and irrelevant *Noah's Ark* lacked. Now almost everything is plain and harsh—the characters, the writing, the design, the lighting. After the enormous expense and trouble of gearing up for sound, Warner

Brothers is cheap and Warner Brothers is fast. As if making up for the sluggish camera work and idle chatter of the first talkies, the studio excels in the furious drive and vivid lingo of the genre it was to develop uniquely, the crime film.

This field has its subdivisions—gangster, prison, newspaper, shyster, boxing, detective, and lawman pictures. And of course the crime film itself was invented and supported by other studios. But Warners administered the genre in its prime, made most of the exemplary entries, and propounded most of the key elements. The very casting of the Warners crime film marked a historical break with Hollywood procedure, which favored the employment of general-use contractees—Paramount's George Bancroft and Evelyn Brent, for instance. These two became celebrated, in their brief heyday, for underworld charisma, but they were just as plausible in non-gangster roles. *Little Caesar*'s Edward G. Robinson is a new sort altogether, an actor who was scarcely plausible in any role *but* that of a gangster. The trope works in reverse as well, when Robinson plays a pathetic worm in Universal's classic film noir *Scarlet Street* in the mid-1940s, Robinson all the wormier precisely because we know that the ruthless Little Caesar lies under the façade. The news that Robinson was in fact mild-mannered and culturally minded is amusing but beside the point, as is the legend that *Little Caesar*'s producer, Hal Wallis, couldn't see Robinson in the role till the actor clomped into Wallis's office in fedora and overcoat, leering behind a cigar.

"*Nyahhh*," Robinson rasps. "You and me can do business. *Nyahhh*."

And Wallis says, "You've got the part."

Cute but unlikely. Robinson's movie career till then consisted almost entirely of gangster roles. What else had Warners hired him for? At the time, they had George Arliss for prestige costume bios—*Disraeli* (1929), *Alexander Hamilton* (1931), *Voltaire* (1933)—and John Barrymore for romantic bizarrerie. Everyone else was, again, plain and harsh, some meaner, like Robinson, and some nicer, like Edward Woods, whom Zanuck put into Warners' next major gangster title after *Little Caesar*, *The Public Enemy* (1931). Woods played a cop's son who goes bad, joins the mob, and dies the death. He has one mitigating quality, love of his mother, and one friend, a sidekick from the neighborhood who follows him through his criminal career and also

*One advantage of the talkie was the chance to see if the stars'
sound matched their looks. Here's Richard Barthelmess in
Weary River (1929); note the use of a favorite Warners
genre, the prison picture. The ads emphasized Vitaphone
fun in that Barthelmess not only talked but sang and played
the piano. Well, Barthelmess could talk, but the music was
dubbed by others. Some fun.*

gets killed in a mob war. James Cagney played the sidekick. After viewing the first few days' rushes, producer Zanuck told Woods and Cagney to switch parts.

As *Little Caesar* made Robinson Warners' reigning Italian hood, with the flavor of Chicago, *The Public Enemy* made Cagney Warners' New York hood, Irish, with the ecumenical savor of the melting pot —every so often he'll throw out a phrase or two in Yiddish, reminding us that the old Irish and Jewish ghettos not only abutted but sometimes interlocked. Already we sense Warner Brothers' unusually downtown atmosphere. Paramount's Bancroft and MGM's Gable never played ethnic. But Warner Brothers, remember, is the studio that wagered its very future on the tale of a Jewish boy caught between patriarchal insularity and babes-and-booze Americana, a Jakie Rabinowitz turning into one Jack Robin: *The Jazz Singer*. And Warners wagered this future not through the deputy of some WASP engagingly "doing" Jewish (as Cornel Wilde, say, does Chopin) but through Al Jolson, one of the most Jewish entertainers of the day— he throws out even more Yiddish than Cagney—and, typically, a big Warners star.

Like *Little Caesar*, *The Public Enemy* is not concerned with the politics of the underworld, only with its character. Both Robinson's Rico and Cagney's Tom Powers simply want to "be somebody," to exercise free will and take what can be got. Nor does *The Public Enemy* moralize in favor of Cagney's taking. Yet why are all the film's good guys so dreary? Cagney's policeman father's a brute; his brother, Donald Cook, a pill; his mother, Beryl Mercer, an idiot. Cook is made to seem a fool for having done his Army stint and returned to a low-paying honest job; if his is the right way, why is he so gloomy? Even Mother Mercer doesn't seem to like him. And if *Little Caesar*'s Robinson is shown very much cut off from family and romantic life —*his* sidekick, Douglas Fairbanks, Jr., deserts him to dance with Glenda Farrell, and Robinson's "mother," the atrocious hag Ma Magdalena, cheats him of his loot and locks him in a womb-like closet—Cagney's public enemy is a romantic hero. A Warners sort of hero, with back-alley patter and a half-grapefruit to slam in Mae Clarke's kisser. "I ain't so tough," he observes contemptuously when his rival's bullets hit and he totters. No, that's just it: he *is* tough. He dies hard. Director William Wellman closes on Cagney's corpse, dropped off at his mother's door, falling to the floor as brother Cook sanctimoniously stalks away. This is a glamorous anti-glamour.

Robinson's grotesquely uncouth and Cagney's charmingly insensitive heroes attracted a wide public. The gangster cycle that Warners thought had commenced with *Lights of New York* actually began with Robinson and Cagney. *No one* was in *Lights of New York*. *Little Caesar* and *The Public Enemy* introduced high-powered versions of what had been Warners' stock-in-trade for the first two years of sound (four years, if we count Jolson and Brice from the part-talkie years): real people. Or, let's say, imaginary people with real faces and voices. Their dynamic personalities made them so appealing that the entire gangster cycle was thrown into disrepute, especially with the Production Code people. Whose side, as the old leftist anthem runs, are you on?

As the leader in the field,* Warners took most of the heat. Now comes a cycle of retractions, first in hortatory notes tacked onto rereleases, next in purifying recastings of Robinson and Cagney. "The public enemy is not a man, nor is it a character," we learn in the doctored print (still in use today). "It is a PROBLEM that, sooner or later, we, the public, must solve." No sooner have we taken this in than Robinson plays a cop in *Bullets or Ballots* (1936) and Cagney appears as a lawyer so honest that he decides he can best uphold justice as one of the—yes!—*G-Men* (1935).

Here's another way out: cast the *nyahhh*-wild Little Caesar as a soigné author interested in crime, in *The Amazing Dr. Clitterhouse* (1938). From the first sequence, a fancy party attending to a florid soprano singing "Una voce poco fa," from *The Barber of Seville* (but note the filleted version—Warners is still moving quickly, can't waste a moment), we take in the activity from a new plane of observation. *Little Caesar* and *The Public Enemy* led us into the streets with the street people. Now we see the world through leadership-class eyes. Like Robinson's Dr. Clitterhouse, we are not partakers but witnesses. Interesting, too, that only the studio that virtually owned the

---

*The gangster cycle ran through Hollywood generally, but Warners claimed most of the talent best suited to it. What other studio had a Robinson or Cagney on hand, or the writers equipped to work that terrain, not to mention the sheer guts of realism in the *mise-en-scène*? There were plenty of good films of the cops-versus-criminals sort, but in the more essential genre of the gangster's rise and fall, popular in 1931 and 1932, the only film to share the Warners impact was *Scarface* (1932), an independent production released by United Artists.

crime film could make a spoof of crime *cast with its standard criminal roster*—not only Robinson but Humphrey Bogart, Allen Jenkins, various rogues of secondary familiarity, and, as the gang leader, Claire Trevor.

Still, all crime films are, ultimately, crime films. In a pinch, Warners might turn out a prison film, but with Robinson, Cagney, George Raft, and the usual suspects on hand, the difference was of setting, not character. We note the assistance of Paramount's former Dangerous Man, George Bancroft, as the warden in *Each Dawn I Die* (1939), but otherwise this is pure Warner Brothers, with Cagney a crusading reporter framed by a corrupt D.A. and brutalized in the Big House. This is Tom Powers, the Public Enemy, with morality and a motive. And what of the ex-convict? George Raft bears a veritable mark of Cain as a parolee in *Invisible Stripes* (1939), hunted from job to job, even arrested for a crime he didn't commit because he *could* have done it.

At Warner Brothers, all crime films conduce to political film. Despite the lack of position points in *Little Caesar* and *The Public Enemy*, the Warners crime series aims at a Statement, and finally stated it most clearly in *The Roaring Twenties* (1939), for many the climax of a genre. We are of course looking back, from a generation's vantage, distanced from the start by John Deering's "march of time" voice-over and by the sound track of '20s tunes pumped out in late-'30s swing tones rather than authentically, as we had heard them when they were fresh. Moreover, the Warners style has filled out over the decade, moving more grandly, less tensely, than in the early talkies. Thus, a mere eight years after the gangster-protagonist cycle began, after sliding its key gangster characters into home as lawmen and injured innocents, Warners now proposes that we sit back and "witness" the event nostalgically.

No way. *The Roaring Twenties* bears Cagney himself as the hero under Raoul Walsh, a master of the action genre who directs to bring his audience into the adventure, not keep them at a remove. And in form *The Roaring Twenties* observes the gangster conventions, reintroducing us to places and figures we first met when Robinson went *Nyahhh* and Cagney muttered, "I ain't so tough!" Here again—or, rather, still—are the clubs and molls and hijackings and intramural duels.

Here also is an explicit view of the outlaw as a good man dispossessed, a Jean Valjean who doesn't live long enough to reform. The movie begins as Cagney returns from his war service. Not only is he unable to reclaim his old job, but the men who replaced him—who took it easy while he fought—razz him as a chump. A concentration of such encounters between the good man and the corrupt system sends Cagney into the rackets. Thus the film reasons out his criminal career, even dubs him a "crusader" mediating between, in Deering's authoritative voice-over, "an unpopular law and an unwilling public."

The Roaring Twenties is heavily freighted with such dualisms—"honest" crime versus Fascist law, the honorable gangster versus the gangster heel, loyalty versus received morality . . . the film itself is a Socialist outburst disguised as slick nostalgia. *High Sierra* (1941), also directed by Walsh, is sometimes called the "last" of the old gangster films for its sentimental view of an aging hood and for its institutionalization of Humphrey Bogart as Robinson's and Cagney's replacement as the studio's outlaw hero. And *High Sierra* does have its touch of social commentary, especially in its view of the rich, seen as irritable, stingy, and stupid. During a heist at a resort hotel, one couple enters in clothes—his white jacket, her flouncy cape—that would have marked them as madcaps at Paramount. At Warners, the clothes tell us that they're jerks. And indeed she tries to goad her date into being a hero and precipitates the murder of a law officer.

The Roaring Twenties, however, is far more precisely the last of the gangster films, more respectful of the atmosphere of the originals and something of a sermon on how social conditions frame human action. Certainly "Mad Dog" Earle, Humphrey Bogart's character in *High Sierra*, is likable but not, as far as we learn, a good guy who wants to stay clean. Like all the nasties Bogart played in the 1930s, often in gangs headed by Robinson or Cagney, he went bad by choice. But *The Roaring Twenties* furiously takes us through Cagney's degradation as if making a connection between the Public Enemy and the Public Victim, between all Warners crime films and all Warners socially conscious films—and, in the 1930s, few Warners films weren't. The picture is retrospective not of the 1920s but the 1930s—as experienced at Warner Brothers. *The Roaring Twenties'* air of tragic vitality is so surely felt that the famous climax—in which the mortally wounded

Cagney staggers onto the steps of a church to die—feels like bene-
diction rather than irony. In *High Sierra*, Bogart is shot down by a
sniper as his girlfriend Ida Lupino looks on in despair. *The Roaring
Twenties* similarly has a loving moll on hand, Gladys George. But
note that Lupino is cut off from Bogart geographically, setting off his
alienation existentially but not historically. Bogart is a dead man,
Cagney a broken icon. For as George cradles the dead Cagney in the
snow, a cop asks her who just died.

"He used to be somebody," says George—an unmistakable reference to Little Caesar's itchy mission. *Be* somebody. Thus *The Roaring
Twenties* closes Warners' gangster cycle, full term. It is not only the
last gangster film, but the first, the primary entry, abstracting the data
from earlier films into a position paper.

We must as well take into account Warners' innumerable "alternate" underworld films—on crooked lawyers, newspapermen,
boxers. Now we have Robinson, say, in a film of social criticism, *Five
Star Final* (1931), on the corrupt recklessness of the tabloid. Then we
have Robinson in sheer entertainment, in *Kid Galahad* (1937), with
Wayne Morris as a bellhop-turned-prizefighter, Bette Davis as Robinson's girlfriend, and Bogart as the hood who tries to muscle in.
Now we have a film in which a social problem is laid out and solved:
Star Witness (1931), wherein the mob tries to terrorize a family out of
testifying in court; courageous citizenship wins out. Then we have a
problem without a solution: *They Won't Forget* (1937), in which a
scapegoat is lynched—judicially; then, upon pardoning, spontane-
ously by mob action—for the murder of a high-school girl. Yet all
these very different films share a politicized atmosphere, an awareness of class as fate.

All studios are class-conscious, but not necessarily for political
confrontation. Paramount believes in class as setting, a style; MGM
offers class as décor, or, in Crawford's shopgirl-princess vehicles, class
as adventure in self-affirmation. Warner Brothers' class-as-fate may
sentimentalize itself as didactically compassionate, but it is as often
provocative, even incendiary. The most innocent-seeming film will
suddenly crack wise, even something as silly as *Gold Diggers of 1937*
(1936), a backstager in which insurance salesman Dick Powell strives
to keep policyholder Victor Moore alive while Moore's business
partners plot to kill him. They grant him a nice way to go, all told,

hiring gold digger Glenda Farrell to love him to death. Sighting her prey, Farrell dons a weisenheimer grin and sails off observing, "It's so hard to be good under the capitalistic system."

The moment startles; some Warners movies startle all the way through. Leave it to Warners, in *They Won't Forget*, to counter Hollywood's traditional view of the American South as a paradise of wisteria, juleps, and dashing gamblers. At Warners, at least in the 1930s, the South is bigots and chain gangs. When teenager Lana Turner is raped and murdered, District Attorney Claude Rains sets out to find not the culprit but a defendant who will inflame the public and get Rains into the newspapers. A black would do nicely; but that's so *usé*. How about a white man, a teacher . . . a Northerner? Oh *yes*.

What is unnerving about *They Won't Forget* is the pure sociopathic ambition it portrays in Rains, the ease with which he manipulates press and public. Bad enough that a mob can get its hands on you—Warners shows that the law itself can lynch. The trial is so unfair that the governor of the state pardons the condemned man—reluctantly, as it will mean the end of the governor's career. Thus defied, the public pulls the victim of Southern justice off his train and strings him up. It is a credit to the realism of the Warners style that we are so caught up in the politics of the event, in feeling out our own awareness, that not till the very end of the film do we realize that we still don't know who killed Turner.

Historians will remind me now of Fritz Lang's *Fury* (1936), a comparable film, from Metro—made a year before *They Won't Forget*. And let it be said that Lang terrifies us with the experience of a lynching far more than Mervyn LeRoy does in *They Won't Forget*. The sequence in which a mob marches on the jail that holds Spencer Tracy is justly famous. As they try to burn the jailhouse, burn Tracy alive, Lang picks out details—a woman holding her infant up to see, another woman falling to her knees in prayer, a child gobbling a hot dog—that chillingly naturalize the event.

However, MGM's lynching is strictly a law-and-order matter, lacking the regional bigotry that Warners expresses (though even Warners dared not get to the heart of the case the film was based on: Southern anti-Semitism). "I had a scene showing a group of Negroes," Lang later recalled, "sitting in a dilapidated Ford car in the South listening on the radio to a transcription of a lynching trial. As the state attorney spoke about the high incidence of lynching in the U.S. each year, I had the old Negro just nod his head silently without a word. Mayer had this scene, and others like it, removed." Note, too, that Lang's sheriff attempts to stop the lynching, while Warners' Claude Rains in effect leads it. Most important in terms of the impression the two films make, at Metro the intended victim gets away. At Warners he is hanged.

Warners' key film of this kind is *I Am a Fugitive from a Chain Gang* (1932), directed, like *Little Caesar* and *They Won't Forget*, by Mervyn LeRoy. The setting is again the South, and the story is basic Warner Brothers: a working-class man, wrongfully implicated in a holdup, is sentenced to hard labor in iron. He escapes and creates a new life for himself, till someone exposes him and he is returned to the chain gang. Again he escapes, this time to the life of a nomad outlaw. (Consider another Warners title: *They Made Me a Criminal* [1939].) Simple action, no personable stars or production values or even a grand song in a cabaret scene. Unthinkable at Metro or Paramount, Goldwyn or Selznick. Unnecessary. Movies aren't supposed to remind you of life's ills; movies soothe them.

I Am a Fugitive soothes less than any Warners film. We check off the political inflections of the tale: when protagonist Paul Muni tries to pawn his war medal, the pawnbroker shows him a display case full of them. When he is whipped for muttering "Skunk!" at a sadistic prison warden, LeRoy pans past Muni's fellow convicts on their cots, all sullenly expressionless. Just after breaking out, Muni, in the barber chair, hears a policeman describing him—so Muni, daring the lot, gets out of the chair and turns to stare the cop down. He's not even looking. He's reading *Liberty* magazine.

Political inflections. How loathsome authority figures are in this movie—the judge who condemns Muni, the chain-gang guards, or the lawyer for the state, a hypocrite who lectures on the beneficial effect of what is clearly shown to be legal slavery. Even Muni's brother, a minister, is a collaborator in the repressive system. When the state promises to treat Muni lightly in order to get him back, then slams the iron on him for what is more or less going to be a life sentence, Muni cries, "They're the ones who should be in chains, not me!" This is what is called recognizing the Socialist moment—but the minister brother does little more than murmur a homily.

The fade-out is absolute talkie, sound without a visual, a story missing its hero. Daring a visit to the woman he loved, Muni shares a tender moment, hears a car approach, then slithers away. His girl frantically tries to call him back. Doesn't he need money? Food? Help? By now we can't even see Muni; we can't see anything. "How do you live?" she asks him, and in the blackness he replies, "I steal."

Apparently the stage lights failed, throwing the set into darkness. But it was very Warners of LeRoy to keep the cameras rolling, not only because the studio liked one-take shooting but because the social implications of the picture of a man erased into a non-person suited the Warners approach. Critics underrate the film, assuming that no production of the fat-cat Studio Age could serve as a social indictment on a par with Eisenstein or De Sica. There is a grip of Rooseveltian loyalty about Warners generally; how critical of systemic iniquity can an FDR sponsor be?

But how much more critical does *I Am a Fugitive* have to be than to show an innocent man swept into a trap of ruthless brutality from which neither church nor state wants to save him? LeRoy makes it plain that those who don't shrug Muni's case away actually want him back in chains out of vindictive fury: simply because their power to do evil has been threatened. *They Won't Forget* is comparable for this view of democracy as a fraud run by thugs; but at least there the protagonist is one of the scoundrels, distancing us from the suffering. We never quite touch base emotionally with the victim, a supporting player. But *I Am a Fugitive* travels with the victim, makes us his confidants in that grouchy Warners naturalism that prefers subjective to omniscient narration. Muni is no plop, no born casualty, Warners cautions us. He is a veteran, energetic, fair-minded. It could happen to you. What stronger critique could one ask for? "I steal."

Why was Warners in particular so alert to the politics of culture? A studio as bound as this one to city stories might easily have taken on the perceptions of the urban proletariat, which do not tend to the compassionate left. On the contrary, the urban proletariat vote with L. B. Mayer. It would seem that the Warners themselves were the only moguls who felt some responsibility about their Jewish background, and the Jewish prole tends to the liberal.

Warner Brothers is in fact the only studio with a Jewish identity. Fleeting glimpses of the Jewish subculture run through Hollywood

King of the Lot: James Cagney in a surprisingly characteristic PR shot, even for the central figure of Warners' social-problem films.

studio history, whether in seriously humanistic situations or for cheap-shot laughs. But Warners, especially in the 1930s, is very aware of its own background. It maintained a heavy complement of Jewish stars (Jolson, Robinson, and Muni, among others; and John Garfield, later, played romantic leads) and fiercely defied anti-Semitism in its films. One can imagine MGM making *The Life of Emile Zola* (1937), but not building up Zola's defense of Alfred Dreyfus the way Warners did (though it's never mentioned that Dreyfus was Jewish); and one can't imagine MGM making *Disraeli*. Even the notion of MGM's letting a star feast his eyes on a Yiddish newspaper, as Jolson does in the vision of heaven in *Wonder Bar* (1934), is beyond conceiving. Moreover, Warner Brothers was one of the few studios to cut Nazi Germany out of its foreign market—most of the other lots, though run by Jewish producers, had to be banned by the Nazis before they would give up this lucrative arena.

Oddly, the man most responsible for Warners political films was the only major Studio Age mogul who *wasn't* Jewish, Darryl Zanuck. A corn-fed Midwestern daredevil who broke in as a writer during the Third Era and rose to claim power just short of that of a birthright Warner brother, Zanuck believed in plugging the movies into the social currents of the day. A headline would inspire him—FEDS HUNT LAMMING KILLER, or BOXING FIX SCANDAL, or SOCIETY QUEEN IN LOVE NEST RAID. Books prompted him as well; he was one of the few moguls who read more than the title. *Little Caesar*, the film that most truly launched Warners' gangster cycle, is a close adaptation of W. R. Burnett's novel, itself a fictionalized account of life in the Chicago underworld. Robert E. Burns, author of the book on which *I Am a Fugitive* is based, was in fact a fugitive from a chain gang when the film was made: his book was autobiography, not fiction.

This is Zanuck at his best, quick to seize the day, give it a picture and caption.* Certainly the future will refer to the Warners films of the Zanuck era to get a reflection of life in the Great American Depression, not Paramount's *Trouble in Paradise* or Metro's *Grand Hotel*. This is not to visualize Zanuck in his office exhorting his staff to expedite the revolution, to characterize bankers as grubby sneaks and the workers as Jimmy Cagney. Indeed, it isn't clear exactly who

Little Caesar and *I Am a Fugitive* were both Hal Wallis productions, but they nevertheless bear Zanuck's stamp: his kind of movies, if not his movies precisely.

Paul Muni bids adieu to Helen Vinson in the last scene of I
Am a Fugitive from a Chain Gang. *Muni's big mistake was
letting Glenda Farrell denounce him to the police, a
strangely passive act for a Warners hero. What would the
film have been like if James Cagney had played the part?
More violent, no doubt, more heroically tragic—but using
the unassuming Muni intensifies the message: it could happen to anyone.*

at Warners supplied the political input. It seems likely that the studio itself provided a tolerant climate, and that the projects it favored encouraged certain writers and directors to look at life from the underdog's perspective. Zanuck's people of the headlines—his criminals and boxers and slumming society queens—have an unusual take on things. They have been to the world. Perhaps Zanuck, a writer himself, gave his writers extra leeway; most writers tend to the liberal side. It is indisputable that Zanuck's writers did.

Then too, Zanuck liked controversy, enjoyed the suspense of seeing how a touchy proposition would go over. In the contemporary style of iconoclastic retrospective, our picture of Zanuck focuses on that damn polo mallet he swaggered around with, his chorus of yesmen (most Hollywood executives had them, but Zanuck actually strolled the lot wagging these tails behind him), and his daily afternoon date with some starlet, during which the office was closed, the phones were let ring, and the secretaries sat red-faced waiting for the 4:30 resumption.

That's Hollywood. But Zanuck does seem to have loved movies for their own sake; and that's not Hollywood. He was a man of his word as well; that's not even the planet earth. Zanuck left Warner Brothers after the industry-wide salary cut of 1933, because Warners extended the cut after Zanuck had given his word that the studio would restore full pay when the other lots did.

Zanuck's steerage of his own studio, Twentieth Century, and of the ensuing amalgamation of Twentieth Century–Fox, yielded a somewhat different approach from that of his Warners days. Yet he left a mark that showed into the 1940s. Take the Warners musical. This was a Zanuck creation, for the form, overexploited in the first years of sound, had been alienating audiences by late 1930. Few musicals were made in 1931 and 1932, especially at Warners, badly burned by such expensive Technicolor musicals as *On with the Show!* and *The Show of Shows*, both flops. In late 1932, Zanuck sensed a lucrative cycle in the offing if he could bring the musical back. He used the backstager format, and qualified the risk by bunching most of the numbers at the end; if preview audiences didn't like them, they could be cut without hurting the narrative flow. Better yet, Zanuck outlawed the two-bit excrescence that bedeviled so many early musicals, the shticky comics and let-me-sing-and-I'm-happy honkers. In fact, Zanuck simply applied the Warners city music to the moribund song-and-dance genre, with all the wiseass slang and hustling ambition that any Warners movie exploited. The politics are understated, just a few references to the number of jobs riding on the show's success. But the underworld is just a phone call away when the show's director needs a thug to break up a back-street romance involving his star.

This is, of course, *42nd Street* (1933), forerunner of the great series that included *Footlight Parade* (1933) and *Dames* (1934), as well as *Gold Diggers* annuals of 1933, 1935, and 1937. The form is not totally Zanuck's, or even Warners'. Its most apparent source is the very first movie musical, MGM's *The Broadway Melody*, which has some of the low-down Backstage Confidential atmosphere that perfuses *42nd Street*. But *The Broadway Melody* is almost entirely about three performers who happen to be putting on a show, while *42nd Street* is about Putting On a Show. It also has a large cast of principals, thirteen names, all below the title (even veterans Warner Baxter and Bebe Daniels didn't get star billing), each of them introduced in live action during the credits in that characteristic Warners cameo style that MGM borrowed for *Grand Hotel* and *Dinner at Eight*.

Actually, *42nd Street* appears to look back to Warners' own *On with the Show!*, a backstager set, like the last third of *42nd Street*, during the out-of-town tryout of a troubled musical. *On with the Show!*, too, has a large cast of principals. But otherwise the two films have almost nothing in common. It is particularly notable that *On with the Show!*'s show, *The Phantom Sweetheart*, is a book musical just like the kind Broadway was producing at the time, a story show with plot and character and scene numbers—notable because Hollywood virtually never attempted that again. Why trouble to think up a story show when a revue allows you to throw in any number you choose, without explanatory context? There is something wonderfully bemusing in *On with the Show!*'s backstage shots. Terrible as the film is (and *The Phantom Sweetheart* is no better than it should be), we have the sensation of peeping in through the stage door of a Broadway theatre in 1929. For once, the show they're putting on really could have been produced as we see it. But *42nd Street*'s *Pretty Lady* is a revue, with self-contained numbers performed for their own sake, and thus Zanuck affirmed Hollywood's growing distrust of authenticity in dealing with Broadway. As of *42nd Street*, every Broadway musical—in Hollywood—is a revue.

Zanuck underlined the break between Hollywood's Broadway and the real thing in letting Busby Berkeley film the numbers. Like most of Hollywood's dance directors, Berkeley had come from Broadway. But unlike his colleagues he quickly seized the advantage of the camera. In Samuel Goldwyn's *Whoopee!*, Berkeley is still wrestling with the possibilities: he has discovered overhead pattern shots, but ends the "Stetson" number with a line of girls dancing off the screen as if the edge of the frame led to the wings.

By *42nd Street*, Berkeley is ready to party. Director Lloyd Bacon gives us one very brief shot of the title number, *Pretty Lady*'s finale, in the dress rehearsal; and this is pure Broadway, with the cast ranged across the stage in front of a painted flat, arms raised and curtain falling. But when Berkeley gives us the number proper, we move out of the theatre's confines into Hollywoodland, in a set larger than any Broadway house could accommodate, with the spectator's eye led not by the sweep of the stage but the take of the camera. Nor does Berkeley bother to match his last shot—Ruby Keeler and Dick Powell pulling down a shade as if it were the theatre curtain—to what Bacon showed us of the number's finish. This is a movie.

Not till after *42nd Street* did Berkeley really exploit the camera, thinking up numbers that didn't just depart from stage procedure but defied it—"Lullaby of Broadway," for instance, more a dream sequence than a "staging"; or "Dames," special effects rather than choreography. Berkeley's big numbers, usually set to songs by Harry Warren and Al Dubin, and generally sung by Dick Powell, Ruby Keeler, or Joan Blondell, comprised one of the Hollywood musical's unique styles, instantly recognizable. Even more basic to these films, however, is the characteristic Warners political reading that shapes the titles that followed *42nd Street*—*Gold Diggers of 1933*, the immediately succeeding entry, is suffused with Depression panic. In *42nd Street*, Warner Baxter wants to put on his show for professional satisfaction. In *Gold Diggers of 1933*, performing is work; one works to eat. And, lest we forget, the film closes with "Remember My Forgotten Man," a Berkeley phantasmagoria on the socially disinherited war veteran.

In short, all Warners movies of the 1930s are the same movie, fast, hip, contemporary, political, urban: even when they aren't. *Val-*

ley of the Giants (1938) isn't urban or contemporary. The giants are redwoods and the time is 1902. Yet as early as in the opening title cards, we are fugitives from a chain gang: "Backed by limitless power and wealth, the timber barons moved in . . . " While enjoying our first Technicolor view of Claire Trevor's hair (it is *very* red; so is Charles Bickford's), we note good guy Wayne Morris's use of "reforestation" and bad guy Bickford snarling, "What do you care what happens fifty years from now?"

There is almost no Warners film of this decade that is not somehow concerned with the problems of social disintegration, whether in race or class prejudice, in inequities of opportunity, in money-boss corruption, or in simple unemployment. Other studios, taking up the practice, would lecture—a bane of late-'40s RKO especially. At Warners, a villain rasps out a credo of opportunism, Wayne Morris goes rigid, and the story *moves*. No lecture. As in the Bible, the lesson lies in the story itself, in the clash of characters. At Warners, during but also after Zanuck, the science was storytelling—and keep it clear and quick. I don't want it good, I want it *active*: short scenes, shorter ones, montage narration, wipes and fast cutting instead of the temperate fade, sets changed so fast that no one has a chance to see how dull they are, lit as if by bare bulb. Let Metro have its production values, Paramount its elegance. Warner Brothers is fast and plain and that is hot stuff. That has bite; and when it's over, you remember it.

One reason why is the memorable look of the city people. Only MGM was as readily identifiable by its stars—because they were so opulently presented. Warners' people could be the men and women you passed in apartment hallways, dressed so, lit so, speaking so. There were exceptions, especially in generic casting: Joe E. Brown for slapstick, Ruth Chatterton to serve as Queen of the Lot in weepies, George Brent to wear a tuxedo in a world-weary manner in Chatterton's weepies (and marry her; but that's his business), Douglas Fairbanks, Jr., for light comedy, Errol Flynn and Olivia de Havilland for costume action, Richard Barthelmess for prestige—he had been a Griffith star and wore his dignity nicely—and the very young Loretta Young for reasons that have never been made clear.

By far, however, Warner Brothers was the house where "character people" played leads—Al Jolson, Edward G. Robinson, Humphrey Bogart, Warren William (ideal as a shyster or detective but embarrassing as a romancer), Aline MacMahon, Joan Blondell,

Other choreographers set a song dancing; Berkeley turns it
into a short story. "Lullaby of Broadway" (above), from
Gold Diggers of 1935, is his masterpiece, a night in the life
of "Broadway baby" Wini Shaw, who sleeps by day, dates
Dick Powell in a gigantic art deco nightclub, then tumbles
through a window to her death. "All's Fair in Love and
War" (right), from Gold Diggers of 1937, is a sequence of
puns on the song's title, as Powell and Joan Blondell lead the

boys and girls in a gender war till a cannon explodes into a
rocking chair, yielding, through the Berkeley kaleidoscope,
a pride of rocking couples. (Note Lee Dixon, the original
Broadway Will Parker in Oklahoma!, to Blondell's immedi-
ate left.) Last (overleaf), "By a Waterfall" from Footlight
Parade (1933) is Berkeley at his simplest: no story, no puns,
just the girls frolicking in the wet.

Ruth Donnelly. It was a studio of tough broads, too, in Bette Davis, Claire Dodd, Ann Sheridan, Ida Lupino; and of sidekick people born to play cabdrivers and gunsels, like Allen Jenkins and Alan Hale. In the 1940s, casting would plume up a bit, go Hollywood, with Ronald Reagan, Dennis Morgan, Lauren Bacall, and Doris Day. But Warners made its reputation on real faces and voices.

It was the antithesis of MGM's grooming faculties, also of MGM's "woman's studio" touches. Warners was a man's place, perhaps the only studio in which Marlene Dietrich could get lost between Edward G. Robinson and George Raft, in *Manpower* (1941). Warners had no Clarence Brown or George Cukor, adept at drawing performances out of actors (though Warners did bring Edmund Goulding in for some of Bette Davis's vehicles). Warners had Raoul Walsh and Michael Curtiz and Lloyd Bacon: okay, let's make it. Let's get this thing lit and shot, and you actors—shut up and do it. I mean, think of it—Walsh wore an eye patch. We're talking major Tough Guys here, charged with bringing every film off with the efficient fury of a pirate raid.

Without question, the essential Warner star was James Cagney. "Women love bums!" is how Zanuck explained it. Cagney was nasty but lovable, taking energy and a crass self-esteem as the first virtues. Looking back much later, Cagney stated that he put "a hunk of hoodlum" into everything he played. That is, building on the boys he had grown up with in New York, the heroes and punks, the wastrels and calculators, the loners and bunch runners, Cagney slipped a bit of it all into his portrayals, and that "all" bore a heavy input of male aggression. Cagney isn't just forceful; he swaggers, force as an art form. In *The Roaring Twenties*, when the two guys who took his job while he was overseas taunt him with a spoof of an Army marching rhyme, Cagney slugs one so deftly the punch bounces off the other. Both drop. "Two for one," Cagney sneers.

It was an original conception, as much of air as of earth, but it meshed perfectly with the Warners tension. Cagney is fast stuff, impetuous in war or peace, ready with a comeback or a punch on the money, not to mention that half-grapefruit. Maybe Cagney wasn't as sexy as Gable, but he was as physical; and he got there first, a star as of *The Public Enemy* while Gable was still third-lining it at MGM.

The New Yorker's theatre man, Wolcott Gibbs, said of Beatrice Lillie that she performed "as if all human aspiration were absurd." Cagney performed as if all American aspiration were forgivable. Energy and self-esteem. "You don't give, you take," Jean Harlow tells Cagney in *The Public Enemy*, observing that most women look for men who are gentle and considerate. Not Harlow. "Oh, Tom," she cries, "I could love you to death!" But Gladys George in *The Roaring Twenties* tells Cagney, "I think you're a pretty decent guy. I like to talk to decent guys. They're pretty hard to find."

Like Gable's Dangerous Man, Cagney's is ambiguously mixed of good and bad intentions, an honorable rat, a helter-skelter knight. But Cagney brought a bit of the picturesque to the type, for while Gable seemed a mid-American ace, more or less conventionally derived—"common, pleasing, vigorous," as Sophie Treadwell put it —Cagney was a shantytown Irish cockerel, his voice a city snarl and his features almost demonic.

This is Warner Brothers on the absolute. None of the studio's other action heroes had anything like Cagney's agility, originality, charm. Robinson was somebody's uncle. Bogart took a decade to establish himself. Raft was slow and dull. And Errol Flynn, a genuinely romantic hero, couldn't match Cagney for smarts. (Flynn, as we'll see, comes into a different Warner Brothers altogether.) In fact, none of these stars could place, as Cagney could, that good bad man that much of Warners' moral code depended on. Even Gable in his prime did not easily switch from total bad guy to total good guy and back; something bluntly mean in him pushed all his characters, no matter how loyal, courageous, or affectionate, back to the bad side of the dividing line. "You're not so tough," Carole Lombard tells Gable in Paramount's *No Man of Her Own* (echoing Cagney's "I ain't so tough" in *The Public Enemy*). She's wrong. He's so tough that on their honeymoon he can sport a dressing gown Mae West would have thought gaudy, and still look vicious. He's a scoundrel, one way or another.

But Cagney could jump from the brutal and selfish Tom Powers of *The Public Enemy* to the victimized Eddie Bartlett of *The Roaring Twenties*, from *Footlight Parade*'s musical-comedy director energetically thinking up ways to keep everyone off the breadlines to the engagingly arrogant George M. Cohan in *Yankee Doodle Dandy*, from

a G-man to a cowboy* to the meanest gangster of all, Cody Jarrett in
White Heat (1949). Gable played a similar range of roles, but not with
Cagney's range of personality. Nor of course did Gable have Cag-
ney's hoofing ability, another reason why Cagney's was the most
richly inflected Dangerous Man in Hollywood. But then Gable's
MGM observed a somewhat conventional morality, whereas
Warners' more naturalistic purview looked for nuances, ironies,
exceptions. Gable suited MGM because Gable was larger than life.
Cagney suited Warner Brothers because Cagney was life.

It is instructive that the studio's most typical star found himself
constantly at war with Jack Warner. Several times in the 1930s, Cagney not only walked off the lot but moved back to New York in symbolic defiance of the factory town of Los Angeles. His problems were
inherent in the very structure of the low-budget studio—long hours
(six-day weeks and, often, night work as well), low pay, hectic working conditions, three rotten pictures to every decent one. It was
treadmill stardom: no money, no patience, no quality.

Look how long it took Warners to make Humphrey Bogart
bankable—twenty-seven films, not counting those he made for other
studios—before he got to *High Sierra*. He had been a gangster in most
of these twenty-seven. "I played more scenes writhing around on the
floor," he later recalled, "than I did standing up." *High Sierra* made
him sympathetic, as an over-the-hill gangster with a strong sense of
charity and a strain of autumnal romance. Here too, he ends up shot,
but now it is tragedy rather than just deserts. For twenty-seven films,
Bogart had been just a criminal or a dude. In *High Sierra* he became a
Dangerous Man, ready for *The Maltese Falcon* (1941), *Casablanca*
(1943), *To Have and Have Not* (1944), *The Big Sleep* (1946). Yet Bogart
owed it all to chance: *High Sierra* was another of the important films
that George Raft spent his career turning down. But for Raft, Bogart
might have writhed around on the floor for life.

One wonders what would have happened to Gable had he forged
his career at Warners instead of at MGM. We get a glimpse of a
Warners Gable in *Night Nurse* (1931), on loan-out from Metro, playing a chauffeur trying to murder two little girls while he romances

---

*As Jim Kincaid, the eponymous protagonist of *The Oklahoma Kid* (1939). Humphrey Bogart's
in it, too. You don't realize how essentially urban Warners is till you see Cagney and Bogart
riding horses and wearing ten-gallon hats.

their alcoholic mother and takes over the house. The young Bogart might have done the part. And we can see why Bogart spent twenty-seven movies paying dues, because little of the Gable we know comes through here. We get none of his sensuality and wit, just the meanness. He's no Dangerous Man here; he's a creep. Gable made *Night Nurse* the same year he made *A Free Soul* back at Metro. Yet where Norma Shearer goes into a rhapsody when Gable shoves her around in the latter film, his bullying of Barbara Stanwyck in *Night Nurse* is ghastly.

No wonder Cagney lived in a permanent state of war with his studio. No other lot remotely approached Warners' record for disciplining and even suing its own top breadwinners. One Warners actress virtually made her career on her battles with Jack Warner—one ongoing battle, really, on the quality of the films she had to make. At least Bogart and Cagney and Dick Powell and Ruth Chatterton and Edward G. Robinson quickly found their type. The pictures may not have been rousers, but their personalities had something to bite on.

This particular woman star had something special to get rebellious about: Warners couldn't type her. She played society flappers, working-class girls, tramps, little sisters. The pictures were at best competent, more often abysmal. Warners gave her star billing to shut her up, on something called *Ex-Lady* (1933), so terrible that, she said, "my shame was only exceeded by my fury." She begged and bullied Jack Warner to lend her to RKO for the utterly unsympathetic kind of role that kills a career: being nasty to Leslie Howard. Finally her boss agreed. "Go hang yourself," says Jack Warner. But no. This RKO film gave her her first major notice; and some of her Warners pictures picked up in quality. She actually managed to win a Best Actress Oscar in 1935, though many felt she really won it for the RKO the previous year.

The RKO was *Of Human Bondage*, the star was Bette Davis, and the film that first alerts us to her ascendancy in the studio hierarchy is *Marked Woman* (1937), about a bunch of "nightclub hostesses" who tackle their mobster boss in court and send him to prison. Typical Warners, in the Zanuck Effect: the film is based on a headline item, the Lucky Luciano case, despite the opening disclaimer that the characters and events are fictitious. Also typical Warners is the use of the sordid and even brutal milieu for a star's vehicle; only at Warner Brothers did you become Queen of the Lot playing a B-girl—without any romance to speak of at that. District Attorney Humphrey Bogart tries to spark one, but Davis takes the fade-out walking into city fog with her fellow heroines, an arrestingly feminist conclusion.

Davis gives a rangy performance in *Marked Woman*—irate, terrified, disgusted, hysterical, every scene a Big Scene, fully punctuated. Warners is getting big, too. The films have opened up somewhat, taking more time than they did in the *Little Caesar* days. We're getting fewer montages, more fully spelled out episodes. We note the opulent orchestral track, not just accompanying but propelling the action. Warners is growing up.

Davis is growing along with the studio, specializing in "high and mighty comedown" parts, as a diva who must learn grace. In *Jezebel* (1938) she's an inflamed Southern flirt who matures through unselfish love—and the death of love. In *Dark Victory* (1939) she herself dies, as a young plutocrat stricken in her heedless prime. We see a more imaginative Davis now, far more skillful at reading the nuances than in *Marked Woman*. She softens the grain of melodrama, tightens up the weepie. Then, faced with the challenge of historical romance-*cum*-melodrama-weepie, she says the hell with it and really lets fly in *The Private Lives of Elizabeth and Essex* (1939), a study in take-no-prisoners, stand-and-deliver star quality. She was not yet Queen of sufficient power to get a more sympathetic Essex than Errol Flynn, despite her demands for one. But then she was the only woman in Hollywood who didn't like him; and the film is in Technicolor, a rare splurge for Warners, a Queen's due. Davis had made it to the top.

All the more amusing, then, to watch Miriam Hopkins defy Davis's supremacy in *The Old Maid* (1939). Ostensibly the rivalry of cousins in love with George Brent and co-"mothers" to his daughter, the film is in fact a rivalry of divas, spiced by Davis's ultra-pro resistance of Hopkins's many tedious little difficulties during shooting, perhaps inspired by her resentment of having played a mere four weeks on Broadway in *Jezebel*—the property that gave Davis her second Oscar.

La, the duels! Of hairdo: with Davis in a giant snood and Hopkins in enough corkscrew curls to outfit fifty Little Evas. Of costume: as Hopkins grabs Orry-Kelly's velvet-and-lace décolleté while Davis, in

The range of Davis: above, contemporary melodrama in
Dark Victory (note President McKinley in a small role),
then (right) costume pageant in The Private Lives of Elizabeth and Essex, *as Bette reprovingly eyes the impedient*
Flynn.

the spinster part, makes do with aprons and shawls and a high neck. All goes well at first, for Hopkins can preen and Davis can act, a suitable separation of gifts. Comes then Davis's big confession scene— unmarried, *she* bore Brent's daughter—and Hopkins pales with jealousy. She didn't know they were dueling over portrayal, too.

Just as well, for Hopkins is utterly outclassed. This is what being Queen of the Lot is about: overwhelming force of personality. Given a heavy line, Hopkins storms. Davis knows how to fling an accusation in a whisper, as we marvel. Granted, Davis's role is a knockout as written. She has the best bits: sitting alone in her room listening to party music, dancing by herself, stopping, sitting, and sighing for the late George Brent; being hurt again and again by her unwitting daughter, who calls Miriam Hopkins "Mummy" to Davis's "Aunt Charlotte"; playing mother in soliloquy by her fireside, chiding her by now virtually imaginary daughter. It's a Queen's part especially in that it successfully contradicts Hollywood's first and second principles of stardom: (1) Look your best no matter what, and (2) Don't have competition. Maybe Hopkins isn't competition in any true sense, but Bette really turns into an old maid here, gray and pinched, fussing about the disposition of the doilies for the daughter's wedding. Yet Davis has us in her grip, if only by startling us with the rightness, the profound pain, of her feelings as never-wife and near-mother. After "Aunt" Charlotte, Davis can play anything, and so she does in *The Letter* (1940), breaking yet another principle of stardom: (3) Be accused of murder, but innocent.

Bette's guilty. We see as much in the opening sequence, one of the most prestigious star showcases in all film. It's Malaya. It's hot. Natives lie about in hammocks, unable to stir. Then: gunfire! The camera pulls back on a woman shooting a man as he escapes from a house. She shoots him repeatedly. We move in: it's Bette! A close-up on her fury. The natives gather; they all saw it. So did we—and what focuses attention on a star more than committing cold-blooded murder? For once, we have a Dangerous Woman.

This is High Warners, a lot at last imposing enough to deserve a Queen. There is a luxurious Max Steiner score, atmospheric décor, a budget beyond reproach, and cinematography to rival Metro's, letting light and darkness play parts in the show as exposure and menace, rendering people as shadows. There is a Paramount touch in the use of William Wyler—in the Old Hollywood belief that a wise director makes a wise film.* There is the self-importance of the property itself, from Somerset Maugham through Katharine Cornell (on Broadway) and Jeanne Eagels (as a silent). And there is Bette, her name not over the title but *before* it, by itself. Queen of the Lot.

True, there are no gala fashions. No ball gowns, no important jewelry. This is not Norma Shearer's idea of a Queen's role. Not MGM's. But Shearer would never have played *Of Human Bondage* or *Marked Woman*, either. Bette Davis's idea of a Queen's role is *acting*, especially with Bette Davis eyes. When her lawyer hands her a copy of the title's incriminating letter, we watch as she reads, Steiner bellowing in agony. She swears she didn't write it; the lawyer knows she did. Yes! She wrote it! *Yes!* But she was afraid! Unsure! We think back to the opening. Afraid? The lawyer reads the letter aloud. They must retrieve the original. If it's produced in court, it will hang her. So Bette calls in one of the Queen's most essential perquisites and faints dead on the spot with exceptional prestige. Another Oscar nomination for Bette—and if she hadn't already copped two, she would have won.

High Warners, widening its sociopolitical survey with these grander, richer, and more dexterous films, begins in the mid-1930s with *A Midsummer Night's Dream* (1935) and *Anthony Adverse* (1936). The latter title is the more negotiable vehicle for image enhancement: a somewhat sensational best-seller with enough plot to fill out a picture the length of a Metro Big One. The production itself was rather big-deal for Warners, not only in the substantial capital outlay involved but in its need for actors and staff of some elegance and fashion, especially a prestigious star. The studio talent pool, used to the gritty style of gangster pictures and backstagers, nonetheless included the lustrous Anita Louise and Claude Rains, so versatile he could play the D.A. in *They Won't Forget*, Prince John in *The Adventures of Robin*

---

*Wyler had directed a previous Warners film, *Jezebel*. Still, he was a most uncharacteristic choice for the studio of fast setups and single-take printings, even in its grander phase in the 1940s. Wyler habitually shot and reshot scenes without ever telling the actors what he wanted instead. He caught thirty-three takes of *The Letter*'s first sequence, and Hal Wallis called him into the projection room to see the take they had chosen. The dourly scintillant night sky, baleful in its beauty, the hammocks and the heat, and Bette shooting, shooting. Perfect. "Now you see," Wyler smugly tells Wallis, "why it was worth thirty-three takes." And Wallis replies, "We printed the first take."

Hood, a detective (badly, for once—but he fights valiantly against the miscasting) in *They Made Me a Criminal*, and Napoleon III in *Juarez*. The hero, Fredric March, and most of the character roles signed up on loan-out or free-lance contracts. But otherwise *Anthony Adverse* was manufactured in house: Mervyn LeRoy directed, Sheridan Gibney wrote the screenplay (to the praise of the novel's author, Hervey Allen), and Erich Wolfgang Korngold composed the score.

Korngold was one of the pioneers of the big symphonic track score. The first years of sound generally depended on orchestral medleys of atmospheric tunes more or less autonomously lilting away in the background, rather like a salon trio stroking an afternoon's teatime. Dance bands would crank out hits from a studio's earlier movies for contemporary films; costume shows would call upon the classics. Korngold, a distinguished classical composer, developed the possibilities of the dramatic track score, psychologically commentative, opera without voices.

Korngold was not the first to do so; Max Steiner preceded him. (Listen to RKO's *King Kong* sometime: *listen* to it. Steiner's sweep and terror should be counted among *Kong*'s special effects.) But Korngold's imposing reputation lent honor to the profession, underlined the *responsibility* of the track composer. Most important, these new-style Hollywood scores of the late 1930s not only exploit the atmosphere of melody but key the music so closely to the action that they assist the camera, heighten the effect of a shot—stopping on a dime, say, at the crashing open of a door. Korngold refused to exhaust himself by falling into the Warners schedule, and composed at leisure. But the indefatigable Max Steiner joined him in setting a style for the Warners score that influenced all Hollywood.

Korngold came to Los Angeles specifically to rearrange Mendelssohn for Warners' *A Midsummer Night's Dream*. Now, here was a project to confer honor on a studio: the game is to *be* somebody, as Little Caesar warned us. The illustrious Max Reinhardt had staged the play at the Hollywood Bowl, and Warners offered to let him film it. Reinhardt adapted uneasily to the mechanics of filmmaking, however, and William Dieterle was called in to collaborate on the direction. This was a brilliant stroke, as the two men were fellow campaigners from their Berlin past, and what they worked out was, essentially, Dieterle's filming of Reinhardt's production.

So far, so good, for Reinhardt was a genius and Dieterle very gifted. But if *Anthony Adverse* needed the prestigious borrowing of high-class actors, *A Midsummer Night's Dream* was cast almost exclusively on the lot, with the figures of the Berkeley extravaganza and the urban melodrama intoning Shakespeare in tights and ruffs. Dick Powell as Lysander? Billy Barty—the bizarre midget of "Pettin' in the Park" and "Honeymoon Hotel"—as Mustardseed? Olivia de Havilland as Hermia? Historians jeer. Oddly, some of the casting succeeds in spite of itself, Warner Brothers pulling itself out of its mean-streets past through the vivacity of the personalities it has nurtured. The *Pyramus and Thisbe* amateurs may lack the Shakespearean ring, but Joe E. Brown, Hugh Herbert, Frank McHugh, Arthur Treacher, and especially James Cagney (as Bottom) create a proletarian comix neither contemporary nor antique that contrasts wonderfully with Reinhardt's opulent fairyland. Mickey Rooney, borrowed from MGM, makes a savagely capering Puck that many of the film's admirers hail as Reinhardt's key invention, certainly his most noticeable break with Shakespearean tradition. At the time, Warners was simply "doing an MGM" in producing the film at all. Half a century later, side by side with MGM's own Shakespeare, the Norma Shearer–Leslie Howard *Romeo and Juliet*, Warners' film betters MGM, with a more daring approach (forgiving the miscasting, that is) and more vivacious cinema.

The most striking evidence of the studio's bid to relax its underdog stance and join other lots in the making of Big Ones is the costume-adventure series built around Errol Flynn and launched in the mid-1930s, simultaneously with *A Midsummer Night's Dream* and *Anthony Adverse*. The latter two films were one-shots, specials. But to institute escapist romances in defiance of the dark, brisk, urban naturalism that *was* the Warners talkie is something like self-subversion.

True, the first Flynn, *Captain Blood* (1935), is not unlike a lighter and more positive *I Am a Fugitive from a Chain Gang*, reset on the high seas. Flynn's Dr. Peter Blood is convicted of treason against King James for treating a wounded rebel, and is deported to Port Royal for hard labor. As so often before, Warners analyzes the cruelty of the system's overseers—the judge suavely vicious in his wig, the king remarking that "hangings are splendid, aren't they?" We see one prisoner branded on the face, whereupon director Michael Curtiz cuts to another wig saying, "What a shame, that any man should suffer so!" Pity from a tyrant? No: Curtiz dips down for a shot of the wig's foot, crippled with gout. The wig was speaking of himself.

Compare *Captain Blood* with MGM's immediately contemporaneous *Mutiny on the Bounty* and one sees how political the former is. The two pictures share a premise: a group of men, driven beyond endurance, became outlaws, led by a hero. But MGM never regards the brutal Captain Bligh as a symbol of the institution of oppression. He is corrupt. He is a sadist. He is a murderer. But at MGM he is just a man. *Mutiny on the Bounty* is so unable to answer Lenin's *Kto kowo*—who does what to whom—that it shows us Clark Gable, the hero of the piece, forcibly impressing innocent seamen for the *Bounty*'s crew, taking them away from their homes for two years of what they know will be terrible hardship. Worse yet, the mutineers who return to England, justified (they think) in their case, are hanged—except Franchot Tone, pardoned because he's of noble family. It doesn't take much imagination to see the socialistic ironies in this, but MGM ham-and-eggs its way around it. *Captain Blood*, for all its whimsical flirtation and revenge-and-piracy plot center, is very aware of the advantages of birth.

Flynn, in his first lead part to speak of as Peter Blood, is energetically tentative, now earnest and now empty, not yet realizing—as he soon would—that he was at his best when he let his natural charm shine through. He has Olivia de Havilland for a Lusty Lady heroine, Lionel Atwill and Basil Rathbone for villainous adversaries, and a call to piracy to express his radicalization against injustice. What more Public an Enemy than a pirate? Yet Flynn is not cut off from society, as Paul Muni was in *Chain Gang*. It is villains he hates, not England or its system. And he has Erich Wolfgang Korngold's surging symphony, spacious backlot sets and stock galleon footage, and a certain grandeur of narrative tempo to exhilarate his tale. We are far, far from the claustrophobic city of *Little Caesar*.

Director Curtiz, heroine de Havilland, the snarling Brit Villain (Claude Rains, most frequently), and the galvanizing Korngold formed Flynn's stock company, and the ensemble gave Warners a kind of second style, perhaps a style-within-style, like Paramount's vaudevillian comedies or MGM's Freed Unit musicals typifying a studio yet unique of themselves. By *The Adventures of Robin Hood* (1938),

Warners was indulging in Technicolor, the expense alone the signet of a major studio. This time we get both Rains and Rathbone, so artfully nasty that it's a letdown when Ian Hunter finally shows up as Richard Coeur de Lion. All the more so when we realize that the very rebellious hero is quite happy with the return of his king. It wasn't Saxon-Norman race war that had worried him, apparently, nor the atrocities of the police state—both of which have been made most evident—but simply the greed and treachery of Rains and Rathbone.

By the time of *The Private Lives of Elizabeth and Essex*, the following year, there is scarcely a trace of politics as such—this in a tale that questions rulers' ability to retain their balance as human beings. Instead, we are treated to a film that questions the Queen of the Lot's ability to retain her prestige when she's thrust into a Flynn–de Havilland–Curtiz–Korngold spectacle.

She does, we know. If Queen Elizabeth I had not existed, Bette Davis would have had to invent her. Maybe Davis did invent her; this pouting, fan-smacking, mirror-smashing, grabbily shy puppet is most people's image of the Virgin Queen. Davis's audacity runs to excess, but it is admirable excess, a talismanic portrayal. She thinks *Elizabeth and Essex* is The Big One, Warner Brothers' *Gone With the Wind* and *The Wizard of Oz* at once. Flynn thinks it's a Flynn vehicle, and he hurts the film by refusing to respond to Davis. To save it, Davis plays seven things at once: queen as woman, queen as warrior, warrior as sweetheart, sweetheart as virago, virago as Lusty Lady with Slight Character Disorder, Lusty Lady as sweetheart, sweetheart as Queen. "I never knew from day to day who me mother was," she tells Flynn. "Shook me nerves." She laughs—then, in a terror, reaches for him.

He isn't there. Granted, it must be a challenge to enact love scenes with a woman whose subtext is I love him but I love history more. Granted too, it must have grated on him to have her intruding into his cycle, with the amenably complementary de Havilland demoted to a secondary part. I mean: who is the protagonist of this film? Or even: what is it about? We are given the makings of an essay in politics, and end with an aborted love story. No wonder Flynn's succeeding pictures largely abandoned the historical context for simple World War II tales, wherein we know who's good and who's bad. Even *Santa Fe Trail* (1940), pictorially a look at Bleeding Kansas during John Brown's abolitionist raids, is a World War II movie, in

The Sea Hawk *(1940) is another Flynn costumer with a message to hearten a people facing war. Spain is bad because it exploits criminals as galley slaves; England is good because Flynn is English. Anyway, Claude Rains is always the villain, and he's Spain's ambassador to England, here talking over spying and treachery with King Philip II (Montagu Love). Flora Robson plays a zesty Elizabeth I, closing the film with a democratic pep talk: "When the ruthless determination of one man threatens to engulf the world . . ." And she doesn't mean Montagu Love. Note the High Warners décor, with atmospheric map.*

which we do not reason why: we just do. "It isn't our job," Flynn tells a concerned Ronald Reagan (as George Armstrong Custer; this is witty casting *avant la lettre*), "to decide who's right and wrong about slavery any more than it's John Brown's."

Thus Warner Brothers began to go back on its worldview. Paul Muni didn't escape from the chain gang because he didn't like the life—he knew he was right and They were wrong. But wartime was approaching. Charles Lindbergh may not have thought so, but the Rooseveltian Jack Warner did. So his studio put by its subversive aesthetic of bare-bulb lighting, downtown faces, and leftist politics for the duration: not only of the war, but of the studio itself. It was a real major now, big enough to have two Queens of the Lot, with Mildred Pierce challenging Good Queen Bette.

It's interesting to see how much of Davis's tigress sensibility— the *Dangerous* and *Jezebel* Davis—Joan Crawford adopts in her new house. We get no real sense of a jump from Metro to Warners in Crawford's late-'40s films, as we would have if Eleanor Powell had left her *Broadway Melody* for the *Gold Diggers*, or if Clark Gable had made *The Maltese Falcon*. Perhaps by the 1940s Warners was somewhat like Metro and vice versa; perhaps Crawford herself was less like Crawford. But we definitely lose the heroistic Crawford for a down-and-dirty noir character. As at Metro, Crawford's cleaver-sharp diction enables her to be as unbelievable playing a society matron as playing a waitress. However, Warners emphasizes Crawford's violence, her ferocious feelings that swerve from admiration to vindictiveness almost for the fun of it. *Humoresque* (1946), Warners' follow-up to *Mildred Pierce*, finds her playing protégeuse to slum-kid violinist John Garfield. Crawford makes a star entrance, thirty-four minutes into the action, as the hostess of a superb party, surrounded by men—some five or six flash lighters for her cigarette. Yet we are not meant to like her:

JOHN GARFIELD: (to a party guest) What's her husband like?

CRAWFORD'S HUSBAND: Weak. Not a bad sort. Just weak.

Sure. But what's his wife like? Venomously sexy, virulent in a way the Metro Crawford wasn't: a rich bitch. Metro didn't like the type. Rich is good. Warners, even after Errol Flynn and World War II, hasn't changed enough to approve of women who have five or six men to light their cigarettes.

A touch of Humoresque. *John Garfield wants to act, but Crawford knows a star is always a star: with shadowed face, penetrating look, and a cosmic sense of self.*

The studio has grown big by 1940, but not fat-cat. In fact, it has stayed the most compact of all the major studios, the least versatile but the most consistent. It continues to emphasize city settings and crime genres. It's still cutting corners, employing Technicolor less often than any other major except Universal and RKO. It is strapped for a musical form, unable to find a successor to the Berkeley Depression backstager in the aftermath of a Depression. (Berkeley himself moved to MGM.) *Night and Day* (1946) is as slipshod a Cole Porter bio as any of MGM's bios, with songs thrown into any old show and a marquee reading "*Paris*, music by Cole Porter." Who wrote the lyrics, Lorenz Hart? (A touch of *Yankee Doodle Dandy*'s authenticity, however, in "My Heart Belongs to Daddy," sung by its creator, Mary Martin, and staged in facsimile décor.) One expects a sanguine view of the marriage of Linda Lee and Porter—one of the gayest men who ever lived, insistently and amusedly and penetratingly gay, and he didn't care who knew it. Okay, this is not for 1946. But does Cary Grant have to walk through the role? He could have been a dynamite Porter; he had the charm and the wit, and he's one of the few actors who could look at home on a piano bench. Clearly, the idiotic script discouraged him.

Musicals aren't the only problem. Warners also has yet to get the hang of social comedy, mainly because this studio put so much of its satiric energy into all its scripts. MGM's Eleanor Powell vehicles never enjoyed the wisecracking zip of Berkeley's backstagers. As for mannered comedy, here was one studio that couldn't pull off a screwballer. *Four's a Crowd* (1938), at the height of the screwball era, is a charming failure as early as in the opening credits, when Errol Flynn, Olivia de Havilland, Rosalind Russell, and Patric Knowles march arm in arm like the stars of MGM's *Libeled Lady*. *Libeled Lady* had a classic screwball cast. *Four's a Crowd* sounds like *They Died with Their Boots On* with emergency loan-outs from a Columbia divorce-remarriage spoof.

Screwball comedy, at heart, is about having money and fun. Warners is against both. The studio can fabricate genre, with the vapidly handsome other man (Knowles), the silly heiress (de Havilland), the irascible plutocrat (de Havilland's father, Walter Connolly), the rich-at-play hobby (Connolly's model railroad), even the devious wirehaired terrier, established across studio boundaries in

MGM's *The Thin Man* (Asta), Columbia's *The Awful Truth* (Mr. Smith), and RKO's *Bringing Up Baby* (George), all played by the same lucky animal. But Warner Brothers doesn't *believe* in this genre—doesn't believe that the rich are redeemable or that a heroine can be as madcap as an heiress. *Four's a Crowd* even gets socially preachy, one thing screwballers never are.

Warners is still Warners, which is why *The Maltese Falcon* (1941), one of the most typical films of the reconstituted wartime Warners, feels somewhat correspondent to the dangerous city music we heard in Warners' first talkies. The political readings are missing, for a nation gearing up for defensive solidarity would not likely support Warners' ontology of common-man alienation. Still, we have the bleak urban milieu, the anti-glamour naturalism, and the sharp tough-guy writing that marked Warners from the start of sound. We have as well Humphrey Bogart, one of the studio's most official personalities. After *High Sierra*, he has been graduated from his outlaw stage. (At that, the sneaks have appeal, too, as a rogues' gallery of screwball eccentrics: sniveling, scented Peter Lorre, unctuously jovial Sydney Greenstreet, sullenly farouche Elisha Cook, Jr.) A friend of the sneaky and righteous alike, Bogart is no longer rapacious, but noble and charming. The gang is gone; Bogart is now a loner. And, at Warners, that's as noble as a guy can get.

The Maltese Falcon marks another rehabilitation, that of the crime film into noir, complete with Treacherous Woman Mary Astor. In a way, Warners had been making noir right through the 1930s, if only because of its emphasis on mystery and violence in darkly lit places. It had in fact already made *The Maltese Falcon* twice, in 1931 with Ricardo Cortez and Bebe Daniels, and again in 1936, as *Satan Met a Lady*, with Warren William and Bette Davis. The first version, directed by Roy Del Ruth, is faithful to Dashiell Hammett's novel, as is the third version, written as well as directed by John Huston. But *Satan Met a Lady* is so asinine one gawks at the screen; it recalls to us the cheapjack quickie-lot Warners elbowed aside in history by the incisiveness of *Little Caesar* and *42nd Street* or the luxury of *The Letter* and *The Adventures of Robin Hood*.

By the time of the Huston–Bogart *Maltese Falcon*, this other Warners is fading out. Prestige bans these fast-buck features that Warners built its fortunes on; it has won too much respect in Holly-

wood to grind out many more *Satan Met a Lady*s. Like any other studio, it continues to foster its profitable B units. Cheap movies make
money. But Warners can no longer hope to hit jackpots with slap-
dash B films that bear an A vitality, as it did in the early 1930s. Why
can't it? Perhaps the early-talkie years, energized by the very novelty
of the technology, have ceded to a more reflective—or even more
simply confident—age. Perhaps directors like Michael Curtiz and
stars like Bogart realized that they could work more successfully on a
less grueling schedule and less stingy budgets. Perhaps the overpowering example of MGM, the velvet Oz, inspired Jack Warner to emu-
lation. The game is to *be* somebody. For we find a kind of MGM
prototype in what may be Warner Brothers' most popular film, and
surely one of the ten or twelve most basic American movies, *Casablanca* (1943).

Warners gives us the political slant, the clever grip of repartee,
and the administrative symphonic narration that we seldom find at
Metro. And a heroically cynical Humphrey Bogart is pure Warners.
But consider the film's premise—do-or-die intrigue centered on the
hero's bar and back-room gambling club, the pleasantly illicit relationship with the authorities shattered by historical upheaval, and a
triangle love plot further to stir the blood. This is suggestive of the
grander Gable films—*China Seas* with some colorful minor characters and suaver bad guys, *San Francisco* without opera, *Idiot's Delight*
(note the parallel erotic flashbacks) in Rick's Club Américain. MGM
would not have fielded both Peter Lorre and Sydney Greenstreet in
brief but crucial roles designed to fill out the apprehensive quality of
life in Vichy Casablanca. Either Lorre or Greenstreet might do for
MGM—as each, indeed, did. But the two together were simply too
flavorful for Mayer's applehood-and-mother-pie operation. MGM
would not have put so much of the action into Rick's café, either;
with such an exotic setting, MGM's designers must give us some
backlot Casbah footage. Warners is content to keep it simple till the
spacious airfield sequence at the climax. And surely MGM would not
have torn Ingrid Bergman from Humphrey Bogart, even for the sake
of letting Paul Henreid carry on his anti-Nazi Resistance work. At
MGM, only Garbo's romances could end in tragedy.

Nevertheless, *Casablanca* is in outline the kind of movie MGM
made—might easily have done, in 1942, with Gable as Rick, Lana

Turner (miscast; but she often was in her Metro years) in Ingrid Bergman's role, Franchot Tone as her Resistance-fighter husband, and Frank Morgan in Claude Rains's role as the urbanely corrupt chief of police. After Henreid drowns out the Germans' singing by leading the rest of the club habitués in the "Marseillaise," Rains is ordered to close the club. On what grounds? "I'm shocked," Rains replies, *"shocked,"* he insists, "to find that gambling goes on here!" One of Bogart's men runs up with some money. "Your winnings, sir," he tells Rains. "Oh, thank you so much," says Rains, pocketing the cash and proceeding to direct the raid. It's nearly impossible to see the waspishly bumbling Morgan in the part, but then Morgan played a lot of parts that might have come off with greater point in Rains's hands. It's not that MGM could have made a better film than Warner Brothers; it's that Warner Brothers could now make an MGM film in the Warners style.

The essential difference between the two lots lies in Hollywood glamour. Metro found it in star personality while Warners found it in a good story, in the characters that personalities played. A good story: *Casablanca* is one of the best. It may have one flaw, in the beveling of tone accommodating a very serious love plot, a very melodramatic political intrigue, and a very satiric view of secondary-level corruption. So Bergman and Henreid are ultra-solemn, Lorre and Greenstreet as eccentric as ever, and Rains does his wry devil. At times, the writing fails to hold the parts separate, as when Bergman tells Henreid, "Victor, please don't go to the underground meeting tonight." This sounds like satire. At other times, the blend—or confrontation—of the serious and the satiric is nicely mixed, as when Nazi general Conrad Veidt dismisses Bogart as a "blundering American." "You mustn't overestimate this American blundering," Rains warns him. "I was with them when they blundered into Berlin in 1918." Touché!

Of course, it is just this mixture of adventure, the erotic, and the comic that has kept *Casablanca* vital long after its time. It is a rich mix, making the film one that gets better the more you see it. No doubt the element that holds it together is Bogart's Rick, tough and scarred enough to be a true Warners protagonist but endowed with the genial grandeur of the all-Hollywood hero. Gable couldn't have done it as well, because MGM heroes are born heroes. Warners heroes are born losers who refuse not to win. This gives MGM films their confidence, Warners films their balls. Then too, MGM's idea of the human comedy is everybody getting along because everybody wants to. Warners believes we have to work at it, sacrifice some sense of self to defeat evil. The good fight is a communal undertaking.

So if Bogart begins *Casablanca* wryly neutral in a city of hustlers and innocents, of Nazis, French collaborators, and Resistance fighters, Bogart ends the film by taking on the bad guys single-handed and giving up his personal happiness to join the war. "The problems of three little people," he explains, "don't amount to a hill of beans in this crazy world."

That's the city music expanded to cover the globe.

A classic Fox threesome: Alice Faye, Tyrone Power, and Don Ameche in Alexander's Ragtime Band *(1938).*

FOX

The Rube

Fox is two studios, separate but connected. The first is Fox Film, an Old Hollywood firm run by mogul William Fox on a medium-size budget with mostly second-rank stars and a conservative aesthetic. A successful studio: not an important one.

The second Fox is Twentieth Century–Fox, William Fox's studio merged with Darryl Zanuck's independent outfit for big-budget production with major stars and a conservative aesthetic now and again broken by defiant social critique.

The difference between the two Foxes is strategic, for it shows how influential a mogul can be. We see the makings of Studio Age Paramount in its Famous Players silents, its Little Mary and Wallace Reid vehicles. We get a strong sense of MGM style in the very first

MGM release, *He Who Gets Slapped*. But who could have foreseen *The Grapes of Wrath* or Betty Grable's backstagers in Fox's first major series, the Vamp films of Theda Bara?

Bara, who was actually a nice Jewish girl named Theodosia Goodman, played a character few of her audience had ever seen, the implacable temptress who destroys men of caste and wealth for fun and profit; but mainly fun. Running through her Vamp cycle was one of the most basic energies of the American film: cinema takes you out of your limited existence into worlds you have no practical access to, where you experience life with admirable people on terms of extraordinary intimacy. It is no accident that the movies always drew their largest audiences from the classes traditionally least well traveled, well read, well seen. Poor, they could taste wealth. Lonely, they might fancy themselves loved. Cold, they would watch how passion felt.

Theda Bara stimulated this vicarious adventurism as she posed, threatened, devoured. It's shocking to look in on her first film, *A Fool There Was* (1915). How primitive it is. How unreal. And as Vamp avatar, Bara's no Garbo. Her voluptuous rejoinder to some mewling victim, "Kiss me, my fool!," inspires not delicious awe but laughter in the house. Still, given the language spoken in the Second Era American silent, she was as eloquent as Paramount's Gloria Swanson was in her glorious DeMille bathrooms and dinner parties in dinner clothes. William Fox had a good thing, and he kept it going; when Bara ran out of customers, Fox instituted other Vamps—Betty Blythe, for example, in *The Queen of Sheba* (1921). The very notion of the congenital ruiner of men was getting painfully silly. But Blythe looked devastating and, for all her costume changes, wore a grand total of very, very little.

This was early Fox: following the available trend, whether original with the studio or picked up from some other lot in the periodic cycles; exploiting the potential star who won't cost too much, then replacing him; comprehending cinema as a culture-widener, not because this is socially worthy but because it's good for business. Class and culture were very stratified when William Fox opened shop, and his shop shook them up somewhat, showed folks what else there was in the world. In effect, every movie was a newsreel. But where Paramount seized on this and put forth a cinema of the most spectacular people committing greatly forbidden acts, Fox simply ran with an expedient concept. Now it's the Vamp, then it's the Folk Hero; now it's the Wife and Mother, then it's the Tough Nice Guy. Whatever went over, Fox pursued.

But why do we get a strong sense of close-knit Americana in the Fox output, of films about the family, the land, the history? Much of Fox film has vanished. Yet as far as we can reconstruct it, there seems a clear if inadvertent movement within the studio to show us not new places and people but what we already know. We consider that Fox's contribution to the cycle of Big Ones at the start of the Third Era is *The Iron Horse* (1924), on the transcontinental railroad, a piece of John Ford Americana of such naturalistic fiction that the great scene in which the rails meet to join the continent has the ecstatic wonder of an epic poem and the honesty of an old photograph. We point out that most of Fox's presiding eminences during the Studio Age came from rural or small-town environments—directors Ford, Henry King, Henry Hathaway, and Frank Borzage (from Salt Lake City— just as bad as a small town, if not worse), writers Nunnally Johnson and Dudley Nichols, and producer Darryl Zanuck. We note that Fox's stars almost never came of the glamour ranks, that Fox liked them attractive but uncomplicated—like the studio's big draws of the late 1920s and early 1930s, Janet Gaynor and Charles Farrell, she pretty and he handsome, like 4-H Club devotees rather than movie stars. Speak of Studio Age movie teams, and one thinks of Gable and Harlow, Gable and Crawford, Cooper and Dietrich—only twice, in *Morocco* and *Desire*, but so hot they singed the lobby cards. Yet here was Fox's demure little couple, top box-office for years. One of the biggest Gaynor–Farrell hits, *Seventh Heaven* (1927), finds them as Par- isians, he a street cleaner and she a prostitute. Director Borzage instills the metropolitan scene in his crane shots of the seven floors of stairs they climb to their apartment; and Paris is Paris. Yet Gaynor and Farrell seem like country waifs, not city dwellers. They are basic, sweet, unknowing.

Country people: that's the melody of Fox. Despite its luxurious presentations of the Vamp, this was a circumspect house, never dar- ing the electricity of contact that Metro and Paramount made their stock-in-trade. It may be coincidental, but when Fox decided to buy a little prestige and brought F. W. Murnau over for *Sunrise* (1927)—the first major Fox film since *The Iron Horse*—the result was a potent argument for the country against the city. Murnau cast entirely from the lot: hulking husband George O'Brien, dowdy wife Janet Gaynor, and remorseless Vamp Margaret Livingston. But Murnau built the biggest sets Fox had ever seen, a village by a river and a roaring art deco city. The Vamp of course is of the city; she wants O'Brien to drown Gaynor, so Livingston and O'Brien can move to the city and live on jazz passion. She shimmies as she schemes, wild about sex and death. And, sure enough, the city that Murnau shows us is something of a dangerous theme park, a place of amusement but also of traffic speeding toward its next accident. Murnau's picture of a jazz band is like something out of Fritz Lang's *Metropolis*, and even a trip to the barbershop threatens Gaynor, waiting for O'Brien, with a nasty-looking masher. The city bears contemporary evil. The town lives more simply, on timeless truth.

Fox got in on one contemporary evil, sound: in its Movietone newsreels and the occasional music-and-effects track. (The *Sunrise* seen today carries the same symphonic commentary put on it sixty years ago.) But even in the talkie years the studio continues to emphasize country themes—as in remakes of outdated Second Era titles in *Rebecca of Sunnybrook Farm* (1932) and *Way Down East* (1935), or in films like *The Farmer Takes a Wife* (1935) or *Chad Hanna* (1940), difficult to imagine on other lots. It's not that no studio but Fox would want to make pictures set in nineteenth-century, upstate New York, as these last two are. *Chad Hanna* even gives us a backstage look at the circus, a valid visual novelty. But surely no studio but Fox would relax into this setting so contentedly. MGM, which doted on such tales in the Mayer years, would have found some way to glamorize them. Even Andy Hardy's Carvel, Idaho, allowed such totsies as Esther Williams, Lana Turner, and Kathryn Grayson to pass through; and Judy Garland would sing. Yes, *Chad Hanna* gives us Dorothy Lamour, but it's still a dud.

At Fox the country really is the country, a big, plain, empty place. Because it plays host to the epic of life, it needs epic characters, Folk Heroes. Fox had two, the wise old humorist Folk Hero Will Rogers, in the early 1930s, and the rustically dashing young Folk Hero Henry Fonda, in the late 1930s. Fonda hated Fox, and contrived to play most of his contract on loan-outs to studios with more ambitious directors

One usually gets the same five or six shots of Sunrise, but here's a rare one, as Margaret Livingston urges George O'Brien on to the destruction of his nuclear family: wife Janet Gaynor will drown as O'Brien coasts back to shore on bulrushes.

and writers. But at home Fonda played many a symbolic character, and he was so persuasively epic about it that he enacted Abe Lincoln for John Ford. Now, that's epic.

Fonda did not hit his stride of fame till his post-Fox years. But Rogers, a failure in silents because his act was so verbally pointed, became one of Hollywood's biggest stars exclusively in talkies at Fox. Given his wily/relaxed, cynical/forgiving, parson/horse-trader persona, Rogers had come to the right studio. In the theatre, he had prospered in an alien environment, the *Ziegfeld Follies*, sharing the stage with representatives of the new upstart immigrant city culture in mountings celebrated above all for sophistication of taste. Coming alone before the curtain, apparently unmindful of the priceless collection of womanly beauty and music and comic talent that stood just behind him in the stage house, Rogers would twirl his lariat and expatiate on just about anything, like a loafer on the courthouse steps.

In the realism of sound film, however, Rogers needed a hostly background, settings in which he could symbolically gather into himself the better qualities of American tribal life or in which he could reject the qualities of other systems. Authoritarians, snobs, bullies, and hypocrites are his set targets, but he doesn't defy them as much as outwit or razz them. (Similarly, his famous "I never met a man I didn't like" turned out to be disarming diplomacy rather than confession; Rogers disliked plenty of men, and was outspoken about it: in private.) Rogers will also drop a line or two on the more forgivable foibles that most of us can own up to without shame. In *Judge Priest* (1934), at a party, a Civil War veteran—still in uniform decades after Appomattox—is holding forth on his war adventures. There he was in the river, surrounded by Yankee gunboats . . . and Rogers passes. "Gunboats?" he echoes thoughtfully, in that matchless off-hand delivery that gave his portrayals an improvisational naturalism. "Puttin' them gunboats in there is a new touch, ain't it?"

The Civil War is an active memory in the Rogers village, typically Southern, strongly demarcated by class, and much less the misty paradise we see in other studios' Southern tales. Everyone is solvent middle class, poor white, or black. Everyone knows everyone else; all are related, old friends, or lifelong enemies. The town in *David Harum* (1934) is actually called Homeville. If Rogers's forte was the gentle honesty of his humor, his great appeal lay in his representation of the old ways, the world much of America took for granted before there was a World War or immigration "troubles," or women's rights . . . or movies. Fox launched its history by breaking taboos in the unveiling of Theda Bara; but Fox continued its history by reaffirming age-old cultural pieties. Even references to contemporary life come off as the opening of a vault of relics, as when *Steamboat Round the Bend* (1935) starts with a duel of orators, a revivalist and Rogers selling alcoholic medicine. Prohibition was only two years dead by then, yet we think not of closed saloons or racketeer wars but of the little Temperance Unions of the 1870s. Rogers isn't ageless; he is of a vanished age.

His Fox films follow two patterns. In one, Rogers travels out of his village to comment on the vain ways of the outside world, usually in the company of a wife of comparable vanity. In the other pattern, Rogers, as village honcho, plays Dutch uncle to a young couple while saving the day in some incidental plot contrivance. The latter format has proved the more enduring, partly because John Ford directed three titles. It was one of Ford's few experiences in dealing with an actor whose standing and independence put him absolutely out of Ford's control. Outfoxed, Ford glumly put up with it but they are among Rogers's best. Ford's, too.

"Hear! Hear!" Rogers cries, looking up and banging his gavel. "Court's called to order!" Then the credits file past and *Judge Priest* begins as a windbag lawyer performs a verbose harangue about a chicken thief. The accused, Stepin Fetchit, is asleep. The judge, Will Rogers, is reading the comic page. He has Fetchit awakened. "If anyone's going to sleep in this court," says Rogers, "it's going to be me."

This is a Rogers pattern 2 film, but the young couple (Tom Brown and Anita Louise) and the plot contrivance (the trial of Louise's father less for a crime than because he is an outsider in the village) are mere fronts for an evocation of a lost style of life. There are wonderful touches, as in Rogers's maid Hattie McDaniel's habit of singing conversational blues, extemporizing lyrics to reflect what's on her mind. Taking in the laundry, she utters a work song, but when Tom Brown returns from law school up North, she switches her lyric to the subject of homecoming celebrations. Later, McDaniel gives us another song as she dusts, and Rogers falls right in antiphonally, singing responses to her queries. An astonishing moment.

Much of the atmosphere of the Rogers village, and of certain of Ford's Fox films and Fox's rural films generally, recalls D. W. Griffith. It is no accident that America's only sound remake of a Griffith classic was Fox's *Way Down East.* Nor can it be coincidence that Shirley Temple, Fox's biggest star in the post-Rogers late 1930s, remade a number of Little Mary's films. Griffith and Pickford were the key exponents of rural, nostalgic, historical America in the Second and Third Eras—and we should remark that Henry B. Walthall, the closest thing to a protagonist in *The Birth of a Nation,* turns up in *Judge Priest* to say, when asked if he was in the "War of the Rebellion": "No sir—the War for the Southern Confederacy." Whereupon, cheers from the house.

Rogers's two patterns combine yet transcend each other in *State Fair* (1933), one of the most relevant titles in Fox's rural Americana. For once, Rogers is not the central figure: the *rite* is, of just folks communing expansively, with fixed points of recreation and solemnity to be made: hitting the road, falling in love, choosing the blue-ribbon pig and the ultimate mincemeat and pickles. Instead of a young couple to protect, Rogers has two, for each of his children falls into romantic company on their visit to the state fair; and the plot contrivance involves the coronation of Rogers's hog, Blue Boy. Yet none of this matters as much as going along with Rogers's family on this once-a-year outing wherein Rogers is set down in an outside-world version of his village, the American pastoral made into a nation. As one reviewer said when *State Fair* was released, "[Rogers] is what Americans think other Americans are like." Thus Fox wants to show us not new places and people, but the kind of people we trust in the places we are sure of. If much of Hollywood's history involves the revelation of out-of-reach places, Fox seeks to affirm the public's personal experience—at least for that segment of the public that can visualize itself as figures in a panorama. The approach directly opposes that of Warner Brothers, where all activity is roiled in the needfulness of *now.* Fox is pacific, retrospective, self-sufficient. Everything is already there, in the village. One has only to look for it.

Rogers's films were immensely profitable, and kept the studio floating in its rocky early-talkie days. Winfield Sheehan, who had been running the West Coast lot since the Third Era of Silent Film, was still in charge, and while he kept Fox going, he could not quite promote it from its secondary status. Fox's releases lacked the excitement of Metro's, Paramount's, and Warner Brothers'. There was too much an air of the twice-told tale about its features, of the nonentity in most of its second-rank players. In desperation, Sheehan would throw out a surprise, daring a Big One in *Cavalcade* (1933), from Noël Coward's Drury Lane extravaganza viewing British history through the fortunes of a family, upstairs, downstairs. It's scarcely a Fox film at all, given its West End source and almost entirely West End cast.

Similarly curious is *Music in the Air* (1934), from the Jerome Kern–Oscar Hammerstein II musical about a Bavarian village songwriter who journeys to Munich to sell "I've Told Every Little Star" and nearly loses his girl-next-door to an operetta impresario. That the property is a backstager, and a Broadway hit, does not surprise; all the studios were making such movies then. But the cast is unexpected: has-been Gloria Swanson as the impresario's diva, for instance, reminding us that she can, too, sing; or the obscure old troupers Al Shean and Joseph Cawthorn in small parts. Then we realize that *Music in the Air* is virtually *Sunrise* as a musical: in the city lie snares of culture and sensuality that the pure in heart must flee, as Douglass Montgomery and June Lang do. But are they victors over urban *Angst* or simply not big enough for the big time? It might be the latter, as both of them had to be dubbed in their songs, an annoying technique that became, as we'll see, virtually a Fox specialty.

In 1935, Darryl Zanuck's Twentieth Century impressed what remained of Fox's staff and facilities to form Twentieth Century–Fox; immediately the logo of a movie-city Egyptian monument swept by spotlights was adopted and Zanuck's voluble input was fed into the repertory. The former boy wonder of the most urban studio, Warner Brothers, joins the most rural lot in town. Zanuck had other adjustments to make. The capital foundation of the merger gave him considerable financial leeway; and instead of playing production chief to Jack Warner, as he had done on his last big lot, Zanuck was now his own Jack Warner. But Zanuck was less a businessman than a moviemaker, more a Thalberg than a Mayer, even if he did favor the Mayer domination of stars' personal lives.

He was unquestionably in control of every facet of studio operation. "Brilliant," Ida Lupino called him, in conversation with John Kobal for his book *People Will Talk*. "That man could, *had* read every script on the lot; he watched every wardrobe test of every male star, every female star; he could remember—with all the people under contract!—that he didn't like a spotted tie on a man in test number three, or he didn't like the cut of a skirt on me in test number four."

Zanuck was a first-rate mogul on a second-rate lot. Warners was cheap but it was loaded with talent. Fox had no major directors besides John Ford and no major writers besides Dudley Nichols and Nunnally Johnson. Zanuck is known as a "writer's producer," appreciative of good text. Yet he made no great effort to attract the best writers. The typical Twentieth writing byline was that of the tireless Lamar Trotti, a sound storyteller short on wit and guts.

The Fox that Zanuck took over was also poor in stars. Will Rogers had died in a plane crash before his last two Sheehan projects were even released, so Zanuck never dealt with him. Nor did he deal with Janet Gaynor, by choice: Zanuck preferred to build his own stars, not attempt to maintain stars already heavily exploited. Zanuck kept on Warner Baxter, Fox's biggest male star after Rogers. But, like Gaynor, Baxter had already been seen a great deal, and he was reaching the age that turns the romantic lead into the character man.

Zanuck brought Loretta Young with him from Twentieth Century, and there were a few new names on the lot he felt he could use, particularly Alice Faye, Henry Fonda, and Shirley Temple. As the 1930s wore on, Zanuck pulled off a major coup in the fashioning of a genre for ice skater Sonja Henie and the framing of a very successful and varied career for Tyrone Power. With Richard Greene as a second-level Power, Don Ameche a dependable sidekick, and John Payne a kind of Dangerous Man—he had the attributes but seldom played the parts—Zanuck found himself with a personality pool vastly different from the one he drew on at Warners. Putting it simply, Zanuck is now fielding soft blonde women and big dark men—even more so in the next decade or so, when Betty Grable, June Haver, Marilyn Monroe, Sheree North, Victor Mature, Cornel Wilde, Dana Andrews, George Montgomery, Cesar Romero, Mark Stevens, Anthony Quinn, and Fred MacMurray (who had left Paramount) appear. Even the exceptions—Jeanne Crain, Linda Darnell, Anne Baxter, Dan Dailey, and Dick Haymes—aren't far off the type.

These are the people for whom Zanuck created Twentieth's genres, drafting energies already in play when he took over and occasionally nudging them with the Zanuck Touch as aimed in his Warners years. The results made Twentieth as big as MGM and Paramount, as profitable, as notable. But not as admirable.

One of the worst aspects of Zanuck's Fox is the tendency to lock certain stars in formats so unyielding that their films are a series of remakes. All studios are guilty of this to some extent; it is the principle by which the B star (if that's not a contradiction) thrives. But to make A-star pictures that doggedly resemble each other is not the act of a leadership lot, as witness the fact that, of the other majors, only the backward-looking Universal did this as often.

No doubt Zanuck simply ran out of things to do with a tyke star, who couldn't do most of the things stars do in movies. Shirley Temple was seven years old when Zanuck arrived, already so important that she had been given a special Oscar for being—well, so important. The film in process as Zanuck came in was *Curly Top* (1935), a remake of Little Mary's *Daddy Long Legs*. As Zanuck saw it, this picture held the key to the Temple form: nice Daddy, no Mommy, a bit of menace, and four songs, especially the title tune, which Daddy John Boles plays and sings as Shirley dances atop the piano. It may be that Zanuck had a hand in the production, even unto ordering rewrites and retakes, for Temple's films under Sheehan were much less confident. The one immediately preceding *Curly Top*, *Our Little Girl* (1935), is atrocious. Joel McCrea is Daddy, Rosemary Ames is Mommy, nothing happens, and Shirley doesn't sing. Instead, she performs cute stunts, such as playing seesaw with her little black Scottie, Sniffy. The dog runs off and Shirley faws down and goes boom, director John Robertson celebrating with a shot of her little behind. The cuteness is verbal, too, when Mommy asks Shirley whom she works for. "You," says Shirley. Whom does Mommy work for? Daddy. Whom does Daddy work for? Counting fingers, Shirley replies, "The butcher, the grocer, the tax collector, and the telephone company!" Add to this more adoring close-ups of Our Little Girl than von Sternberg gave Dietrich in their whole cycle.

Zanuck gave Temple stories and music, also Bill Robinson to dance with in some unforgettable callouts in the history of American race relations. Zanuck took away the parents and made Temple an orphan or the near-equivalent, so she could be all America's Little Girl. Zanuck gave the mode a bit of variety. Now it's a period adventure; now it's a contemporary fairy-tale backstager. With audiences dwindling, Zanuck lured them back with Technicolor, in *The Little Princess* (1939). We're in London during the Boer War, and Shirley has been haunting the local hospital for a sight of Daddy Ian Hunter, supposedly killed in action; but Shirley knows better. She has been demoted to slavey in her fancy girls' school by a wicked headmistress, and almost everyone's mean to her, but she stays nice. For all the color and costume, it's the same little Temple show. Even a dream sequence that finds Shirley as a real little princess, dancing with ballerinas, is embarrassingly modest for a Technicolor A feature.

But then Zanuck seldom made his Temples on an A budget. It didn't take much in the way of mogul smarts to reckon that Temple's public was largely unsophisticated, easily pleased. Only as a last resort, when it looked like do or die, did Zanuck go for it, in *The Blue Bird* (1940), from Maurice Maeterlinck's play but clearly an imitation of Metro's *The Wizard of Oz* from the year before. So, at last, Zanuck spent the money (though not remotely as much as MGM had) and took Temple out of her accustomed milieus. The film itself is a disaster, a *Wizard* that never gets out of Kansas. The European setting is utterly beyond Fox's capabilities in atmosphere. The recasting of Wizard roles—Laura Hope Crews "as" Billie Burke, Eddie Collins "as" Bert Lahr, Gale Sondergaard "as" Margaret Hamilton—is feeble, except for Sondergaard's roguish cat. The music is perfunctory —didn't *The Wizard* teach Zanuck how music illuminates fantasy? The change from black-and-white to color occurs not as the heroine stumbles into the magic (as in *The Wizard*) but in such a drab scene that we think, Oh color. Worst of all, Temple has reached an awkward stage between seesaw with Sniffy and marriage to John Agar. It was all a dream and there's no place like home, yes; but in the end all we have seen is a thirty-five-cent version of a Metro Big One.

When in doubt, do a backstager: this could be the motto of the Twentieth Century–Fox musical, for Alice Faye scarcely sang a note except in a performing context, whether on stage, in rehearsal, or, in a pinch, to cheer someone up. We have none of musical comedy's sheer exuberance of song bursting out of story, as in RKO's Fred Astaire–Ginger Rogers musicals or MGM's Freed Unit specials. No "Let's Call the Whole Thing Off," no "Trolley Song." Nor does Fox have RKO's or MGM's choreographers or arrangers or song-

On the set with capering Shirley: Dimples *(1936). One can see why the nation adored her, but Frank Morgan (left) has his back against the wall and director William A. Seiter (seated) appears somewhat less than enthused. I think she's neat.*

writers or directors. Zanuck did give Faye the benefit of his big dark
men, so these musicals usually have high-powered stars—just not
high-powered song-and-dance talents. Most of Faye's co-stars can't
sing. Henry Fonda is so disgusted to be in *Lillian Russell* (1940) that he
doesn't even act.

Who can blame him, with a bio historically wayward even by
Hollywood standards? First, we have to address Fox's philosophy of
costume, which may be described as early-middle Come As You Are,
and its sense of responsibility to the music of the day, which may not
even be described. Faye doesn't register as an antique personage; Faye
is contemporary, earthy, the queen of Hell's Kitchen. Not only is the
role of Lillian Russell beyond her grasp culturally, it never was written, so she has nothing to play. It's too serious. Faye doesn't do a good
serious. She needs to truck and jive and throw tantrums. We do get a
taste of Russell's involvement in women's rights, and we are
reminded of Russell's background in Gilbert and Sullivan. But after
displaying a poster announcing Russell at the Savoy Theatre—the
Grauman's Chinese of G & S—Zanuck gives us Faye in an evening
gown and tiara bearing a Lullyesque bonking stick singing a modern
ballad. You know the old puzzle with the caption "What's wrong
with this picture?" Well, *everything is wrong with this picture!* The costume is wrong, and Faye carries herself wildly out of style, and they
didn't sing top forty at the Savoy: they sang Gilbert and Sullivan.

One of Zanuck's inventions was the third-billed olio of house
entertainers, literally vaudeville acts plopped in to fill out a thin story:
the hectic Ritz Brothers for (alleged) comedy, Borrah Minnevitch
and His Harmonica Rascals, the dancing Condos Brothers, wisecracking Joan Davis, singing Dixie Dunbar, the Flores Brothers, the
Paxter Sisters, the Brewster Twins, the Four Playboys, Maida and
Ray, Tip, Tap, and Toe—the list, as the poet quoth, is endless. Faye's
pre-Zanuck musicals are a touch lean in musical entertainment, perhaps—but then Zanuck fills them out with extraneous people.

Zanuck's choice interloper was Carmen Miranda, so delightful
she was written into the scripts as a character. In *That Night in Rio*
(1941), Miranda and Don Ameche are a couple; but Ameche is a dead
ringer for a Brazilian baron (also played by Ameche) married to Alice
Faye . . . and as we take in Faye's icily grand demeanor, we wonder if
we were better off at *Lillian Russell*. We concentrate on the Techni-

"Let's go slumming on Park Avenue," Faye pleads in On the Avenue *(1937), a kind of credo for the Fox musical in general: the heroes are proletarian but the backdrop often reeks of fame and riches. At Warner Brothers, everyone just wants to stay employed. At Fox, we're looking for the Big Time.*

color décor, but even this bears the sameness of the series: every set looks like a nightclub. The Brazilian stock exchange looks like a nightclub. The Baron's house looks like a nightclub. And the night-club looks like heaven with chairs.

Sonja Henie's films were even more generic than Temple's or Faye's. Henie didn't share Faye's irregularity of costume, as Henie's were modern-dress films; the dress was storm-warning overcoats. An Olympic skater, Henie could be called a form of dancer. But she didn't sing and she couldn't act. So it was on with the Tyrone Power and the Don Ameche; go with the Joan Davis and the Ethel Merman; bring on the specialty acts: anything to take the pressure off Henie.

Once again, Zanuck held his star to a set situation—her simple country ways in confrontation with show-biz slickers. And once again we miss the vision of a Paramount or Warners or Metro direc-tor. Zanuck had helped pioneer the Berkeley "camera number," in which the frame danced as much as the performers. But that was then; this is now, so Henie's big ice ballets are photographed straight on, with inserts here and there. *One in a Million* (1936), Henie's American film debut, comes off as a proto-Zanuck picture in its backstage texture, olio incidentals, and unimaginative production. Don Ameche is Henie's romantic lead, Jean Hersholt her Norwegian innkeeper father, a former skating champ readying Henie for the Olympics. Hersholt is touching, of course, but unfortunately not in a cameo: he's all over the place. Henie is cute, and if nothing else she is a superb skater. But she is nothing else. At least Temple and Faye sing, dance, and act. At an informal after-dinner entertainment, Dixie Dunbar starts "Who's Afraid of Love?" Ameche takes it up. But all Henie can do is beam as he sings. Before we get too annoyed at the odd sense of balance in the actors' talents, Zanuck hustles Borrah Minnevitch and His Harmonica Rascals onto the scene—in Alpine costume!—to perform. This is the Zanuck musical: irrelevant but spicy entertainment surrounding the star. Suddenly director Sidney Lanfield remembers that it's Henie's film and has Minnevitch hand her a rose.

By contrast, Zanuck's handling of Tyrone Power stands among the most creative programming in Hollywood history. There was no Power genre. He started out as a romantic lead on the light side, the sort who gets the girl Don Ameche can only dream of. As Power rose in popularity, he was paired with the lot's reigning women—Loretta Young, Sonja Henie, Alice Faye. Film by film, Power triumphed in every sort Fox turned out, whether costume romances, action adventures, contemporary comedies, or musicals—though he couldn't sing and didn't try to. Power's natural elegance, strangely, did not limit but extended him; he seemed confident in any setting.

Forget the "women love bums" that Zanuck propounded at Warners. Power was a gentleman, at home playing smooth mobsters and weighty historical figures alike. He had that much over Clark Gable, who had to play virtually everything contemporary. We take the comparison most strongly when Power plays the Gable role of *San Francisco* in Zanuck's imitation, *In Old Chicago* (1938). Though MGM takes its usual pains to re-create the past, Gable's breezy directness roots the film in the present. At Fox, where authenticity of atmosphere is not stressed, especially in Alice Faye's numbers, Power's sweetness—even in the role of a rakehell—recalls a lost, mannered age. Thus ideal for costume shows, Power led Twentieth to specialize despite itself. Power ended up playing so many youthful versions of the George Arliss man of history and so many challenges to the Errol Flynn soldier of fortune (note the reference to Warners characters) that Zanuck's studio was jokingly known as "Nineteenth Century–Fox."

But whatever happened to the Warners Zanuck? He didn't vanish. We recall his "headline" plot premises in, of all things, a Sonja Henie vehicle, *Second Fiddle* (1939), a spoof of David Selznick's search for a Scarlett O'Hara. We remark a Warners aperçu in a Faye musical, *Weekend in Havana* (1941), when Faye's vacation is ruined in some accident and she refuses to sign a waiver liberating a steamship company from responsibility. "You can't be too careful with these big corporations," says Faye.

We even get full-length, out-and-out political films of the kind that Warners developed. One of Zanuck's first projects at Twentieth, *The Prisoner of Shark Island* (1936), recalls the tragic victimization of the doctor who unwittingly attended the most unpopular man in America, John Wilkes Booth, just after his assassination of President Lincoln. Nunnally Johnson and John Ford treat Dr. Mudd (Warner Baxter) much as Warners' writers and directors treated Paul Muni or James Cagney in certain roles: as the prey of a ruthless and vindictive system. However, Baxter plays his role as a Job, with none of the hopped-up defiance of the Warners hero.

The outstanding political-problem film of Zanuck's regime at Twentieth gives us only the problem, not—as Warners so often does —the solution. This is *The Ox-Bow Incident* (1943), a polemical view of a lynching. It is to Zanuck's credit that the film was made at all, for no one in Hollywood would touch it. William Wellman had bought the rights to the property and had run through every contact he had. Only Zanuck was left, and Zanuck was just the hotspur to dare it; but Wellman and Zanuck had quarreled and weren't speaking. Wellman gave him a try anyway, and Zanuck went for it, even though he was heavily involved in war work and was letting other Fox producers run the studio.

The Ox-Bow Incident has been criticized lately for shallowness of argument. The studio-bound décor cripples Wellman's realism, especially in the perfunctory layout of the forest clearing in which the lynching takes place. The three victims are eventually discovered to be innocent—in fact, the man they supposedly killed is very much alive. There has been no crime—and this allegedly weakens Wellman's theme (as scripted by trusty Lamar Trotti), as if he were saying that it's okay to lynch the *guilty*. The use of Dana Andrews as one of the victims is called manipulative, even glamorous, a "going Hollywood." And Wellman has made it all too simple for us to identify the self-righteous vigilantes (including a professional Civil War veteran who turns out to be a fraud), the ineffectual do-gooders, and the clear-cut good guys in Henry Fonda and Harry Morgan. "There's always some crazy fool," Folk Hero Fonda warns us, "loses his head and starts hanging everyone in sight."

In truth, the stagey clearing set is a letdown, especially after the Midwestern location shooting Twentieth put in on *Jesse James* a few years earlier; and yes, the members of the posse are somewhat stereotyped. But why do the victims have to be guilty for us to recognize the horror of mob justice? Isn't it just as bad—isn't it, in fact, a very great deal worse—if the lynched men are innocent?

However Wellman trains his argument, he has very fiercely and truly caught the brutality of the story—in the posse's virtually cold-blooded hysteria, its sullen eagerness not to believe the three men's defense and get the rope looped over their heads, even in the unnerving use of Jane Darwell, a Fox regular in comic-aunt parts and an official Folk Heroine through her Ma Joad in *The Grapes of Wrath* three years earlier, as one of the posse. "Keep your chin up," she tells Dana Andrews. "You can only die once, son." And Wellman does not fail to point up the theme contemporaneously, for when the posse votes on whether to hold off for due process or hang their prisoners, a black man joins the minority vote to wait for justice.

The Grapes of Wrath (1940) is the masterpiece of Zanuck's limited output of compassionate cinema at Twentieth. But it is not a political-problem film, despite the Socialist apprehension of John Steinbeck's novel. As Nunnally Johnson wrote it and Ford directed it (and as Zanuck emended it), *The Grapes of Wrath* comes off less as a study in economic oppression than as a family melodrama in the old Fox tradition. It is the opposite of, say, the Will Rogers *State Fair*, certainly, in almost every point of comparison: wiry rather than soft, enacted by thespians rather than personalities, directed and photographed (by Gregg Toland) for keenness of drama rather than folksy self-affirmation, epic by theme rather than by grandeur of illusion. Yet it is just as unlike anything Zanuck turned out at Warners, except possibly in one sequence—oddly out of kilter with the tone and even the look of the rest of the movie—in which the Joad family finds refuge in a federal camp that is fair and clean and even loving. The camp is pictured as being surrounded by hostile natives, the American peasant-class male as thug. This is a long way from Will Rogers's village, from the Griffithian heartland.

Yet *The Grapes of Wrath* is the work of Fox's and Twentieth Century–Fox's post-Griffith Griffith, John Ford. Here is the main linking figure between the studio's two eras, from silent programmers in the very early 1920s right up to *What Price Glory?* in 1952, as the Studio Age was breaking apart. It is a cliché of movie history that Ford made a great variety of films, far more rustic family studies, contemporary comedies, urban melodramas, and contemporary wartime adventures than the westerns for which he is best known. But more than that, most of his famous westerns were made away from his home studio. *The Iron Horse* (1924) and *Three Bad Men* (1926), both for Fox and both famous in Ford's canon, are westerns. But almost all of Ford's work in the first decade of sound emphasizes country themes (or contemporary tales) rather than westerns. Ford's work for Fox really reflects the lot's down-home sentimentality and its occasional attempts to update and urbanize. *Stagecoach*, in 1939, right at the apex of Ford's greatness at Fox, was made for independent producer Walter Wanger and released by United Artists. Ford's celebrated cavalry epics of the late 1940s were with one exception produced for Ford's own firm, Argosy. At that, when Ford determined to try the unusual in films of little commercial potential, he had to leave Fox temporarily for RKO, daring enough to see the possibilities in *The Informer* and *The Plough and the Stars*.

Ford's long tenure at Fox tells us as much about the studio itself as it does about Ford. Not till Zanuck arrived was Ford regularly assigned projects uniquely apt for him: *The Prisoner of Shark Island*, *Young Mr. Lincoln* (1939), *Drums Along the Mohawk* (1939), *Tobacco Road* (1941), *How Green Was My Valley* (1941). Fox under William Fox and Winfield Sheehan was a studio of genre just as Paramount was a studio of directors and MGM a studio of stars and Warner Brothers a studio of politics. Now the genres inspired Ford's gifts; now they didn't. But we do notice that studio and director aligned best in films of rural family life, and that Ford continued to make such films after Zanuck arrived. In other words, Fox and Twentieth Century–Fox was a lot organized around a nineteenth-century worldview, an aesthetic largely unmindful of Paramount's sybarites and Warners' loners and rebels. The lot's seminal talents left so strong an impression that even the intrusion of Zanuck and the corrective patterns of wartime moviemaking did not overwhelm the studio's basic character.

On the contrary. Depression escapism and wartime affirmation seem to have given Fox's archaic and domestic idylls a renewed vitality. Nor did the studio need essentially rustic personalities like Will Rogers to keep the concern in trim. Two typical (and typically unimportant) films of the early Zanuck years, *Ramona* (1936) and *Kentucky* (1938), present Fox's historical and modern-dress country tales. The two films share some elements and dispute others, but it makes little difference one way or the other. Both are in Technicolor, and both star Loretta Young, who brings absolutely no feeling of time or place to the very different roles. She has Don Ameche (playing an Indian!) as co-star in *Ramona*, Richard Greene in *Kentucky*. The generally undistinguished Henry King directed *Ramona*; the

The artist of Fox: this still reminds us how hard times can
get in The Grapes of Wrath, a Fordian Americana to complement his folk comedy and Wild West. Note the touch of
Pirandello as Henry Fonda seems to glare at the photographer who caught the shot.

even less distinguished David Butler directed *Kentucky*. Character bits include Jane Darwell's dear old soul in *Ramona* and Walter Brennan's crabby grandpa in *Kentucky*. *Ramona*'s subject is racism and *Kentucky* treats horse-breeding. Both films are dull and vapid. Even the color lacks the depth of tint and highly charged pastels we appreciate in MGM's color shows, not to mention Rouben Mamoulian's thematic use of shade in the first feature made in Technicolor's improved three-strip process, *Becky Sharp*, made independently in 1935 for RKO release.

Twentieth did better with *Jesse James* (1939) and *The Return of Frank James* (1940), with Tyrone Power as Jesse, Henry Fonda as brother Frank, and John Carradine as Jesse's killer, Bob Ford. Fonda "returned" more or less at Zanuck's gunpoint, but both films yield vital entertainment, and both are in Technicolor; and while *Jesse James* endures the business-as-usual Henry King, *The Return* rings in Fritz Lang. *Ramona* and *Kentucky* find Zanuck coasting; in the *James* pair he asserts himself. There's even an *hommage* to Warners' "motivation for rebellion" in *Jesse James* when railroad money bosses, hot for land, instigate a feud with the Jameses and kill their mother, Jane Darwell. However, at Warners Jesse would confront the issue of corporation land-grabbing; here he simply becomes a criminal, starting with polite robberies of train riders (urging them to sue the railroad, because they started it) but running to gala bank robberies, crime not as statement or revenge (as at Warners) but for its own sake.

A favorite American irony finds the yokel outwitting the slicker; this was a natural at Fox. In *The Magnificent Dope* (1942), Folk Hero Henry Fonda takes on city shill Don Ameche. America, we learn, is ailing from get-rich-quick and how-to-succeed obsessions. Fonda teaches New York the arts of relaxation, self-belief, and humor. Even the college musical, so narrow a genre that they all look alike no matter what studio makes them, takes on the Fox philosophy in *Pigskin Parade* (1936). This film is more yokel than Will Rogers: Texas State University's football team is so backwoods that its quarterback (Stuart Erwin) got his training hurling watermelons. Yet Texas State beats Yale. It's a great silly delight of a show, with so many principals that loan-outs turn it into a kind of state-of-the-art in the Hollywood musical: Betty Grable from RKO, Johnny Downs from Paramount, Judy Garland (in her first feature) from MGM, free-lancer Erwin, and

Fox locals Patsy Kelly, Jack Haley, Tony Martin, and Dixie Dunbar (with bits from Lynn Bari and Paramount's future Dangerous Man Alan Ladd).

Pigskin Parade's large cast is exceptional at Twentieth, for Zanuck was so genre-oriented in the musical that he wanted nothing but woman-star backstagers, with a big dark man for the love plot and a sidekick or comic and the usual contributions from variety artists. The Alice Faye film. But Zanuck also liked to shadow his stars with a younger version of themselves, an implied blackmail to keep the stars in line. If Power balked at a role, Zanuck might give it to Richard Greene, along with a big Greene PR buildup and, for all Power knew, all the rest of Power's parts and fame and career. Sonja Henie and Shirley Temple were one-of-a-kind players by virtue of the one's skates and the other's age. But Faye was shadowed by Betty Grable, and when the time came, Grable took over the Faye musical.

There was a change in format, and the result is what many people attending movies in the 1940s thought of as "the Twentieth Century–Fox musical," as compared with "the MGM musical" turned out by the Freed Unit. Because all other studios but these two had generally given up on regular musical production except as programmers, the Twentieth and MGM forms bear historical comparison.

In terms of composition, the writers' contribution, MGM is supreme, particularly in songwriters. MGM's musicals can tell a story through their scores, like a Broadway show; the Grable musical is most often a backstager with pop tunes. The song-and-dance cameos that littered Faye's films have vanished, strengthening the storytelling; but even here MGM is ahead with more surely narrative scripts while Twentieth often seems to be dodging from bit to bit, as in: Now we do comic drunk, now we do Charlotte Greenwood's high-kick specialty, now Grable does a love scene, now the silky curtains part on a floor number. And if Metro, for all its fine male dancers, is strapped for fine male singers, Zanuck's insistent use of his big dark men sabotages a level of musicality in Grable's films, for Victor Mature, George Montgomery, and John Payne must be dubbed or left out of the music. Dick Haymes, at least, is a singer, Cesar Romero is a ballroom dancer, and Dan Dailey, Grable's most frequent partner, is an accomplished musical-comedy man. But Metro has Fred Astaire and Gene Kelly.

In choreography, too, MGM outperforms Twentieth. When the Hollywood musical got started, American show-biz dance was enjoying an era of self-inventing talents. Everyone stole from everyone else, yes; but it was a rule that the choreographer arranged the traditional "combinations" for the corps while the featured dancer came up with his or her own routines. Thus Ann Pennington, Marilyn Miller, Fred Astaire, Bill Robinson, and Eleanor Powell—all introduced to Hollywood in the early talkie—danced unlike anyone else. Their styles were unique. By the 1940s, this had broken down, and there were few new dance stars. The stars were now choreographers: Agnes de Mille, Michael Kidd, Jack Cole, Jerome Robbins. At MGM we see the tail end of the individual dance talent. At Twentieth we see no unique dance talents, only choreographers, and no individuals at that. Not only is there nothing at Twentieth to compare to *Yolanda and the Thief*'s dream ballets or to *Easter Parade*'s recreations of vaudeville, Twentieth can't even equal what Columbia came up with in *Cover Girl*.

Nevertheless, the Grable musicals are pleasurable. Consider *Coney Island* (1943). This is absolute Grable: a costume show (in as many incorrect costumes as possible), a Technicolor show (in a far more vivid palette than Fox dabbed in the 1930s), a backstage show (with all numbers in a performing context). It moves, it's funny, and it has everything: old standards ("When Irish Eyes Are Smiling," "Pretty Baby"), old novelties ("In My Harem"), and some new songs; two big dark men (Montgomery and Romero); two stage-trained comics (Charles Winninger and Phil Silvers); some Irish savor; a competent director (Walter Lang); and Grable. Nothing unusual here. These films ran not on surprise but on familiarity. This very film was remade seven years later, as *Wabash Avenue*, with no loss of appeal. It is not the form that matters in the Grable musical, but the details.

Look at the handling of *Coney Island*'s "Cuddle Up a Little Closer." Grable might easily just get up and do it, sock it home in quickstep tempo with a bit of footwork on the side. And that's exactly how she wants to do it—but Montgomery, running the show in Romero's club, wants her to try it slowly, as a love song, without dancing. Grable refuses. So just before she goes on, Montgomery handcuffs her hands and feet, edits the overflounced trim on her dress, and plants her onstage. Trapped, Grable sings the song as he wants it, and of course it's a triumph. Granted, the number looks and sounds like a spot at the Copacabana, not an act of the ragtime era. But then Grable's films are no more authentically appointed than Faye's were. The thing is that the "Cuddle" scene works as entertainment yet relates something of the story in its depiction of the Grable–Montgomery challenge romance.

Buffs of the MGM musical fine Fox not only for its unambitious aesthetic but for its star, Grable herself. She is not a distinctive talent —as, say, Gene Kelly was in dance or Jeanette MacDonald in song, or, for that matter, Judy Garland in all-around expertise. Yet Grable handles everything with competence at the very least, which puts her one up on the slight-voiced Kelly and the non-dancing MacDonald. In her prime, much was made of Grable's looks, especially her legs, and she was certainly among the most attractive musical stars, in a class with Rita Hayworth and almost no one else. But Grable's ace is none of the above. She is, more than anything else, very pleasant company. It's an "uncomplicated" talent, which would probably have made her uncomfortable in the tensely detailed MGM form, and is probably why Zanuck let her make so many similar movies.

There were Twentieth musicals without Grable, but they usually followed the Grable line. June Haver seems to have found a home at Fox specifically as a second-line Grable; not once did Haver make it into one of Zanuck's personal productions. One can see why, too: unlike the immediately appealing Grable, Haver never seems to know what she is playing. She'll be pensive in a charm role, glum in comedy, enervated in song-and-dance. She manages to be all of these at once in her worst film (for Warner Brothers, albeit), *Look for the Silver Lining* (1949), miscast as the elfin delight Marilyn Miller.

At least Haver enjoyed Twentieth's heavy use of Technicolor. Vivian Blaine was stuck in mostly black-and-white backstagers that are even less well remembered than Haver's. Blaine is an arresting anomaly at Twentieth, dark-haired, hard-edged, and city-flavored on a lot that liked its women stars moist, dear, and corn-fed. *Doll Face* (1945), apparently a response to Columbia's *Cover Girl*, finds burlesque queen Blaine trying to graduate herself to the Broadway big time. But for the presence of lot regulars Carmen Miranda and Perry Como, one would scarcely take this for a Fox musical. It has the irritated hustle of Warner Brothers. And Blaine's boyfriend and employer, Dennis O'Keefe, is a seedy knockdown of Zanuck's big dark man. The Zanuck backstager favored tough-guy heroes, yes, and the erotic violence in Betty Grable's attraction to George Montgomery or Victor Mature is strongly felt. But O'Keefe, advising Perry Como in couch artistry, actually suggests that women like a good beating now and then. More: Como's song, "Dig You Later," a take-off on jive, treats the bombing of Japan with unspeakable crassness even in a time of advanced patriotism. "I got it from a guy who's in the know," Como sings, "it was mighty smoky over To-ki-o."

The rough talk and sexy squabbling are what most truly set the Fox musical apart from the MGM. MGM's performers put on cute shows in barns or play the Palace or thrill Broadway with a revue. Fox's show biz is strip shows and beer gardens. Blaine launches *Doll Face* by auditioning for a fancy "Flo Hartman" musical, and director Lewis Seiler cuts to four men in the auditorium who look at Blaine as if she's porn and they're her co-stars. Hartman tells her to go back to burlesque, and Blaine, hurt and angry, calls out, "Do you mean to stand there and tell me I ain't got class?"

The Fox musical in general ain't got class—not, at least, compared with MGM. The setup organized for Alice Faye in the mid-1930s overcame even Fox's tradition of family Americana. The studio did unearth *State Fair* for a musical adaptation by Rodgers and Hammerstein in 1945—in response, one presumes, to another studio's hit, MGM's *Meet Me in St. Louis*. The story material is pure Fox. So is the casting—Jeanne Crain, Dana Andrews, Vivian Blaine, and Dick Haymes as the kids—especially because Crain, who's in most of the numbers, has to be dubbed. The Freed Unit sought out real singers or coached questionable voices (in *Good News*, wherein even non-singers carry their own freight). Fox hires the personalities, then deals with the music. Such thinking resulted in *Centennial Summer* (1946), the only Hollywood musical with seven stars who can neither sing nor dance—Jeanne Crain, Cornel Wilde, Linda Darnell, William Eythe, Walter Brennan, Constance Bennett, and Dorothy Gish. This is worse than reckless: it's erroneous. When, late in the picture, Avon Long struts in for "Cinderella Sue," it's as if Henry Irving had popped up as Dogberry in an amateur production of *Much Ado About Nothing*.

State Fair and *Centennial Summer* at least mark an innovation for Fox in their use of top-class Broadway songwriters and scores dealing in story and character as well as performance numbers. It often happened that Broadwayites experimented with form far more in their few movies than in their many stage shows. Sigmund Romberg and Oscar Hammerstein II wrote something of a pop opera for Warners' early talkie *Children of Dreams*, so made of music that it has lyrics rather than a screenplay. Rodgers and Hart developed their "rhythmic dialogue"—lyrics *spoken* to music—at Paramount, and expanded this to run right through United Artists' *Hallelujah, I'm a Bum*. In this tradition, Rodgers and Hammerstein integrated *State Fair*'s songs into the action so deftly it makes *Oklahoma!* look like a vaudeville—as in the way "Our State Fair" is tossed from character to character in the opening montage of citizens gearing up for the trip (the prize pig, Blue Boy, takes one chorus), or in the bits of reprise that wander in and out of the dialogue. Jerome Kern did nothing unusual in *Centennial Summer*, but the very use of this greatest of great Broadway composers is notable in the Fox context, which rigorously depended on humdrum Hollywood pros.

Even more notable is the use of Kurt Weill, Broadway's Weimar jazzman, on *Where Do We Go from Here?* (1945). The film, alas, is notable only as a piquant idea that utterly misfires. Fred MacMurray, a loser who can't get a date, even with his draft board, rubs a magic lamp and asks the genie to put him in the war. The genie, a little rusty, sends MacMurray to the Revolutionary War, at Valley Forge. The Hessians are about to shoot MacMurray as a spy when the genie plucks him up and drops him on board with Columbus. And so on, till MacMurray succeeds in enlisting and drops eternal tease June Haver for eternal sweetheart Joan Leslie.

Truth is, the light fantastic style the tale needs is beyond Fox. Even Metro bungled it in the coeval *Yolanda and the Thief*. We never feel that we have traveled with MacMurray to another time, just to another set, and the casting is utterly wrong. MacMurray as a 4-F? His draft board should have consulted with Mitchell Leisen and Claudette Colbert. Haver once again doesn't know what to play; she tries for Vamp and ends up as a grouchy prom queen. Leslie is okay but has nothing to do. Gene Sheldon's genie is atrociously frisky. The only interesting aspect of the film is that here, for the first time,

Weill succeeded in writing a score wholly purged of his Brechtian cabaret bite. Even his takeoff on German oompah in the Hessian scene sounds like an American's takeoff.

Betty Grable got a chance at a story musical with a score by big Broadway names in *The Shocking Miss Pilgrim* (1947), playing a feminist of old Boston trying to reform reactionary Dick Haymes. Ira Gershwin set new lyrics to his late brother George's trunk material, and the whole thing has a peaceable charm. But after a while we see why Twentieth emphasized the backstager. We miss watching Grable bounce around a stage; we miss the wonderfully irrelevant Carmen Miranda singing "Chattanooga Choo-Choo" in Portuguese, as she does in *Springtime in the Rockies* (1942). The studio simply didn't have the talent or staff to bring off the unusual musical, like *The Pirate*, or even something like *Singin' in the Rain*, usual but ingenious. Zanuck had reorganized a failing system by keying production to stars, and keying new stars to the old genres. And he did make Twentieth Century–Fox one of the big studios, something William Fox never was able to do.

Indeed, Zanuck outlasted most of the moguls of his generation. He left Twentieth in 1956 but returned after the mismanagement of *Cleopatra* (1963), a remake, one might say, of the 1917 *Cleopatra* starring Theda Bara, who virtually built William Fox's studio. By 1963, of course, little of the studio's output resembled anything that Fox, Sheehan, or Zanuck had set up during the Studio Age. There are glimmers here and there—a second remake of *State Fair* (1962), for instance, retaining most of the Rodgers and Hammerstein score with new songs by Rodgers alone. But listen to the cast—Pat Boone, Ann-Margret, Bobby Darin, and Pamela Tiffin. True, there was Fox's own Alice Faye at last playing the essential Fox role that she never played in her backstagers, the rural housewife. But otherwise there is nothing in the film that recalls the look or the sound of Fox, save that Tiffin, like Jeanne Crain, had to be dubbed by a singer.

It's a terrible film, too, but that's incidental. Even the realization that Fox has lost its grip on one of its basic genres is incidental, for this is typical of all the studios. The enforced disintegration of the Hollywood studios' theatre chains was the most apparent problem, for the collapse of monopolistic exhibition led to retrenching, loss of traditions, schemes to reattract the public with new kinds of films, and other developments that changed the business of moviemaking. There was another problem—a lack of new moguls equipped with the vision and smarts to do what men like Zanuck had done.

At least Fox survived. Our next studio was so hard hit that it literally vanished from sight.

Ginger Rogers "going" art deco sums up RKO in its prime.

RKO

The New Yorker

R KO is in many ways the anoma-
lous studio. First of all, it was
formed specifically to market the talkie, and thus had no background
in silence, no experience of the movies' history. All the other major
studios go back in one form or another to Old Hollywood. Paramount, Fox, and Universal virtually founded the place. RKO
marched in on a wave of big Eastern money and started cranking.

Second, RKO is the studio without an overwhelming mogul
eminence. It had no Mayer, no Goldwyn, no Zanuck—no chief
stayed long enough to earn renown. RKO did have David Selznick
for a while, and a very valuable and long-term producer in Pandro S.

Berman. Dore Schary's era of social critique in the late 1940s is worthy, too. But there was no clear and lasting stylist. This makes it difficult to get a fix on RKO; its identity changes as each new presider moves onto the throne with a plan for recovery and renewal. Even the budget philosophy varies wildly, at times emphasizing the programmer almost to the extinction of all A films, at other times risking fortunes on doubtful projects. For much of its history, RKO survives not on its production output but on the distribution deals it made with such independent producers as Walt Disney, Samuel Goldwyn, John Ford's Argosy Pictures, Frank Capra's Liberty Films, and quite a number of smaller operators.

One other thing sets RKO apart: it no longer exists. Alone among the majors it collapsed, in 1957, twenty-eight years after it began production.

RKO begins in 1928 with the merger of three companies: Radio Corporation of America, which wanted to move in on Hollywood to sell its sound equipment; the Film Booking Office, a quickie lot that RCA bought as a foothold; and the Keith-Albee-Orpheum circuit of vaudeville theatres, to provide the firm with its exhibition real estate. The new firm called itself RKO Radio Pictures (a tautology, as RKO stood for Radio-Keith-Orpheum), and used as its logo a beeping radio tower atop a revolving globe. The Keith-Orpheum chain was situated mainly in the Northeast, especially in the New York metropolitan area, and this became RKO's targeted public.

Only Paramount's Adolph Zukor, back in Old Hollywood, could make movies for everyone: Zukor had all the theatres. By 1929, when RKO began releasing, the acute producer knew precisely who would attend his pictures, based on who made them, what they were about, and where they would play. RKO's appeal seemed, to RKO, to address the smart money in the metropolitan Northeast, not only its public but its critics and bankers. This is going to be uptown trade, challenging Paramount at its most Lubitsch—but the idea was to make a virtue out of a loophole: tight money. "RKO was never a rich company," Pandro Berman recalled later. "We couldn't compete with the Thalbergs and the Warners, who were buying great thick books and Broadway plays and making movies out of them. We were making ours out of spit and paper."

Stage Door (1937) looks like it, though it was in fact based on one of the Broadway plays that the Thalbergs and Warners were buying up. In the wastrel mood of the 1930s, RKO bought the property just for the title and setting, a young actresses' boardinghouse in Manhattan, for the George S. Kaufman–Edna Ferber script was thrown out and an almost entirely new one by Morrie Ryskind and Anthony Veiller substituted. There's a suggestion of Warner Brothers in the premise of kids pushing for employment, in the non-stop wisecracking, in the drab décor of boardinghouse lobby, halls, and rooms, a producer's office, and on stage in the theatre. But Gregory La Cava's direction shows a loving care Warners seldom tolerated, and the faces of Katharine Hepburn, Ginger Rogers, Lucille Ball, Eve Arden, Ann Miller, and Gail Patrick suggest a style of New York rather than the rude city itself, the New York of Midwestern ingénues. Rogers always seemed at home on her Warners jobs, and Miller had the Warners energy. But Ball, one of RKO's most enduring contractees, never quite caught the edge of the Warners gold digger, and Arden's timing is a bit sure, a bit studied, for Warners, where Arden's lines would be delivered, sloppily but more naturalistically, by Joan Blondell or Aline MacMahon.

In fact, *Stage Door* is sophisticated—sharp, wise, elegantly quick. This is RKO. It *knows* too much, as we'll see again and again. Its best films are flop films; it's too sharp and wise even for most New Yorkers. Its best conceptions often run past spectators the first time around, which is why RKO lives a second life as a source of television and revival-house viewing when the same films died on their first release. In backstagers like *Stage Door*, a favorite touch of Hollywood bric-a-brac was the old has-been; I see May Robson at Paramount. La Cava gives us Constance Collier in the part—first of all, a genuine has-been herself, a London stage star and Lady to Herbert Beerbohm Tree's Macbeth in Triangle's Shakespearean film in 1916; second, no cheap sentimentalist. Collier's portrait of an Anglophile veteran has a pathetic majesty that even Paramount might have feared. Either pathos or majesty works, but to mix them is to tell people that actors end up obscure and hungry. Collier tenses at Hepburn's arrival at the boardinghouse—someone new to play to. She dips into her handbag for her faded notices—"Oh look, they're right on top!"—and skins Hepburn for coaching lessons. Collier, a beauty of her day and a very, very expert actress, plays it vain and touching and embarrassing in the way New York arts-world wreckage is. This is New York and this is RKO, and this is the story of a studio that never quite realized where it was.

In Hollywood.

This is not to say that RKO never turned out product. As we'll see, twenty-five years of a heavy B-movie schedule kept it alive. But no studio can be known by its garbage, and it was the struggle to distinguish itself in inexpensive A material that makes RKO's history so fascinating and disappointing—fascinating because of the many audacious entries, and disappointing because again and again the studio overestimates the daring of its public. Add to this the money problems Pandro Berman mentioned, the constant scrabbling around for a budget to afford the choice properties, the secure performers, the motivated staff. Add to that the eternal administrative upheaval as sliding profits force out one regime after another, each one changing production and marketing policies. The result was a lot that was, almost from the beginning, permanently in chaos.

RKO started out well. William Le Baron was head of production, and his small corps of stars, directors, and writers turned out reasonably competent examples of the available genres—a boxing film, a Latin Lover romance, a three-brothers melodrama (one is a doctor, one a cop, one a gangster), and a number of musicals to exploit the microphone. Nothing here suggests a nonconformist aesthetic. About the most innovative element in the whole caboodle was the casting of three real-life brothers, Owen, Tom, and Matt Moore, in the melodrama.* There was one major effort, *Rio Rita*, from a Ziegfeld show and in Ziegfeld style, with the last third in Technicolor. It has the defects of the early film musical—sluggish camera work, off-kilter dubbing, a crackly sound track, and actors making bizarre lunges at concealed mikes. But it was handsome and lively and RKO gave it the road-show treatment for prestige and profits.

Fine. But another musical of RKO's first year, *The Vagabond Lover*, sounds an ominous note, for this is an unforgivably incompetent piece of work. Pop-music buffs will recognize the title as a Rudy Vallee tune; *The Vagabond Lover* was planned to adhere to the singing

---

*The Moores, mildly popular second-rank stars of the silent era, had never acted together before. Owen was the best known, because he was the man Little Mary had had to divorce to marry Douglas Fairbanks.

bandleader's radio prominence. It's not a bad idea on paper. Vallee will sing his old favorites and a few new ones, lead his Connecticut Yankees, and have a romance with Sally Blane. There'll be some nugatory plotting, and Marie Dressler, as Blane's aunt, will preside with shtick. On screen, however, only Dressler tells. Vallee is so stiff we can't blame him for a poor performance: he never tries to perform. Blane is terrible, too. What must Le Baron have thought as he screened the footage?

There are too many wrong guesses in RKO's first years—or right guesses that led to disaster. An attempt to turn out a second *Rio Rita* in *Dixiana* (1930) failed miserably with the same star (Bebe Daniels), comics (Bert Wheeler and Robert Woolsey), ingénue (Dorothy Lee), composer (Harry Tierney), director (Luther Reed), choreographer (Pearl Eaton), and producer (Le Baron) plus another Technicolor finale. *Dixiana* starts promisingly, as Metropolitan Opera baritone Everett Marshall sings the amusingly "Ol' Man River"–inspired "Mr. and Mrs. Sippi" over the credits and Daniels—playing a circus performer who will become romantically involved with plantation scion Marshall—makes her entrance hatching out of an egg, as Wheeler and Woolsey cavort in ostrich outfits. But the film quickly deteriorates, as the ungainly Marshall keeps looking away from the probing camera, as the script traps itself in corners, as the score thuds and blunders.

Worried, the studio begins to pull in different directions. Appealing to a low audience, RKO concocts a vehicle for Freeman Fisher Gosden and Charles Correll, enormously popular on radio as Amos 'n' Andy: *Check and Double Check* (1930). At the same time, RKO finalizes plans to absorb the ailing Pathé studio, taking in such talents as stars Constance Bennett and Ann Harding and director Gregory La Cava—all of them much too special for the Amos 'n' Andy crowd. Indeed, Bennett was at the time regarded as the most sophisticated star in Hollywood. On the other hand, RKO won a Best Picture Oscar for its first Big One, *Cimarron* (1931), with Richard Dix and Irene Dunne (both nominees for Oscars, as was director Wesley Ruggles). Good news: except that the movie cost so much it lost money. Big Ones can break you.

After a while, we get the feeling that RKO just isn't good at judging the ordinary fare on which Hollywood does most of its business, those medium-A features between the Big Ones and the B's like MGM's *Three Comrades* or *Little Nellie Kelly* or Paramount's *The Bride Comes Home* or *This Gun for Hire*. These are a studio's bread-and-butter films, to be turned out with no special effort, without financial risk or artistic embarrassment. One way a studio learns just which forms it can treat in this manner is sheer survival, being around long enough to know your potential and sift your instincts.

RKO had not been around long, and could make errors that Paramount, MGM, Fox, Goldwyn, Warner Brothers, Columbia, and Universal wouldn't. At the height of the adaptation-from-classic-lit cycle that hit Hollywood in the early-middle 1930s, RKO chose *Little Women* (1933), not wisely perhaps—but in the event the film did excellent business. Even quickie lots were running with the trend (not least because, for once, they could film a novel for free), and most of the hot titles were snapped up and registered. So RKO saddled itself with Edward Bulwer-Lytton's *The Last Days of Pompeii* (1935).

Surely this was the sort of thing that went out with the DeMillian tribal flashback. It might have worked with some fetching stars; at least that was DeMille's approach in invigorating the antique over at Paramount—Claudette Colbert as Poppaea and Cleopatra, Charles Laughton as Nero. RKO scared up Preston Foster, Basil Rathbone, David Holt, John Wood, Dorothy Wilson, Louis Calhern, and Wyrley Birch, not exactly household names. DeMille also applied plenty of spectacle to subjects of this kind, as he did to everything. RKO's Pompeiian spectacle is acceptable, but no more. Spectacle must dazzle.

Producer Merian C. Cooper and director Ernest B. Schoedsack, RKO's experts in special-effects films, used next to nothing of the book. They devised the tale of a blacksmith-turned-gladiator who adopts the son of a man he killed, laced in Pilate, Christ, and the Crucifixion, and sealed it with a Vesuvius disaster finale. The final sequence is enjoyable, with a dandy gladitorial arena (everyone in Pompeii is at the games at zero hour) surmounted by the usual colossus doomed to topple, a nice long shot of the volcano smoking over its wreckage, and lots of screaming, cringing, shoving, and dying. But the bulk of the film, the Story of Preston Foster, Gladiator, so to say, is a mess. It's not that RKO can't compete with Paramount in historical adventure. It can't; but that's not the problem. The problem is that RKO hasn't decided what historical adventure is about. At Paramount, it's about sex. At MGM, it's pure heroism. At Warner Brothers, it's (in the 1930s) revolt against oppression and (later) pure heroism. At RKO, the story's implications vary so much we never get a chance to care what is happening to Foster or even what is happening in his general vicinity. Now he's sensitive; then he's callous. Here he helps the bosses subdue a rebellious slave; there he rails at the brutality of slavery. Confused, RKO throws in everything that went over in Gospel two-reelers, as if Cooper and Schoedsack were reliving the matinees of childhood. We even see the march up to Calvary. Jesus doesn't appear, but his toted cross sways before our eyes.

It's not terrible, in all. But it's not a good showing for a form that most studios could have reeled out with a crank or two. What is typical, and delightful, and thrilling about RKO is that it excels in unusual movies, the kind that any studio can botch. Take *Bringing Up Baby* (1938). This is screwball comedy, already a tricky genre; the studios made hundreds of them, yet only a dozen or so are outstanding. RKO is so confident that it places all the essential elements and then goes on to add others that seem so correct that *Baby* in effect reinvents the form.

Consider: RKO presents the madcap heiress (Katharine Hepburn), the square with the dull fiancée who must be reclaimed on the eve of his wedding (Cary Grant), the devious screwball terrier ("a perfect little fiend," as one character puts it), the foolish cops, the crazed psychiatrist, the impatient judge. We also get the hurtling, overlapped dialogue, as much an element of director Howard Hawks as of screwball.

All this is standard issue. But the new elements are so fetching we take them for conventions: the country house and grounds as essential neighborhood; the spontaneous take (another Hawks trademark), as in Hepburn and Grant's improvising story-line lyrics to "I Can't Give You Anything But Love, Baby" while unloading Baby the leopard; and the use of transvestism and other inappropriate getups as signets of the transformational character of the screwball experience. (Grant tries out a frilly negligée, then a riding habit without a shirt, from froufrou to he-man entirely in caricature; while Hepburn runs around in a coolie outfit, as if rendering a takeoff on Luise Rainer in

MGM's *The Good Earth* the year before.) Some quasi-familiar characters are epitomized, in May Robson's crusty aunt and Charles Ruggles's fatuous expert on big-game hunting. RKO leaves no possibility unexplored—there's big game here, too. Three wild animals, anyway: two leopards and Hepburn.

Baby is the most absurd of the screwballers. Columbia counts the classics of strict genre; but of the errant and dangerous exception that tests the rule, *Baby* is the exemplar. It is the only screwballer that deserves to have been put together for real-life screwballs—not Columbia's Irene Dunne and Melvyn Douglas, not Universal's William Powell, not Paramount's Mary Boland, but genuine crazies. Hepburn tells Grant, "You're so good-looking without your glasses," meaning without his dignity. This might have been said in any screwball comedy. But look how far Hepburn is willing to go to demolish that dignity, luring Grant into a stream that, she says, is shallow enough to wade through. She ought to know—she grew up on the property. Both step in and immediately plunge to their necks.

"The riverbed's changed," she tells him, not even bothering to sound surprised. Why should she? By that time, Grant knows that everything she says is banter.

Everything in this movie is banter, which is why it takes prime place in the screwball cycle. Its eccentrics are not merely décor, as in so many lesser screwballers, but take active part in the proceedings. Even the screwball terrier, a familiar sight from his earlier outings at MGM and Columbia, has been graduated from bit player with a good moment or two to crucial featured role. All the great screwballers have strong scripts, for this was one of Hollywood's most literate genres. But *Baby*'s script, by Dudley Nichols and Hagar Wilde, must be the only one to derive its point not from elegance of wit but elegance of violence. The title character himself warns us: the baby is a leopard. Some of this is Hawks's doing; he often presents love as a battle. Some of this is Hepburn's doing, in the aggressive way she stalks Grant, playing his ball at golf, driving off in his car, purloining his clothes, stealing Grant's dinosaur bone—the intercostal clavicle (through her familiar, George the terrier)—and finally wrecking Grant's life-size dinosaur model.

Some of *Baby*'s unique flavor lies in its revision of screwball's class complex, its normalization of Philip Barry's aristos as a country-club bourgeoisie. Barry's Broadway comedies established screwball's setting, but Barry's people can be tiresomely stylized. In Columbia's *Holiday*, directly from Barry, Hepburn and Grant are much less attractive than they are in *Baby*. It's not their fault; it's Barry's. "Linda," crows a party guest, in flawless Locust Valley lockjaw, as Grant's engagement to Hepburn's grasping sister is announced, "isn't it *too* mahvelous!" "Too, too mahvelous," the distracted Hepburn must reply. It's like Rome ten minutes before the Visigoths walked in.

Bringing Up Baby is more engaging than *Holiday* because it has more life, more zany enjoyment of life, and this is what screwball uniquely prefers. In all, *Baby* comes off as the ultimate screwball comedy. It is typical of RKO to have made it, and typical of RKO to have lost money on it in its original release, for this is the studio that is celebrated today for its "mistakes."

At least some of RKO's unique ventures were commercially successful. Despite the usual money troubles, the Selznick regime managed to bring off the most unexpected Big One of its day, *King Kong* (1933). The auteurs are producer-directors Merian C. Cooper and Ernest B. Schoedsack and special-effects chief Willis O'Brien, for it's the concept rather than the script that matters here, and the actors are of such little moment that the best performance is that of the ape, a rich character as sadistic and pathetic as he is sexual and heroic.*

However, technology is the star of the show, especially in the way the fantastic is assimilated into live-action photography. Many a sight is extraordinary for 1933—the pterodactyl-like birds flapping through the air on our first view of Skull Island; the gigantic wall with its double doors, secured by a bolt thirty feet long; the brontosaurus attack, so deftly blended of miniatures and full-scale footage that it's impossible to spot the sutures, even in close-ups; the approach of the Third Avenue El, roaring down the track right into the hands of the berserk monster; the shocking long view of Kong bouncing down the side of the Empire State Building. It seems amusingly inevitable that, after showing us how Kong rules his island domain, RKO ups the stakes by testing this king of beasts in RKO's island domain,

*The rerelease print, dating from after the revitalization of the Production Code, cut away most of Kong's sadism and sexuality—his curious pulling off of Fay Wray's clothes, his vicious trampling of harmless people after he breaks into the native village, and the famous moment in New York when he pulls a woman out of an apartment building, sees it's not Wray, and carelessly dashes her to the street far below.

*A trick still: Kong and the plane have been doubled onto a
stock Manhattan skyline shot. It conceptualizes the "trick"
by which a small, underpowered lot pulled off the Big One
of 1933.*

Manhattan. It is almost as if the studio thinks of locale as being either New York or jungle, either sophistication or everything else.

The jungle came in handy, having been used in two films the previous year, *Bird of Paradise* and *The Most Dangerous Game*; and RKO used it again for a sequel, *The Son of Kong* (1933). Cooper, Schoedsack, O'Brien, composer Max Steiner, and a few of the actors were retained, but the film is a disappointment, an attempt to make a quickie Big One. Fleeing civil and criminal proceedings, Robert Armstrong (who brought Kong to New York) goes back to Skull Island, where he meets Kong's son, smaller and sweeter, even comic. It must have seemed like a valid novelty in all, especially with O'Brien's process monsters. But what really fueled *King Kong* was its second half, its view of the beast unable to comprehend industrial-age civilization. *The Son of Kong* never leaves Skull Island; Skull Island itself leaves, vanishing beneath the sea in a convulsion as little Kong sees the humans to safety, sinking into the deep himself. At least we get a sense of atonement when Armstrong bandages little Kong's wounded finger and saves him from quicksand. "This is sort of an apology," Armstrong explains—for it was not beauty killed the beast, as he said at *King Kong*'s fade-out. It was Armstrong.

How often can a basically small studio go on making unusual films? Yet RKO did. Its version of cowboys-and-Indians, subclass British imperialist adventure, *Gunga Din* (1939), set a new style in war films for the finesse of its satiric-romantic tone, somewhat derived from *What Price Glory?* yet original in the end, emphasizing the jests and guts of men of rank and polish. Similarly, RKO's horror unit under producer Val Lewton in the 1940s contrived to avoid the exhibition of creatures favored by Universal, Hollywood's leader in horror, for a subtle suspense based not on what one sees but what one senses—as when, in *Cat People* (1942), we never glimpse Simone Simon in her transformation as a beast but hear her purring and the clicking of her claws.

Even the woman's picture, surely the form least agreeable to upgrading, would be reinvented at RKO. *Ann Vickers* (1933), from Sinclair Lewis's novel, with Irene Dunne and Walter Huston, looks like another of those weepies made by Universal, especially with Dunne—though at Universal the source would be Fannie Hurst and the co-star someone less intense than Huston. Scenarist Jane Murfin clearly has more to work with here; we are constantly enlightened by details of characterization, of the habits and oddities of American life that Lewis treated. In fact, Huston is a real surprise in this genre, worldly and tolerant, a champion amateur cook, and an aggressive lover where the genre more often made do with Charles Boyer, John Boles, William Powell, and other softies. And look at the odd professions RKO allowed its stars—Dunne is a penologist and Huston a judge. The party scene in which they meet is one of Hollywood's rare attempts to deal with the bemused urbanity of the New York leadership class, especially when Huston tells Dunne she looks melancholy. "You a Communist?" he asks—not suspiciously, but as a joke, poking at her earnest preoccupation and the dark brow of Depression leftism at once. Compare this to the fetid crew that Paramount assembles for *its* New York party scene in *The Scoundrel*. Paramount gives us real-life New Yorkers looking silly, self-conscious, and dull. RKO gives us a roomful of *leaders*.

All of *Ann Vickers* reflects this almost reckless disposition to show the world as it is. At one point, Dunne warns a drug-addicted prisoner that she'll have to give "snow" up "cold turkey." Who knew these terms in 1933 but smart New Yorkers? Dunne even has two illegitimate children, a realism that, for a weepie, verges on the fanatical. But then *Ann Vickers*'s director, John Cromwell, was a hard-nosed storyteller and RKO the perfect studio for him, in its belief in a large-spirited public: a public willing to experiment, to absorb some of the world's meaner truths. One cannot imagine any other studio dealing so frankly at this time with prison life, not even Warner Brothers. Because Lewis's heroine is a reformer of the prison system, Cromwell must show us a system in need of reform, and he doesn't dillydally. We see not only authoritarian brutality but a prison riot— and this is, exceptionally for the day, a view of women's prisons. Most grueling of all Cromwell's pictures is a scene in which a black woman is hanged. Here is a certain case of directorial ingenuity. What could anyone, even Lewis, have written to equal Cromwell's relentless building of terror as the prisoner is forced up the steps of the gallows, mumbling incoherently, eyes fixed on the noose? Cromwell cuts away to a group of officials in suit and tie and holds the camera till one of them keels over in a faint.

RKO even allowed its stars to play unattractive roles, including stars who had established personalities based on impeccable attractiveness. Gregory La Cava's *Primrose Path* (1940) looks in on a kind of West Coast Tobacco Road where the men are liquor-sodden failures and the women prostitutes. Yet the heroine is the star-spangled sweetheart Ginger Rogers. True, RKO provides the very clean-cut Joel McCrea to save her from The Life, but not before she gets a berth in a bordello, complete with lap dog, black maid, flounces and fringes on everything, and a dress so lurid it looks red in black-and-white. Unlike Cromwell's prison, La Cava's skid row is somewhat gently treated. Still, he gives us a family of women—from grandmother (salty Queenie Vassar) to little sister (Joan Carroll)—who not only accept their fate as employees of sex but actively resist McCrea's attempts to rescue the doubting Rogers.

A year later, RKO offered Rogers in yet another unusual item, *Tom, Dick and Harry* (1941). The premise is traditional: Rogers must choose a husband from three suitors. But the director is a Broadwayite, Garson Kanin, and he boldly *stages* the performance, New York–style, as well as films it, Hollywood-style. Takes and shtick give the film a lunatic flavor, though it already has three wacky dream sequences in which Rogers imagines life with each of her beaux. Moreover, Kanin's Rogers gives a theatrical interpretation rather than a naturalistic portrayal; dreamy, murmuring, deliberately mistiming or overlapping her lines, she seems like a knickknack Katharine Hepburn. The film tends to inspire extreme reactions. Some loathe its sly whimsey; others dote on Kanin's startling manipulations. And, New Yorker or not, he does comprehend the motion of pictures. One shot of auto salesman George Murphy reflected in a car window as he watches Rogers and Burgess Meredith reflected in the front overhead mirror is almost more film than film.

All Hollywood studios were more or less fascinated by New York—Warner Brothers and MGM more and Fox and Universal less. But RKO sometimes feels like New York West. Surprisingly, the studio hedged on the adaptation of Arthur Kober's play *Having Wonderful Time* (1938)—the script by Kober himself—turning a cast of Jewish workers on a Catskills holiday into a Protestant parade, with Ginger Rogers, Douglas Fairbanks, Jr., Lucille Ball, Red Skelton, Eve Arden, Jack Carson, and Lee Bowman. But *The Big Street* (1942), after Damon Runyon, the New Yorker's New Yorker, came through with color, flash, and bite. Other studios turned Runyon's quaintly tense comedy into farce or fairy tale—look at Paramount's versions of *Little Miss Marker* in 1934 and 1949 (as *Sorrowful Jones*). One has Shirley Temple and the other Bob Hope. *The Big Street* seeks out the ambitions and angers of The City, grinding away the feelings of innocents. Henry Fonda, in another of his many relieved loan-outs from his cheerless duties at Fox, is an innocent. He has a crush on nightclub singer Lucille Ball, a real Runyon broad—demanding, unresponsive, a gorgeous creep. Ball never quite masters the hard-tongued idiom, but she really goes for the character. She's so mean that the picture hates her—till hood Barton MacLane cripples her, giving Fonda his main chance as her nurse, benefactor, and solace. Now the picture loves Ball—too much, perhaps. It forgives her everything, even her ratty treatment of Fonda. But the Runyon bite holds firm in the many secondary characters, the guys and dolls, and we even get a real New York traffic jam, with the horns and the tempers, when Fonda tries to take Ball through the Holland Tunnel in her wheelchair. They're on their way to Florida. When they arrive, RKO's technology fails us, with back projections so phony that a beach scene looks like two different movies going on at once.

This was always a problem at studios strapped for funds: they were humiliated by the suaver science of MGM and Paramount, the one for its budget and the other for its directorial élan. RKO's distinction was its originality, its bent for the unusual. Not only unusual pictures, but an unusual Queen of the Lot, Katharine Hepburn. Today it's common to think of Hepburn as a natural, even as inevitable. But when she was new she was thought strange-looking, affected, and possibly nutty. Hollywood likes outstanding versions of the norm, not outstanding versions of the outstanding, and the nonconformist Hepburn, blurting out The Oddest Things to the press, dodging photographers, and failing to be spotted on the right arms at the orthodox places, acted as strangely as she looked.

She played strange roles, too, no one like another: and played them not as if the studio made her do it but because she wanted to. How to get a handle on this woman? In *Christopher Strong* (1933) she is Lady Cynthia Darrington, world-famous aviatrix. The very noun itself bespeaks a pride of glamour. But Hepburn shows up in silver lamé sheath with a Dracula collar and antennae. Maybe it's supposed to suggest Garbo, but it makes Hepburn look like a Martian lounge singer. Then, in *Spitfire* (1934), she's a mountain girl, a genuine boondocks crazy under the tutelage of the go-for-broke John Cromwell. There's more vitality in these two portrayals than in the entire career of Norma Shearer, and more sheer stuff in them than a Janet Gaynor or a Loretta Young ever got to show. Still, they are rather—well, versatile for a common-denominator audience to comprehend.

RKO isn't producing Hepburn's pictures for that audience. But how sophisticated an audience is there for film? George Stevens's *Quality Street* (1937) enters, through James M. Barrie's play, the world of Jane Austen—"Quality Street," the opening credits announce: "where a gentleman passerby is an event." But the real Austen has wit. James Barrie is as affected as Philip Barry, as affected as Hepburn. When Franchot Tone asks her to a ball, she wonders if the men will adore her. "I should so love," she goes on, "to inspire a frenzy in the men."

This is one of the campiest straight lines in film, and it tells us something of why Hepburn and RKO didn't have a hit every time. "You're different, that's all," Andrea Leeds tells Hepburn in *Stage Door*. Give them time, Leeds suggests, and they'll accept you. But they're wondering if Hepburn and her frenzies are—like her stage name, "Eva Lovelace," in *Morning Glory* (1933)—"partly made up and partly real." Another key line, from *Alice Adams* (1935), this from Hepburn herself: "I guess all talented people are a bit peculiar."

In fact they needed no time to accept Hepburn in *Little Women*, as the tomboy Jo. This is a curious item for Hepburn and for RKO, a film to inspire a frenzy only in Louisa May Alcott fans. Yet it was a smash, the bluenoses' exhibit of *summum bonum* in the year they brought cultural suit against Hollywood for lubricious subjects and randy behavior. It's historical. It also seems to be the product of Selznick's regime and his devotion to classic children's books, though he had left RKO for MGM before *Little Women* went into production.

George Cukor's direction saves the film, for once again this master of atmosphere develops the sense of time and place as if he had been there. The picture delights against impossible odds. Among the four March girls and "Marmee" (Papa is off at the Civil War), love pours out in such quantity that if someone goes out of the room for a moment, the others have to kiss her when she comes back. Marmee

Kate the absolute. Even in hypocritical PR poses, Hepburn is truth.

(Spring Byington) is a horror of a dear, cheerlessly smiling and full of senseless wisdom. She is so insensitive that as her nearly starving daughters slaver over their first blue-ribbon breakfast in years, Marmee bustles in to suggest they send the food over to some family no more unfortunate than they. The script (probably heavily overseen by Selznick) captures all the constipated gamboling and monstrously elfin piety of Alcott, yet Cukor keeps it charming and frolicsome. One enjoys it incredulously.

Alice Adams better fixes Hepburn for us—RKO, too. It is sophisticated precisely because of its small-town, Booth Tarkington setting —because of the way it disapproves of the mean-spirited character of village social life. Fox's Will Rogers merely poked at snobs and cheats, benignly improved them. RKO can't stand them. Then too, director George Stevens balances the snobs and the unbearably cleancut, upper-class love interest (Fred MacMurray) with a close look at Alice's family. After the pasty symmetry of *Little Women*'s March girls, here is something genuine, in the loving and dimly ambitious but sorrowfully failed father (Fred Stone), the mother (Ann Shoemaker), a good soul driven to nagging and fury by Stone's weakness, and the brother (Frank Albertson), who has good instincts but is essentially a bum.

Then there's Alice herself, so sympathetically portrayed that her social designs and poses make her not comical but interesting. There are worse crimes than wanting to be liked. Indeed, the big set piece of the country-club dance—where Alice makes her most desperate lunges at acceptance and suffers her most wretched rebuffs—renders her all the more admirable. She is fighting for something; that puts her ahead of everyone else at the dance. Stevens takes the scene with devastating clarity, till we feel as hurt as Hepburn: as Everyone Who Matters cuts her; as a huge plop (Grady Sutton) humiliates her on the dance floor; as she tries to enhance her charisma with pathetic affectations to attract attention; as Stevens pulls back for a long shot of a roomful of young people coupling up to take the festive floor, leaving Hepburn entirely alone. What a relief we all feel—we and Hepburn —when MacMurray asks her to dance.

Alice Adams is RKO at its best—in writing, directing, and casting. Pandro Berman, its producer, is the man responsible for many of the studio's most enduring efforts, and this film, we sense, was Berman's, and thus RKO's, idea of a prestige picture. Not a load of Brits or a big Broadway bash or anything over two hours, but something unusual for an unusual actress. This is how to "be somebody," as Little Caesar put it. The film stints only in the ending. Tarkington left his defeated heroine trudging up the steps of a secretarial school, steps that lead to a life of subsistence survival, not only financially but emotionally. RKO can't let the tank-town snobs win, and brings MacMurray back for a romantic fade-out. This ending seems more fitting than Tarkington's, given Hepburn's spirit and resourcefulness. It may well be her best performance.

Berman also stood behind RKO's unique contribution to the musical in the Fred Astaire–Ginger Rogers films. We have already catalogued RKO's unusual one-shots and unusual star; here's RKO's unusual genre, so familiar to today's movie buffs that few realize how avant-garde the form was in its day. Berman, RKO, and Astaire created the musical that uses dance characterologically and even (as in the "Night and Day" dance) narratively. This was a breakaway for Hollywood, as choreography in the earliest musicals largely reflected Broadway techniques.

It was in fact largely laid out by Broadway technicians—Bobby Connolly, Seymour Felix, Albertina Rasch, Sammy Lee, and even Busby Berkeley, who for all his cinematic zing launched his Hollywood years by going Broadway: first you sing, then you do the dance. Whether the latter called for hoofing, an "eccentric," or a "bring on the boys and girls" routine, it was a charming excrescence, dance for its own sake rather than pointed, thematic. Astaire was one of the few great originals in Broadway choreography at this time, and in his last stage show, *Gay Divorce*, he sought ways to blend dance into the scenario, not only devising choreography to suit his character but leaning on the evocative power of dance so that his numbers needed movement as much as song.

Astaire is just an accoutrement in *Flying Down to Rio* (1933), the first Astaire and Rogers teaming. But it's not a teaming. They take each other for granted. Astaire's romantic dance duet, "Orchids in the Moonlight," pairs him with Dolores del Rio, and there's no great black-and-white art deco expanse for a big number or a passionate flirtation, no Edward Everett Horton and the merest snatch of Eric Blore. The concept of Astaire–Rogers is as yet unimagined.

But *The Gay Divorcee* (1934), the adaptation of *Gay Divorce*, pulls many of the parts of Astaire–Rogers into play, and its suave pacification of the film musical's interior contradictions suggests that RKO's staff enjoyed an incomparable expertise. There is no shame whatever about people jumping into song; Astaire slides into "Needle in a Haystack" so casually we begin to feel inferior because we never do that. And RKO finds ways of ending numbers without that telltale pose and pause that works nicely as punctuation in the theatre but that threw the makers of the first film musicals into tizzies. A *stage* wait in a talkie? Watch how smoothly "Let's K-nock K-neez" ends (rather, subsides) when Astaire wanders in, reacts to the absurdity of Horton trying the dance, and rallies the plot as the boys and girls make themselves scarce and the music halts for a beat or two, only to slip back in to catch up with the story. No pose; no waiting. Smooth.

By the time of *Top Hat* (1935), the form was fixed, and if this one is virtually a remake of *The Gay Divorcee*, only historians care. Cole Porter's *Gay Divorce* songs all but disappeared in the film, but RKO did better by Jerome Kern and Otto Harbach in *Roberta* (1935), and commissioned a new score from Irving Berlin for *Top Hat*. This in particular sets RKO's dance musical apart from other musical cycles of the 1930s. Warners' Berkeley backstager ran on Harry Warren and Al Dubin, enchanting tunesmiths but not up to Broadway's top level. MGM's house team, Nacio Herb Brown and Arthur Freed, were primitives, and Fox's Harry Revel and Mack Gordon, admitting Revel's vitality, suffered from Gordon's prosaic poetry.

RKO offered more Berlin and went on to inveigle scores from Kern and Dorothy Fields and from the Gershwins. Moreover, RKO's musical arrangements are ingenious at matching sound to action. In *Follow the Fleet* (1936), during "Let Yourself Go," just as the camera jumps from three backup singers to Ginger Rogers, the orchestra jumps up a step in key, a very exuberant sensation. Comparably, as Harriet Hilliard leaves the dance hall to tryst with Randolph Scott, a piano, noodling during the preceding dialogue, goes into a vamp, the orchestra takes it up, and, without the slightest hitch in credibility, Hilliard starts "Get Thee Behind Me, Satan" as if she'd been born to hear that vamp and sing that ballad. This is craftsmanship that rivals the more vaunted Freed Unit.

The Astaire–Rogers format was a rich one, especially when com-

Swing Time *(1936) might be the best of the Astaire–Rogers series. It starts sluggishly, lacks a big ensemble number like "The Continental" or "The Piccolino," and, but for Helen Broderick and Victor Moore, needs a sense of humor. However, it boasts a superb Jerome Kern–Dorothy Fields score, a tasty sense of the place RKO loved—art deco New York— and an almost unnerving earnestness about the love plot; nowhere else do the two stars seem so crestfallen when boy loses girl. An informal contest: what was the picture called till just before release? (Hint: the movie title comes from one of the song titles. No, not "The Way You Look Tonight.")*

pared with Fox's Faye, Henie, or Grable musicals. The style was capable of modification, too. Because Rogers had been playing roles in other sorts of films right through the 1930s, but Astaire made his musicals only with Rogers, it was decided to give Astaire another partner for once, in *A Damsel in Distress* (1937). She couldn't have been more different from Rogers: Joan Fontaine. But suddenly everything is different—the setting, the supporting cast, the thrust of the story, the tone of the humor—yet the form's virtues accommodate the shift beautifully.

We still have the transatlantic Astaire, an American in England, singing a Gershwin score not above a British inflection, in "Stiff Upper Lip" and a madrigal, "The Jolly Tar and the Milk Maid." But instead of the hotels and ballrooms Astaire frequents with Rogers, RKO sends him to the country, to Totleigh Castle and, for novelty, to an amusement park. Joan Fontaine's dragon aunt Constance Collier and some more or less eccentric relations and servants replace the dithering Horton and Blore, and—this is real novelty—George Burns and Gracie Allen sign up as Astaire's PR man and secretary. What Burns and Allen did at Paramount, they do here. On a tour of Totleigh, Gracie learns, "Oliver Cromwell passed through here in 1628."

GRACIE: That was pretty fast time for those days.

Or: "His Lordship gave more than five thousand pounds for that portrait."

GRACIE: Five thousand pounds of what?

Burns and Allen are extraneous pleasures here, but otherwise the *Damsel* script is much more tightly plotted than was usual for Astaire and Rogers. The story per se is so solidly laid out that the unmusical Fontaine fits in nicely, emboldened to try a little leap and some twirls in "Things Are Looking Up." The film did not go over well—once again, RKO had done the unusual, in so gracefully establishing the stiff-upper-lip whimsey and the madrigal milieu. But we realize how deft RKO's dance musical was in viewing the films Astaire made after he left for other studios. Excepting MGM's *Broadway Melody of 1940* and Columbia's *You Were Never Lovelier*, Astaire had to ham-and-egg it for years till he reclaimed a worthy berth with Freed's people.

All this perdurable RKO—the unusual lot—obscures something of the studio's self-image. Various regimes shifted the image, from nonconformist studio to popular lot and back again. Through it all, RKO's survival money lay in its distribution facilities and its sizable B units, more varied than those of much larger studios.

American film has been running on B movies since movies began. The B is older than the A, which developed toward the end of the First Era, in the features, by D. W. Griffith and others, that led up to *The Birth of a Nation* and in the burgeoning star system. The very term "B movie" has lost its vitality, especially among armchair critics, who apply it to any film they don't like—along with the incoherent "C movie," a description without a meaning.*

The B first of all denotes a low-budget feature, not just less expensive than an A, but very much less: a really cheap film. It is almost invariably a programmer, made to fill out a show as the second feature. B movies are genre films, the kind that can be turned out by the least gifted writers, directors, and staff. Westerns, mysteries, shtick comedy, and backstage musicals are typical, each with its recurring names of modest celebrity—Warner Oland, for instance, of Fox's *Charlie Chan* series, or Ann Sothern of MGM's *Maisie*.

Series B's are a cinch, because each is a remake of the last. There are no compositional adventures to make, no logistical problems to work out. Standing sets, scripts pounded out by the yard, back-projected exteriors, and team players insure brisk production. In 1935, when the average A feature cost between two and six hundred thousand dollars, and took four weeks to shoot, a B might cost forty thousand and wrap in five days.

RKO's B's are a heady mix. For westerns it had Tom Keene and later Tim Holt; as distributor for George Hurliman's star George O'Brien, RKO took O'Brien over for its own series. For comedy it had Bert Wheeler and Robert Woolsey, spun off from their *Rio Rita* roles (as sap and sharp lawyer) along with darling Dorothy Lee; and Lupe Velez as the Mexican Spitfire, with foil Leon Errol. In mystery there was *The Falcon* and *Dick Tracy*, in heart-warming melodrama the *Dr. Christian* cycle with Jean Hersholt, tired of his MGM cameos but still nauseously touching. An odd series was the Bobby Breen

---

*No doubt they mean that a C is so terrible it's even worse than a B. But a cheap B movie is so cheap that nothing is cheaper, and the cheapest B movies are the worst movies. There is nothing worse than the worst, and there is no such thing as a C movie. B says all you need.

musical, modeled on Zanuck's Shirley Temple format, with another singing kid who rights wrongs.

The most telling illustration of the B film's character is RKO's *Tarzan* series, a follow-up to MGM's retaining Johnny Weissmuller (without Maureen O'Sullivan, unfortunately). The first thing we notice about RKO's *Tarzan* is the studied studio look, a terrible comedown from MGM's luxurious backlot jungle and location footage. Where MGM gave us teeming native extras, hordes of elephants, compelling narratives, and that amazing fight with the crocodile, RKO can't get up more than a little band of players, the odd animal, jagged plotting, and mainly human adversaries, because humans are cheaper than jungle. Most notably, we have lost the sexy-comic thug that MGM devised. At Metro, Weissmuller was unlikably arresting, pushy and stupid but a man true to his code. B features have no time to delve into character, and at RKO Weissmuller seems cantankerous and unmotivated. He has various women to play to, but the occasional jabs at romance have none of the fervor with which he took O'Sullivan; and the directors are so unalert that whole scenes go by without a center. At one point in the series, Weissmuller stands near a quicksand pit as some villains struggle for life. Will he save them? Just stand there? He looks confused, as if no one has told him what he's supposed to do. The villains sink into doom; now Weissmuller's glowering. Was he counting on their sinking, or was this a chance treat? As filmed, the take is not clear, and we start to wonder what code Tarzan is true to.

This combination of incessant quickie series and never-say-die art, as well as the uncompromising honesty of much that lay between—in *Ann Vickers*'s look at prison life, for example—finds no reflection in the programs of other studios. No doubt RKO's lack of experience kept it from turning cynical. Perhaps the turmoil of floundering regimes in the front office left gaps that artists, seizing their moment, rushed to fill. Surely the strong grosses in the Northeast led the lot to think it must break through sooner or later on the national level. RKO's idea of show biz seems more like Broadway's than Hollywood's: it believes that cheap pop can lay the foundation for more audacious endeavors, that sophistication is an acquired habit. At the time that RKO was founded, the American theatre was a vast enterprise, counting a leadership class of playwrights and producers as well as a sub-industry of low commercial operations—Eugene O'Neill, say, playing next to *Abie's Irish Rose*. Hollywood, founded on a distinctly commercial approach, did film O'Neill in the Studio Age, but sparsely, and mainly in prestige emergencies. *Abie's Irish Rose* was more to its taste—Paramount bought it in the 1920s for half a million and a percentage deal, one of the highest prices paid for a property to that time.

RKO seems to have been formed, and tried to survive, on the belief that the art mattered as much as the pop, a notion more suitable to an elite theatre system with its audience-flattering epochs behind it (as Broadway saw itself in the 1920s and 1930s) than a movie world still tied to majority taste. How else to explain RKO's making—even more, releasing—*Citizen Kane* (1941)? Called the greatest film of its era, the very midpoint of the Studio Age, *Citizen Kane* had popular potential, for all its artistry. George J. Schaefer, running the studio at the time, did not make it because it was a doubtful proposition. He had no doubts. Like many of RKO's producers before and after, Schaefer had a producer's head but an adventurer's soul. Still, bringing theatre-and-radio wonder boy Orson Welles to Hollywood with his own unit, the Mercury Theatre, was asking for trouble. Hire a pack of untried New Yorkers to make a movie? Hollywood saw it as an arrogant invasion—especially as Welles produced, co-wrote (this is questioned; but he took the credit), directed, and played the lead. Most infuriating to the business was Schaefer's agreement to give Welles the right of final cut, one of the most damaging precedents in the history of mogul-artist relations.

On top of all this was *Citizen Kane*'s unmistakable *à clef* derogation of Hollywood's *bête noire* Santa Claus, William Randolph Hearst. Many Hollywood honchos would have been glad to see the overbearing tycoon held up to public ridicule. But Hearst threatened to expose Hollywood's backstage secrets in his papers if *Citizen Kane* was released. Facing the greatest security threat since the bluenose attack of 1933 that led to the strict censorship of the Production Code, Hollywood leaders acting through Nicholas Schenck offered to reimburse RKO for *Citizen Kane*'s negative cost if Schaefer would vault the film. Schaefer refused. He was also stonewalling a threatened boycott of all RKO releases in Hearst's paper empire, as well as attacks, in the form of "news" stories, on Welles and himself.

History is being made here: Citizen Kane *in process. Note Orson Welles's markings, and Everett Sloane in full cry. End of* Swing Time *contest (see p. 312): the original title was* Never Gonna Dance—*retained so late that* Swing Time*'s production stills are coded NGD (RKO used initials rather than the usual Hollywood serial numbers), not ST.*

Citizen Kane was released, to spectacular critical acclaim and—that old RKO story—good business in metropolitan places. Provincial road-show tests disappointed, and fear of Hearst led many exhibitors to pass the film up. Grateful as we are to Schaefer for having made *Citizen Kane* (and he doggedly pursued his alliance with Welles), it was a startling act for a Hollywood businessman. So was Selznick's *What Price Hollywood* in 1932, or Dore Schary's *Crossfire* in 1947. All three of these RKOs challenged Hollywood pieties, Selznick's in his doubting look at glamour, Schaefer's in his allowing an outsider to outrage a dangerous eminence, Schary's in his fierce treatment of anti-Semitism.

As of the rise of the big studios in the Second Era, most moguls were Jewish, and anti-Semitic writers enjoyed attacking them as a "foreign" element in American culture. Genetic memory told the moguls that these controversies were no-win situations, so they staved them off by avoiding as much as possible any telling reference to Jewishness or anti-Semitism. (Warner Brothers was truly exceptional in this, but, again, was careful to change the lynching victim in *They Won't Forget* from a Jewish man to a Northerner.) It took a Christian mogul, Fox's Darryl Zanuck, to issue perhaps the first film in the Studio Age to deal with this prejudice, *Gentleman's Agreement*, released just before *Crossfire*. But *Gentleman's Agreement* goes rather gently; RKO's *Crossfire* more truly enters that bad night, in the psychotic violence of noir. Fox sees anti-Semitism as keeping Gregory Peck from checking into a restricted hotel. *Crossfire* sees anti-Semitism as inspiring Robert Ryan to beat Sam Levene to death.

There may be profit in quality, for *Crossfire*, made on a tight budget, brought in a fortune. Perhaps RKO's chiefs saw the distinctive as being a way to compete with other studios' big budgets and genres and remakes; perhaps the unusual is lucrative. Certainly RKO chose some of Broadway's most out-of-the-way properties while other studios grabbed the hot stuff—*Grand Hotel, Dead End, The Little Foxes, The Philadelphia Story, Born Yesterday*. Surely if RKO hadn't filmed Maxwell Anderson's *Winterset* (1936), no one would have, for this verse play on the aftermath of a trial modeled on the Sacco and Vanzetti case comprised lyrical conversations more than a story. There is a touch of Goldwyn in the production, with a faithful script (the actors speak most of the poetry as if it were prose) and the three key actors from Broadway—Eduardo Ciannelli as the gangster Trock, and Burgess Meredith and Margo as the romantic couple. Similarly, RKO brought over Abbey Theatre players for *The Plough and the Stars* (1937), from Sean O'Casey's play on Dublin's Easter Rebellion of 1916. Again, is RKO on stage or at the movies, even with John Ford directing? It appears to be in both places, with rowdy action scenes spliced into O'Casey's personal drama, the playwright's critical dissection of the Irish spirit romanticized into a cavalry western that for some reason takes place in Dublin. By far the most disastrous of RKO's films of big theatre names was *Mourning Becomes Electra* (1947), O'Neill's Aeschylean epic so self-consciously realized that the film lost over two million dollars.

Even the filming of novels, a Hollywood routine that yielded thousands of successfully routine films, gave RKO some of its strangest entries. Take Ford's *The Informer* (1935), from Liam O'Flaherty's tale of a loser who betrays a comrade in the Irish underground to the Brits for steamship passage to America. Ford's highly stylized approach, a kind of fantasy-naturalism, should have guaranteed a respectable flop. Previews did not go well, and the first booking, at Radio City Music Hall, was a disaster. Yet in smaller theatres *The Informer* did good business. Critics praised it, and it won four Oscars, including Best Director, Writer (Dudley Nichols), and Actor (Victor McLaglen). In fact, until *Citizen Kane* came along, *The Informer* was regarded as the movies' major artistic breakthrough since the introduction of the talkie.

That was RKO's luck, surviving on its distribution contracts and B series, every so often earning out on the profit in quality. But previews for *Sylvia Scarlett* (1936) went so poorly that producer Pandro Berman told director Cukor and star Hepburn that he'd never work with them again. Compton Mackenzie, whose early novels bespoke a serious, poetic intent, suddenly turned to comedy after World War I, and *The Early Life and Adventures of Sylvia Scarlett* suggests a raffish sensibility exploding with first loves and whimseys. The novel is indescribable except to say that it offered Hepburn the chance to spend most of the action disguised as a boy. She and Cukor apparently thought this marvelous sport, and the whole RKO team wallowed in Mackenzie. So the film is indescribable, too, except to say that Hepburn as a boy reminds us of the great role she never got to play, Peter

Pan. She looks terrific. But the very strange story, now dire, now waggish, gives her too much to do and she tries to do all of it.

Sylvia Scarlett is a one-of-a-kind movie, but then that's the theme of this chapter, it seems. Some thirty minutes along—and very little has happened thus far; or, rather, everything has happened but a story—a maid is searching for her mistress's lost pearls. Tipsy Kate leaps grandly off a couch onto the floor. "Dive for them!" she cries. "They've gone back into the sea!" One imagines crowds of preview spectators slipping out as Berman fumes. But Hepburn's transvestite gambol provisions striking erotic puns. Flirty Dennie Moore grabs her and kisses her full on the mouth. Moments later, Hepburn is trying to worm out of sharing a bed with cockney con man Cary Grant. "It's a bit nippy tonight," says Grant. "You'll make a proper hot-water bottle." Kate flees, along with the rest of the preview audience.

Even pre-sold titles like Somerset Maugham's *Of Human Bondage* (1934) end up, in RKO's hands, as too faithful, too strong, to be popular. Here's a self-hating, self-effacing dolt of a man courting a vicious opportunistic woman. Hollywood in the 1930s just did not film such stories without substantial modifications. No doubt when Berman gave the project to the sharp-edged director John Cromwell he was asking for a wild magic. But then it's just this artistic audacity that characterizes RKO. Lack of deep-pocket capitalization also characterizes it, and the tight finances not only strapped production and PR budgets but forbade the studio from assembling a competitive contract roster. To cast *Of Human Bondage*, RKO had to borrow the two leads from Warner Brothers: Leslie Howard and Bette Davis.

Maugham's tale is in a sense a weepie from the man's point of view. But there is none of the luxuriating in misery that Hollywood condones in soap opera. Howard is made utterly miserable, but not because love is too beautiful to bear: because love is humiliating. The downward spiral of Howard's "romance" with Davis's cockney waitress is so honestly depicted, and Cromwell's control of the English atmosphere so telling, that at times we wonder if the picture didn't come to RKO on one of its distribution deals, from an English outfit.

No: hooray for Hollywood. But this is an extravagantly artistic Hollywood. Howard does nothing to ingratiate himself with us, makes no reference to the debonair Philip Barry aristo he usually played; he is simply a mesmerized fool. Davis is no heroine slumming for an Oscar. She *is* Mildred, pushing the rudeness of her lines to the limit, snarling out a smile, sadistically loveless—all the more so in comparison with Howard's other girlfriends, Kay Johnson and Frances Dee. To force the point, Cromwell gives us Howard's dream of an ideal; Mildred, polite and responsive, grateful for his attention. It's shocking in the context of the real-life Mildred. After she throws Howard over, he takes up with Johnson, and comes home to find Davis waiting for him. Howard says, "I didn't think I'd ever see you again." And says it quietly terrified.

RKO shares one thing with the other lots. During the Studio Age itself, it had no one period of glory. The 1930s, era of Astaire–Rogers and Hepburn, may count the greatest number of great RKOs, but the 1940s brought Orson Welles's *Citizen Kane* and *The Magnificent Ambersons* (1942); the uncompromisingly tragic *None But the Lonely Heart* (1944); *Crossfire*; and the testily sentimental *I Remember Mama* (1948), a nostalgic domestic drama with a tender honesty far beyond what Fox might have made of similar material—and with one of Irene Dunne's most beautifully judged performances.

Perhaps RKO might have run along into the post–Studio Age, like its fellows, on this strange agglomeration of the unusual and the ordinary. But in 1948 Howard Hughes bought control of RKO. Living up to his legend, Hughes fired, canceled, delayed, disorganized, exasperated, destroyed. In 1957, what was left of the lot collapsed, productions stopped where they stood, and other studios enlisted to distribute completed films. Later that year, two former RKO contractees, Lucille Ball and Desi Arnaz, purchased the lot for their Desilu company, and regeared it for television production.

The monster of monsters at the studio of horror: Boris Kar-loff in Bride of Frankenstein. *A superb shot, but Universal films seldom if ever looked this good. There's a fetching incongruity in the demon's embracing the saint, and the shaft of light upon Our Father reminds us that Karloff is the only man without One. But—as we shall see—Universal's supernatural mainly comprises ethnic paradox, slow-motion storytelling, and Lon Chaney, Jr.*

UNIVERSAL

The Old Monster

T here is something shocking and wonderful about Universal, shocking because it has lasted three-quarters of a century despite the least ambitious aesthetic of all the major studios; and wonderful because it opens a door on the movies' deepest history, back in the First Era when D. W. Griffith was making two-reelers with Little Mary and the Gish girls in a brownstone on Manhattan's Fourteenth Street. Universal is *old* Old Hollywood, older even than Paramount. It is not only the oldest surviving studio but the *last* surviving studio, the last to function more or less in the way that studios functioned in the Golden Age, even unto providing tours of the lot for the curious.

Perhaps Universal outlasted its coevals precisely because it had the least ambitious aesthetic. Certainly its stylistics reveal an insistent conservatism—no, *reactionary* tendencies. Where Paramount and MGM stand out for their leadership of the industry, and where Warner Brothers, Fox, RKO, Columbia, Goldwyn, and Selznick are as interesting in their imitative responses to that leadership as in their inventions, Universal often seems to be rooting helplessly in the past. In the mid-1920s, next to Paramount's *A Kiss for Cinderella* or MGM's *He Who Gets Slapped* or Buster Keaton's *The General* or Douglas Fairbanks's *The Thief of Bagdad*, most of Universal's output resembles the work of mid-1910s Hollywood. This is a mere ten years' default—but in art and technology this was Hollywood's most decisive decade, from the flickers over into cinema.

Sometimes we feel that Universal simply can't keep up with Hollywood, that its judgment calls never catch on to the ontogeny of film, the unceasing tempo of development. Was it misapprehension or resistance that led Universal to grind out woman-protagonist serials long after their vogue had passed?* Was it stinginess or wait-and-see wisdom that inspired the studio to boycott the full-length feature long after the two-reeler had gone under? It was certainly stinginess, and a lack of wisdom, that allowed such key personnel as production chief Irving Thalberg, director John Ford, and actors Lon Chaney, Rudolph Valentino, and Mae Murray (among a great many others) to move to rival studios offering more money. Similarly, Universal steered wide of the exhibition oligarchy buying up theatre chains, crippling its exposure in the key metropolitan centers, and was dragged kicking and screaming into the talkie era. If Universal's founding mogul Carl Laemmle had had his way, the American film would still consist of a fifty-minute program comprising one two-reel drama, one single-reel comedy, and one split reel of documentary instruction, changed for your delectation and faithful attendance each day.

All of the above marks a self-aggravating disease: the more old-fashioned Universal was, the more old-fashioned Universal perforce became. The dowdy subject matter—hurly-burly serials in the late

*It might have been feminism. To its credit, Universal was the only major studio that, for a time, routinely employed women directors; and the cliff-hanger serial originated as a feminist fantasy, the heroine very energetically routing the villains and saving some bumbling boyfriend.

1920s!—alienated critics. The refusal to bank on stars eroded credibility in a star-oriented age. The lack of urban theatres and sophisticated audiences affirmed the retroactive aesthetic. The need to cultivate the rustic patrons of the outback further limited Universal's originality.

Worst of all, Universal's nickelodeon mind-set cut it off from Broadway just when the stage was a fertile supplier of Hollywood's needs—in the transition into talkies. Paramount and RKO devour literacy and golden tones. Warner Brothers taps them. MGM worships them. Universal is virtually unaware of them—except in defensive postures. Like all Old Hollywood moguls, Laemmle did everything while looking over his shoulder at Adolph Zukor. If Paramount had Famous Players, Laemmle would have the Broadway Universal Feature—Jane Cowl in *Garden of Lies* (1915) or Marie Cahill in *Judy Forgot* (1915), direct from Broadway. Later, in the 1930s, we find Universal still making kowtow to Paramount's acumen, buying up its rejects in Marlene Dietrich, W. C. Fields, Mae West, and Martha Raye. Throughout, we sense Laemmle's fury at having to expand, energize, retool. He doesn't *want* to make Broadway Universal Features. He doesn't want to hire anything that's been at Paramount. He will never understand why Dietrich is sexy, why Raye is loud. All Laemmle wanted from his work was to make two-reel dramas, one-reel comedies, and split-reel documentaries. He built the first *big* Hollywood studio. Yet all he could see in it was a sprawling outdoor American Biograph, the city brownstone opened up, pushed west, spread out.

Ironically enough, Laemmle began as a rebel, a defier of status quo, when Edison's Patents Trust attempted to bind the movie business with sweeping policies covering production, distribution, and exhibition. Backed by a court decision, Edison's syndicate proposed not only to run the lives of all in the industry but to ban anyone who tried to go independent. Laemmle had started out as a theatre owner, then moved into distribution. He was one of the most constant customers of the Patents Trust studios' output. Outraged by the Trust's high-handedness—and, like many moguls of his generation, offended by the haughtily waspish character of Edison's cohort—Laemmle went outlaw.

He also went into production, since breaking with the Trust cut off his supply of films. In a nice turn of history (and a bold move, considering that Trust tactics extended to the use of hired bravos to disrupt filming, destroy equipment, and threaten the staff), Laemmle set up shop just a block east of American Biograph. His first picture, typical of the day in its bid for elocution-parlor prestige and its marketing of a pre-sold title, was *Hiawatha* (1909). ("You can bet it is classy," Laemmle announced in his prospectus, "or I wouldn't make it my first release.") Seeing himself as the leader of the independents fighting the Trust, Laemmle dubbed his firm the Independent Motion Picture Company: the IMP. In 1912, Laemmle's operation merged with a few other independent studios, concentrated the bulk of its production in Los Angeles, renamed itself the Universal Film Manufacturing Company, and three years later officially opened the first of the big Hollywood studios, Universal City. The Trust was dead and the independents would inherit the industry as, one by one, Edison's conspirators faded away.

Yet Laemmle had never planned to make films different from those of the Trust. He was not *artistically* independent. Looking at the kind of films Biograph, Kalem, Lubin, Essanay, and the other Trust studios issued, a *Hiawatha* is not only not a breakaway proposition but an aggressive imitation. Laemmle couldn't join the Trust, so he beat it. But he had every intention of continuing, so to say, their work.

So first we find him fulminating against Trust greed. Then we find him raging against Zukor's use of expensive stars in five- and six-reel features, turning the assembly line of two-reelers into a vast competition of helter-skelter and adventurism. *The Birth of a Nation?* How about the death of a business? Laemmle had seen how the vanity of a popular performer drains his employer's profits, for Laemmle had stolen Little Mary from Biograph for a raise in salary, only to see Little Mary dance off to another independent studio, Majestic—for a raise in salary. Laemmle had also seen the fortune a feature could earn, when he dared a six-reel exposé of New York prostitution, *Traffic in Souls* (1913), and took in half a million dollars on a film that cost less than ten thousand. But he didn't like the way these fancy productions gummed up the schedule and stymied distribution techniques any more than he approved of highfalutin stars bouncing from studio to studio. Let us forge ahead, one hears Laemmle cry, to yesterday!

Laemmle's yesterday, which dominated Universal's production

through the silent period, is quaint and primitive. Universal was Hollywood's biggest production center, yet culturally it was an outpost. Looking back to 1916, we see Hollywood's Second Era of Silent Film taking shape in the work of such as Geraldine Farrar, Wallace Reid, Charlie Chaplin, the Gishes, Blanche Sweet, Theda Bara, the Barrymores, Harold Lloyd, Pearl White, Nazimova, William S. Hart, Douglas Fairbanks, and Little Mary. At Universal, we find not names with the ring of the future but such obscure billings they were not known enough then to be fairly called forgotten now. They were forgotten then.

Laemmle published a list of his players in 1916. "Week after week," he crowed, "you get the cream of the world's biggest Box Office attractions." Some one hundred ten names follow, a catalogue of the piquant: Little Clara Horton, Fatty Voss, Billy Human, W. F. Musgrave, Flora Parker de Haven, Lule Warrenton, Myrtle Gonzales, Doc Crane, Harry Depp, Mother Benson, Rex de Rosselli. Laemmle does cite a few who achieved renown: Betty Compson, Lois Wilson, Harry Carey, and Lon Chaney. Yet it's typical of Universal's approach to moviemaking that the first three left early on, enervated by the lackluster stories and eager to test their potential at the more ambitious lots; and Chaney, who became Universal's big draw in the early 1920s, left to develop his fame with Mayer and Thalberg.

Even those actors in Laemmle's list who were notable stars in 1916—King Baggot, J. Warren Kerrigan, and Grace Cunard—have the bizarre ineffability we sense in Fatty Voss and Flora Parker de Haven. In this same year, 1916, Universal ran an advertisement in the form of an open letter from King Baggot to his fans, offering five dollars "to any person who will suggest a new character role that I can make use of in a photoplay." To freshen contestants' memories, the ad lists all Baggot's roles heretofore, some fifty-five. (Remember, these were two-reelers, turned out in less than a week.) They suggest the innocent, uncouth versatility of the anonymous stock companies of the earliest studios: Ancient Grandee, Protean Detective, Shabby Genteel Swell, Punch and Judy Show Operator, Train Wrecker, Irishman, Italian, Tramp, Burglar, Village Bully, and, in one film, ten parts, including a Dutch Policeman, an Old Millionaire, a Grand Dame Mother, and the Wayward and Prodigal Son.

All the same, Universal made a bid to join the new wave in Erich von Stroheim's quartet of *Blind Husbands* (1919), *The Devil's Pass Key* (1920), *Foolish Wives* (1922), and *Merry-Go-Round* (1923), though Laemmle hired the director without knowing what he was in for and though von Stroheim increasingly indulged his taste for overshooting till Laemmle's studio chief, Irving Thalberg, threw von Stroheim off *Merry-Go-Round* in the middle of production. Von Stroheim's naturalistically erotic and at times debauched view of life proved especially galling to the old-folks-at-home mentality of the critics and public that Universal normally played to. But Laemmle enjoyed being, for once, the envy of the industry. After all, he was the mogul who had beaten down the patents men and cleared the way for Hollywood, yet his fellow independents William Fox, Jesse Lasky, and Adolph Zukor had disinherited Laemmle of his just honors, had eclipsed him with definitions of prestige that Laemmle didn't believe in and could not practically compete with.

He was not sorry to see von Stroheim go. For *Foolish Wives*, the director had built a pointlessly precise re-creation of Monte Carlo on the backlot—the biggest set till then in Universal's history—and had shot well over three hundred reels on a picture that was released at fourteen. This was already too long—remember, this was the last studio to make two-reelers, and was still doing so during von Stroheim's era there. And what was this foolishness with three hundred reels? In Laemmle's day, you shot so many feet, called cut, and gave it to the lab for developing.

It wasn't Laemmle's day anymore. Thalberg sacked von Stroheim just at the start of the Third Era, the day of the Big One; and under Thalberg's prodding, Laemmle had to compete, spending more on his A's and trying another spectacle in *The Hunchback of Notre Dame* (1923). This was much less of a departure for Universal than von Stroheim's perverse satires: another reference to the classics, sheer family fun. Nor was it quite as Big as Laemmle would have everyone believe. Contrary to a legend that refuses to die, Notre Dame cathedral was not reconstructed on the lot. Not even the façade was. Warming to the wonders of technology—that is, facing up to the present—Universal built only the cathedral's door front (in painstaking duplication) and filled in the towers with a glass shot.

The Hunchback of Notre Dame did bring forth a real star in Lon Chaney, and it turned out to be one of the year's top-grossing films, with road-show engagements, big urban business, and, finally, saturation play-offs in the small houses where most Universals played their only bookings. So Laemmle had been over into the future, even if it worked better for studios like Paramount and Metro, with their huge theatre circuits tuning into the volatile city culture that was redefining the American style. Two years after *The Hunchback of Notre Dame*, Laemmle dared *The Phantom of the Opera* (1925), again with Chaney, again with an exaggerated legend about a reconstruction of Paris architecture, this time of the auditorium of the Opéra. In fact, all we see is about fifteen rows of the orchestra.

We do get a lot of backstage and lobby, not to mention the underground vaults where the Phantom grouches and sulks. We also get a strong sense of how backward the studio *still* is. The acting of everyone but Chaney is School of Edwin S. Porter: why walk when you can lurch, glance when you might stare? The titles make D. W. Griffith's Victorian samplers seem like the wisecracking of Anita Loos. "I can never leave the Opera, Raoul," Mary Philbin announces. "You must forget our love!" Perhaps it's movie license that allows the tenor to join her in *Faust*'s rising-to-heaven apotheosis, though in the opera only the soprano dies. But why, just after, do we find her in her dressing room costumed for the Garden Scene, which ended two intermissions earlier? It's a small point, perhaps, but it wouldn't have happened at MGM or Paramount—not because these studios were crazed for authenticity but because the sloppy mistake that undercuts the action typifies the movies' earliest days, and the 1920s stressed credibility. Certainly Paramount and MGM would never have released the Technicolor *bal masqué* reel (in which the Phantom stalks through the ball costumed as Death), with the absurd long shot of revelers hyperactively gamboling on the Opéra stairs. It looks phony and silly. It looks, like so much First Era film, as if no one involved in the production had the remotest idea what the world is like. But this is the Third Era. Think of King Baggot blithely taking on the Irishman, the Italian, the Punch and Judy Show Operator, the Train Wrecker, the Ancient Grandee; think, even, of Fatty Voss and Mother Benson. It sounds like American Biograph—but Biograph, remember, had D. W. Griffith.

Griffith shares with Universal an affection for old-fashioned stories. He astonished Hollywood with *Way Down East* in 1920, making compelling cinema out of outmoded melodrama. Universal did not astonish Hollywood with *Uncle Tom's Cabin*, the studio's Big One for 1927. This melodrama was dismally outmoded, and seemed to pilfer *Way Down East* in the chase scene on the ice floes. Another problem was Universal's continuing lack of star power, despite its proud boast that accompanied the closing credit list for over two decades: "A good cast is worth repeating." As the silent era neared its end, with Lon Chaney gone to MGM, Universal's big draws were Laura La Plante, Priscilla Dean, Reginald Denny, and Jean Hersholt, just ahead of his touching-cameo period at Metro. Even Fox and Warner Brothers had more to offer in personalities, let alone Paramount and MGM. Characteristically, Universal's part-talkie Big One of 1929, *Show Boat*, suffered from the underpowered La Plante as Magnolia, the alien Joseph Schildkraut as Ravenal (to understand how miscast he was, consider that twenty-six years later he played Anne's father in *The Diary of Anne Frank* on Broadway), the pushy Otis Harlan as Captain Andy, the acceptable Emily Fitzroy as Parthy Ann, and only Alma Rubens commanding as the tragic Julie. (And no wonder: Rubens died shortly after, a victim of drug addiction.)

Notice again the antique nature of the property. Edna Ferber's novel had been published in 1926, but her setting, characters, and story line look back to traditions of romantic adventure laid down in the late 1800s. And note Universal's antique approach to an unusual problem: the Jerome Kern–Oscar Hammerstein II adaptation, in Florenz Ziegfeld's spectacular mounting, had totally overshadowed the novel. Though the show had opened in late 1927, *after* Warner Brothers' *Don Juan* and *The Jazz Singer* had signaled the emergence of the musical track, Universal still went ahead with a silent *Show Boat*. At the last minute, sound sequences were spliced in to make a frantic part-talkie—a silent film braced with boring new songs and preceded by a prologue in which some of Ziegfeld's New York performers delivered highlights of the Kern–Hammerstein score. This is going for it and fleeing it at the same time.

Once again, Universal had tried to stonewall the future, dragging into the talkie era with a prefabricated museum piece.* *Show Boat*'s premiere coincided with that of MGM's *The Broadway Melody*, and

*This was not entirely *passéiste* thinking, for Universal's major customers were the smaller theatres that could least afford the retooling necessary for talkie exhibition. Most of them ran through 1929, playing the alternate silent versions of talkies that the studios put out as stopgaps. Universal naturally stayed on the longest, printing these if-you-must silents well into 1930.

the aural energy of MGM's backstager utterly foreclosed on Universal's sluggish, semi-mute *Show Boat*. Why commission new songs when the Kern–Hammerstein score had become so closely associated with the story? Why not borrow a star or two to urge the action onward? Why retain the typical dreary Universal director—Harry Pollard, who had finished off *Uncle Tom's Cabin*—instead of daring one of the new bloods in town?

Universal was already inadequate in silents. Talkies direly tested it. Defensive imitation buoyed it along. We constantly sense that Universals of the early sound years are re-creations of other studios' films—if not a copy of a certain title, then surely the mugging of a genre. We find, for instance, a typical Warner Brothers shyster study in *Counsellor at Law* (1933), with Warners' own John Barrymore as a Jewish lawyer torn between ethnic honesty and upward mobility among the heartless rich. We miss the driving Warners tempo and the fast cutting and montages. (Virtually all the action takes place in Barrymore's office, apparently at the insistence of Elmer Rice, author of the original play and the film script.) But there are the city people, rich and poor, in their texture of accents; and of course the political worldview. One of Barrymore's clients is a young Jewish man, arrested and beaten by the police for giving a Communist speech in Union Square. While he's sitting in Barrymore's waiting room, Barrymore's bratty son tells Barrymore's assistant, a Harvard law graduate, to hand him a magazine. Done—and the Communist, outraged at the youngster's moneyed-class hauteur, rises shaking with fury. It's a great moment; it would be outspoken even in a Warners film. Even better is the scene in which the Communist tells Barrymore off for pandering to the bosses and indulging his "kept parasite of a wife." The young man gets so angry that—crying "you dirty *traitor*, you!" —he actually spits in Barrymore's face.

Counsellor at Law is, no doubt, less an imitation of the Warners style than a faithful adaptation of Rice's play. But many of Universal's *hommages* to rival studios' formats feel like remakes of then current films, clumsy at that. *Love Before Breakfast* (1936), one of those naughty-come-on titles that have nothing to do with the story, offers Preston Foster as a tycoon after Carole Lombard, who's in love with Cesar Romero—already testing credulity. The style is pure Paramount, specifically Mitchell Leisen's Claudette Colbert–Ray Milland sex comedies that had just got under way the year before—except Universal's director Walter Lang lacks Leisen's lightness of touch, his wit, his designer's imagination of place (this though Universal troubled to hire Paramount's Travis Banton to dress Lombard).

Universal even attempts MGM's "two buddies and the woman they chase" comic adventure, the kind of thing Clark Gable and Spencer Tracy might do with Myrna Loy. Universal's version is *Pittsburgh* (1942). With Marlene Dietrich on hand, the studio borrowed John Wayne and Randolph Scott, which is not up to MGM in charisma; and loaded the tale with clichés, which is not how MGM kept the formula alive for trio after trio. Universal's boldest allusion to *Pittsburgh*'s matrix is Wayne's repetition of "I love ya, baby, I love ya," a Gable trademark. It's irritating on Gable, but at least it's authoritative. Wayne, at this stage of his career, doesn't have the affable majesty to pull it off. Perhaps the worst aspect of *Pittsburgh* is not a pilfering, but a true example of Universal's "two reels good" mentality in the sound-track score, a blundering medley of tunes in the manner of the early talkies rather than the tone poems pioneered at RKO and Warner Brothers in the early-middle 1930s. In some scenes, Universal's orchestra just stands there and plays a theme over and over regardless of what is occurring on screen. This is backward even for 1930.

In at least one instance, Universal's reactionary aesthetic delivered it of a classic: its 1936 remake of *Show Boat*. There are two reasons for this *Show Boat*'s excellence: authenticity of adaptation and sharp casting, virtues lacking in the 1929 version and also in the 1951 version (one of Arthur Freed's less entrancing efforts over at MGM). First of all, rather than fool with a great show, Universal hired the authors, Jerome Kern and Oscar Hammerstein II, to knock out the new text. Too much of the score is dropped, including "Why Do I Love You?"—filmed but cut before release. (A tiny bit of the scene remains, in the automobile-ride episode during the Chicago sequence.) But three superb new songs were added. And surely Kern and Hammerstein were consulted on the casting, for most of the leads are veterans of important *Show Boat* productions, including the key performers of the 1927 original, Helen Morgan and Charles Winninger, Paul Robeson of London and Ziegfeld's 1932 New York revival, and Irene Dunne of the first national tour. One deplores the lack of Edna May Oliver, the original Parthy Ann and working in Hollywood at the time. But Helen Westley is fine, though comically rather than dourly menacing. Add to this group Allan Jones, arguably the best of Hollywood's operetta heroes, and Hattie McDaniel in one of her few chances to play a lead, and it almost doesn't matter whether or not James Whale brings any imagination to the direction: the production is already secure as composition and performance.

In fact, looking at other films of Broadway musicals in the late-middle 1930s, we cherish Universal's *Show Boat* all the more. Fidelity to the original is rare in these times, and the rewritten scripts and new songs are not impressive. MGM's *Rose Marie*, the same year as *Show Boat*, typifies the approach. The alterations begin with the title, which has lost the hyphen used in New York, and run right through the score, which has vanished except for a few central numbers. Most revised is the story. MGM filmed a silent *Rose Marie* with Joan Crawford in 1928, following the show's plot, but for Jeanette MacDonald and Nelson Eddy it changed the plot around. Rose Marie, a backwoods hellcat, is now a prim opera singer; her lover, Jim, becomes her brother; and her paternal Mountie friend, Sergeant Malone, now supplies the love interest as Sergeant Bruce. Why the change of name?

At least MGM determined to do a lot of location shooting, a significant point in a movie musical that, but for opening and closing sequences onstage at the opera, takes place almost entirely out of doors. However, even there MGM hedged, relying on far too much back projection. "The Mounties," Eddy's big entrance song at the head of a column of law officers on horseback, looks particularly suspicious. We have the feeling that if the camera pulled back, we would find Eddy on a treadmilled horse singing, "Here come the *Mounties!*" in front of a screen.

Here come the Mountie—and remember that *Rose Marie* is only typical of its day. It is not the worst by any means. MGM's *Rosalie*, adapted for Eleanor Powell and Nelson Eddy, retained its story but lost its *entire* score (by two of Broadway's greatest composers, George Gershwin and Sigmund Romberg; MGM brings in a third when Cole Porter writes the new songs). Fox's *Sally, Irene and Mary* lost score *and* story. All they kept was the title.

The question is: why was it Universal that made the outstanding faithful adaptation of a great show in this period? Filming musicals with some authenticity was common in the first two years of the talkies, when studios weren't sure how else to handle Broadway. Warner Brothers' *Sally*, MGM's *Good News*, Goldwyn's *Whoopee!*, Paramount's *The Vagabond King*, and RKO's *Rio Rita* held quite close to the originals, even unto hiring original performers. The practice fell away as the musical cycle ended in late 1930, and when Warners' Berkeley backstager revved it up in 1933, each studio began to work particular approaches of no reference to Broadway—Fox's show-biz tales filled out with specialty acts, Columbia's pop-and-classical romances for Grace Moore, MGM's operettas, RKO's dance musicals.

This is exactly why Universal made a faithful *Show Boat*. Unoriginal as always, the studio had developed no musical genre; backward as usual, it did what had proved doable a decade earlier. Universal's 1936 *Show Boat* is like an early talkie. It even sounds like one, the microphone technology not up to MGM's and RKO's clarity and density. For a final irony, it would seem that Laemmle initiated the project to get his money's worth out of an old contract. Edna Ferber opposed selling her books to Hollywood outright: she leased them for a certain period. Universal's 1929 *Show Boat* hadn't earned much in the first place, and Laemmle's option was about to run out. He seized the advantage virtually out of *force majeure*.

Yet Universal does at times pull off a coup of originality. One of its earliest talkies, *Broadway* (1929), came from the New York stage hit about the nightclub world of hoods and hoofers. Set in the Paradise Club's back room, not on the main floor, the play was literally a backstager: no music. Universal reset it at the center of its activity, *on* stage, with plenty of song-and-dance. The main set, an eye-filling art deco monstrosity dressed by chorus girls in bizarre skyscraperish costumes, was a wonder of the year, especially since cameraman Hal Mohr devised a special crane that freed the frame of that fixed stare so common to the first talkies. Roving through the club, darting from on high to close-up in seconds, Mohr and director Paul Fejos gave Universal's *Broadway* a cinematic exuberance no real Broadway could hope to counter. And note that the subject was very contemporary, unlike the melodramas that had served Universal for its Big Ones heretofore.

The "Wow" number of the Paradise Night Club revue.

Universal does a Warners backstager: Broadway, a musical version of the George Abbott–Philip Dunning "crook show" (as they were known), anticipates the style of the Berkeley backstager.

Universal reverted to tradition in its Big One of 1930, *All Quiet on the Western Front*, a look at the Great War in terms reminiscent of D. W. Griffith more than Erich Maria Remarque's novel would have suggested. Director Lewis Milestone lyricizes Remarque's edgy ironies; the sorrowful last shots of Lew Ayres's hand reaching out of the trenches to touch a butterfly, shaking at the report of a rifle, and then lying still echo the rhapsodic pathos of Griffith's small-town epics. This is Universal managing to make a great film on its own terms—and doggedly furnishing its little neighborhood cinemas with a silent version in case they, like Laemmle, deeply resent the talkie revolution.

Yet again that same year, 1930, Universal came up with the very capstone of a cycle that had run through Hollywood: the musical revue. Designed to display each studio's expertise in the talkie, the revues in fact revealed too much fake versatility (MGM's Norma Shearer and John Gilbert doing *Romeo and Juliet*'s Balcony Scene in '20s slang in *The Hollywood Revue of 1929*) or too much stagestruck production (Warner Brothers' John Adolfi filming *The Show of Shows* from, apparently, fifth row center). What could poor Universal do? Somehow, it made the right choices throughout and unveiled that rarest of gems, a one-of-a-kind genre piece.

First of all, there is no all-star approach—wise, because Universal has few genuine stars and no versatile ones, especially no musical ones. Second, the whole film is in Technicolor—an unheard-of splurge for a studio that left its heart in Fort Lee, New Jersey, where you could make *Hiawatha* inside of a week and still have time to knock off a couple of Fatty Voss comedy shorts and a heart-petting *semiseria* with Little Clara Horton and Mother Benson. Third, for novelty Universal drafts talent from the East—a breakaway act for a lot that regarded thespians as wholly unabsorbable. Fourth, instead of a rota of unrelated spiels, the entertainment will adhere lightly to a theme.

The Easterners are director and designer John Murray Anderson and bandleader Paul Whiteman; the theme is Paul Whiteman's Scrap Book (the pages turn to announce each episode); and the film is *King of Jazz*. Nothing in it typifies Universal; even the use of Laura La Plante, the one house diva who appears, is limited to brief comedy sketches. Still, *someone* in Laemmle's crew had the vision to invite

Anderson and Whiteman over, Whiteman for the delight his troupe could offer on the sound track (Bing Crosby appears with the band's vocal trio, the Rhythm Boys) and Anderson because he had made his name in New York as a master of revue. Who would have thought how easily the two would adapt to cinema? Whiteman is an endearing movie personality, totally at ease, and Anderson directs the only Hollywood revue that is *entirely* visual. This is spectacle and surprise —in an animated cartoon on Whiteman's discovery of jazz in the African jungle; in the players' arrival in Whiteman's satchel (through double exposure in perfect registration); in the coordination of the color design, shifting act by act but generally observing white, silver, and pink; in portly Whiteman's tap demonstration, startlingly agile till the real Whiteman comes out and pulls the fake mustache off his exact double; in a view of Times Square that we take for a photograph till the girls dance in and we realize it's a miniature. Moreover, Anderson smartly kept the comedy to a minimum—feckless jokes were the bane of the form—and held out for the best songs of all the revues.

In a way, Universal's history in the Studio Age accords with this odd catalogue of films, this odd mixture of, primarily, the old-fashioned; generally, the imitative; and, occasionally, the unique. We sense, too, a break in Universal's style in 1936, when money problems ended the Laemmle family regime at Laemmle's studio. Since the arrival of the talkie, Laemmle's son Junior had headed production; but Junior could not muster a 1930s worldview out of a tradition that was born to look backward. As with Metro's Thalberg, the Laemmle family Effect held on for some years after their passing, and many of the studio's best efforts in the 1940s appear to draw on the Laemmle energy of retroaction, the tendency to follow after having taken the lead. What studio but Universal would have appropriated Paramount's Marlene Dietrich, only to strip away the exoticism and mystery that made her compelling? Seeing von Sternberg's *Morocco* or *The Scarlet Empress*, could anyone have imagined that by the decade's end Dietrich would have been turned into Frenchy, the kick-and-spittle hostess of a western saloon in *Destry Rides Again* (1939) at Universal, with the ultra-American good guy James Stewart and villain Brian Donlevy? At least *Destry* is lively fun. The aforementioned *Pittsburgh*, with John Wayne and Randolph Scott, is twaddle. Universal took

Dietrich out of erotic films, women's films, directors' films, and put her into sexy films, men's films, producers' films.

What is one to say, then, of *Seven Sinners* (1940), which somehow gives Dietrich one of her best films even within the flat Universal formula? What a heavy-handed aesthetic! Universal is so eager to tell us that this is an action picture that we get the first of several tavern brawls even before the credits; and Dietrich enters the movie by finishing off a smutty story—". . . And that's what happened to the farmer's daughter"—and striding into a courtroom, her bag rudely aswing. Lumpy comics like Billy Gilbert and Mischa Auer abound. It's hopeless. Or it should be. Actually, this tale of naval officer John Wayne and café singer Dietrich loving and parting in the South Seas is almost a spoof of the kind of films Dietrich made at Paramount, and as such has something of a purposeless purpose, a mission without an aim. Inadvertently or not, Universal has created a new genre for Dietrich, an American Vamp comedy-romance. At Paramount, Dietrich played by European rules of timeless fatalism: you cannot evade destiny. At Universal, Dietrich plays by American rules of democratic self-sacrifice: you can remake the world. At Paramount, Dietrich would have destroyed Wayne. At Universal, Dietrich lets him go to a more fitting mistress, the Navy.

Universal was not agile enough to distinguish itself in screwball comedy, one of the most contemporary forms that the 1930s cultivated. No matter what the year, Universal was anything but contemporary. Yet again, somehow or other, the studio made one of screwball's classics, *My Man Godfrey* (1936), with a demonstration-level cast at that: William Powell, Carole Lombard, Alice Brady, Eugene Pallette, Gail Patrick, and Jean Dixon. Similarly, Universal's *Scarlet Street* (1945), only a year after Paramount's *Double Indemnity*, proved one of the essential noir entries. Perhaps this is because of a long-standing Universal tradition, the émigré auteur. Back in the 1920s, Universal made a home away from Germany for German directors and cameramen—Karl Freund excelled as both. This was not unique to Universal; in the same period, Warner Brothers had Ernst Lubitsch, Fox F. W. Murnau, Paramount Josef von Sternberg. Still, Universal may have led off with Erich von Stroheim, who made *Blind Husbands* back in 1919. Fritz Lang had free-lanced all over Hollywood for a decade before he made *Scarlet Street*; and as Lang produced as well as directed this is far more his triumph than the studio's. Nevertheless, here's our eternal has-been of a lot releasing a key film, not only for its incisive atmosphere as a thriller but for its appalling honesty in the exposure of noir archetypes: the wormy husband (Edward G. Robinson) with the termagant wife (Rosalind Ivan), the Treacherous Woman (Joan Bennett) who seduces him, and her crumb-bun boyfriend (Dan Duryea). Dudley Nichols's script traps Robinson in a terrifying snare in that the people he should count on the most are the most withholding while the people he should avoid are the ones who tantalize. Lang's direction plays wonderfully on all this, especially in Bennett's manipulation of Robinson—and Duryea, in his bow tie, straw hat, and egregious smile, is the epitome of the destructive good-for-nothing. Well, good for one thing:

JOAN BENNETT: I don't know why I'm so crazy about you.

DAN DURYEA: (carelessly) Yes, you do.

Some critics prefer the Universal noirs that followed *Scarlet Street* —*Black Angel* (1946), *The Dark Mirror* (1946), *The Killers* (1946), and *Criss Cross* (1949) among them. (And note the continuing German émigré influence: all these but *Black Angel* were directed by Robert Siodmak.) The point is that, for once, Universal was quick to explore the latest trend instead of waiting for it to go away and, five to ten years after it fails to, awkwardly trying to adopt it. Noir analysts will further round up Siodmak's *Phantom Lady* and *Christmas Holiday*, both for Universal in 1944, early enough in noir's history to be called avant-garde.

In one form, beyond question, Universal was an innovator: horror. The fantasy of the grotesque, ideal for cinema, is even older than Universal. When Laemmle was still in his IMP days, film had already started on the classic titles. Edison made *Frankenstein* in 1910, Universal *The Werewolf* and *Dr. Jekyll and Mr. Hyde* (with King Baggot in the dual role) in 1913. Lon Chaney's work at the studio obviously bore influence, especially in his fascination with the transformational power of his makeup box. But Chaney spent most of his stardom at MGM with director Tod Browning, disturbing Universal's flow of development in horror. It started up again when Paul Leni directed a "haunted house" classic in *The Cat and the Canary* (1927)—again the Germanic guide, texturing a basically comic tale with a morbid *Expressionismus*. The heiress heroine spends a night in a spooky man-

*Universal American and emigrant: My Man Godfrey's cast
—as we set up for a shot not in the film—was almost
entirely borrowed: William Powell, Carole Lombard, Gail
Patrick, Mischa Auer, Alice Brady, Eugene Pallette. (Only*

'Auer and Pallette were on contract.) Above, the German
effect, in The Last Performance (1929), directed by Paul
Fejos to look like a bite of UFA, with (center) Conrad Veidt
and (flanking him) Mary Philbin and Leslie Fenton.

sion with a more or less hostile claque, one of whom sneaks along creaky halls and through secret panels in monster costume. So there is real menace: yet in the end nothing unearthly. Similarly, Leni's *The Man Who Laughs* (1928), with Conrad Veidt, his face fixed by torture surgery in a maniacal grin, treats the grotesque without fantasy. The very gifted Leni died in 1929, never having made a full-fledged talkie, and Universal's horror took a different turn, setting Chaney's goblin guises in the realm of the supernatural.

Universal horror is, above all, a monster picture. The talkie cycle begins in 1931 with *Dracula,* as much an adaptation of the 1927 Broadway hit as a reflection of Universal's fright-night traditions. But the studio explored its new-old genre in 1932 with *Frankenstein, Murders in the Rue Morgue,* and *The Mummy. The Invisible Man* (1933) and *The Black Cat* (1934) led to a festival in 1935: *Bride of Frankenstein, Werewolf of London,* and *The Raven.* Then 1936 saw a tapering off in *The Invisible Ray* and *Dracula's Daughter.* The cycle temporarily stalled.

It is this first wave of Universal talkie horror, from *Dracula* to *Dracula's Daughter,* that most affected the genre, not only in Hollywood but throughout the movie industry, then and since. A paradigm of the Universal horror stock company would give us James Whale directing and Karl Freund at the camera, working with stories whose atmosphere is a strange blend of Middle Europe and England, not only in setting and casting but in dialogue. One scene will be veddy transatlantic, with, say, vapid good guy David Manners, cockney hysteric Una O'Connor, and wise demon killer Edward Van Sloan. The next scene will feature a peasants' gambol in dirndls and lederhosen with plenty of yodeling and knee-slapping. This bifocal tone becomes absurd when, in *Frankenstein,* a maid calls Colin Clive's father "Herr *Bah*-ron" and the Burgomaster calls him "Herr Ba-*rohn.*"

The use of music, however, quotes the symphonic Romantics of Middle Europe, from the big A-minor theme of Tchaikofsky's *Swan Lake* during the credits of *Dracula* and *Murders in the Rue Morgue* to the Chopin, Brahms, Rachmaninof, and Beethoven (the slow movement of the Seventh Symphony) running through *The Black Cat.* This is all stirringly mealymouthed, for while the music is certainly effective, it comes through too faintly to make much of an impression. By *Bride of*

Frankenstein, however, Universal has finally made the bold move of commissioning a new score, from Franz Waxman.

Like the innocents, the fiends are a cosmopolitan bunch: mad doctor Ernest Thesiger, apprentice ghoul Dwight Frye, and, of course, Bela Lugosi and Boris Karloff, made available to terror by makeup man Jack Pierce. Perhaps Lugosi's lurid Transylvanian and Karloff's brandy-and-cigars English essentialize not only the splintered tone of Universal horror but that of Universal itself, the Hollywood studio with star-spangled actors and a sauerbraten staff. One wonders if Whale—a sharp satirist by nature—ever thought of his golems and vampires as pointing up his own situation in Hollywood, with himself and Karl Freund as the scientists in too deep and the moguls as the monsters who are Coming to Get Them.*

Heaven knows, plenty of Hollywood's bosses hailed from the Danubian outback in which Tod Browning's *Dracula* begins. Browning must have been spoiled by his years in MGM's workshop of experts, for in this, his sole entry in Universal talkie horror, he is unable to energize his former studio's dowdy facilities. The opening sequence, in which Dwight Frye journeys to Lugosi's castle and falls under his spell, is beautifully set and lit. But the acting is stilted, shots fade out before their wonted climax, and the rest of the film, set in London, is drab and stagey.

Dracula is in fact extraordinarily old-fashioned for 1931, when we consider the immediately contemporary *Arrowsmith, The Public Enemy, Monkey Business, Possessed,* or *Dishonored.* At seventy-five minutes, *Dracula* seems to be retreating from the ninety that the talkie recognized as regulation (not to mention the longer running times favored in the late 1920s), and much of the actors' behavior refers to silent procedures, pantomimic rather than naturalistic. Lugosi's transformation as a bat is technically poor, almost laughable. Even the makeup is antique.

After the Transylvanian opening, but one moment gives us something to bite on, when Edward Van Sloan warns his fellow mortals, "The strength of the vampire is that people will not believe in him." This identification of the horrifying as beyond the natural, the probable, the sane—in effect, beyond reality—proved to be Universal's

---

*They certainly got Whale, a gay man who disdained cover procedures to live openly with his lover. He was run out of the business in 1941 and died, a suicide, in 1957.

salient thematic invention. Much of Continental horror fiction depends on the use of horror as something terrible but omnipresent, especially as a metaphor for evil, sexuality, heresy, or guilt. The characters in most European horror tales suffer no crisis in belief. They know the evil is there. The vampire *is*. Universal's approach, particularly when Lugosi and Karloff begin playing mortals as well as monsters, alienates horror from human patterns. Horror is no longer a metaphor for worldly disorders; it is the aggression of an underworld. The vampire is *not*. The strength of the monster is that most people are too pure to believe in evil.

This is made clear when James Whale follows Browning as director, on *Frankenstein*, *Dracula*'s successor. Whale's sophistication textures the action far more than Browning had done. Sometimes we see the man-made monster as human: he is Frankenstein's *child*, delighted by the sun, terrified of fire, enchanted by little Marilyn Harris's game of tossing flowers onto a stream to watch them float. But the monster is also a freak of creation, his brain that of a psychotic criminal. His "father," Colin Clive, exults in his unnatural power: "Now I know what it's like to *be* God!" he cries, upon the electrical "birth" of his son. A shocking concept—audience hostility in previews convinced Universal to cut the passage. "Only evil can come of it," Clive's former professor warns him: only something inhuman, of another world, something that cannot connect to mortal patterns.

Thus in the opening credits we learn the real-life identities of all the characters except the creation, billed as "The Monster . . . ?" Baron Frankenstein has manufactured life without humanity, so much so that, in the game with Marilyn Harris, when the thing runs out of flowers, it grabs the girl and flings her into the water to drown —another scandal at the previews, another shot cut in defense of taboo.

Such is Whale's amusement at the possibilities in Mary Shelley's tale that he bends Universal's monster imagery back upon itself, allows sympathy for the ghoul in his anger, bewilderment, torment. Yet he bends it once again to admire the beauty of the night sky as screaming peasants burn the monster in a windmill. A good cast is worth not only repeating but celebrating: at the end, Universal names Boris Karloff, and a star is born.

It was ironic that a studio that never seemed to have enough genuine stars in the usual genres threw several off in these monster roles. After Lugosi and Karloff came Claude Rains, not only without Jack Pierce's fascinating makeup but utterly unseen till a moment before the fade-out: *The Invisible Man*. This is Universal's breakaway item in horror, the first wholly self-assured film, partly because Whale worked with the relatively distinguished playwright, R. C. Sherriff, Whale's old campaigner since Whale had directed Sherriff's war play *Journey's End* (the movie adaptation brought Whale to Hollywood); partly because Whale and Sherriff settled the preceding confusion of ethnicity into a sturdy English atmosphere; and partly because this one develops horror out of constantly surprising special effects rather than a makeup job.

The Invisible Man yields other blessings: the David Manners callow juvenile figure is absent, while the indispensable Una O'Connor enjoys her greatest role in the series in a veritable cavalcade of cowering, shrieking, and tumultuous dropping of trays. Dwight Frye, Dracula's slavey and Frankenstein's sadistic tormentor, is here demoted to a bit role among a group of reporters. This is sad; Frye doesn't project as a square.

Rains, of course, is the great discovery. While Lugosi soon sank into quickie-lot horror rip-offs and Karloff eventually joined him, Rains carved a niche as Warner Brothers' Character Brit—not to mention such complementary distinctions as the corrupt senator in *Mr. Smith Goes to Washington* (at Columbia) or *Casablanca*'s randy French police chief. Rains brings a mortal desperation to the Universal monster, for now the human world has invaded the supernatural rather than the reverse. "There *must* be a way back!" Rains cries. *The Invisible Man* thus bears a moral might where *Dracula* and *Frankenstein* simply illustrate the temporary overwhelming of the real by the unreal. Here the grotesque is not psychological but scientific— though the film sounds a prophetic note in its view that chemistry alters not only matter but character. Rains, whose experiments have made him terminally invisible, is like a modern-day cocaine crank, unstable and murderous, trying a little defensive blackmail here, a train wreck for the sport of it there, as he dances along a country lane singing, "Here We Go Gathering Nuts in May." This is Whale at his capers, the mitigating influence in an otherwise bitterly gloomy cycle.

There *must* be a way back: there is none. Universal horror does not view the supernatural and the real as coexistent. Other studios, dipping into the lunatic trend, tried to harmonize the two worlds. Paramount, appalled at the very notion of a monster (except for an overtly erotic one like Mr. Hyde, filmed with John Barrymore and then Fredric March), bought *The Cat and the Canary* to turn it into a laff fest for Bob Hope (1939), then demonstrated the grace of ghostly visitation in *The Uninvited* (1944). Warner Brothers turned monster horror into a crime picture in *Mystery of the Wax Museum*, ghoulish but strictly downtown, with reporter Glenda Farrell tracking very mortal fiend Lionel Atwill amid a load of slang and moxie and police brutality. Val Lewton's unit at RKO dealt in the supernatural, but his style preferred the suspense of the unseen menace rather than the lurking golem or slithery goblin. MGM was willing to rival Universal, if only because Tod Browning was on hand; but MGM's idea of a monster was nothing worse than Lionel Barrymore. Bela Lugosi is in MGM's *Mark of the Vampire* (1935), but no vampire is: it turns out that Jean Hersholt was playing the ghoul as a cover for his murders. (Barrymore unmasks him.) *The Devil-Doll* (1936) at least deals in the scientific surreal. But the highly motivated revenge plot (Barrymore gets even with the men who framed him) gives us the MGM human comedy, not a fantasy of the grotesque.

This Universal did, particularly in several mid-1930s teamings of its two house monsters Karloff and Lugosi as antagonists in good-versus-evil matches. They are humans in *The Black Cat, The Raven,* and *The Invisible Ray,* yet of a fiendish bent. The castles and stone towers of old now give way to futuristic forts and laboratories; science-fictional elements and torture gizmos, useless in *Dracula* and *The Mummy,* offer machinery of doom. It is as if the whole world is *Frankenstein,* all monsters—not ghouls who live to destroy and destroy to live, but men who want to know what it's like to be God. Lugosi and Karloff switch off the good guys' parts from film to film, but even as heroes they follow a vicious hidden agenda, and we usually get a David Manners figure, if not Manners himself, to remind us that, human or inhuman, Lugosi and Karloff are not human. The strength of the monster is that David Manners won't believe in him: that he *is* a monster. Even giving *The Black Cat*'s Lugosi a sympathetic revenge motive like Barrymore's in *The Devil-Doll* doesn't naturalize him—naturalize *Lugosi?*—and he closes the film tying Karloff up to skin him alive. It seems radical; but Karloff has stolen Lugosi's wife and kept Lugosi's daughter prisoner with vile intentions. Worse, he conducts Black Masses. David Manners, who never does anything right, mistakes Lugosi for a villain during the skinning and shoots him.

These Lugosi–Karloff pairings generally call up sleazy movies, in Universal's worst smash-and-grab style—*The Raven*, like *The Black Cat* bearing an Edgar Allan Poe title but little of Poe's handiwork, lasts scarcely sixty minutes. But David Boehm's *Raven* script touches importantly on Universal's alienation effect, its view of evil as something from beyond our world, irresponsible and amoral, a thing-in-itself. Karloff is a vicious criminal who wants plastic surgeon Lugosi to enhance his features.

KARLOFF: Maybe if a man looks ugly, he does ugly things.

LUGOSI: You say something profound.

No, Karloff says something prophetic, for Lugosi makes Karloff even uglier than before, a tearoom Frankenstein.

KARLOFF: Do I look . . . different?

LUGOSI: Yes.

KARLOFF: Something's the matter . . .

Director Louis Friedlander films Karloff's rediscovery of self with a series of curtains pulled aside to reveal mirror after mirror, Karloff frantically shooting the glass before settling down as Lugosi's slave of terror. The normal-looking Lugosi and the monstrous Karloff are one: deformity and madness are both forms of evil. More alienation, more Their World Against Ours.

James Whale, still amused by how easily this nonsense goes over, made Universal's ultimate statement on the theme in *Bride of Frankenstein*, generally regarded as the high point of Universal horror. "It's a perfect night for mystery and horror," coos Mary Shelley (Elsa Lanchester) to her husband and Lord Byron as she spins a sequel to Whale's 1932 *Frankenstein* with the credentials of footage of the earlier film. Back we go to the burned windmill. There, lurking in the watery wreckage, is the monster, Boris Karloff, now so famous that Universal bills him by his last name alone: a *sui generis* classic like Nazimova and Garbo. Whale doesn't waste time telling us what monsters do. Karloff slams out and kills the parents of the drowned flower, Marilyn Harris, as an owl looks on.

Whale apparently decided to make *Bride of Frankenstein* Universal's most ghoulish horror film, also its funniest and psychologically most endearing. It's something of an old-home-week of the stock company, with Colin Clive, Ernest Thesiger, and Dwight Frye—and Una O'Connor upholds the studio's split-personality aesthetic by dressing in early-middle goosegirl but screaming, gasping, and fainting in Brit. There's even a "Frau Newman" in the cast, the height of Universal's Esperanto. Some commentators favor the sequence in which a blind man befriends the monster, feeding him, soothing him with violin music, and teaching him words like "good," "bad," "alone," and, fatally, "friend." The blind man prays (as an organ Ave Marias on the track) and the monster drops a tear. It's touching and disturbing, the monster made human—the ghoul and mortal worlds harmonized.

Wait. Other commentators prefer the sequence in which mad doctor Ernest Thesiger displays his own monsters, six miniature people squeaking in jars. "This isn't science!" cries Colin Clive. "It's more like black magic!" Just the point, that. For all Karloff's tears and love of violin music, his deformity marks him as a non-person. Even his bride, Elsa Lanchester again, rejects him—and, through her Mary Shelley in the prologue, she is also his creator: a double rejection. Science, though a hostile power, treats natural phenomena. Monsters are black magic, unnatural.

It is sometimes suggested that Hollywood's horror movies contributed to the stylization of film noir. But Universal horror is the opposite of noir. Noir sights evil in the most sacred precincts of human fellowship, the middle-class marriage. Universal horror defines evil as a thing apart—though, as the things it stands apart from are usually David Manners and Zita Johann, we end up rooting for the monsters.

No doubt Universal's horror photography, with its skewed angles and biased narration, gave something to the early-'40s crime film, the direct progenitor of noir. But Universal itself lent its horror style, especially in casting, music, and design, to films that did not deal with the supernatural, such as *The Old Dark House* (1932), with its batch of crazies, and *The Mystery of Edwin Drood* (1935), with Claude Rains and a fright of brooding camera angles. By far the most interesting of this lot is the uncelebrated but fascinatingly louche *Tower of London* (1939), directed by Rowland V. Lee. Here is England in the time of Richard III (Basil Rathbone), a great era for political murder. Planning to usurp the throne, Rathbone keeps a puppet theatre dressed with dolls representing the royal family, placed in order of succession. At each new killing, Rathbone deposes the appropriate doll and moves himself up a notch.

Boris Karloff is the central figure, as Mord, executioner of the Tower and Rathbone's hireling. Karloff loves his work, especially when it gives him the chance to torment attractive males. The film's opening sequence, twelve minutes long, covers in loving detail the public execution of a haughtily poetic-looking fellow. The charge is treason—meaning that he opposed Rathbone's succession over the dead bodies of his relatives. But we sense that Karloff's homoerotic sadism is the real energy urging on Rathbone's assassinations. At times Karloff is amusingly offhand about his capers, as when he opens an iron maiden and a corpse falls out. Karloff scarcely glances at the body. But he spends most of the film exquisitely relishing his duties. When Tower guards chase another Rathbone-hating juvenile, Karloff trips him up and grabs him, purring, "My pretty, you'll not escape Mord!" Follows then a torture montage of Karloff at his sport, whipping, scorching, and racking the young hero. Director Lee keeps it all in good taste: Karloff feigns professional interest and his victim endures the torture without reaction. Not even a whimper. But we get a more involved Karloff in the murder of the two little princes. When Karloff picks one up, the boy sleepily puts a hand on Karloff's shoulder. Stung by his own pity, Karloff runs off to commission a few thugs, amusingly pantomiming the size of Rathbone's latest victims with "fish that got away" hands. And there's Karloff in on the kill, shuddering in delight as the children scream.

Of course, the classic sexual image in horror is that of the monster bearing the limp form of the heroine. The trope blends two notions of Edgar Allan Poe, one of the fathers of modern horror, who elegized "the unselfish and self-sacrificing love of a brute" and thought "the death of a beautiful woman . . . the most poetical topic in the world." The loving brute was Chaney's favorite role, one he played in both his Universal Big Ones; and *Dracula* and *Frankenstein* honor the image. Male-to-male terror sadism, however, was sneaking into the picture. Back in 1932, in MGM's *The Mask of Fu Manchu*, Karloff had done quite a little riff on the theme while bedeviling the implausibly handsome Charles Starrett, and Lugosi's skinning of the bound Karloff in *The Black Cat*, though dully photographed, seems an epic moment in the two monsters' careers. We should note as well the lesbian nature of Gloria Holden's encounters in *Dracula's Daughter*, directed by Lambert Hillyer and amazingly forthright for 1936, when reinforced Production Code censorship was biting down tightly on Hollywood releases of every kind. No wonder critics find so much to analyze in horror movies, particularly the first wave at Universal, from 1931 to 1936.

Unfortunately, the second wave is drudgery, a mere replaying of the old characters and themes. Here's image without art. Whale and Freund are gone, Lugosi and Karloff seldom seen, the décor and camera work perfunctory. The colorful featured players of the 1930s have been replaced by people like Lionel Atwill and John Carradine. We almost begin to miss David Manners.

The second series took off in 1939 with *Son of Frankenstein*, and upheld the "retread" concept with such titles as *The Invisible Man Returns* (1940), *The Invisible Woman* (1941), *The Ghost of Frankenstein* (1942), *Son of Dracula* (1943), *Frankenstein Meets the Wolf Man* (1943), and *The Invisible Man's Revenge* (1944). The worst aspect of these films is the introduction of Lon Chaney, Jr., as the new Universal monster. Yes, Chaney inherited the post by right of genes. But Chaney is no Chaney. With his toneless voice and Mr. Potato Head features, he prefigures the B-movie actors of the 1950s, those who played everything, and everything badly. There is simply no terror in this man: no evil, no *Angst*, no frisson. Poe would have looked right through him. Lugosi and Karloff, whatever their thespian talents, were genuine macabre personalities. And Rains was, no question, a fine actor. But to watch the junior Chaney pathetically galumphing his way through *The Wolf Man* (1941) is to keen for a cashed-in tradition—not least when the evocative Maria Ouspenskaya takes the screen with her gypsy predictions, and Universal horror, briefly, comes alive again.

One other genre particularly interested Universal, the weepie. All major studios kept the woman's picture in repertory, but Universal stands out somewhat, partly because auteurist critics have been discovering Universal weepie directors John M. Stahl and Douglas Sirk, and partly because the Stahl years counted such resourceful protagonists as Irene Dunne, Margaret Sullavan, and Claudette Colbert. Stahl's classics hail from the 1930s: *Back Street* (1932), *Imitation of Life* (1934), *Magnificent Obsession* (1935), and *When Tomorrow Comes* (1939); along with Edward Sloman's *There's Always Tomorrow* (1934) and Edward H. Griffith's *Next Time We Love* (1936). Sirk's output, in the 1950s, depended on remakes: *Magnificent Obsession* (1954), *There's Always Tomorrow* (1956), *Imitation of Life* (1959), along with David Miller's *Back Street* (1961), which had already been remade by Robert Stevenson in 1941.

Actually there is little to discover in Stahl besides the expertise of actors fondling silly material. Most of these films derived from unimportantly popular novels in which heroines hurt not because love doesn't last but because it does—note the emphasis on "tomorrow" in Universal's '30s titles. Irene Dunne must pine for John Boles in her back-street digs, the love of his life but a woman without a family because Boles already has one. Alternatively, Dunne can pine for Charles Boyer because it isn't fair for him to dump his demented wife; Dunne and Boyer will wait it out to unite, perhaps, when tomorrow comes. Even the optimistic films paint in broad strokes— Robert Taylor's magnificent obsession is to master ophthalmologic surgery in order to restore Dunne's eyesight, lost in an accident but really because Taylor is a playboy.

For all the discussions of Stahl's worldview, these are relatively unnuanced films, briskly moping when there's no love handy, then gently recoiling from the terror of extramarital sex. Yet, we ask, what else is there when all the men are either married or playboys? Also, the insistence on elegant love objects dulls the series. As *When Tomorrow Comes* opens, in a middle-class beanery, Dunne is a waitress and Boyer her customer. Universal tells us he's sophisticated by having him ask for bouillabaisse. In a glorified hash house? Later, with Dunne on an East River pier, Boyer looks out on Queens and decides he's reminded of Venice.

True, Stahl's weepies have outlasted Ruth Chatterton's for Warner Brothers and Ann Harding's for RKO (among countless others). But Chatterton's have an impressive passion and Harding's have Harding. Stahl's weepies meander, giggle, pussyfoot. They . . . stall. We have only to compare Stahl's *Back Street* with Paramount's *Jennie Gerhardt*, made a year later on a very similar story, to see how unstylish Stahl is. He and Paramount's director, Marion Gering, have vapid leading men in John Boles and Donald Cook, respectively; both directors wisely focus their affect on their heroines, Dunne and Sylvia Sidney. But that said, Stahl simply goes about filming the script methodically and cleanly, keeping the view brightly lit, the surroundings uncluttered, and the sadness—the waiting for tomorrow—palpable. Gering, who came from Russia, working in Paramount's weepie department in the early 1930s, is less concerned with storytelling than with how the story feels to the heroine at any given moment. Time and place must have visual impact, the lighting must illuminate, the sadness is not a generic prop but an antithesis: now, what is the thesis?

Gering has the advantage over Stahl in that *Back Street*'s source is Fannie Hurst while *Jennie Gerhardt*'s is Theodore Dreiser. Still, none of *Back Street*'s big scenes has the visual force of one in *Jennie Gerhardt* that is utterly directorial, not literary, in concept. Senator Edward Arnold has used his influence to get Sidney's brother out of jail. She is in his power—worse: his room. Poor thing, she must lie down, he says. As she does, Arnold approaches the bed—and Gering closes in to frame only Sidney's head and Arnold's hand, underlining her loveliness, his grasp. The hand caresses her, moving from her hair to her shoulder as she flinches. Gering shows us the appeal of a vulnerable girl, conveys the man's inability to withstand temptation, even his erotic enjoyment of her fear. His arm pushes into view now, pulling her to him, and she thrusts out her own arm, looking like a broken puppet.

If Stahl's work is ordinary, the Sirk remakes are atrocious. They look garish, take forever to do nothing, and depend on some of the worst performers of the day. *There's Always Tomorrow* at least has Barbara Stanwyck and Fred MacMurray, and *Magnificent Obsession*, for all its drag, has a certain tidy clarity (though this makes the absurd story all the more absurd). However, Sirk's *Imitation of Life*, with Lana Turner, John Gavin, Juanita Moore, Sandra Dee, and Susan Kohner, is a blot even to Stahl's minor memory—and this entry is the only one with some bite in its plot. Its subplot, actually: Turner's servant Moore is black but Moore's daughter Kohner is so light that she tries to live as a white woman, cutting her heartbroken mother off in desperation. Stahl got more out of it, as in the scene in which mothers

Claudette Colbert and Louise Beavers powwow empathically over the generation gap, then bid each other good night. In a famous shot, Colbert mounts a stairway to the *piano nobile* as Beavers trudges down to her basement maid's room.

What's most irritating about Sirk's *Imitation of Life* is its blithe disregard for credibility. (Sirk's comment on the idiocies of the weepie? Then why did he make so many?) This film doesn't fail to be logical —it doesn't *bother* to be. In the Stahl original, Colbert ran a flapjack parlor (on Beavers's personal recipe, by the bye). This isn't glamorous enough for Turner; besides, it would recall *Mildred Pierce*. So this time out the heroine is an actress. Now, this is dangerous, because to portray an actress you have to be one. Turner isn't. She is also much harder than Stahl's heroines were. "I'm going *up* and *up* and *up!*" she rants at Gavin, who just wants a housewife. "And no one's going to pull me down!"

Turner does a lot of ranting. We see her, at the start of her career, in rehearsal. The script reads as absurdly comical, yet Turner plays it almost without inflection. Surely she will be fired for underacting. No: the playwright-director chews her out for *overdoing*. His lines call for delicacy, he says, "not loud, goggle-eyed takes."

Lana Turner couldn't play a take to bring L. B. Mayer back to life. Now she chews the playwright out. No one could play this terrible scene, she avers. Of course he's impressed by her probity. What would she do? She considers, then says she'd cut the scene, as if recommending to Goethe that he add a love plot to *Faust*. Imitation of Life is right.

One recurring problem at Universal was its shortage of bankable stars on contract. Most of the big names that turn up in Universals during the Laemmle years were loan-outs from other lots. Here was another legacy of Laemmle's antiquated approach, his resistance to Zukorism, Thalbergism. After Laemmle's "good old days" philosophy lost him and his son control of their lot, Laemmle's successors steadily built up a contract roster of stars who could draw huge audiences in essentially simple films, inexpensive and of a fixed format. That is, unlike a Hepburn or Gable or Davis or Cagney, who textured their fame in a variety of subjects and forms, Universal's stars would play a specialty over and over. Maria Montez, queen of sarong-and-volcano melodrama, was one such, a distinctly '40s figure whose vehicles would nevertheless not have been out of place in the silent period. The *Ma and Pa Kettle* series of the early 1950s also applies, as a kind of spoof of Fox's *Jones Family* and Metro's *Andy Hardy*, with Marjorie Main and Percy Kilbride as boondocks cutups. Audie Murphy, the war hero turned cowboy star, was another shoo-in; nothing's easier, or surer at the box office, than a western. But the most unusual attraction of this set was Bud Abbott and Lou Costello, basically radio comics—the verbal without the visual—who ran through the 1940s in cheap films of almost no story content that earned stupendous profits.

Abbott and Costello entered Hollywood in *One Night in the Tropics* (1940), a musical with the usual Universal bumblings. It's humdrum and interesting at once, sometimes elaborate and sometimes shabby, counting the effervescent Nancy Kelly and Mary Boland but also the bland Robert Cummings, and boasting a Jerome Kern–Dorothy Fields score (plus one lyric by Oscar Hammerstein II and Otto Harbach) that finds all hands off form. Abbott and Costello are ringed in, somewhat as the Ritz Brothers were in the late-'30s Fox backstager; they have roles in the plot but mainly provide excrescent gambado, set routines drawn from their radio and stage work. This is reminiscent of the Paramount vaudevillians, especially Burns and Allen and W. C. Fields. So there was some precedent for Universal's folding Abbott and Costello into an otherwise conventional form. However, Abbott and Costello are more active in the narrative than Fox's troupers, and they share none of Fields's antiquely mannered self-portrayal. What could be more contemporary than their famous "Who's on First?" sketch, set into *One Night in the Tropics* without context, except for a taxi driver who watches the whole thing with a frozen face.

He was one of the few, for if Abbott and Costello's comedy was low, it struck a national nerve, not least in the second-run houses that Universal was still pitching to. Their next film, *Buck Privates* (1941), was a smash. Now they're the stars, and here Universal sets the format for an entire era of Abbott and Costello films: plop the boys down in a hostile environment and give them a bully to confuse (Nat Pendleton as their sergeant), a cliché love plot between routines (USO hostess is chased by two soldiers, one a rich boy who must prove himself by democratically mixing in), and an assortment of extraneous musical numbers (the Andrews Sisters and some champion jitterbugging).

The form held through such titles as *In the Navy* (1941), *Hold That Ghost* (1941), *Ride 'Em Cowboy* (1942), *Pardon My Sarong* (1942), and *In Society* (1944). After the war, the series took an unexpected turn in *Bud Abbott and Lou Costello Meet Frankenstein* (1948), two backlist low-budget units thus combined for a new cycle. *Abbott and Costello* would *Meet: the Killer Boris Karloff* (1949), *the Invisible Man* (1951), *Dr. Jekyll and Mr. Hyde* (1953), and *the Mummy* (1955). But the first outing holds classic status for its historically cast grab bag of Dracula (Bela Lugosi), the Wolf Man (Lon Chaney, Jr.), Frankenstein's monster (Glenn Strange), and, at the very end, the Invisible Man, via the voice of Vincent Price. As with all Abbott and Costello, you either enjoy its elemental whimsy or despise its crude corn:

ABBOTT: *I* know there's no such a person as Dracula. *You* know there's no such a person.

COSTELLO: But does *Dracula* know it?

Costello, the more visually silly of the pair, has some good moments. Of course, he is the first to spot the ghouls while everyone else is oblivious. Too terrified to speak, Costello tries to give off a warning in mime, even aping Frankenstein's lumbering march and Lugosi's face-shrouding cape. The monsters themselves are not camped, but the humor is pervasive. It surrounds them. Only Lugosi resists. "Ah, you young people," he says. "Making the most out of life . . . while it lasts." The almost casual jab of menace in his tone is nicely judged, as if he were back with Karloff in their prime rather than in a burlesque knockdown. On the other hand, Universal's *mise-en-scène* is catching up to Hollywood state-of-the-art: the décor, lighting, and music are acceptable, and a touch of animation to turn a flying bat into Lugosi is a vast improvement on the effects in the 1931 *Dracula*.

Of all the lot's post-Laemmle stars during the Studio Age, Deanna Durbin was the most lucrative. Like Maria Montez, Audie Murphy, the Kettles, and Abbott and Costello, Durbin worked within strait format. But the wholesome Miss Fix-It teenager with stripling boyfriends and puppy crushes on older men, ideal for 1936 when the series began, aged into a heroine with respectable romances. Thus *One Hundred Men and a Girl* (1937) finds Durbin racing around capitalizing a concert for unemployed musicians. *That Certain Age* (1938) shows her debonair Melvyn Douglas but demands that she accept callow Jackie Cooper, and allows her mother to hassle her over what dress she can wear to a party. By *Nice Girl?* (1941), Durbin is trying on slinky black pajamas complete with matching cloche hat and hurdy-gurdy jewelry belt, and in *Hers to Hold* (1943) she is Joseph Cotten's official fiancée, reluctant to let him enlist in the Air Force till her father delivers a patriotic lecture. Durbin herself works in an aircraft factory, and comes around in time. "Got it all figured out," she tells Cotten as they say goodbye. "I'll build 'em. You fly 'em."

Durbin's vehicles stand out from all other Universal series by nature of their distinguished casts—again, with much free-lancing and borrowing. The studio even got Leopold Stokowski for *One Hundred Men and a Girl*, along with Adolphe Menjou as Durbin's father and Alice Brady as the dizzy society matron whom Durbin bemuses. "Don't go, little girl!" cries Brady, when Durbin, having crashed Brady's party, starts to leave. "You're too original and charming!" Who but Brady could have brought off a line like that? *Nice Girl?* is a festival of second-line favorites: Robert Benchley (the father), Franchot Tone (the grown-up love object), Robert Stack (the adolescent boyfriend), Walter Brennan (the postman), and Helen Broderick (the maid).

Obviously, Universal was extending itself, celebrating one of the few times it had hit upon a unique form. The stories may not be innovative, but Durbin herself was: in her music. Like almost all Hollywood's trained voices, she does both opera and pop. She has neither the Metropolitan grandeur of Lawrence Tibbett or Gladys Swarthout in the one nor the put-it-over zing of Bing Crosby or Judy Garland in the other. Durbin splits the difference. But her opera has a confidence one misses in the coeval Kathryn Grayson and Jane Powell and her pop is pleasurable. The odd little scores Universal gave her are unlike anything in other films, usually two or three new ditties and a legit showpiece or two. *That Certain Age* is typical: "Be a Good Scout," sung to the accompaniment of a Boy Scout marching band (and it deserves to be); Delibes's chanson "Les Filles de Cadiz"; "Pretty as a Picture," to her mother's piano; and, for an eleven-o'clock song, the coloratura waltz from Gounod's *Roméo et Juliette*. Another oddity:

Durbin must be the only musical star who went through twenty-one films—all for Universal—only very rarely sharing the musical honors with anyone else. Nor did Durbin have the advantage of the high-toned Broadway masters RKO gave Astaire and Rogers, or that MGM gave Freed's people, or that Fox used in its story musicals. Yes, *That Certain Age* has Delibes and Gounod, but the new songs are by Jimmy McHugh and Harold Adamson, of the third rank. Only once did Universal go for it, on *Can't Help Singing* (1944), with a new Kern–Harburg score of six numbers, plus baritone Robert Paige and an eager chorus—Durbin's sole all-out musical.

There is something we must consider about Universal's approach to stars throughout its history to this point, the mid-1940s. Carl Laemmle helped create the movie star—for a brief time, his IMP gang were the best-known performers in American cinema. But Laemmle doggedly insisted that movies needed only familiar faces, not the most familiar, or the newest, or the most glamorous. Laemmle never caught on to the "loss leader" approach to the star system, by which a few outstanding actors would be hired at near-ruinous salaries in order to put over an entire year's worth of films by second-raters and walk-ins. This was Zukor's Little Mary strategy—to get her pictures, exhibitors bought Zukor's line in toto. Finally Little Mary became so expensive that even Zukor couldn't afford her. One imagines Laemmle shaking his head over this extravagant expansion: See? he says. Two-reelers weren't good enough. Mother Benson and Fatty Voss weren't good enough. *Hiawatha* wasn't good enough. You had to go do Big Ones, Big Hollywood, Big Stars, till you don't know even what's a film anymore!

Laemmle's resistance to the star system comprised not only distaste for blackmail salaries but an unwillingness to disturb his machinery to develop, mollify, aggrandize, deify. Why can't they just do it? When Laemmle began, the cameraman turned a crank and photographed the players on coarse stock. You looked your worst. When Laemmle finally acceded to the end of silence, cameramen were so accomplished and their materials so rich that they could paint like Titian. Add to this the Warner Brothers writer pointing up theme, the Paramount director making magic, and the MGM producer plotting a fame, and you have a system that not only invents stars but invents people.

These two shots frame Deanna Durbin's career. Above, One Hundred Men and a Girl—note Stoky with the heroine—was Durbin's second feature but the one that proved her salability; Universal raised her take by a very considerable margin during its release. That was Durbin impetuous. Right, Up in Central Park (1948) was Durbin dispirited. Universal took a smash Broadway show with a Sigmund

Romberg–Dorothy Fields score, shredded all but two numbers, threw in a few interpolations, and filmed in black and white. Doing Up in Central Park *without "Close as Pages in a Book" is like doing* My Fair Lady *without "On the Street Where You Live." At least we get Dick Haymes, assisting here on "Carousel in the Park."*

This is a form of cunning that Laemmle never caught on to, and we constantly sense Universal's poverty of dimension in its treatment of actors. There are exceptions, in the collaboration of James Whale and makeup man Jack Pierce on the look of Boris Karloff's Frankenstein, for instance, so special the studio put a copyright on it. But in general Universal cannot texture its stars, present them on anything but coarse stock. Come as you are: it's recording without mixing. It's flat. Deanna Durbin, at Paramount or Metro, would never have been allowed to sing with the deadpan face she invariably offers; someone would have worked with her, developed her body language to match the smile in her musicality. It's odd that such nice music comes out of such a lifeless face. Or think of John Wayne in his Randolph Scott–Marlene Dietrich trios, so unflatteringly presented. Years later, we would learn of the contradictions in Wayne—the raving bigot playing American hero, the beauty so awkward that he trips over his behind, the man's man taking unspeakable guff from John Ford and liking it. And Ford, bless his heart, catches this complex Wayne. Look at Wayne in *Pittsburgh* and *The Spoilers*: cardboard.

This is why the Maria Montez films have become camp classics —not because of the hoary genre she inhabited, but because it is treated with unknowing dull candor. It's insipid camp, without fervor—all the more rollicking therefore. It's tempting to think back to 1936, when Garland and Durbin were both at Metro. They let Durbin go; Garland hung on. What if Garland had gone to Universal and Durbin stayed put? Think of it—Durbin in the Freed Unit, coached and supported to her nth; and Garland trapped at the studio that, ten years after the movie musical was invented, still couldn't figure out how to make one.

At least self-starters like Abbott and Costello didn't suffer; they would have been the same wherever they went. W. C. Fields may have profited by Universal's lack of skill. Where Buster Keaton was ruined by MGM's smothering expertise, Fields was allowed to maintain the format he had developed at Paramount, if only because Universal didn't know what else to do with him beyond pairing him with his fellow Paramount alumna, Mae West, in *My Little Chickadee* (1940). The studio was not Fields's harness as much as his accommodation.

Fields was not only a self-starter but a self-evolver. *The Bank Dick*

(1940) employs the usual Fieldsian small-town frame, as the belea-
guered husband and father wandering from episode to episode. Yet
Fields is expanding somewhat, as in the characters' names, more
bizarre than ever. He himself bears one as descriptive as any in Resto-
ration comedy, Egbert Sousé; we expect this, as well as Fields's necessarily constant reminder to all and sundry that it's "Soo-zay—accent
grave over the 'e'." But the movie director A. Pismo Clam, crook
Loudmouth McNasty, and bank examiner J. Pinkerton Snoopington
suggest a crazier Fields than Paramount knew, and *The Bank Dick*'s
script (credited to Mahatma Kane Jeeves: Fields) originally called for
a raven named Nicodemus who speaks fluent English. The touch of
surrealism was abandoned before shooting.

However, *Never Give a Sucker an Even Break* (1941) is not only
surreal but triumphantly plotless, a celebration of the improvisational. The film is literally indescribable, a movie about the movie
that Fields proposes to make, and neither movie makes sense. Unfortunately, Universal's editors tried to reshape the footage into something reasonable, and only succeeded in dropping some of the best
business. What might have followed *Sucker* is beyond imagining; it
was Fields's last feature vehicle.

By then Universal was over the financial troubles that had
plagued it throughout the Depression. The returns on the Durbin
series had pushed it into the black by 1939, and Abbott and Costello's
profits doubled and even tripled the take. The studio's ingrained nostalgic policies kept it from enjoying the unprecedented boom of wartime moviegoing, and in 1946 it merged with a small independent
outfit and began a second era as Universal International. (An irritating tautology. If it's universal, it's already international; it's down-
right interplanetary.) At first there was no major change in style.
Durbin left in 1948, but Abbott and Costello continued into the
1950s. Cheap monster pictures remained stock-in-trade, following
the form of Junior Chaney's cheap series rather than the classics of
the Whale era. Universal made a name for itself in film noir in the
late 1940s; but *Christmas Holiday* and *Scarlet Street* had predicted as
much. The studio's prime market was the same second-run circuit it
had always played to. It continued to look upon color as a wasteful
extravagance.

However, by the early 1950s Universal International was becom-

ing a completely different studio. The government's enforced separation of production and exhibition hit the other majors badly, since
their budgets had been planned decades before upon a fixed flow of
distribution from lot to theatres. Universal, with no theatre realty to
speak of, found itself, for the first time in its forty-year history, one
up on its rivals.

With the exchequer thus healthy, Universal at last caught up
with its times. Features ran long, Technicolor became routine, and a
large roster of new young stars was assembled. It was not a great roster—not by standards noted earlier in this book in Warner Brothers'
urban tigers, Paramount's sophisticates, Thalberg's beauties, or Zanuck's headliners at Twentieth. However, Universal's roster suited the
era. The 1950s liked uncomplicated people, perky young women and
dully stalwart men. This Universal gave them: Piper Laurie, Yvonne
de Carlo (*sexy*-perky; but still), Sandra Dee, Jeff Chandler, John
Gavin, Tony Curtis, Rock Hudson.

It is characteristic of Universal's product in the 1950s and 1960s
that Curtis and Hudson did their most interesting work elsewhere,
Curtis independently (*The Sweet Smell of Success, The Defiant Ones,
Some Like It Hot*) and at Twentieth (*The Boston Strangler*), and Hudson
at Warner Brothers (*Giant*) and Paramount (*Seconds*). But interesting
is not what Universal was doing in the early post–Studio Age. Its
slick new producer, Ross Hunter, emphasized the pretty, the simple,
the smooth; those vapid remakes of John Stahl's weepies were
Hunter's babies. Furthermore, Hunter's unique contribution to
movie history—Universal's first innovative genre since monster horror and Durbin's soloist pop-and-classical musical—may be the most
reproachably dishonest style in the American movie: the Universal
no-no "sex" comedy.

This very popular series depended on the erotic tease. The sensual
pull had to be patent, or the tease wouldn't work; but the resistance to
sensuality must be strong or you have not a tease but a love affair. Or,
God forbid, sex. So the leading men were big and aggressive and the
leading women were Doris Day. There would be a second man as
well, the Looney Capon figure, sort of a Ralph Bellamy with a psychiatrist, to spoof the sensual pull, and, on and off, a second woman
whose wisecracks affirm the pull. The décor would recall DeMille's
consumerist initiations, but modestly; and Day's fashions would simi-

larly uphold the bourgeois making-it philosophy. But the milieu was of so little importance that the films moved from New York to mid-America, and from the suburbs to the city, without the slightest change in character or tone or politics. *What* politics? There aren't any, because these films see the world as made of nothing but money and sex. Everyone has money, so life consists of trying to score Doris Day.

Pillow Talk (1959) set the mold: Day and Rock Hudson feud over their party line because Hudson, that implacable seducer, monopolizes Day's speaking time to set up his dates. Tony Randall plays the Looney Capon ("As many times as I'll be married, I'll never understand women"), Thelma Ritter the eternally hung-over maid who listens in on Hudson's phone seductions ("He's brightened up many a dreary afternoon for me"). The assaults on Day's right to assert herself as a professional are irritating. "If there's anything worse than a woman living alone," Ritter asserts, "it's a woman saying she likes it." But then Day's fastidious support of received morality makes her the appropriate target of its criticism. She is her own victim because she's her own oppressor. Thus the coyness of writing and directing results in a coy sociology, a sex without penetration. The coyness reaches its apex in a split-screen shot—and remember this is CinemaScope—that finds Day and Hudson facing each other in bathtubs, each in his own apartment. Day of course is almost entirely hidden in bubbles, while Hudson oozes out at the legs and torso. For climax, Universal gives us a touch of footsie at the dividing line of the two setups.

How astonishing to find Universal so acutely judging its times after decades at the rear guard. Perhaps it's astonishing in the first place to find an old studio that still behaves like a studio, though we miss the old-time moguls and their belief in a cinema that could reflect the culture. Universal had no such intention; all Laemmle wanted to do was grind out lively melodramas, poignant romances, and Fatty Voss comedies. Still, until this chapter, this book has recorded a surprising amount of art that is critical, directly or subtly, of American life. The inveigling eroticism of Paramount, the proletarian cynicism of Warner Brothers, the city-fearing pastorals of Fox, the reinvented democracy of Frank Capra's Columbia—and perhaps even Laemmle's Universal, struggling to assert the simplicity of the

Old Ways in an increasingly technophile age—left their mark on the American people and undoubtedly enriched their sense of self. I'll have a few last words to say on what happened after the breakup of the studio system, but in effect this book is now over, because virtually nothing of what seemed valid in the Studio Age has survived to the present day.

The films themselves have survived, of course, and it may be that the current interest in restoring and reviving old films stands in direct reaction to new movies' general lack of . . . what? Fascinating company? Witty language? Resonant song? Instructive heroism? Once, the movies took us places we had never been, among people we longed to know. Perhaps we're too smart now, too experienced. We've seen bloody war on our home entertainment centers. Old movies bring us back to a time when the notion of adventure still had meaning. Even dreary, ancient Universal gave us adventure through monster horror. Nowadays, with a Dracula and a Frankenstein's monster walking the streets of our cities, we can't enjoy them purely, as our grandparents did when they were new. Nor, it seems, do we believe in heroism anymore. Life is noir; we cannot often be moved or invigorated by a cinema that reflects that life.

So we turn to the cinema of the past, the Studio Age. The strength of the movies is that people must believe in them.

The City of Streets
Universal Studio
Universal City, Calif.
Schellenberg Photo

The last performance up in central park: Universal City, oldest yet latest of the Hollywood lots, in 1923. Look for the Monte Carlo of Erich von Stroheim's Foolish Wives, upper far right, then seek left for the bottom floor of Notre Dame cathedral, set up for The Hunchback of Notre Dame. Never Gonna Dance—isn't that a great title for an Astaire and Rogers film?

CLOSING

The Implosion from Without

In 1948, the Supreme Court ruled that the incorporation of production and exhibition facilities was monopolistic, and that the Hollywood studios must dispose of their theatre holdings. The system that had allowed the movies to prosper was dismantled. The biggest studios, such as MGM and Paramount, hurt the most, because they had grown big precisely through the benefit of their theatre circuits. Owning your own theatres guaranteed distribution for your output while it closed the system to outsiders, who might easily capitalize a new studio but, without many new theatres, would not be able to sell their product. For roughly thirty-five years—from the rise of Hollywood and the full-length feature and the picture palace and the star in about 1915—the studios had their way. It *was* a monopoly.

Ironically, the studio bosses did not inflict a narrow art upon the public. On the contrary, the movies opened up the culture, connected diverse regions, revealed willy-nilly the national class structure, aired controversies, extrapolated the parts of the American character, good and bad. (Edward Arnold is bad; James Stewart is good.) The movies must have liberalized the country somewhat, not necessarily by promoting tolerance (which the movies certainly did) but simply by showing segments of the public what other segments were like. Familiarity breeds acceptance.

Most important, the big studios' theatres—hungry for film, new film every week, twice a week, fifty-two weeks a year, year after year for decades—encouraged the studios to swell their facilities with personnel. The more theatres you had, the more film you needed, so the more staff you hired. But it worked backward, too: the more staff you had on hand, the more projects had to be conceived to keep them making good on their salaries. Given this constant outpouring of film, many a project that would have been artistically prohibitive in a more controlled system was sucked in along with the business-as-usual product. Thus the studio system welcomed the most brilliant artists as well as the journeymen, for there were too many movies to be made to leave anything out. King Vidor might have been occupied on some screen-filling dreck, but he wasn't, and he wanted to make *The Crowd*; and Irving Thalberg, who was as much a creation of the studio system as a founder, said okay.

This is how the art got made: by the size and wealth and power that the system gave the studios. When they divested themselves of their theatres, they shattered the innate balance of the structure. With no guarantee of exhibition, fewer movies could be made. The studios had to break their lots down to minimum personnel. This accounts for the bizarrely unambitious character of Hollywood in the 1950s. Boom times tolerate experimentation. The 1950s was a time of bust: of caution.

Another important factor was the rebellion of the most crucial personnel, the stars and the directors. Bored with their assignments, tiring of the way the system had dominated their lives both personally and professionally, and noting how many contract people were being dropped by the now helplessly overextended studios, the big

names increasingly sought independence in short-term contracts or in
setting up their own production companies. It was a great era for
United Artists, Hollywood's prime distributor of independent film
since 1919; and RKO, UA's only rival, was going under just then.

The third factor in the collapse of the Studio Age was the rise of
television. Granted, the tiny black-and-white screens of the day, the
limited public consumption of the novelty, the annoying commer-
cials, and the small-scaled entertainment it offered—domestic sit-
coms, variety hours, and kiddie shows—were not what Hollywood
could reasonably regard as competition. To emphasize the point, the
studios made movies as unlike television as possible, through color
and wide-screen processes, even gimmicks such as Cinerama and 3-D
photography. Yet one aspect of television Hollywood could not
combat: it was handy. Beyond the purchase price, it cost nothing; and
you didn't have to go anywhere to watch it. Throughout the 1950s,
television developed its attractiveness with its own widening of the
screen, its own color. The quality of programming improved. Even:
old movies turned up on it. The public bought television.

By about 1965, the studio system as explored in this book was history. Aside from the major economic and social factors, a crisis of
leadership had developed. The generation that succeeded the Golden
Age moguls lacked the experience and instincts that guided the lots in
the good old days. Not only was there no new Thalberg, no Zanuck,
no Selznick, there was scarcely even a new Carl Laemmle..

Once, a studio was a place governed by a budget set by a mogul
who believed he could market certain kinds of stars who were presented by a staff of experts who held certain social, artistic, and political aperçus in common. As Adolph Zukor, the founder of it all,
looked on, the studio dwindled into a firm governed by various crass
jerks who hold nothing in common but a contempt for everything
but money.

It is thought that a parent's greatest agony is to live to see the
death of his child. But Zukor is not on record as having said anything
on this matter whatsoever.

Index

PHOTOGRAPHIC CREDITS

Photographs on the following pages are from the author's collection:
8, 9, 115, 143, 160, 189, 239, and 359.

All other photographs are from The John Kobal Collection.

A NOTE ON THE TYPE

The text of this book was set in a digitized version of Bembo, a well-known Monotype face. Named for Pietro Bembo, the celebrated Renaissance writer and humanist scholar who was made a cardinal and served as secretary to Pope Leo X, the original cutting of Bembo was made by Francesco Griffo of Bologna only a few years after Columbus discovered America. Sturdy, well balanced, and finely proportioned, Bembo is a face of rare beauty, extremely legible in all of its sizes.

Composed by New England Typographic Service, Inc.,
Bloomfield, Connecticut
Printed and bound by Halliday Lithographers,
West Hanover, Massachusetts

Designed by Julie Duquet